Case Analysis
and Fundamentals
of Legal Writing

Third Edition

Case Analysis and Fundamentals of Legal Writing

Third Edition

William P. Statsky
R. John Wernet, Jr.

West Publishing Company

St. Paul   New York   Los Angeles   San Francisco

Library of Congress Cataloging in Publication Data

Statsky, William P.
    Case analysis and fundamentals of legal writing/William P.
Statsky, R. John Wernet.—3rd ed.
        p.   cm.
    Bibliography: p.
    Includes index.

    1. Legal research—United States.   2. Legal composition.
3. Briefs—United States.   I. Wernet, R. John.
II. Title.
KF240.S78   1989
808'.06634—dc19   88–17048
ISBN 0-314-43754-1
ISBN 0-314-67424-1

For Gabriel Farrell Statsky
W.P.S.

For Robynne Lee Harrington and Hobart House
J.W.

Other books by William P. Statsky:

Legal Research and Writing: Some Starting Points, 3d ed. St. Paul: West Publishing Co., 1986.

Legal Desk Reference. St. Paul: West Publishing Co., 1989 (with B. Hussey, Michael Diamond, & R. Nakamura).

Legal Thesaurus/Dictionary: A Resource for the Writer and Computer Researcher. St. Paul: West Publishing Co., 1985.

Legislative Analysis and Drafting, 2d ed. St. Paul: West Publishing Co., 1984.

Rights of the Imprisoned: Cases, Materials and Directions. Indianapolis: Bobbs-Merrill Co. (Michie), 1974 (with R. Singer).

Contents

Preface

No one has yet devised a universally accepted method of acquiring the skills of reading and applying court opinions. Some would take the view that an exposure to thousands of opinions is all that is needed. At the end of this exposure, the skills somehow emerge. Others maintain that an extended exploration of jurisprudence and legal process is the only meaningful route to intelligent reading and application. Both positions have considerable merit. This book, however, starts with the assumption that much can be learned about opinions and their jurisprudential context *before* confronting thousands of them in the reporters and casebooks.

The beauty of a court opinion is the wealth of learning that it can provide about legal analysis and our legal system. This learning is the foundation for the development of the skills of reading and applying opinions.

The parties who litigated the dispute that led to the opinion are primarily concerned with the result of the opinion and "the law" or legal doctrine on which it is based. Our focus, as students of the law, is broader. While we also want to understand results and doctrines, our primary concern is *how* results and doctrines are reached. This understanding will be our primary route to the skills of case analysis.

The skills are covered at four levels: briefing a case, applying case law in an interoffice memorandum of law, using case law in an advocacy letter, and arguing case law in oral advocacy.

There are many individuals who have been supportive in the preparation of the three editions of this book. Jean and Edgar Cahn, founders of Antioch School of Law, have been most helpful. Wilbur O. Colom assisted in writing the chapter on appellate briefs. Jim Wade, Mary Lynn Perry, and Jim Acoba are fellow teachers who thankfully have continued to be available with their guidance.

William P. Statsky
San Diego, California

R. John Wernet
Grand Ledge, Michigan

Acknowledgments

American Bar Association, *Law and the Courts: A Layman's Handbook of Court Procedures with Glossary of Legal Terminology* (1974). Excerpts reprinted by permission.

Cardozo B., *The Nature of the Judicial Process* (1921). Copyright 1921 by Yale University Press. Excerpts reprinted by permission.

Gregory, H., "Shorter Judicial Opinions," 34 *Virginia Law Review* 362 (1948). Excerpts reprinted by permission.

Prosser, W., *Handbook of the Law of Torts,* Third Edition (1964). Copyright 1964 by West Publishing Co. Excerpts reprinted by permission.

Stevenson, D., "Effective Opinion Writing," 59 *Judicature* 134 (No. 3, Oct. 1975). Excerpts reprinted by permission.

Swift, J., *Gulliver's Travels and Other Writings.* Published by Random House, Inc. Excerpts reprinted by permission.

West Publishing Company, *Corpus Juris Secundum.* Excerpts reprinted by permission.

PART ONE

Background Information on Case Law and the Legal System

Chapter One

Introduction to Court Opinions and the Legal System

Section A. The Pain and the Excitement of Case Analysis

In the early eighteenth century, Jonathan Swift made a very cynical comment about the preoccupation of lawyers with court opinions:

> It is a Maxim that among these Lawyers, that whatever hath been done before may legally be done again: and therefore they take special Care to record all the Decisions formerly made against common Justice and the general Reason of Mankind. These, under the Name of *Precedents,* they produce as Authorities, to justify the most iniquitous Opinions; and the Judges never fail of directing accordingly.[1]

Although some might disagree with Mr. Swift's derogatory comment about how lawyers function, no one can disagree with his suggestion that court opinions are the cornerstone of the law and of our legal system.

This book is about case law and the legal writing that is dependent upon the skill of case analysis. There is no better way to understand our legal system than to understand the use of case law; yet perhaps no component of our legal system is more frequently misused than case law. There is, perhaps, no other aspect of law that is more deserving of the word *art* than case analysis. In short, few undertakings are more frustrating, challenging, and rewarding than the *proper* use of case law.

---

1. Swift, J., *Gulliver's Travels and Other Writings,* p. 203 (R. Quintana, editor), (Random House, The Modern Library, 1958).

The late Supreme Court Justice, Benjamin Cardozo once said:

"Cases do not unfold their principles for the asking. They yield up their kernel slowly and painfully."[2]

Our objective in the following chapters shall be an extensive study of this unfolding. We will examine in detail the reasons why the analysis of case law must be a *slow,* deliberate process. While the *pain* of case analysis can never be totally eliminated, the techniques discussed in this book will assist you in minimizing the pain while maximizing the excitement of the endeavor.

There are over three million court opinions in a comprehensive law library. Each year, tens of thousands of new opinions are added. Although the ability to read a single case intelligently is a difficult skill to achieve, you can take comfort in the fact that if you know how to handle one opinion, you are well on your way to being able to handle them all.

Section B. Definitions and Overview of Case Analysis

A *dispute* is a controversy between two or more parties which may or may not be brought to a court for resolution. A *civil dispute* consists of (a) one private party suing another private party, or (b) a private party suing the government, or (c) the government suing a private party for a matter other than the commission of a crime. A *criminal dispute* is a suit brought by the government against a party for the alleged commission of a crime. The court's resolution of a civil or criminal dispute is called a decision or *judgment.*

How does a court reach its judgment? One can approach this question in two ways: (a) by studying "politics," and (b) by studying structure, form, and process. The focus of this book will be on the latter, although in the next section we will confront, at least in general terms, the delicate topic of "judicial politics."

The judgment of a court in a given dispute depends primarily on two factors: (a) the facts of the dispute, and (b) the rules of law that are applied to these facts. A *fact* is information describing a thing, occurrence, or event. A *rule of law* is an enforceable pronouncement of government, e.g., a statute, a constitutional provision, or a regulation, that directly or indirectly establishes a standard of conduct. The task of the court in resolving the dispute is to *interpret* the appropriate rules of law and to *apply* them to the facts of the dispute. This application is called the *holding* of the court. A holding, therefore, is the court's application of particular rule(s) of law to the particular facts of a dispute. Very often, more than one holding is involved in the litigation. An *opinion* is the court's written explanation of how it reached the holdings.

The words *opinion* and *case* are sometimes used interchangeably. A court, for example, will often refer to another opinion as "the case of ———." Or, the court may refer to the opinion it is writing as "this case." (The current client's problem is often referred to as a *case*).

---

2. Cardozo, B., *The Nature of the Judicial Process,* p. 29 (Yale University Press, 1921).

Suppose that years after an opinion is written, you are in a law library researching the case of a current client and you come across this opinion. You want to know whether the same application of the law in the opinion, i.e., the same holding, will be applied by a court to the client's case. This determination is made through two interrelated sets of comparisons: a *fact comparison*, and a *rule-of-law comparison*.

(a) You must compare the facts in the opinion with the facts of the client's case. We will study fact comparison in chapter 13. More specifically, the comparison must be between the client's facts and the *key* facts in the opinion. Starting with chapter 8, we will focus on the identification of key facts in an opinion. Few skills are more important or more difficult to acquire than the skill of identifying key facts.

(b) You must also undertake a rule-of-law comparison. We said earlier that courts interpret and apply one or more rules of law in their opinions. When you work on a client's case, you also must consider rules of law. Suppose that you want to know whether the client qualifies for a benefit found within § 23 of the bankruptcy code. (The symbol for section used in the law is §.) One way to find out is to locate opinions that interpret the *same* rule of law, i.e., you want to find opinions on § 23. Suppose, however, that you cannot find an opinion that interprets § 23 of the bankruptcy code, but you are able to find an opinion that interprets § 25 of the same code. Can you use this opinion? Can an opinion on § 25 be precedent for a case involving § 23? The answer depends on the results of a rule-of-law comparison. You must compare § 23 with § 25 in the manner described in chapter 14.

You go through these two sets of comparisons between the opinion and the client's case in order to make a prediction. If the facts and the rule of law in the client's case are the same or substantially the same as those in the opinion, then the opinion is said to be *on all fours* with the client's case; you can safely predict that the holding in the opinion will be applied to the client's case. If the facts and the rule of law in the client's case are totally different, you are equally safe in predicting that the holding in the opinion will not be applied to the client. In between these two extremes is a gray area. It is difficult to predict what a court will do when the opinion is somewhat different from, yet also somewhat similar to, the client's case. This book is designed to help you develop the skills needed to make predictions in the gray area.

The term *case analysis* refers to the technique used in predicting the applicability of opinions. Case analysis poses the question of whether a given opinion is *analogous* to the client's case. Analogy means likeness or similarity in corresponding elements. Hence, if there is sufficient likeness between (a) the facts and the rule of law in the opinion and (b) the facts and the rule of law in the client's case, then the holding of the opinion will apply to the client's case. The basic steps, therefore, of case analysis are as follows:

---

(1) Compare the key facts in the opinion with the facts in the client's case;

(2) Compare the rule of law that was interpreted and applied in the opinion to the rule of law that will likely be interpreted and applied in the client's case; and

(3) Draw conclusions as to whether the opinion, in whole or in part, is analogous to the client's case.

This is not to suggest, however, that applying opinions is a simple process of mechanical fact and rule-of-law comparisons. As we shall see in later chapters, a very pronounced and at times complex mix of policy and principle dominates the process.

Administrative agencies, such as the National Labor Relations Board and a state income tax commission, act like courts in that they attempt to resolve disputes between the agency and a citizen or organization. They may, for example, conduct hearings and render decisions on the disputes. We shall refer to these decisions as *administrative decisions*. The techniques of determining whether an administrative decision applies to the facts of a client's case are the same as those used in applying court opinions to a client's case.

Section C. Judicial Politics

Lawyers are reluctant to admit that politics plays any role in judicial decision making. Political scientists, on the other hand, sometimes suggest that little else exists. One of the units within the American Political Science Association that concentrates on the study of law is revealingly called the section on "Judicial Politics." A corresponding unit within the Association of American Law Schools might be called "Judicial Process and Legal Method" or "Jurisprudence."

Judges reach their position on the bench by a variety of routes. They are

- elected by the public;
- appointed by chief executives;
- designated, nominated, or confirmed by special panels, councils, or commissions; or
- selected by a combination of the above.

This diversity is vivid testimony to the fact that our society has no clear idea of the best way to select the best people for the court. Almost all judges will deny that they can be classified as "liberal" or "conservative" either before or after donning the robe; yet few people hesitate to put them in one of these categories. While it is true that judges use their intellect, integrity, and sense of fairness in writing an opinion, no one knows for sure how that opinion might *also* be influenced by a Republican or Democratic background, a prior career in law enforcement, or training at a law school that directly or indirectly promotes an activist role for the judiciary, and it would be naive to ignore the fact that this mix of influences does exist.

It is fascinating to compare the way political scientists study court opinions with the way lawyers study them. There are similarities of approach: for example, both groups closely examine the text of the opinions. Nevertheless, there are differences. Political scientists focus on the background of the judges and on how they reached the court. Lawyers, on the other hand, concentrate more on the opinions themselves and less on the biographies of the judges. Yet both groups would claim that the goals of their study are the same: an appreciation of the judicial process, an understanding of particular opinions, and an ability to predict how existing opinions might be applied in the future. Does either group have a monopoly over the achievement of these goals? It depends on which of the two groups you ask!

There is another dimension to judicial politics. It is often said that judges do not bargain over their votes with fellow judges in the manner that legislators commonly do over river projects and other pork barrel items in their districts. Yet when a court consists of more than one judge (as is usually the case on our higher courts), the ultimate focus of the debate within the chambers of the court is on votes for or against certain positions and litigants. Judges will always maintain that they cast their votes on the basis of principle, and this in large part is true. However, judges are human beings who spend a good deal of time trying to persuade each other to adopt certain points of view. No one can prove whether or not a measure of accommodation takes place on certain votes, particularly when the judges do not feel the same about the importance of the issue under discussion. It is not inconceivable that Judge Smith will vote a certain way on an issue that this judge does not consider vital in order to encourage Judge Jones (who does consider the issue vital) to vote a certain way on another issue that is critically important to Judge Smith. The opinions, of course, are absolutely silent about such accommodation; and judges and lawyers cringe at the suggestion that any of this goes on, or that it is of any significance if it does.

Section D. Why Study Case Law?

Case analysis is an essential skill because it increases:

1. Your understanding of the legal system and the practice of law;

2. Your understanding of constitutions, statutes, ordinances, and regulations;

3. Your understanding of common law;

4. Your ability to do effective legal research;

5. Your ability to write memoranda of law and appellate briefs;

6. Your ability to engage in effective oral advocacy during formal proceedings;

7. Your expertise in conducting client interviews and field investigations.

1. UNDERSTANDING THE LEGAL SYSTEM AND THE PRACTICE OF LAW

A large part (but by no means all) of the law and its practice concerns litigation, present or threatened. *Litigation* is the process by which the parties to a dispute have the controversy resolved by a court. As noted above, the decisions that the court makes in the course of resolving the dispute are often explained in a written opinion. An opinion provides us with a view of a particular litigation and reveals much about the process of litigation generally.

To be sure, most disputants arrive at a settlement without resorting to the courts at all. Moreover, many of the disputes that are initially brought to a court are settled or compromised between the parties before the court has made a decision or written an opinion. This process of compromise and settlement is also a major component of the practice of law. Yet both opinions and the courts that write them are very much a part of the settlement process. One of the most common arguments used by an advocate who is trying to reach a favorable settlement is to point out the probable court decision. "If this case goes to court, we think it is clear that the judge will rule in our favor. If, however, you wish to settle the case, here are our terms." How can you as an advocate obtain ammunition to support this kind of pressure? One way is to find and read the relevant court opinions and then to argue to the other advocate that if the case goes to trial, the court would apply the opinions in a manner favorable to your client. Obviously, to be effective in taking such a position in the negotiation process, you have to be able to convince the other side of your perceptiveness in reading and analogizing opinions.

When a lawyer (in the role of legal counselor) is advising a business client about the legalities of a proposed business transaction, the judicial process again has an impact on the lawyer's advice—even though at the time there are no plaintiffs or defendants about to do battle in court. Expressly or implicitly, the lawyer's advice is phrased in terms of the steps that should be taken now in order to *avoid* litigation in the future. This is the essence of preventive law.

Hence, a thorough understanding of case law will increase your understanding of (a) the counseling role in which advice is given to avoid litigation, (b) the settlement role in which the parties seek to compromise their way out of litigation, and (c) the litigation role itself, which is entered into when preventive law has not worked and no settlement has been achieved.

2. UNDERSTANDING CONSTITUTIONS, STATUTES, ORDINANCES, AND REGULATIONS

Court opinions, of course, are not the only source of law. We need to look briefly at constitutional, statutory, and regulatory law and examine their relationship to case law. Consider the following hypothetical example.

> John Smith is walking down one of the aisles of XYZ Supermarket on January 10, 1977. He slips on a wet spot and sprains his elbow. The floor became wet when a customer opened a jar of apple juice and spilled half the bottle on the floor about fifteen minutes before Smith came down the aisle. The customer has since disappeared.

Within our legal system, the potential problems growing out of these facts could involve three different but interrelated kinds of governmental action: legislative, administrative, and judicial.

(a) Legislative A *legislature* is a branch of government that has responsibility for passing laws. The state legislature, for example, may pass a law or may already have a law requiring all supermarkets in the state to have flooring of a specified quality that resists slipping. Laws passed by legislatures are referred to as *acts* or *statutes* or, more generally, as *legislation*.

City councils and county boards of supervisors are local legislatures. Laws they pass are often called *ordinances*. The city council, for example, may pass an ordiance requiring the City Board of Health and Safety to inspect all supermarkets every six months to ensure that the stores are designed and operated to provide maximum customer safety.

(b) Administrative An *administrative agency* is a unit of government within the *executive branch* whose primary function is to carry out or administer the laws passed by the legislature. The Board of Health and Safety, the police department, and the Internal Revenue Service are examples of such agencies. In addition to the responsibility of administering the laws of the legislature, the agency may be given the power to write rules. The rules that agencies write are usually called *administrative regulations*.

Suppose in our example that the Board of Health and Safety has the power to write regulations. The board may have a regulation requiring that the floors of supermarkets be kept dry while being used by the public.

The board may also have the power to grant and revoke licenses to supermarkets based upon their compliance with the regulations. If the board seeks to revoke a license, it may hold a revocation hearing and, based upon this hearing, may write an *administrative decision*.

(c) Judicial One of the main functions of the courts is to resolve or *adjudicate* disputes by interpreting and applying constitutions, statutes, ordinances, and regulations. As we have seen, the process by which parties present evidence and legal arguments in an attempt to persuade the court to reach a favorable decision is called litigation, and the parties are known as *litigants*. The litigant bringing the dispute to court is called the *plaintiff* and, in the case of a civil dispute, is said to be *suing* the other litigant, who is called the *defendant*. Some examples of litigation that could arise from the supermarket case:

i. Smith (plaintiff) might sue XYZ Supermarket (defendant) for negligence.

ii. Smith (plaintiff) might sue XYZ Supermarket (defendant) for violation of the state *statute* requiring that supermarket floors be of a specified quality.

iii. Smith (plaintiff) might sue XYZ Supermarket (defendant) for violating the Board of Health and Safety *regulation* that supermarket floors be kept dry while being used by the public.

iv. Smith (plaintiff) might sue the Board of Health and Safety (defendant) for failure to inspect supermarkets every six months pursuant to the city council *ordinance* requiring such inspections.

v. The Board of Health and Safety (plaintiff) might sue XYZ Supermarket (defendant) to force it to institute more effective safety practices.

vi. The Board of Health and Safety might revoke the license of XYZ Supermarket. Following a revocation of its business license, XYZ Supermarket (plaintiff) could sue the Board of Health and Safety (defendant) to challenge the board's revocation of its license. One of the supermarket's arguments might be that the board's procedures for revoking licenses are in violation of the federal or state *constitution*.

Over ninety percent of all court decisions involve constitutions, statutes, ordinances, or regulations. Understanding how the courts interpret, cr construe, and apply these different kinds of law is essential to understanding the constitution, statute, ordinance, or regulation itself. You can never be sure of the meaning of a particular statute, for example, until you know how the courts have construed and applied it in their written opinions.

3. UNDERSTANDING COMMON LAW

Suppose that a dispute comes before a court and there are *no* statutes, ordinances, regulations, or constitutional provisions governing the facts of the dispute. Then the judge will rely on prior opinions in which the court has established rules for this type of dispute; if no such opinions exist, the judge may be forced to create new rules to resolve the dispute. Such judicially created rules are referred to collectively as the *common law*. The common law is created by judges in their written opinions. In order to find and understand common law, then, you must be able to read and analyze court opinions.

4. LEGAL RESEARCH

When undertaking legal research, one of your major objectives is to find opinions *on point,* i.e., case law that a court might apply to the facts of the problem the client brings into the law office. But when does an opinion apply to or govern your problem? To answer this question, you need an understanding of the following basic concepts:

- stare decisis
- precedent
- distinguishing a case
- extending a case

These concepts will be among our concerns in Parts III and IV of this text.

Legal research is not simply a matter of *finding* case law. How do you know *what* to find? How do you know *whether* you have found something? How do you *apply* what you have found? The skill of case analysis will help you answer such questions.

5. LEGAL WRITING

A *memorandum of law* is a written explanation of your analysis and research on the problem of a client. An *internal* or interoffice memorandum is addressed to your supervisor, who must decide what advice to give the client and what strategy to pursue in litigation. Your memorandum will be designed to assist the supervisor in making these decisions. If you submit a memorandum that does not contain a discussion of court opinions, the inevitable (and perhaps angry) response of your supervisor will be: "Where's the case law? Aren't there any opinions on point?" For most legal problems, there *will* be court opinions that must be analyzed. If you are working on a problem where this is not so, you must tell the supervisor in the memorandum that no opinions were found.

An *internal* memorandum is seen only by individuals working in the same office. Since its main purpose is to assess the client's case, it must be thoroughly frank about the strengths and weaknesses of all arguments on both sides; there is no need to hide anything or to downplay any weaknesses that may exist in the client's case. It is to the advantage of the supervisor reading the memo to examine *all* aspects of the client's case, positive and negative.

An *external* memorandum, on the other hand, is usually an *advocacy* document; you will be asked to write this type of memorandum for someone outside of the office, e.g., a judge or hearing examiner, in the hope of persuading this person to accept the client's position on a question of law. Such a memorandum might be submitted to a trial court in support of a certain request made of the judge before trial, e.g., a memorandum in support of a motion (a formal request) to force the other party to turn over certain records. Similarly, an external memorandum might be submitted to an administrative agency following an agency hearing but before the hearing officer has made a decision. In both of these situations, the objective of the memo is to influence the decision that will be rendered by the trial judge or hearing officer. This type of memorandum, unlike an internal memorandum, should highlight the strengths of the client's arguments and downplay the weaknesses. In doing so, the memorandum will almost always cite case law in support of the client's positions.

An *appellate brief* is a document submitted to an appeals court. Its purpose is to ask the court either to affirm or to correct what a lower court or agency has done in the litigation thus far. An appellate brief is similar to an external memorandum in that it is an advocacy document and it usually analyzes case law extensively. Very often one or more *internal* memoranda of the law will be written preliminary to the drafting of the appellate brief.

Needless to say, in all these writing ventures, the skill of case analysis is very important.

6. ORAL ADVOCACY

Advocacy on one's feet—oral advocacy—can occur in a number of formal proceedings: at an administrative hearing, at a trial, or at an appellate hearing, to name a few. During these proceedings, the advocate will often cite case law in support of a particular position. Given the need to be brief and to the point in such settings, the case analysis skills of the advocate must be finely tuned.

7. CLIENT INTERVIEWS AND FIELD INVESTIGATION

Students new to the law sometimes ask, "How will I know what questions to ask a client during an interview?" or "what facts should I investigate?" One of the major objectives of interviewing and investigation is to uncover the legally significant facts. What facts are legally significant? To a large degree, the answer depends upon what the law (constitutional provision, statute, ordinance, regulation, or court opinion) says and means. Hence, knowing the law gives *direction* to interviewing and investigation.

Suppose that during an initial client interview you are told certain facts. You use these facts to begin your legal research. You come across a court opinion that appears to be on point. As we have seen, one of the steps you must take in assessing whether an opinion applies is to compare the key facts of the opinion with the facts of the problem you are researching. Suppose, however, that there are certain facts in the opinion that you cannot compare to the facts of the client's problem because the client has never been asked any questions on these facts and no field investigation has been undertaken as to the facts. *You did not know that such facts were significant until you read the opinion.* Now that you are aware of having a fact gap, you conduct a subsequent client interview or you undertake an investigation in order to explore these factual areas which became apparent after you read the opinion. You do this in order to make a better assessment of whether the opinion applies.

Thus the skill of case analysis can help give direction to client interviews and field investigations that follow your initial legal research.

Section E. Judicial Systems

1. JURISDICTION

There are fifty state court systems, a court system for the District of Columbia, and a federal court system. Each court within a system is identified by its *jurisdiction.* The word jurisdiction has three meanings.

First, the word is often used to refer to the *geographic* area over which a particular court has authority. A state trial court, for example, has geographic jurisdiction to hear cases arising in a specific county or district of the state. A state supreme court, in contrast, may have geographic jurisdiction to hear appeals in cases arising anywhere in the state. Thus a state supreme court will often say "in this jurisdiction" when referring to its own state. The phrase has the same meaning as "in this state."

Secondly, the word jurisdiction is used to refer to the *power* of a court to adjudicate a dispute. In order for the court to have the power to order the defendant to do anything (or to refrain from doing something), the court must have *personal jurisdiction* over the defendant. This is also called *in personam* jurisdiction. As we shall see in Chapter 2, one component of acquiring personal jurisdiction is through service of process on the defendant.

Thirdly, jurisdiction means the power that a court must have over the *subject matter,* or over the particular kind of dispute that has been brought before it. Some of the more common classifications of subject matter jurisdiction are:

a. *limited* jurisdiction;

b. *general* jurisdiction;

c. *exclusive* jurisdiction;

d. *concurrent* jurisdiction;

e. *original* jurisdiction;

f. *appellate* jurisdiction.

(a) Limited Jurisdiction A court of *limited* (or *special*) *jurisdiction* can hear only certain kinds of cases. A criminal court of limited jurisdiction is not allowed to take a noncriminal case, and a small claims court is authorized to hear only cases in which the plaintiff claims less than a certain amount of money as damages from the defendant.

Another way to look at a court of limited jurisdiction is to say it has a specified *subject matter jurisdiction*. Its subject matter jurisdiction is limited to cases that deal with designated subject matters only, e.g., criminal cases.

(b) General Jurisdiction A court of *general jurisdiction,* with some exceptions, can hear any kind of case so long as the case arises within the geographic boundaries of that court. A *state* court of general jurisdiction can handle any case that raises state questions (i.e., questions arising from the state constitution, state statutes, or state common law); a *federal* court of general jurisdiction can handle any case that raises federal questions (i.e., questions arising from the federal constitution or federal statutes).

(c) Exclusive Jurisdiction A court of *exclusive jurisdiction* is the only court that can handle a certain kind of case. For example, it may be that the Juvenile Court has exclusive jurisdiction over all cases involving children under a certain age who are charged with acts of delinquency. If this kind of case were brought in another court, there could be a challenge on the ground that the court lacked jurisdiction over the case.

(d) Concurrent Jurisdiction Sometimes two courts have jurisdiction over a case; the case could be brought in either court. In such a situation, both courts are said to have *concurrent jurisdiction* over the case. For example, it could be that both the Family Court and a County Court have jurisdiction to enforce a child custody order.

(e) Original Jurisdiction A court of *original jurisdiction* is the first court to hear and decide a case. It is also called a trial court or a court of first instance. In addition, it can be classified as a court of limited jurisdiction (if it can try only certain kinds of cases), of general jurisdiction (if it can try cases involving any subject matter), of exclusive jurisdiction (if the trial can take place only in that court), or of concurrent jurisdiction (if the trial can take place either in that court or in another court).

(f) Appellate Jurisdiction A court with *appellate jurisdiction* can hear appeals from lower tribunals. An appeal is a review of what a lower court or agency has done to determine if there was any error. Sometimes a party who is dissatisfied with a lower court ruling can appeal to the appellate court as a matter of right (i.e., the court must hear the appeal); in other kinds of cases, the appellate court has discretion as to whether or not it will hear the appeal.

How do you determine what kind of geographic and subject matter jurisdiction a court has? There are three sets of laws that will provide this information: the constitution, the statutory code, and the court's procedural rules. In assignment #1 below, you will be asked to consult these sources *for your state* in order to construct a chart of your state's court system. The following description applies to court systems in many states.

2. STATE COURT SYSTEMS

(a) Courts of Original Jurisdiction Depending upon the particular state, there may be one or more levels of trial courts (i.e., courts of original jurisdiction). These courts hear the dispute, determine the facts of the case, and make the initial determination or ruling. In addition, they may sometimes have the power to review cases that were initially decided by an administrative agency.

The most common arrangement is a two-tier system of trial courts. At the lower level are courts of limited or special jurisdiction, the so-called inferior courts. Local courts, such as city courts, county courts, or justice of the peace courts, often fall into this category. These courts may have original jurisdiction over relatively minor cases such as violations of local ordinances and lawsuits involving small sums of money. Also included in this category are special courts that are limited to specific matters, such as surrogate or probate courts which are limited to hearing matters involving the estates of deceased or mentally incompetent persons.

Immediately above the trial courts of limited jurisdiction are the trial courts of general, original jurisdiction, which usually handle more serious cases such as violations of state laws or lawsuits involving large sums of money. The name given to the trial courts at this second level varies greatly from state to state. They are known as superior courts, courts of common pleas, district courts, or circuit courts. New York is especially confusing. There the trial court of general jurisdiction is called the supreme court, a label reserved in most states for the court of final appeals, the highest court in the system.

This two-tier system is not invariable. Some states may have only one court of original jurisdiction. Moreover, the individual levels may be segmented into divisions. A court of general, original jurisdiction, for example, may be broken up into specialized divisions such as landlord-tenant, family, juvenile, and criminal divisions. The best way to learn the names and duties of the courts in a particular state is to check the state's constitution and statutes. (See Assignment #1 below.)

(b) Courts of Appeal These courts rarely make the initial decision in a case. Their primary function is to *review* decisions made by lower courts in order to correct *errors of law*. That is, they will look to see if the lower court correctly interpreted and applied the law to the facts of the dispute. In this review process, appellate courts do not make their own findings of fact. *No* new evidence is taken and *no* witnesses are called. The court limits itself to an analysis of the record made at the trial court (transcripts of testimony and copies of the various documents that were filed, etc.) in order to determine if any errors of law were made by that lower court. Attorneys submit appellate briefs containing their arguments on the correctness or incorrectness of what the lower court did.

Depending upon the state, there may be not one, but two, levels of appellate courts. The first level is the court of middle appeals, sometimes called an intermediate appellate court. The decisions of this court may in turn be reviewed by a second-level appellate court, the court of final appeals. This latter court, often known as the supreme court, is the highest court in the state, the court of final or last resort.

Figure 1–1 illustrates the organization of and the line of appeal in many state court systems.

FIGURE 1–1.
Hierarchy of State Judicial System. Source: *Law and the Courts,* 20 (American Bar Association, 1974).

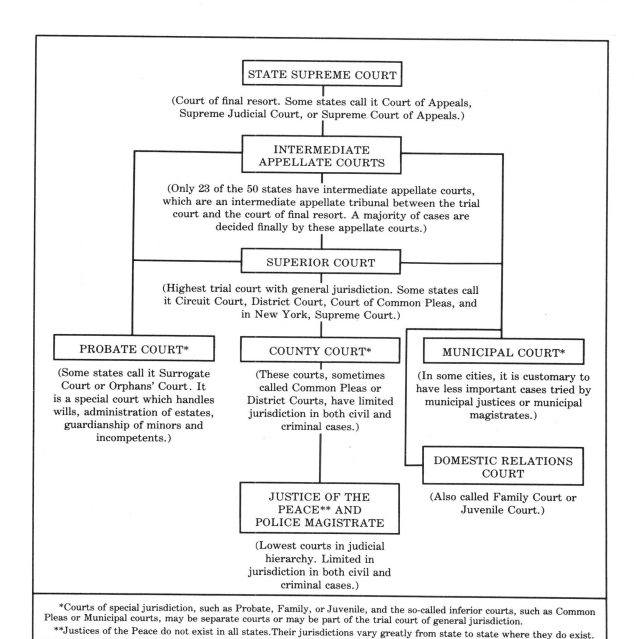

STATE SUPREME COURT

(Court of final resort. Some states call it Court of Appeals, Supreme Judicial Court, or Supreme Court of Appeals.)

INTERMEDIATE APPELLATE COURTS

(Only 23 of the 50 states have intermediate appellate courts, which are an intermediate appellate tribunal between the trial court and the court of final resort. A majority of cases are decided finally by these appellate courts.)

SUPERIOR COURT

(Highest trial court with general jurisdiction. Some states call it Circuit Court, District Court, Court of Common Pleas, and in New York, Supreme Court.)

PROBATE COURT*

(Some states call it Surrogate Court or Orphans' Court. It is a special court which handles wills, administration of estates, guardianship of minors and incompetents.)

COUNTY COURT*

(These courts, sometimes called Common Pleas or District Courts, have limited jurisdiction in both civil and criminal cases.)

MUNICIPAL COURT*

(In some cities, it is customary to have less important cases tried by municipal justices or municipal magistrates.)

DOMESTIC RELATIONS COURT

(Also called Family Court or Juvenile Court.)

JUSTICE OF THE PEACE** AND POLICE MAGISTRATE

(Lowest courts in judicial hierarchy. Limited in jurisdiction in both civil and criminal cases.)

*Courts of special jurisdiction, such as Probate, Family, or Juvenile, and the so-called inferior courts, such as Common Pleas or Municipal courts, may be separate courts or may be part of the trial court of general jurisdiction.
**Justices of the Peace do not exist in all states. Their jurisdictions vary greatly from state to state where they do exist.

Before reading any opinions of your state courts, it would be helpful to have an understanding of the structure of the court system of your state. As litigation proceeds, a dispute might flow into and out of a variety of courts in the hierarchy of the judicial system for your state. Reading an opinion can be confusing if you do not know what this hierarchy is. Assignment #1 is designed to help you overcome this obstacle—at least for your state. A word of caution, however, is needed. States sometimes change the names and powers of their courts. In the law library, you might find an old opinion written by a state court that no longer exists. Or, you may be reading an opinion involving a trial court that today has a different name or function. You will not learn about these changes simply from reading the opinion since they occurred after the opinion was written. Assignment #1 asks you to identify the *current* names and powers of your state courts. As you do the assignment, watch for any references to court reorganizations or to changes in the names of the courts. In your research you may even be lucky enough to come across a brief history of some or all of the courts in your state. Be alert to this kind of information. It may become invaluable later when you study some of the older opinions of your state courts.

Assignment #1

Go to the index of your state statutory code and your state constitution. In many states the state constitution will be found in the first few volumes of the statutory code so that the index for the entire code covers both the statutes and the constitution. In the index at the end of the code or at the end of the individual volumes of the code, look up words such as *court, judiciary, trial courts, jurisdiction, court rules, appeals, Supreme Court, Superior Court, District Court, County Court, Civil Court,* and *Criminal Court* until you locate the statutes and constitutional provisions that govern the establishment and the powers of the courts in your state.

a. Make a list of every court in your state, and give the citation to the statute or constitutional provision establishing that court.

b. State the subject matter jurisdiction or powers of each court. (If the statute or constitutional provision enumerates a long list of powers, just mention what you think are the court's major powers.)

c. For each court, state whether it is a court of original jurisdiction, appellate jurisdiction, limited (special) jurisdiction, general jurisdiction, exclusive jurisdiction, or concurrent jurisdiction. Usually, these terms will not be used in the constitution or statutory code; you will have to infer the kind or kinds of jurisdiction a court has. Furthermore, all of this information may not be found in the constitution and statutory code. Limit yourself to as much information as you do find in these sources.

d. For appellate courts, try to determine the kinds of cases that the court *must* take and the kinds of cases it has the *discretion* to take or to refuse.

e. Draw a chart of the judicial system in your state. Use Figure 1-1 on page 15 as a model, but insert the actual names of the courts and the actual lines of appeal for your state courts. Put the name of the highest state court at the top of your chart.

In your library there may be handbooks and state practice manuals that provide much of the above information. Do *not* consult such handbooks or manuals until you have tried to find the answers yourself directly in the constitution and statutes.

Assignment #2

a. Go to the most comprehensive law library near you. Identify *every* source (including periodicals and legal newspapers) that contains complete or partial reports of the opinions of *any* of your state courts on a regular basis. List each set of books or other source and the names of the courts whose opinions (in whole or in part) are within it. Be sure to check official reporters (see p. 21), unofficial reporters, loose-leaf services, legal newspapers, collections of slip opinions, etc.

b. Choose any three of your state's administrative agencies. For each agency, determine (1) whether the administrative decisions of that agency are published and if so, (2) where these decisions are printed. (Unfortunately, state administrative decisions are not as well organized as decisions of federal agencies. If the state agency you are checking publishes its administrative decisions—and many do not—they are often haphazardly collected in three-ring notebooks rather than in neatly bound volumes.)

Assignment #3

In this Assignment, you will use the information that you collected in Assignments #1(e) and #2(a) above.

In a law library, locate any of the sets of books you listed in Assignment #2(a) as containing complete or partial reports of the opinions of the state courts in your state. Use any of these books to locate three reports on opinions from any state court *other* than the highest court.

Give the names of the three opinions and the names of the courts that wrote them. For each opinion, assume that one of the parties now wants to appeal. To what court or courts could this party appeal? If the chart you prepared in Assignment #1(e) is complete and accurate, you should be able to answer this part of Assignment #3 solely by reading the chart.

3. THE FEDERAL COURT SYSTEM

The federal court system, like those of the states, consists of two basic kinds of courts: courts of original jurisdiction (trial courts) and appellate courts.

(a) Courts of original jurisdiction The basic federal court at the trial level is the United States District Court. There are close to 100 districts throughout the country, at least one for every state, the District of Columbia, Guam, the Virgin Islands, and Puerto Rico. The District Courts exercise original jurisdiction over most federal litigation and also serve as courts of review for many cases that were initially decided by federal administrative agencies.

In addition to the district courts, there are several federal courts that exercise original jurisdiction over specialized cases. These include the United States Tax Court, the United States Claims Court, and the United States Court of International Trade.

(b) Courts of Appeals The federal system, like almost half of the fifty state judicial systems, has two levels of appellate courts: middle appeals and final appeals. The primary courts at the middle level are the United States Courts of Appeals. These courts are divided into twelve geographic circuits, eleven of which are made up of groupings of various states and territories, with a twelfth for the District of Columbia. Their primary function is to review the decisions of the federal courts of original jurisdiction. In addition, the decisions of certain federal agencies, notably the National Labor Relations Board, are reviewed directly by the Court of Appeals without first going to the District Court. Finally, there is a specialized Court of Appeals called the Court of Appeals for the Federal Circuit. This court, created in 1982, reviews decisions of the United States Claims Court and the United States Court of International Trade, rulings of the Patent and Trademark Office, and some decisions of the federal district courts where the United States government is a defendant.

The federal court of final appeals is, of course, the United States Supreme Court, which provides the final review of the decisions of all federal courts and agencies. The Supreme Court may also review certain decisions of the state courts when these decisions raise questions involving the United States Constitution or a federal statute.

Figure 1-2 illustrates the line of appeal for the most common federal courts.

There are a number of exceptions to the basic structure of appeal presented in Figure 1-2. For instance, even the United States Supreme Court has original jurisdiction in certain kinds of cases, for example, in cases involving ambassadors. Also, there are times when opinions of a United States

FIGURE 1-2.
Hierarchy of Federal
Judicial System.

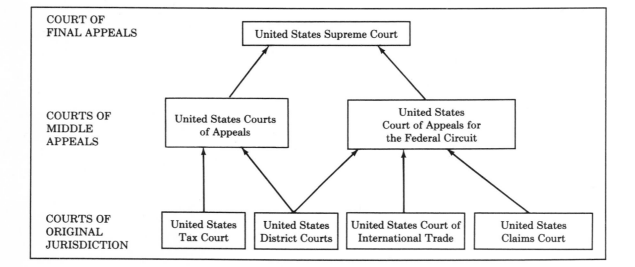

District Court can be appealed directly to the United States Supreme Court without passing through a United States Court of Appeals, e.g., as when the District Court has declared an act of Congress to be unconstitutional.

Figure 1–3 illustrates the division of the federal court system into twelve geographic circuits. Each circuit has its own United States Court of Appeals. The United States District Courts exist within these circuits.

Note on Administrative Agencies

Administrative agencies, both state and federal, are generally part of the executive branch of government. Their function is to carry out or execute legislative statutes and executive orders. Yet in some respects, administrative agencies resemble both the legislative and the judicial branches. Agencies, for example, usually have rule-making powers which closely resemble the legislative or law-making function. And like the judicial branch of government, agencies frequently hear and resolve disputes. A state welfare agency, for example, is empowered to hold hearings, determine the facts of a case, and interpret and apply welfare law to those facts in order to decide whether an individual is eligible for welfare benefits. When an administrative agency functions in this manner, it is said to be acting as a *quasi-judicial* body. Like the courts, the agency may issue a written decision or opinion, which is often called an administrative decision.

An agency exercises its quasi-judicial power at several levels. At the first level there is a *hearing,* which is similar to a trial in a court of original jurisdiction. The presiding agency official—known variously as *hearing examiner, trial examiner,* or *administrative law judge*—will, like the judge in a trial court, take testimony of witnesses and other evidence, determine the facts of the case, and apply the law to those facts in order to render a decision. In many agencies, the findings of fact and the decision of the hearing officer constitute only a recommendation to the Director, Commissioner, Secretary, or other high official who will make the decision at this level. Like the courts, many agencies then provide a second, "appellate" level where a body such as a board or commission reviews the decision of the hearing examiner (or other official) in order to correct errors. In Chapter 2 we will examine these steps in greater detail.

After all these avenues of redress within the agency have been used and a final decision reached, the parties to the dispute are said to have *exhausted their administrative remedies* and may then appeal the final administrative decision to a court. Some of the opinions that we will examine in this book involve a court's review of an administrative decision.

Most administrative agencies are established by and derive their authority from a statute enacted by the legislature. Agency proceedings will be further regulated by the agency's own rules and regulations. Whenever you are working with the decisions of an administrative agency, you should check both of these sources (legislative statutes and the agency's rules and regulations) in order to familiarize yourself with that agency's organization and procedures.

FIGURE 1–3. United States Courts of Appeals and District Courts.

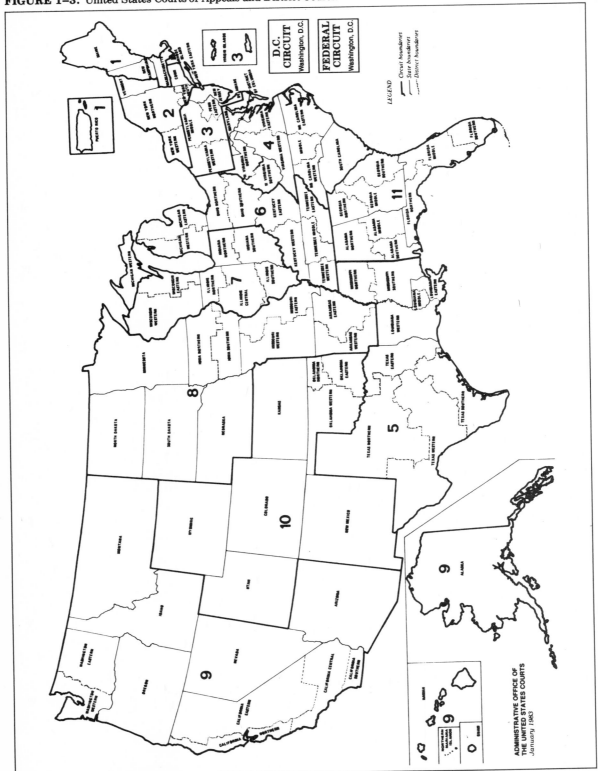

ADMINISTRATIVE OFFICE OF
THE UNITED STATES COURTS
January 1983

Assignment #4

Go to a law library and find the statutes of your state. Use the index to find the statutes on workers' compensation. Read the statues and answer the following questions:

a. What is the name of the administrative agency in your state that administers workers' compensation laws?

b. Briefly describe the steps that can be taken *within* the agency to resolve cases where eligibility for compensation is contested or disputed.

c. Can the parties appeal the agency's decision to the courts? If so, to which court and under what conditions?

d. Ask a law librarian if any administrative decisions of the agency exist in the library. If so, find one of them and briefly summarize the decision.

e. Go to your state digest. Use the index to find any court opinion in which the court took an appeal from an administrative decision of the workers' compensation agency in your state. Go to the opinion itself (in the bound reporter) and briefly summarize the opinion.

Section F. Opinions and Reporters

After an opinion is written by a court, it may be collected with other opinions and published in a set of volumes called *reporters* or *reports*. These volumes are the major source of opinions that you will use in your legal writing.

Reporters containing court opinions are divided into two main categories: *official* and *unofficial*. Often you will be able to locate the same opinion in an official reporter and in one or more unofficial reporters. An official reporter is published under the authority of the government (usually through a statute of the legislature), while unofficial reporters are printed by private companies, e.g., West Publishing Company and the Lawyers Co-Operative Publishing Company. Both kinds of reporters are equally reliable. In fact, some states have discontinued their official reporters and rely on what the private companies print.

The official reporter for opinions of the United States Supreme Court is the *United States Reports* (abbreviated U.S.). There are at least four unofficial reporters for these opinions:

1. *Supreme Court Reporter* (S.Ct.), published by West Publishing Company;

2. *United States Reports, Lawyers Edition,* (L.Ed.), published by the Lawyers Co-Operative Publishing Company;

3. *United States Law Week* (U.S.L.W.), published by the Bureau of National Affairs;

4. *United States Supreme Court Bulletin* (S.Ct.Bull. CCH), published by Commerce Clearing House.

There are no widely used official reporters for the opinions of federal courts other than the United States Supreme Court. The principal source for the opinions of the lower federal courts is West Publishing Company, which prints these opinions in two separate reporters. The *Federal Reporter* (F.) and *Federal Reporter, Second Series* (F.2d) contain the opinions of federal appellate courts, principally the United States Courts of Appeals, while the opinions of the United States District Courts and certain other federal trial courts are found in the *Federal Supplement* (F.Supp.).

The most comprehensive unofficial set of reporters for state court opinions is West Publishing Company's National Reporter System. West has divided the country into seven geographic areas, each consisting of a cluster of states. For each area, a separate reporter is published containing the opinions of the state courts within that geographic area. These *regional reporters*, and the abbreviations used to denote them, are listed below:

- *Pacific Reporter* (P.) and
- *Pacific Reporter, Second Series* (P.2d);
- *North Western Reporter* (N.W.) and
- *North Western Reporter, Second Series* (N.W.2d);
- *South Western Reporter* (S.W.) and
- *South Western Reporter, Second Series* (S.W.2d);
- *North Eastern Reporter* (N.E.) and
- *North Eastern Reporter, Second Series* (N.E.2d);
- *Atlantic Reporter* (A.) and
- *Atlantic Reporter, Second Series* (A.2d);
- *South Eastern Reporter* (S.E.) and
- *South Eastern Reporter, Second Series* (S.E.2d);
- *Southern Reporter* (So.) and
- *Southern Reporter, Second Series* (So.2d).

Note that each of these regional reporters includes a *second series*. This term does *not* mean *second edition*, which refers to a revision of the first edition. Although, as we shall see, an opinion may be overruled, reversed, or otherwise modified by a later opinion, the actual text of the earlier opinion is not amended or revised. Because there are no revisions of opinions, there are no second or succeeding editions of reporters. The opinions are published in a more or less chronological order, and each book is assigned a volume number. When the volume numbers reach a ceratin arbitrary number set by the publisher, a new series is started for all subsequent opinions. The new series will begin with volume one. Thus a second or third series merely contains new and different opinions issued after the prior series of volumes was completed.

In addition to its regional reporters, West Publishing Company also publishes reporters containing opinions from courts in only one state, for example, the *New York Supplement* (N.Y.S.), containing the opinions of New York's state courts, and the *California Reporter* (Cal.Rptr.), containing the opinions of California's state courts.

Other private publishing companies also print state court opinions, but their coverage is much less extensive than that in the West reporters. One of the better known and more useful sets is *American Law Reports* (A.L.R.), published by the Lawyers Co-Operative Publishing Company. That reporter, now into its fourth series, prints selected opinions from state appellate courts. A companion reporter, *American Law Reports, Federal* (A.L.R.Fed.), prints selected opinions from federal courts.

Generally, the organization of the opinions in all of the reporters mentioned thus far is chronological rather than topical. For example, you may find a murder opinion immediately followed by a bankruptcy opinion. There are, however, some reporters that cluster opinions around specified areas of the law. West Publishing Company, for example, has a reporter called *Federal Rules Decisions* (F.R.D.) that is devoted exclusively to opinions deciding procedural questions arising out of federal court rules. Similar reporters exist for virtually every significant legal specialty, such as the *Family Law Reporter* and the *Media Law Reporter*.

Reporters also exist for the written decisions of some administrative agencies, for example, the National Labor Relations Board. These reporters primarily cover federal agencies; it is rare for a state agency to have a comprehensive reporter for its decisions.

Finally, mention should be made of one additional type of opinion. The chief attorney for the federal government is the attorney general. A similar office exists in the government of each state. One of the principal duties of an attorney general is to provide legal advice to agencies and officials of the government, often in response to specific questions sent to the attorney general's office. This advice is issued in the form of opinions which are often published in volumes called *Opinions of the Attorney General.*

Section G. The Structure of a Court Opinion

The opinion of *Cereghino v. Vershum* is reprinted in its entirety in Figure 1–4. It is typical in that it contains most of the basic components of an opinion; it is atypical in that it is very short and relatively uncomplicated. The opinion is taken from *Pacific Reporter, Second Series* (P.2d), an *unofficial* reporter published by West Publishing Company and hence contains features that are peculiar to West reporters, such as the key number system.

In the *Cereghino* opinion, note the phrase "PER CURIAM" just before the opinion begins. This phrase means "by the court." Normally the name of the judge who wrote the opinion would appear at this spot. If the court decides not to name the individual author of the opinion, it will use phrases such as "PER CURIAM," "MEMORANDUM OPINION," or "MEMORANDUM BY THE COURT."

The *Cereghino* opinion contains only one headnote. It is possible for an opinion to have forty to fifty headnotes. Each headnote summarizes only a portion of the opinion. The syllabus, on the other hand, summarizes the entire opinion. In *Cereghino* since there is only one headnote, it, in effect, is almost as comprehensive as the syllabus. If another publisher had printed this opinion (e.g., the Lawyers Co-Operative Publishing Co.), it would have written its own syllabus and headnotes. The latter would summarize the same

FIGURE 1–4.
Structure of a Typical
Unofficial Opinion.:
Cereghino v. Vershum,
538 P.2d 97(1975).

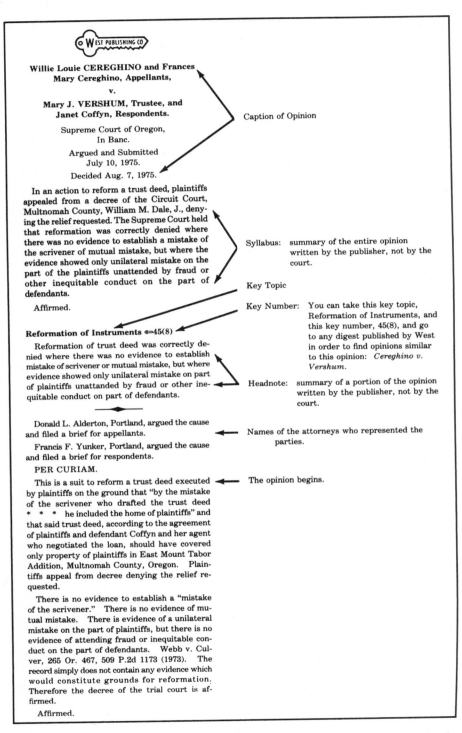

opinion, but the summaries would be worded differently from those in the West reporter since they were prepared by different people.

Suppose that you were reading *Cereghino* in an *official* reporter. Would there be a syllabus and headnotes, and if so, who would have written them?

Occasionally opinions in official reporters will have a syllabus and headnotes. They are usually written by the clerk of the court and not by the judges themselves.

Private publishers are always trying to improve the style and format of their unofficial reporters. Hence, you should not be surprised to find opinions providing features that differ from and add to those found at the beginning of the *Cereghino* opinion, particularly if a publisher other than West has prepared the reporter.

Keep in mind that whether you are reading from an unofficial or an official reporter, you are reading the same opinion. The only differences between unofficial and official opinions are the headnotes and other research features appearing in addition to the language of the court.

Section H. Rules for the Citation of Court Opinions

A *citation* (also called a *cite*) is descriptive information about a legal document that will enable you to find the document in a law library. As we shall see later, one of the basic rules in legal writing is to provide complete citations to all materials relied upon in your writing. Rules for citing the most common kinds of legal documents are found in Appendix C. Throughout this book there will be numerous citations to court opinions. To be able to read these citations, you need at least a general understanding of the structure of a case cite. Hence we will give the basic citation format here. The components of a citation to a court opinion are outlined in Figure 1–5 which diagrams *Cashen v. Spann*, 66 N.J. 541, 334 A.2d 8 (1975). The *Cashen v. Spann* citation format is typical of most citations to court opinions, although there are variations. Many of these variations are illustrated in Appendix C.

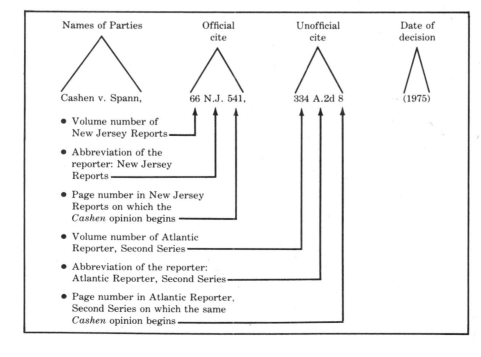

FIGURE 1–5. Components of a Typical Citation.

Chapter Two

Terminology: the Process of Litigation

The following excerpts are from two different court opinions. Examine them and determine how many words and phrases you do *not* understand:

PER CURIAM:

Kirskey McCord Nix, Jr. appeals from the judgment of the district court dismissing his petition for writ of habeas corpus, prohibition and stay in connection with his incarceration in the New Orleans City Jail pending prosecution on both state and federal charges. . . .

AINSWORTH, Circuit Judge:

On August 25, 1971, we considered the appeal and remanded the case with direction that the District Court issue a rule nisi to defendants as to why. . . .

Many new students are overwhelmed by the number of unfamiliar words and phrases they come across in the opinions they read. For example you may not know the precise legal definitions of the following words from the above two excerpts:

From first excerpt:

- per curiam
- judgment
- dismissing
- petition
- writ of habeas corpus
- prohibition
- stay
- pending
- prosecution

From second excerpt:

- remanded
- rule nisi

Another difficulty that might exist is not understanding the legal proceedings that have already occurred in the case. Most of the opinions you will be reading are appellate opinions, i.e., opinions that review prior proceedings in the same litigation. Being able to understand the opinion is in part dependent on your ability to understand the proceedings (at the administrative agency level or in a lower court) that preceded the writing of the opinion before you.

The objectives of this chapter are (1) to increase your vocabulary so that you will be more familiar with the terminology used in case law and (2) to provide you with an overview of the civil and the criminal litigation process so that you can identify the *context* of the opinion you are reading, i.e., what took place, if anything, at what court and/or at what administrative agency before this opinion was written. We started our study of this contεxt in the overview of judicial systems presented in Chapter 1, and we will return to this topic again when we cover prior proceedings in Chapter 7.

We cannot introduce you to every word or phrase that is unclear to you; nor can we cover every conceivable step in the litigation process for every court system in the United States. Hence the following advice:

1. WHEN YOU ARE READING AN OPINION, ALWAYS HAVE A LEGAL DICTIONARY AT YOUR SIDE

You should use a legal dictionary not only for the words that appear Greek to you, but also for the legal terms that you *think* you know. Double-check your own definitions to make sure that you are aware of words that have special meanings. Commonly used legal dictionaries include *Black's Law Dictionary* (West), *Ballantine's Law Dictionary* (Lawyers Co-Operative), and *Oran's Law Dictionary* (West). If the dictionary does not have an extensive abbreviations table, you can obtain explanations for many abbreviations in each volume of *Corpus Juris Secundum,* a legal encyclopedia published by West.

It is important that you always keep in mind the limitations of legal dictionaries. There are dangers in relying too much on the definitions in them:

a. A word may have one meaning in one state and another meaning in another state (the dictionary will usually *not* point out this difference).

b. A word may have one meaning in one area of the law but a different meaning in another area of the law (the dictionary *may not* point out this difference).

c. Special factual circumstances may give the word different meanings (the dictionary *may not* point out these variances).

Of what value, then, is a legal dictionary? It is simply a point of departure. The dictionary may be helpful in giving the *general* meaning of a word. Remain suspicious of *any* definition from a legal dictionary until you have satisfied yourself that the court had this definition in mind when using the word.

2. ALWAYS BE PREPARED TO UNDERTAKE LEGAL RESEARCH TO OBTAIN A BACKGROUND UNDERSTANDING OF THE AREA OF LAW COVERED BY THE OPINION

There will be times when you need more than a legal dictionary at your side. The area of law discussed in the opinion may be so foreign to you that you will need extra help. There are two main sources that can provide this help. First, a legal encyclopedia (p. 209): *Corpus Juris Secundum* or *American Jurisprudence 2d*. Second, a standard hornbook (p. 157) that covers this area of the law. Each of these sources will give you an overview. This background information will usually be very helpful in understanding the opinion. A half hour of your time in these sources may be all that is needed, depending on the complexity of the area and on how much you already know about it.

3. ALWAYS BE PREPARED TO UNDERTAKE LEGAL RESEARCH TO OBTAIN AN OVERVIEW OF THE LEGAL SYSTEM (AGENCIES AND COURTS) IN WHICH THE COURT THAT WROTE THE OPINION YOU ARE EXAMINING IS FOUND

Another major uncertainty that you may have when reading an opinion concerns the various stages of litigation that have occurred in the dispute prior to the opinion you are reading. Eliminating this uncertainty involves (a) being able to identify the various courts and administrative agencies that have been involved in the dispute and (b) understanding the nature of the proceedings that occurred in each court and agency. To understand an opinion, you have to understand its procedural context. As pointed out in Chapter 1, the names of the courts, their powers, and their responsibilities can differ from state to state as well as from federal judicial system to state judicial system. The authority of a court's opinion and its applicability to future litigation will in part depend upon the particular hierarchy of courts within the same judicial system. Hence the significance of assignment #1 (p. 16), which asked you to research the constitution and statutes of your state in order to be thoroughly familiar with your state court structure at the outset.

In the remainder of this chapter you will find two charts on civil and criminal litigation plus a chronological description of the hypothetical (i.e., fictitious) case of Michael Brown. The purpose of the charts and of the hypothetical example is to increase your understanding of the stages of litigation and of some of the basic terminology used at these stages.

The definitions provided in the charts and in the hypothetical case, are, of course, subject to the same infirmities listed above for definitions found in legal dictionaries. You must always be skeptical of general definitions because when you later come across the words in an opinion, more precise definitions than those provided here may be needed. As to the stages of litigation listed in the charts and in the hypothetical case, you must be prepared to make the adjustments needed in order to conform to the precise judicial system of the court that wrote any particular opinion you will be reading.

Chart #1 and Chart #2 present an outline of civil and criminal litigation. In the far left column of each chart there is a statement of the typical events in the litigation process; in the far right column there is an *example* of the kind of decision or opinion that *might* be written in the course of that event or sequence of events. Each of these charts involves one hypothetical litigation sequence. As you can see, the litigation of one case could easily result in a number of separate decisions and opinions.

	Chart #1 **Civil Litigation**	
(Possible proceedings where administrative decisions and court opinions could be written. The events and their sequence presented below are examples only.)		
Event	**Definitions**	**Decisions, Opinions, and Rulings**
	I. Agency Stage	
(If no agency is involved, the litigation begins in court at the pretrial stage.) 1. Someone protests an action taken by the *administrative agency.* 2. *Agency Hearing.* 3. *Intra-Agency Appeal* to a Commission or Board within the agency or to the Director or Secretary of the agency.	*Administrative Agency:* a governmental body whose primary function is to carry out or administer statutes passed by the legislature. *Agency Hearing:* a proceeding, similar to a trial, in which the agency listens to evidence and legal arguments before deciding the case. *Intra-Agency Appeal:* a review within the agency of the earlier decision to determine if that decision was correct.	A mid-level agency official, e.g., Hearing Officer, writes a *recommended decision.* The Commission, Board, Director, or Secretary issues an *administrative decision.*
	II. Pretrial Stage	
4. Plaintiff files a *complaint.* 5. Clerk issues a *summons.* 6. *Service of process* on defendant. 7. Defendant files an *answer.* 8. *Discovery* by written *interrogatories.* 9. *Discovery* by *deposition.* 10. Pretrial *motions.* 11. *Settlement* efforts.	*Complaint:* a pleading in which the plaintiff states claim(s) against defendant. *Summons:* a court notice requiring the defendant to appear and answer the complaint. *Service of process:* the delivery of the summons to the defendant. *Answer:* a pleading in which the defendant gives a response to the plaintiff's complaint. *Discovery:* methods by which one party obtains information from the other party about the litigation prior to trial. *Interrogatories:* a method of discovery through written questions submitted by one party to another before trial. *Deposition:* a method of discovery through a question-and-answer session usually conducted in the offices of one of the attorneys. Parties and prospective witnesses are questioned by the attorneys without a judge being present.	The trial court will often be making rulings concerning these events but rarely will write an opinion on any of the rulings. Occasionally, a party may be allowed to appeal a pretrial ruling to an appeals court which may write an opinion affirming, modifying, or reversing the ruling. Such an appeal is called an *interlocutory* appeal. It takes place before the trial court reaches a final judgment.

Event	Definitions	Decisions, Opinions, and Rulings
II. Pretrial Stage—Continued		
	Their testimony is recorded or transcribed for possible later use. *Motion:* a formal request to the court, e.g., a motion to dismiss. *Settlement:* a resolution of the dispute, making the trial unnecessary.	
III. Trial Stage		

12. *Voir dire.*
 13. *Opening statement* of plaintiff.
 14. *Opening statement* of defendant.
 15. Plaintiff presents its case.
  (a) *evidence* introduced
  (b) *direct examination*
  (c) *cross-examination*
 16. *Motions* to dismiss.
 17. Defendant presents its case.
  (a) *evidence* introduced
  (b) *direct examination*
  (c) *cross-examination*
 18. Closing arguments to jury by counsel.
 19. *Charge* to jury.
 20. *Verdict* of jury.
 21. *Judgment* of court.
	Voir dire: selection of the jury. (Not all cases are tried by a jury).
	
	Opening statement: a summary of the facts the attorney will try to prove during the trial.
	
	Evidence: that which tends to prove or disprove a fact involved in the dispute.
	
	Direct examination: questioning by an attorney of his or her own witnesses.
	
	Cross-examination: questioning of witness by an attorney for the other side.
	
	Charge: the judge's instructions to the jury on how it should go about reaching its verdict.
	
	Verdict: the results of the jury's deliberation.
	
	Judgment: the final statement of the trial court on the rights and responsibilities of the parties.
		The trial court will often be making rulings concerning these events, but rarely will write an opinion on any of the rulings.
		
		After the trial, the trial court will deliver its judgment. Usually an opinion (explaining the judgment) will *not* be written. Several trial courts, however, do sometimes write opinions, e.g., federal trial courts (U.S. District Courts) and New York State trial courts.

IV. Appeal Stage		
22. Filing of *notice of appeal.* 23. Filing of *appellant's brief.* 24. Filing of *appellee's brief.* 25. Filing of reply *brief.* 26. Oral argument by counsel. 27. Decision of court.	*Notice of appeal:* a statement of the intention to seek a review of the trial court's judgment. *Appellant:* the party bringing the appeal because of dissatisfaction with the trial court's judgment. *Appellee:* the party against whom the appeal is brought. *Brief:* written arguments by the attorney on why the trial court acted correctly or incorrectly.	An opinion of the middle appeals court (intermediate appellate court) will often be written. This opinion of the middle appeals court might be further appealed to the highest court, in which event another opinion could be written. [Note that in some states there is no middle appeals court; the appeal goes directly from the trial court to the highest state court.]

Chart #2 Criminal Litigation

(Possible proceedings where court opinions could be written. The events and their sequence presented below are examples only.)

Event	Definitions	Decisions, Opinions, and Rulings
I. Pretrial Stage		
1. *Arrest.* 2. *Initial appearance* before a judge or a magistrate. 3. *Preliminary Hearing.* 4. *Indictment* by Grand Jury. 5. *Arraignment.* 6. Limited pretrial discovery. 7. Pretrial motions.	*Arrest:* to take someone into custody in order to bring him or her before the proper authorities. *Initial appearance:* a court proceeding during which the accused is told of the charges, a bail decision is made, and arrangements for the next proceeding are specified. *Preliminary hearing:* a court proceeding during which a decision is made as to whether there is probable cause to believe that the accused committed the crime(s) charged. *Indictment:* a formal charge issued by the grand jury accusing the defendant of a crime. (If no grand jury is involved in the case, the accusation is contained in a document called an information.) *Arraignment:* a court proceeding in which the defendant is formally charged with the crime and enters a plea. Arrangements are then made for the trial.	The trial court will often be making rulings concerning these events but rarely will write an opinion on any of the rulings. Occasionally, a party may be allowed to appeal a pretrial ruling immediately to an appeals court which may write an opinion affirming, modifying, or reversing the ruling. This interlocutory appeal takes place before the trial court reaches a final judgment.
II. Trial Stage		
8. *Voir dire.* 9. *Opening statements* of attorneys. 10. Government presents its case against the defendant. (a) *evidence* introduced (b) *direct examination* (c) *cross-examination* 11. Motions to dismiss. 12. Defendant presents its case. (a) *evidence* introduced (b) *direct examination* (c) *cross-examination*	*Voir dire:* selection of the jury (not all cases are tried by a jury). *Opening statements:* a summary of the facts the attorney will try to prove during the trial. *Evidence:* that which tends to prove or disprove a fact involved in the dispute. *Direct examination:* questioning by an attorney of his or her own witnesses. *Cross-examination:* questioning of witness by an attorney for the other side.	The trial court will often be making rulings concerning these events but rarely will write an opinion on any of the rulings. After the trial, the trial court will deliver its judgment. Usually no opinion (explaining the judgment) will be written. Several trial courts, however, do sometimes write opinions, e.g., federal trial courts (U.S. District Courts) and New York State trial courts.

Event	Definitions	Decisions, Opinions, and Rulings
13. Arguments to jury by attorneys 14. *Charge* to jury. 15. *Verdict* to jury. 16. *Judgment* of court, including the sentence if defendant is convicted.	*Charge:* the judge's instructions to the jury on how it should go about reaching its verdict. *Verdict:* the results of the jury's deliberation. *Judgment:* the final statement of the trial court disposing of the criminal charges stated in the indictment or information.	
III. Appeal Stage		
17. Filing of *notice of appeal.* 18. Filing of *appellant's brief.* 19. Filing of *appellee's brief.* 20. Filing of reply *brief.* 21. Oral argument by counsel. 22. Decision of court.	*Notice of appeal:* a statement of the intention to seek a review of the trial court's judgment. *Appellant:* the party bringing the appeal because of dissatisfaction with the trial court's judgment. *Appellee:* the party against whom the appeal is brought. *Brief:* written arguments by the attorney on why the trial court acted correctly or incorrectly.	An opinion in the middle appeals court (intermediate appellate court) will often be written. This opinion in the middle appeals court might be appealed to the highest court, in which event another opinion could be written. [Note that in some states, there is no middle court; the appeal goes directly from the trial court to the highest state court.]

The Legal Odyssey of Michael Brown:
An Anatomy of the Litigation Process

Michael Brown is a truck driver for the Best Bread Company. Several years ago, as Brown was walking home from work, Harold Clay, an old friend from the past, stopped and offered him a ride. They had not seen each other since Clay had moved out of state a number of years ago. They carried on an excited conversation as Clay drove. After a few blocks, a car driven by George Miller, a resident of a neighboring state, ran through a red light and struck Clay's car. All three individuals were seriously injured and were taken to a local hospital. Clay died two weeks later from injuries received in the crash.

Several days after the accident, Brown's boss, Frank Best, wrote Brown a letter. In it, Best said that he had learned that the police had found about one-half ounce of heroin under the front seat of Clay's car and were planning to charge Brown with possession of narcotics with intent to distribute. Best also stated that several thefts had occurred at the company warehouse recently and that he now suspected Brown of having been involved in them. For these reasons, he decided to fire Brown, effective immediately.

There are at least three different legal disputes involving Brown that could arise out of this fact situation:

1. A dispute among Brown, Miller, and Clay's estate regarding liability for the accident;

2. A dispute between Brown and the government regarding the criminal charges;

3. A dispute among Brown, the Best Bread Company, and the State Unemployment Compensation Board concerning Brown's entitlement to unemployment compensation benefits.

Each of these disputes could lead to a number of court opinions. The third dispute might involve an administrative decision, possibly followed by one or more court opinions, all concerning Brown's unemployment compensation claim.

1. LIABILITY FOR THE ACCIDENT

Brown suffered substantial injury as a result of the crash. From whom could he collect *damages?* Who was *liable* for the accident. Was Miller at fault? Clay? Was each of them *jointly* and *severally* liable?

Damages:
> An award of money (paid by the wrongdoer) to compensate the person who has been harmed.

Liable:
> Legally responsible.

Joint and several liability:
> When two or more persons are jointly and severally liable, they are legally responsible, together and individually. Each wrongdoer is individually responsible for the entire judgment. The person who has been wronged can collect from one of them or from all of them together.

Brown hired Brenda Davis, Esq. to represent him. Once Brown signed the *retainer,* Davis would later enter an *appearance* and become the *attorney of record.*

Retainer:
> A contract between attorney and client stating the nature of the services to be rendered and the cost of the services.

Appearance:
> Going to court on behalf of. The attorney usually appears by filing a "notice of appearance" in court, which is often accomplished through a *praecipe.* A praecipe is a formal request to the court that something be done. Here the request is that the attorney become the attorney of record.

Attorney of record:
> An attorney who has filed a notice of appearance (e.g., through a praecipe) and who hence is formally mentioned in court records as the official attorney of the party. Once this occurs, the attorney may not be able to withdraw from the case without court permission.

The attorney explained that a number of factors had to be considered before deciding on the *forum* in which to sue Miller and Clay's *estate.* Brown might be able to bring the suit in a number of places: (a) in a state trial court where Brown lives, (b) in a state trial court where Miller lives, (c) in a state trial court where Clay's estate is located, (d) in the federal trial court sitting in Brown's state, (e) in the federal trial court sitting in Miller's state, or (f) in the federal trial court sitting in the state where Clay's estate is located. The reason Brown could sue in a federal court was the existence of *diversity of citizenship:* all the parties involved in the litigation came from different states. Davis advised Brown to sue in federal court. The suit would be brought in the U.S. District Court sitting in Brown's own state since this would be most convenient *venue* for Brown.

Forum:
  The court where the case is to be tried.

Estate:
  All the property left by a decedent (one who has died) from which any obligations or debts of the decedent must be paid.

Diversity of citizenship:
  A kind of jurisdiction giving a federal court the power to hear a case based upon the fact that (a) the parties to the litigation are from different states, and (b) the amount of money involved exceeds the amount specified by federal statute.

Venue:
  The place of the trial. In most judicial systems, there is more than one trial court, e.g., one for each county or district. The selection of a particular trial court within a judicial system is referred to as a *choice of venue.*

Having decided on a court, Davis was ready to begin the lawsuit. She drafted a *complaint,* naming Brown as the *plaintiff* and *stating a cause of action* in tort for negligence against Miller and Clay's estate as *codefendants.* The complaint was the first *pleading* of the case. In the complaint, Davis stated the facts that she felt constituted a cause of action for negligence. Some of the factual *allegations* were based upon personal knowledge of Brown, while others were based upon *information and belief.* The *ad damnum* clause of the complaint asked for $100,000 in damages. When she finished drafting the complaint, Ms. Davis signed the pleading, attached a written demand for a *jury trial,* and *filed* both documents with the clerk of the court.

Complaint:
  A pleading (see definition below) filed by the plaintiff stating his or her version of the facts concerning the defendant's alleged wrongdoing.

Plaintiff:
  The party initiating the lawsuit.

Cause of action:
  A legally acceptable reason for suing.

Stating a cause of action:
Including in the complaint all the facts which, if proved at trial, would entitle the plaintiff to win (assuming the defendant could not establish any defenses that would defeat the case).

Codefendants:
More than one defendant being sued in the same litigation.

Pleading:
A paper or document, e.g., a complaint, filed in court stating the position of one of the parties on the cause(s) of action or on the defenses.

Allegation:
A claimed fact; a fact that a party will try to prove at trial.

Information and belief:
A standard legal term used to indicate that the allegation is not based on the firsthand knowledge of the person making the allegation but that the person, nevertheless, in good faith believes the allegation to be true.

Ad damnum:
A statement in the complaint in which the plaintiff asks for a specified sum of money as damages.

Jury trial:
A jury is a group of citizens who will decide the issues or questions of fact at the trial. The judge decides the issues or questions of law. If there is no jury at the trial, then the judge decides both the questions of law and the questions of fact.

Filed:
Formally presented to a court (usually to the clerk of the court) or to an opposing party.

Service of process came next. It was accomplished when a copy of the complaint, along with the *summons,* was served on both Miller and on the legal representative of Clay's estate. Davis did not serve these parties herself. She used a *process server* who then had to file an *affidavit* of service with the court indicating the circumstances under which service was achieved. Service was made before the *statute of limitations* on the negligence cause of action had run out. Once the defendants were properly served, the court acquired *in personam jurisdiction* over them.

Service of process:
The delivery of a formal notice to a defendant ordering him or her to appear in court in order to answer the allegations made by the plaintiff.

Summons:
The formal notice from the court ordering the defendant to appear. The summons is *served* on the defendant. The words summons and process are often used interchangeably.

Process server:
A person who charges a fee for serving process.

Affidavit:
> A written statement of fact in which the person (called the *affiant*) swears that the written statement is true.

Statute of limitations:
> The law establishing the period within which the lawsuit must be commenced; if it is not brought within that time, it can never be brought.

In personam jurisdiction:
> Personal jurisdiction: the power of the court over the person of the defendant obtained in part by proper service of process.

Both Miller and Clay's estate filed *motions to dismiss* for *failure to state a cause of action.* The motions were denied by the court.

Motion to dismiss:
> A request that the court decide that a party may not further litigate a claim, i.e., that the case on that claim be dropped.

Failure to state a cause of action:
> Failure of the plaintiff to allege enough facts in the complaint. Even if the plaintiff proved all the facts alleged in the complaint, the facts would not establish a cause of action entitling the plaintiff to recover against the defendant. The motion to dismiss for failure to state a cause of action is sometimes referred to as (a) a *demurrer* or (b) a *failure to state a claim upon which relief can be granted.*

Because the case had been filed in a federal court, the *procedural law* governing the case would be found in the *Federal Rules of Civil Procedure.* (The *substantive law* of the case would be the state law of negligence.) According to the Federal Rules of Civil Procedure, Miller and Clay's estate were each required to file an *answer* to Brown's complaint within twenty days. Miller filed his answer almost immediately. Since Clay was dead and unable to tell his attorney what had happened at the accident, the attorney for the estate had some difficulty in *drafting* an answer and was unable to file it within the twenty days. In order to avoid a *default judgment* against the estate, the attorney filed a *motion* asking for an extension of thirty days within which to file the answer. The motion was granted by the court, and the answer was filed within the new deadline.

Procedural law:
> The technical rules setting forth the steps required to conduct a lawsuit.

Federal Rules of Civil Procedure:
> The technical rules governing the manner in which civil cases are brought in and progress through the federal trial courts.

Substantive law:
> The rights and duties imposed by law (e.g., the duty to use reasonable care) other than procedural rights and duties.

Answer:
> The pleading that responds to or answers allegations of the complaint.

Draft:
> To write.

Default judgment:
> An order of the court deciding the case in favor of the plaintiff because the defendant failed to appear or to file an answer before the deadline.

Motion:
> A request made to the court, e.g., a motion to dismiss. The party making the motion is called the *movant*. The verb is *move*, as in "I move that the court permit the demonstration."

The answer filed on behalf of Clay's estate denied all allegations of negligence and raised an *affirmative defense* of contributory negligence against Brown on the theory that if Clay had been partially responsible for the collision, it was because Brown had distracted him through his conversation in the car. Finally, the answer of Clay's estate raised a *cross-claim* against the codefendant Miller, alleging that the accident had been caused solely by Miller's negligence. The estated asked $1,000,000 in damages.

Defense:
> A response to the claims of the other party setting forth reasons why the claims should not be granted. The defense may be as simple as a flat denial of the other party's factual allegations or may involve entirely new factual allegations. (In the latter situation, the defense is an *affirmative defense.*)

Affirmative defense:
> A defense that is based on new factual allegations by the defendant not contained in the plaintiff's allegations.

Cross-claim:
> Usually, a claim by one codefendant against another codefendant.

Miller's answer also raised the defense of contributory negligence against Brown and stated a cross-claim against Clay's estate, alleging that the accident had been caused solely by the negligence of Clay or of Clay and Brown together. On this same theory, that Brown together with Clay had negligently caused the accident, Miller's answer also stated a *counterclaim* against Brown. Miller sought $20,000 from Brown and $20,000 against Clay's estate as damages.

Counterclaim:
> A claim or a cause of action against the plaintiff stated in the defendant's answer.

For a time, Miller and his attorney considered filing a *third-party complaint* against his own insurance company since the company would be liable for any judgment against him. They decided against this strategy since they did not want to let the jury know that Miller was insured. If the jury knew this fact, it might be more inclined to reach a verdict in favor of the plaintiff and for a high amount of damages. The strategy was also unnecessary because there was no indication that Miller's insurer would *contest* its obligation to compensate Miller for any damages that he might have to pay Brown or Clay's estate in the event that the trial resulted in an *adverse judgment* against him.

Third-party complaint:
> A complaint filed by the defendant against a third party (i.e., a person not presently a party to the lawsuit). This complaint alleges that the third party is or may be liable for all or part of the damages that the plaintiff may win from the defendant.

Contest:
> To challenge.

Adverse judgment:
> A judgment or decision against you.

At this point five assorted claims, cross-claims and counterclaims had been filed by the parties. A sixth, Miller's third-party claim against his insurer, had been considered but ultimately had not been filed. These claims and their relationship to each other are illustrated in Figure 2–1.

1. Brown's original complaint for negligence against Miller and

2. against Clay's Estate, as codefendants.

3. Defendant Miller's counterclaim for negligence against plaintiff, Brown.

4. Defendant Miller's cross-claim for negligence against his codefendant, the Estate.

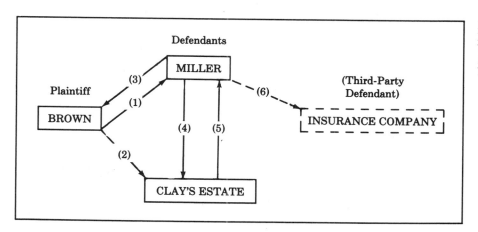

FIGURE 2–1.
Diagram of the Various Claims in the Brown/Miller/Estate Litigation.

5. Defendant Estate's cross-claim for negligence against its codefendant, Miller.

6. Third-party complaint which defendant Miller considered but ultimately decided *not* to file against his insurance company.

Once the pleadings were filed, all three parties began to seek *discovery.* Each attorney first served written *interrogatories* on the opposing parties. These were followed by *depositions* and *requests for admissions.* Miller refused to answer several questions during his deposition in his attorney's office. As a result, Brown's attorney had to file a discovery motion, seeking an *order* from the court compelling Miller to answer. A *hearing* was subsequently held on the motion, and after listening to arguments by all of the attorneys, the judge granted the motion in full, ordering Miller to answer the questions. Faced with the court's order, Miller answered the remaining questions.

Each party then filed a *motion for summary judgment.* The judge denied these motions, and the case was ready for trial.

Discovery:
> The pretrial devices that can be used by one party to obtain facts and information about the case from the other party in order to assist in preparing for trial.

Interrogatories:
> A discovery device consisting of written questions about the case submitted by one party to the other party. The answers to the interrogatories are usually given under oath, i.e., the person answering the questions signs a sworn statement that the answers are true.

Deposition:
> A discovery device by which one party asks oral questions of the other party or of a witness for the other party. The person who is *deposed* is called the *deponent.* The deposition is conducted under oath outside of the courtroom, usually in one of the lawyer's offices. (A recording or transcript—a word-for-word account—is made of the deposition.)

Requests for admissions:
> Written statements of facts concerning the case which are submitted to an adverse party and which that party is required to admit or deny; those statements that are admitted will be treated by the court as having been established and need not be proven at trial.

Order:
> An official command by the court requiring, allowing, or forbidding some act to be done.

Hearing:
> A proceeding in which the judge or presiding officer examines some aspect of the dispute. An *adversary hearing* exists when both parties are present at the hearing to argue their respective positions. An *ex parte hearing* exists when only one party is present at the hearing. Hearings occur in court as well as in administrative agencies.

Summary:

Done relatively quickly and informally without going through an entire adversary hearing or an entire trial.

Motion for a summary judgment:

A request by a party that a decision be reached on the basis of the pleadings alone without having to go through with the entire trial. A summary judgment is normally allowed only when there is no dispute between the parties as to any of the material or significant facts. Summary judgment can be granted on the entire case or on some of the claims raised within it.

As the trial date neared, each of the attorneys received a notice asking them to appear before a *magistrate* for a *pretrial conference.* On the appointed day, the attorneys met with the magistrate to prepare the case for trial. During the conference, the magistrate, with the help of the attorneys, prepared a pretrial statement for the trial judge on the case. It contained a statement of those facts that had been *stipulated* by the attorneys, the facts that were still *in issue,* and a list describing the *tangible evidence* and witnesses that each attorney intended to *introduce* at the trial.

Magistrate:

A judicial officer having some but not all of the powers of a judge. In the federal trial courts (the U.S. District Courts), the magistrate may conduct many of the preliminary or pretrial proceedings in both civil and criminal cases.

Pretrial conference:

A conference held between the judge (or magistrate) and the attorneys to prepare the case for trial. At this conference, the presiding officer often encourages the parties to settle the dispute on their own in order to avoid a trial.

Stipulated:

Agreed to. A *stipulation* of fact will not be *contested* or disputed so that no evidence need be presented as to the truth or falsity of that fact at trial.

In issue:

In question. A question or issue *of fact* means that the truth or falsity of that fact must be established at the trial. A question or issue *of law* means that the judge must rule on what the law is or how the law applies to the facts.

Tangible evidence:

Physical evidence; evidence that can be seen or touched, e.g., letters, photographs, skeletons. *Testimonial evidence* is evidence that can be heard, e.g., the statements made by anyone sitting in the witness box.

Introduce:

To place evidence formally before the court so that it will become part of the record for consideration by the judge and jury.

After some delay, the case was finally *set for trial*. All of the parties, their attorneys, and the witnesses assembled in the courtroom. The judge entered, took the bench, and ordered the *bailiff* to summon a *jury panel* for the trial. Once the potential or prospective jurors were seated in the courtroom, *voir dire* began. Several jurors were *challenged for cause* and dismissed—one because she worked for the insurance company that had issued the policy on Miller's car. The position as to this prospective juror was that she might be *biased*. Several other jurors were dismissed as a result of *peremptory challenges*. A panel of twelve jurors plus two *alternates* was eventually selected and seated in the jury box.

Set for trial:
>   To schedule a date when the trial is to begin.

Bailiff:
>   A court employee who keeps order in the courtroom and renders general assistance to the judge.

Jury panel:
>   A group of citizens who have been called to jury duty. From this group, juries for particular trials will be selected.

Voir dire:
>   The oral examination of prospective jurors by the lawyers, by the judge, or by both the lawyers and the judge for purposes of selecting a jury.

Challenge for cause:
>   A request from a party to a judge that a prospective juror *not* be allowed to become a member of this jury because of specified causes or reasons.

Peremptory challenge:
>   A request from a party to a judge that a prospective juror *not* be allowed to become a member of this jury. No reason or "cause" need be stated for this type of challenge. Both sides are allowed a limited number of peremptory challenges, but they will be granted as many challenges for cause as they can establish.

Bias:
>   The potential for unfairness because of prior knowledge or involvement leading to possible preconceptions and a lack of open-mindedness.

Alternate:
>   An extra juror who will sit with the regular jurors and who will take the place of a regular juror if one becomes incapacitated during the trial.

When the jury was seated, Brown's attorney rose and told the judge that she wished to invoke the *rule on witnesses*. The judge nodded to the bailiff who then led all of the witnesses (except for the parties themselves) out of the courtroom. Brown's attorney then began the trial with her *opening statement* to the jury. When she finished, Miller's attorney also delivered an opening statement. The attorney for Clay's estate, however, decided to reserve his opening statement until it was time for him to present the estate's case.

Rule on witnesses:
    A rule that requires certain witnesses to be removed from the court-room until it is time for their individual testimony so that they will not be able to hear each other's testimony.

Opening statement:
    A speech or presentation made by each attorney to the jury summariz-ing the facts the attorney intends to try to prove during the trial.

Brown's attorney, whose client had the *burden of proof,* called her first witness, a ten-year-old boy who had seen the accident. Miller's attorney im-mediately rose and requested a *bench conference.* When all the attorneys had gathered around the bench, he stated that he *objected* to the witness on the basis of *competency.* The judge then *excused the jury* temporarily while he conducted a brief *examination* of the witness. The judge *overruled* the objec-tion upon being satisfied that the boy was old enough to understand the obli-gation to tell the truth and had the ability to communicate what he knew.

Burden of proof:
    The responsibility of proving a fact at the trial. Generally, the party making the factual allegation has the burden of proof as to that allegation.

Bench conference:
    A discussion between the judge and the attorneys held at the judge's bench so that the jury cannot hear what is being said.

Objection:
    A formal challenge usually directed at the evidence that the other side is trying to pursue or introduce.

Competency:
    Legal capacity to testify.

Excused the jury:
    Asked the jury to leave the room.

Examination:
    Questioning, asking questions of.

Overrule:
    Deny. (The word *overrule* is also used when a court repudiates the hold-ing of a prior opinion written by the same court.)

The jury was brought back into the courtroom, and Brown's attorney began her *direct examination.* After a few questions, Miller's attorney again objected, this time on the *ground* that the child's answer had been *hearsay.* The judge *sustained* the objection and, after instructing the jury to disregard the boy's answer, ordered it *stricken from the record.* Brown's attorney con-tinued her examination of the witness for a few minutes before announcing that she had no further questions. The attorney for the estate then rose to conduct a brief *cross-examination* of the boy. He was followed by Miller's attorney, whose cross-examination was also brief. There was no *re-direct examination.*

Direct examination:
Questioning the witness first. Normally the attorney who *calls* the witness to the stand conducts the direct examination.

Ground:
Reason.

Hearsay:
Testimony in court on a statement asserted or made by someone else out of court when the statement is being offered to establish the truth of the statement, and thus its value is based on the credibility of the out-of-court asserter.

Sustain:
To grant or uphold the objection.

Strike from the record:
To remove the testimony or evidence from the written record or *transcript* of the trial.

Cross-examination:
Questioning the witness after the other side has completed the direct examination. Generally, the person conducting the cross-examination must limit himself or herself to the topics or subject matters raised during the direct examination of this witness by the other side.

Re-direct examination:
Questioning the witness after the cross-examination. The attorney who conducted the direct examination conducts the redirect examination.

Brown's attorney, Davis, called several other witnesses who had seen the accident occur. Each witness was examined and cross-examined in much the same fashion as the boy had been. Davis was about to call her fourth witness, Dr. Hadley, when the judge announced a brief recess for lunch. The judge admonished the jury not to discuss the case with anyone, even among themselves, and ordered everyone to be back in the courtroom by 2:00 P.M.

Dr. Hadley was called to the stand immediately after the lunch recess. Brown's attorney began her direct examination with a series of questions about the doctor's medical training and experience in order to *qualify* him as an *expert witness.* She then moved that Dr. Hadley be recognized as an expert witness. The *court,* with no objections by either defense counsel, granted the motion.

Qualify:
To demonstrate background and experience sufficient to convince the court that the witness has expertise in a particular area.

Expert witness:
A witness who has been *qualified* as an expert and who, therefore, will be allowed to give his or her expert opinion in order to assist the jury in

understanding those technical subjects not within the understanding of the average lay person.

Court:

Here refers to the judge trying the case.

Brown's attorney then asked the doctor to testify as to the nature and extent of the injuries that the plaintiff, Brown, had suffered as a result of the accident. In addition to multiple cuts and bruises, the doctor stated that Brown had suffered a broken knee. The knee, in the doctor's opinion, had been permanently injured and Brown would continue to suffer periodic pain and stiffness due to the injury. In order to show the expense that these injuries had cost Brown, the attorney produced the original copies of the bills that the doctor had sent to Brown. She handed the bills to the *clerk* who marked them as plaintiff's *exhibit* number one. After allowing defense counsel to inspect the bills, Brown's attorney handed them to the doctor who promptly identified them. The attorney then *moved the bills into evidence* and turned the witness over to defense counsel for cross-examination.

Clerk:

The court employee who assists the judge in record keeping at the trial.

Exhibit:

An item of physical or tangible evidence that is to be or has been offered to the court for inspection.

Move . . . into evidence:

To request that the items be formally declared *admissible* (which is not the same as declaring them to be true; they are admitted simply for consideration as to their truth or falsity).

It was late in the afternoon when Brown's attorney finished with her final witness, Brown himself. The judge did not want to recess for the day, however, until the defendants completed their cross-examination of Brown. After about an hour, all the defense attorneys completed their questioning of Brown, and Brown's attorney *rested her case.* The judge *adjourned* the trial until the following morning.

Rest one's case:

To announce formally that you have concluded the presentation of evidence (e.g., through the introduction of tangible evidence, through direct examination of your own witnesses). While the other side presents its case, however, you will be entitled to cross-examine its witnesses.

Adjourn:

To halt the proceedings temporarily.

On the following morning, the attorney for Clay's estate advised the judge that he had a preliminary matter to bring up before the jury was brought into the courtroom. He then proceeded to make a motion for a *directed verdict* in favor of the estate on Brown's claim of negligence. Miller's attorney made a similar motion on behalf of his client. The judge listened to arguments by the attorneys and then stated his decision. As to defendant Miller, the motion was denied because the plaintiff had introduced sufficient evidence to make out a *prima facie case* of negligence which should go to the jury. As to the estate, the judge would neither grant nor deny the motion but would *take it under advisement.*

Directed verdict:
>   To order the jury to reach a verdict for the party making the motion on the ground that the other side, who has just rested its case, has failed to produce enough convincing evidence to establish a cause of action.

Prima facie case:
>   The party's evidence, if believed by the jury, would be legally sufficient to support a verdict in favor of that party, i.e., the party has introduced evidence which, if believed, would include all the facts necessary to establish a cause of action. If the plaintiff *fails* to establish a prima facie case, the judge will decide the case in favor of the defendant without any further proceedings. If the judge finds that there *is* a prima facie case, the defendant will be allowed an opportunity to produce contrary evidence. The case will then go to the jury to decide which version of the facts is true.

Take under advisement:
>   To delay ruling on the motion until another time.

The jury was summoned into the courtroom and seated in the jury box for the second day of the trial. The attorney for the estate began his case by making an opening statement to the jury, reserved from the previous day. He then proceeded to call his witnesses. He had only a few witnesses and was able to conclude his case just before noon, at which time he introduced Clay's death certificate into evidence. The judge then declared a recess for lunch.

Miller's attorney began to present his case in the afternoon, and by late afternoon he too had rested his case. The judge dismissed the jury until the following morning and told the attorneys to be prepared for *closing arguments* at that time. He also asked them to submit any *jury instructions* that they would like to request, so that he could review them. Brown's attorney requested an instruction that the codefendants had to overcome a *presumption* of negligence against them. The judge denied this request. Finally, he announced that he had decided to deny the estate's earlier motion for a directed verdict.

Closing argument:
>   The final statements by the attorneys summarizing the evidence that they think they have established and the evidence that they think the other side has failed to establish.

Jury instructions:
>   A statement of the guidelines and law given by the judge to the jury which they are to use in deciding the issues of fact. The instructions to the jury are also referred to as the *charge* to the jury. The attorneys are

usually allowed to submit proposed instructions for consideration by the judge.

Presumption:

An assumption that a certain fact is true. A *rebuttable presumption* is an assumption that can be overcome or changed if the other side introduces enough facts to overcome it. If the other side does not rebut the presumption, then the assumption stands. A *nonrebuttable* presumption cannot be overcome no matter how convincing the evidence of the other side against the assumption.

Closing arguments began late the following morning. Each attorney carefully reviewed the evidence for the jury and argued for a *verdict* in favor of his or her client. Following a brief recess for lunch, the judge thanked the alternate jurors for their time and dismissed them. He then began to instruct the remaining twelve jurors as to the law they were to follow in finding the facts and in reaching a verdict. He said that they, as jurors, were the finders of fact and were to base their decision solely upon the testimony and exhibits introduced during the trial. He explained the concept of burden of proof and stated which party had to carry this burden as to each of the various *elements* of negligence. Each element had to be proved by a *preponderance of the evidence.* This was the *standard of proof* for this kind of case. Finally, he described the manner in which they should compute the amount of damages, if any, suffered by the parties. The jury was then led out of the courtroom to deliberate on its verdict. The judge retired to his chambers, and the attorneys settled back with their clients to wait.

Verdict:

The final decision of the jury.

Elements:

Here, the components of a cause of action.

Preponderance of the evidence:

A standard of proof (used in many civil suits) that is met when a party's evidence on a fact indicates that it is "more likely than not" that the fact is as the party alleges it to be.

Standard of proof:

A statement of how convincing the evidence must be in order for a party to comply with his or her burden of proof. The main standards of proof are proof *beyond a reasonable doubt* (in criminal cases only), proof *by clear and convincing evidence,* and proof by *preponderance of the evidence.*

After about an hour, the judge received a note from the foreman of the jury, asking that the jury be allowed to view several of the exhibits. The items requested consisted largely of the various medical bills allegedly incurred by Brown and by Clay. The attorneys for Brown and for the estate took this as a good sign—the jury had probably decided the case against Miller and were now trying to compute damages.

A second note arrived in another hour, announcing that the jury had reached a verdict. The bailiff summoned everyone back to the courtroom, and the jury came in a few minutes later. At the clerk's request, the foreman rose to read the verdict. On Brown's original complaint against Miller for negligence, the jury found for Brown and against Miller, awarding Brown $30,000 in damages. However, on Brown's complaint against Clay's estate (the codefendant), the jury decided in favor of the estate, finding that Clay had not been negligent. The jury found for the estate on its cross-claim against its codefendant, Miller, awarding $750,000 in damages to the estate. Finally, the jury found against Miller on his own cross-claim against the estate, as well as on his counterclaim against Brown. The judge entered a judgment against Miller in the amounts awarded by the jury. After denying a motion by Miller for a *judgment notwithstanding the verdict,* he thanked the jurors and dismissed them.

Judgment:
> The final decision of the court resolving the dispute and determining the rights and obligations of the parties. Many judgments order the losing party to do something (e.g., pay damages) or to refrain from doing something. A *declaratory judgment* establishes the rights and obligations of the parties, but it does not order the parties to do or refrain from doing anything.

Judgment notwithstanding the verdict:
> A judgment by the court that is opposite to the verdict reached by the jury, in effect, overruling the jury. (Also referred to as a judgment n.o.v.)

Miller's attorney immediately made a *motion for a new trial,* arguing several possible grounds. When this motion was denied by the trial judge, he moved for a *reduction of the verdict* on the grounds that the amounts awarded were excessive. This motion was also denied, and the attorney announced his intention to *appeal.* The judge did, however, grant Miller a *stay* of the judgment, conditioned upon his filing a *timely notice of appeal* and posting the appropriate *bond.*

Motion for a new trial:
> A request that the judge set aside the judgment and order a new trial on the basis that the trial was improper or unfair due to specified prejudicial errors that occurred.

Reduction of the verdict:
> Lowering the amount of the damage award reached by the jury.

Appeal:
> To ask a court of *appellate jurisdiction* (a higher court within the same judicial system as the trial court) to *review* or examine the decision of the lower court on the basis that the lower court made some errors of law in conducting the trial.

Stay:
> To delay enforcement or *execution* of the court's judgment.

Timely:
> On time, according to the time specified by law.

Notice of appeal:
> A document announcing an intention to appeal filed with the appellate court and served on the opposing party.

Bond:
> A sum of money deposited with the court to assure compliance with some requirement.

Miller asked his attorney what the $30,000 verdict against him meant. Since Brown had originally sued for $100,000, could Brown later sue Miller again for the rest of the amount he claimed? The attorney explained that, because of the stay granted by the judge, Miller would not have to pay anything until a decision on appeal had been reached. Furthermore, Brown could not sue Miller again on the same cause of action because Brown had received a *judgment on the merits* which would be *res judicata* and would *bar* any later suit on the same negligence cause of action. The same would be true of a later negligence action by Clay's estate against Miller.

Judgment on the merits:
> A decision on the substance of the claims raised. Normally, a judgment of dismissal based solely on some procedural error is *not* a judgment on the merits. The latter kind of judgment is often referred to as a *dismissal without prejudice.* A party who has received a judgment on the merits cannot bring the same suit again. A party whose case has been dismissed without prejudice can bring the same suit again so long as the procedural errors are corrected (i.e., cured) in the later action.

Res judicata:
> The legal doctrine that a judgment on the merits will prevent the same parties from relitigating the same cause of action on the same facts; the parties have already had their day in court.

Bar:
> Prevent or stop.

Miller's attorney filed his notice of appeal with the United States Court of Appeals and posted bond the following week. As attorney for the *appellant,* it was also his duty to see to it that the *record,* including *transcripts* and copies of exhibits, was transmitted to the Court of Appeals and that the case was *docketed* by the clerk of that court. Miller's attorney then had forty days in which to draft and file his *brief* with the Court of Appeals. He served copies of the brief on the attorneys for the *appellees,* Brown and Clay's estate, who in turn filed their briefs concerning the *issues on appeal.*

Appellant:
> The party initiating the appeal; the party who is complaining of error(s) made by the lower court.

Record:
> The official collection of all the trial pleadings, exhibits, orders, and word-for-word testimony that took place during the trial.

Transcript:
> Word-for-word typed record of everything that was said "on the record" during the trial. The court reporter types this transcription, which is paid for by the parties requesting it.

Docket:
> The court's official calendar of pending cases. Once all of the necessary papers have been filed, the appeal is "docketed" by the clerk, i.e., placed on the court's official calendar.

Brief:
> A written argument presented to the appeals court by a party stating the legal issues on appeal and the positions of the party on those issues—all relating to the claimed errors that occurred during the trial.

Appellee:
> The party against whom the appeal is brought. (Also called the respondent.) Generally the appellee is satisfied with what the trial court did and wishes the appellate court to approve of or *affirm* the trial court's judgment.

Issues on appeal:
> The claimed errors of law committed by the trial judge below. The appellate court does not retry the case. No witnesses are called, and no testimony is taken by the appellate court. The court examines the record and determines whether errors of law were committed by the trial judge.

Several months passed before the attorneys finally received a notice from the clerk of the court of appeals that the appeal had been scheduled for *oral argument* before a three-judge *panel* of the court. The arguments were heard a few weeks later. Six months after oral argument, the attorneys received the decision of the court in its written *opinion*. By a vote of two to one (one judge *dissenting*), the court *affirmed* the judgments against Miller. The only error which the majority found was the admission of certain testimony offered by Brown's expert witness. However, because Miller's attorney had not objected to this testimony at trial, the opinion stated, he had *waived* this defect.

Oral argument:
> A verbal presentation made by the attorneys before the appellate court during which arguments about the validity or invalidity of what the trial judge did are presented.

Panel:
> The group of appellate judges, usually three, who preside over the appeal of the case and who vote on the result.

Opinion:
> The written decision of the majority of judges on the court which includes the reasons for the decision. One case can contain several opin-

ions: a majority opinion, a concurring opinion (see below), and a dissenting opinion. Opinions are often collected in official and unofficial *reporters*.

Dissent:

Disagree with the decision (the result and the reasons) of the *majority* of the court. If a judge agrees with the result reached by the majority but disagrees with reasons the majority used to support that result, the judge would cast a *concurring* vote and might write a separate concurring opinion.

Affirm:

To agree with or uphold the lower court judgment. If the appellate court *remanded* the case, it would be sending it back to the lower court with instructions to correct the irregularities specified in the appellate opinion. If the appellate court *reversed* the court below, it would have changed the result reached below.

Waive:

To make known expressly or impliedly that you will not exercise a right that you have. Here the court is referring to the well-established rule that failure to object during trial is an implied waiver of the right to complain about the alleged error on appeal.

Miller, undaunted, *petitioned* for a *rehearing* by the court *en banc*. The petition was denied. Miller then discussed the possibility of further appeal with his attorney. The attorney explained that Miller could, if he desired, try to appeal to the United States Supreme Court. He cautioned Miller, however, that he could not *appeal as a matter of right* in this case, but would be limited to a petition for a *writ of certiorari*. He advised Miller that it was extremely unlikely that the Supreme Court would grant the petition and that it probably would not be worth the expense. Miller agreed and no further appeal was attempted. Shortly thereafter the court of appeals issued its *mandate,* and the case was returned to the district court, where Miller, through his insurance company, *satisfied* the judgment.

Petition:

To make a formal request; similar to a motion.

Rehearing:

A second hearing by the appellate court to reconsider the decision it made after the first appellate hearing.

En banc:

By the entire court. The *panel* of judges that heard the first appeal may have consisted of only three judges, yet the number of judges on the full court may be much larger.

Appeal as a matter of right:

An appeal in which the appellate court has no discretion on whether to hear the appeal and thus is *required* to review the decision below.

Writ of Certiorari:
> An order by the appellate court (here the highest court) which is used when the court has discretion on whether to hear an appeal. If the writ is denied, the court refuses to hear the appeal, and, in effect, the judgment below stands unchanged. If the writ is granted, then it has the effect of ordering the lower court to certify the record and send it up to the higher court which has used its discretion to hear the appeal.

Mandate:
> The order of the court. Here the mandate of the appellate court was to affirm the trial court's judgment.

Satisfy:
> To comply with a legal obligation, here to pay the judgment award.

2. THE CRIMINAL CHARGES

Brown was involved in a second legal dispute during the same period of time that the negligence suit was under way. In addition to suing Clay's estate and Miller, Brown was defending himself in a criminal *prosecution* for possession of narcotics.

Prosecution:
> The bringing and processing of a criminal charge by the government. (Occasionally also used to mean the processing of a civil claim by a party.)

As Brown was leaving the hospital after having recovered from his injury, he was met at the door by two police officers. The officers produced a *warrant* and advised Brown that he was under arrest. After he was read his rights, he was taken to the police station.

Warrant:
> An order from a judicial officer authorizing the arrest of an individual, the search of property, etc.

The following morning Brown was taken before a judge for his *initial appearance.* The judge advised Brown that he had been charged with a *felony,* "possession of narcotics with intent to distribute." He then advised Brown of his rights, including his right to be represented by a lawyer. Since Brown was unemployed and without adequate funds to pay an attorney, the judge asked him if he would like the court to appoint a lawyer to handle the case. Brown said yes. An attorney was *assigned* to represent Brown. The judge, at the lawyer's request, then agreed to give Brown a chance to confer with his new attorney before continuing the hearing.

Initial appearance:
> A court proceeding during which (a) the accused is told of the charges, (b) a decision on bail is made, and (c) arrangements for the next judicial proceeding are specified.

Felony:

> A crime that is punishable by a sentence of one year or more. A *misdemeanor* is a crime that is punishable by a sentence of less than a year.

Assigned counsel:

> Attorney appointed to represent an *indigent* (poor) defendant.

When the case was recalled, Brown and his court-appointed attorney again approached the bench and stood before the judge. The attorney handed the clerk a praecipe formally entering his name as attorney of record for Brown and advised the judge that he was prepared to discuss the matter of *bail.* He proceeded to describe for the judge the various details about Brown's background—his education, employment record, length of residence in the city, etc. He concluded by asking that he be released on his own *personal recognizance.* The prosecutor was then given an opportunity to speak. He recommended a high *bond,* pointing out that the defendant was unemployed and had no close relatives in the area. These facts, he argued, coupled with the serious nature of a felony charge, indicated a very real risk that the defendant might try to flee. The judge nevertheless agreed to release Brown on his personal recognizance and set a date for a *preliminary hearing* the following week.

Bail:

> Property or a sum of money deposited with the court in order to insure that the defendant will reappear in court at designated times.

Personal recognizance:

> The defendant's sworn promise that he or she will return to court at the designated times. No bail money is required.

Bail Bond:

> A written obligation to pay a sum of money to the court in the event that the defendant fails to appear at designated times.

Preliminary hearing:

> A hearing during which the state is required to produce sufficient evidence to establish that there is *probable cause* (see definition below) to believe that the defendant committed the crimes charged.

The only witness at the preliminary hearing was the police officer who had been at the scene of the accident. The officer testified that when he helped pull Brown out of the car, he noticed a small paper sack sticking out from under the passenger's side of the front seat. Several glassine envelopes containing a white powdery substance, the officer said, had spilled out of the sack. The substance, totaling about one-half ounce, was tested and proved to be 80 percent pure heroin. Brown's attorney cross-examined the officer briefly but little additional information came out. The judge found that there was *probable cause* to hold the defendant and ordered the case *bound over* for *grand jury* action. He continued Brown's release on person recognizance.

Probable cause:

> A reasonable basis to belief that the defendant is guilty of the crime(s) charged.

Bound over:
   Submitted.

Grand jury:
   A special jury whose duty is to hear evidence of felonies presented by
   the prosecutor in order to determine whether there is sufficient evidence to return an *indictment* (see definition below) against the defendant and cause him or her to stand trial on the charges.

Shortly after the preliminary hearing, Brown's attorney went to the prosecutor to see if he could work out an informal disposition of the charge. He
tried to convince the prosecutor to enter a *nolle prosequi* on the charge, explaining that Brown had simply been offered a ride home and was not aware
of the fact that the heroin was in the car. The prosecutor was unwilling to
drop the charge. However, he was willing to "nolle" the felony charge of possession with intent to distribute if Brown would agree to *plead* guilty to the
lesser offense of simple possession of a dangerous drug, a misdemeanor. The
attorney said he would speak to his client about it.

Nolle prosequi:
   A statement by the prosecutor that he or she is unwilling to prosecute
   the case. The charges, in effect, are dropped.

Plead:
   To deliver a formal answer. In a criminal case, to *plead* means to admit
   or deny the charges made by the prosecutor.

He spoke to Brown that same afternoon, told him about the *plea bargaining* session, and advised him of the prosecutor's offer. Brown was not interested. He felt he was innocent and was unwilling to plead guilty, even to a
misdemeanor.

Plea bargaining:
   Negotiation between the prosecution and defense counsel during which
   an attempt is made to reach a compromise in lieu of a criminal trial.
   Generally the defendant agrees to plead guilty to a lesser charge in return for the state's willingness to drop a more serious charge.

Several weeks went by before Brown's attorney was notified that the
grand jury had returned an *indictment* against his client. The next step would
be the *arraignment* on the following Monday. On this date, Brown and his attorney appeared before the judge, and Brown was formally notified of the indictment. He entered a plea of not guilty to the charge. The judge set a trial
date about two-and-one-half months away and again agreed to continue
Brown's release on personal recognizance.

Indictment:
   A formal document issued by a grand jury accusing the defendant of a
   crime.

Arraignment:
> A court proceeding in which the defendant is formally charged with the crime and enters a plea. Arrangements are then made for the next proceeding.

The day for the trial arrived, and both sides (Brown's attorney and the prosecutor) announced that they were ready. Voir dire was held, and a jury was *impaneled.* The trial itself was relatively uneventful, lasting less than a day. The prosecutor, following a brief opening statement, presented only two witnesses: the police officer who had been at the scene, and an expert from the police lab who identified the substance as heroin. He then rested his case. Brown's attorney then made his opening statement and presented his only witness, Brown himself. The jury listened attentively as Brown, on direct examination, explained the events leading up to the accident and his subsequent arrest. Not only had he been unaware of the heroin, he testified, but he had never even seen it since he had been knocked unconscious by the accident and had not revived until he was in the ambulance. Brown had a previous conviction for shoplifting, and the prosecutor on cross-examination attempted to use this conviction to *impeach* Brown's testimony. Brown's attorney successfully objected, arguing that the conviction, which had occurred eight years previously, was too remote to be *relevant.* The judge agreed and prohibited any mention of the prior conviction. After a few more questions, the prosecutor concluded his cross-examination, and the defense rested its case.

Impaneled:
> Selected, sworn in, and seated.

Impeach:
> To attack or discredit by introducing evidence that the testimony of the witness is not credible (believable).

Relevant:
> Tending to prove or disprove a fact in issue.

Both sides presented their closing arguments following the lunch recess. The judge then instructed the jury; he described the elements of the offense and explained that the burden of proof in a criminal case is on the *government.* That burden, he continued, is to show each element of the offense *beyond a reasonable doubt.* The jury took less than forty-five minutes to reach its verdict. All parties quickly reassembled in the courtroom to hear the foreman announce the verdict *acquitting* Brown of the offense. A *poll* of the jury, requested by the prosecutor, confirmed the result, and the judge advised Brown that he was free to go.

Government:
> Here, the prosecutor.

Beyond a reasonable doubt:
> The standard of proof required for conviction in a criminal case. If any reasonable doubt exists as to any element of the crime, the defendant cannot be convicted.

Acquit:
> Find not guilty; absolve of guilt.

Poll:
> To question jurors individually in open court as to whether each agrees with the verdict announced by the foreman.

Criminal cases in which the defendant is acquitted generally may not be appealed by the prosecutor. Hence, in this case, there was no appeal of the trial judgment.

3. THE UNEMPLOYMENT COMPENSATION DISPUTE

The day after his indictment on the felony charge, Brown went down to the State Unemployment Office to apply for benefits. After being interviewed by a clerk, he filled out an application form. The clerk told Brown that he would receive a letter in about a week notifying him of the agency's initial determination on his eligibility. If he was eligible, his benefits would start in about ten days.

Brown received the letter a few days later. It advised him that, although he was otherwise eligible for benefits, a routine check with his former employer had disclosed that he had been fired for misconduct. For this reason, the letter stated, he would be deemed disqualified for a nine-week period. Moreover, the benefits due for those nine weeks would be deducted from the total amount to which he would otherwise have been entitled. If he wished to appeal this decision, the letter went on, he could request an *administrative hearing* within ten days.

Administrative hearing:
> An agency proceeding usually conducted less formally than a court hearing or trial, at which the presiding officer listens to the evidence and makes a preliminary determination as to how the controversy should be resolved.

Brown felt that he needed some legal advice, but he was still out of work and broke. (The lawsuit in the civil action had not been filed yet—it would be well over a year before the case would be tried, appealed, and the judgment award actually paid.) Brown therefore decided to obtain help from the local legal aid office. He explained his problem to a receptionist and was introduced to the *paralegal* who would be handling his case. The paralegal, an expert in unemployment compensation law, discussed the case with Brown and agreed to represent Brown at the hearing. He helped Brown fill out a form requesting a hearing and promised to let him know as soon as the date was set. Brown left and the paralegal immediately began to research and draft a *memorandum* to submit to the *hearing examiner* on Brown's behalf.

Paralegal:
> A person with legal skills who works under the supervision of an attorney or who is otherwise authorized by law to use these skills. (Some

state and federal agencies allow these nonlawyers to represent clients at administrative hearings.)

Memorandum:

Here, a written presentation of a party's arguments on facts and legal issues in the case. (See discussion of the external memorandum, p. 11.)

Hearing examiner:

A hearing examiner (sometimes called a referee or an administrative law judge) is someone who presides over the hearing and makes findings of fact and rulings of law, or who recommends such findings and rulings to someone else in the agency who will make the final decision.

The hearing, held ten days later, lasted about an hour and a half. The only witnesses were Brown and his former boss, Frank Best. Best told the examiner about Brown's arrest and about the thefts from the warehouse. Taken together, he argued, these events made it impossible for him to trust Brown on the job any longer. Brown, in turn, denied any participation in the thefts and maintained his innocence on the drug charge. (As of this time, Brown had not been acquitted of the felony.) The hearing examiner, at the close of the proceedings, thanked the parties and promised a decision within a few days.

The hearing examiner's decision arrived shortly thereafter in a document labeled "Proposed Findings and Rulings." The last paragraph contained the examiner's recommended decision. The hearing examiner agreed with Brown that his boss's mere suspicion that Brown was involved in the thefts was not enough to justify a finding of misconduct. However, the decision went on, the pending criminal charges for a drug-related offense did provide the employer with good cause to fire Brown since drug involvement could affect his ability to operate a truck safely. The paragraph concluded by recommending a finding of misconduct and the imposition of a nine-week penalty period.

Proposed findings and rulings:

Recommended conclusions presented to someone else in the agency who will make the final decision.

A second letter arrived ten days later giving the *administrative decision* of the agency. The letter, signed by the director of the local agency, adopted the recommended decision of the hearing examiner. This decision, the letter concluded, could be appealed within fifteen days to the State Unemployment Compensation *Board of Appeals.* Brown immediately appealed.

Administrative Decision:

An administrative agency's resolution of a specific controversy involving the application of the agency's regulations or governing statutes. In this case, the decision refers to a determination by a superior of the hearing examiner adopting, modifying, or rejecting the recommended decision of the hearing examiner.

Board of Appeals:

A nonjudicial, administrative tribunal that reviews the decision made by the hearing officer or by the head of the agency.

Copies of the hearing transcript along with memoranda from both sides were filed with the Board of Appeals. The Board, exercising its *discretion,* refused to allow oral arguments before it and *summarily* reversed the decision reached *below.* It issued a short written decision which noted that, while Best may have had cause to be suspicious of Brown, there was no sufficient evidence of actual misconduct on Brown's part. The Board in this final administrative decision ordered the local office to begin paying benefits immediately, including back benefits to cover the period since he had first applied.

Discretion:
> The power to choose among various courses of conduct based solely on one's reasoned judgment or preference.

Summarily:
> Quickly, briefly, without formal proceedings such as a hearing.

Below:
> The lower tribunal.

Best decided to appeal this administrative decision to a court. He was allowed to do so since he had *exhausted* his *administrative remedies.* He filed a complaint in a county court seeking review of the board's decision. He submitted the entire record from the proceedings below and asked the court for a *trial de novo.* Brown, now represented by an attorney from the legal aid office, filed his answer and immediately made a motion for summary judgment. The court, upon a review of the record and the pleadings, granted the motion and affirmed the judgment of the Board of Appeals. Best, after discussing the case at length with his attorney, decided against a further appeal of the case to the court of appeals.

Exhausting one's administrative remedies:
> Pursuing *all* available methods of resolving a dispute at the agency level before asking a court to review the administrative decision of the agency. A court generally will not allow a party to appeal an administrative decision until this process has been completed.

Trial de novo:
> A totally new fact-finding hearing.

Assignment #5

Read the following passage. Rewrite it using some of the technical terms covered in this chapter.

> Tom sues Jim. The theory of Tom's suit is a breach of contract. Jim requests that the court dismiss the case, arguing that even if Tom were able to prove every fact he asserts, he would not establish a breach. The court denies this request. Jim then files a response in which he says that Tom is the one who breached the contract. After the pretrial proceedings to obtain facts needed to prepare for trial, Tom asks the court to rule in his favor without a trial since there are no material facts in dispute. The request is denied.

See Suggested Response to this assignment on page 367.

Assignment #6

Write a fact situation similar to the one presented in Assignment #5 above. You can describe any aspect of the litigation process. Make up any facts you need, including the nature of the litigation. Use nontechnical language to describe the events that could occur in the litigation process. Then write the suggested response which will be a rewrite of your fact situation using technical language (covered in this chapter) to describe the same events. (Your teacher may ask you to read your fact situation aloud so that other class members can try to rephrase it in class using the technical language.)

Chapter Three

Authority: Recognizing the Kinds of Law Found in Court Opinions

Section A. Summary

The primary function of a court is to resolve disputes that are brought to it by litigants or parties. The court's starting point in coming to this resolution is the application of existing law which will lead to the court's holdings. In this Chapter, we will summarize the various kinds of law that can be relied upon by the court as *authority* for the holdings reached in its opinion. Of course, this opinion can in turn become authority that is relied upon by the same court or by other courts in subsequent cases. Our goal here is to explore this diversity.

Below we will briefly examine and define each of the kinds of authority outlined in Figure 3–1. In later chapters we will discuss (i) how to analyze the use of authority in an opinion and (ii) how to use authority in your own writing. You need not concern yourself with these skills at this time. Our concern here is simply that you be able to recognize references in opinions to the various kinds of authority that may be cited and discussed by a court.

Section B. The Distinction between Case Law and Enacted Law

Case law consists of holdings found within court opinions. The distinguishing feature of a holding is that it is the court's specific (and hopefully narrow) answer to a legal issue that is brought before it by a relatively small number

FIGURE 3–1.
Enacted Law and Case
Law.

Kinds of Law That May Be Interpreted and Applied in Court Opinions

1. Enacted Law
   (a) constitutions and charters
   (b) statutes and ordinances
   (c) administrative regulations
   (d) procedural court rules
   (e) a combination of the above
2. Case Law
   (a) opinions applying enacted law
   (b) opinions applying common law
   (c) opinions applying equity
   (d) opinions applying a combination of enacted law, common law, or equity

of named parties (usually two) engaged in litigation. There is only one author of case law: the courts.

Enacted law, on the other hand, can be written by legislatures, by administrative agencies, and by the People through the ballot box. Courts also participate in writing enacted law when they, on their own or with the legislature, produce rules of procedure that govern the conduct of different kinds of litigation in the courts. An enacted law is passed (or enacted) in order to cover a relatively large and often indefinite *class* of people, objects, events, or potential disputes. While enacted law can sometimes be directed at a named person or incident, it usually covers classes or categories. The major examples of enacted law are constitutions, charters, statutes, ordinances, and procedural court rules.

The instigation of case law is the need to resolve a *particular* controversy in litigation. The instigation of enacted law is the need to provide for the *general* welfare, and to identify ground rules and principles of behavior that are broad enough to structure an ordered society and thereby avoid controversies in the future. In later chapters, however, we will see that the amount of case law continues to multiply in part because enacted law is often unclear or nonexistent.

Of course, there is overlap between case law and enacted law. When, for example, a court is creating *common law,* it often uses language that goes beyond the narrow issues before it and produces what looks very much like enacted law as described above. Furthermore, an opinion is capable of straying beyond its particular issues and parties even when it is not creating common law. This results in unnecessarily broad language that is called *dictum.* But these are the exceptions—to be explored later.

Section C. Enacted Law as Authority

The great majority of court opinions involve some form of enacted law. There are four major kinds of enacted law that may be cited as authority in court opinions:

1. constitutions and charters;
2. statutes and ordinances;
3. administrative regulations; and
4. procedural court rules.

1. CONSTITUTIONS AND CHARTERS

Our system consists of fifty state governments, a government for the District of Columbia, and a national or federal government. The word *federalism* is used to encompass the complex variety of interrelationships that exists among these levels of government.

Each level has its own constitution (the United States Constitution at the federal level and the state constitution at the state level), which is the basic legal document of the government, often referred to as its organic document. It allocates powers among the various branches of the government and may also enunciate certain basic rights. As such, the constitution is the authority under which the various branches of government create all other types of law, both enacted law and case law. Thus for any law to be valid, it must be consistent with the constitution. The constitution is enacted through various means—in a constitutional convention, through legislative approval, by vote of the People, or through a combination of the above.

At the local level of government, often a municipality, the organic or fundamental document which lays out its governmental structure is called the charter. The source of the charter is the state legislature, which grants the charter to the municipality.

Because constitutions and charters are the basic law at each level of government, they are frequently used as authority in court opinions. This occurs most often when some other type of law or some action by the government is being challenged on the ground that it violates the constitution or charter. Consider the following hypothetical example from a Maryland court opinion which describes such a challenge involving two Maryland statutes (§ 3 and § 5(a) of the Code), the Maryland Constitution (Art. 46), and another court opinion (*Frontiero*) written by the United States Supreme Court:

> Section 3 of the Code provides: "In cases where a divorce is decreed, alimony may be awarded." Section 5(a) of the Code, however, sets out a proviso: "In all cases where alimony or alimony and counsel fees are claimed, the court shall not award such alimony or counsel fees unless it shall appear from the evidence that the wife's income is insufficient to care for her needs." It is contended that this language by implication excludes a husband from ever receiving alimony or counsel fees from a wife. On 7 November 1972, Art. 46, Declaration of Rights, Constitution of Maryland, was ratified, and became effective 5 December 1972, guaranteeing: "Equality of rights under the law shall not be abridged or denied because of sex." Husband urges that the provisions of § 5(a) offend the constitutional guarantee, relying on Frontiero v. Richardson, 411 U.S. 677, 93 S.Ct. 1764, 36 L.Ed.2d 583.

The example begins with quotations from two statutes: § 3 and § 5(a) of the Maryland statutory Code. The reference to the Constitution of Maryland (Art. 46) occurs approximately halfway through the excerpt. The husband is arguing that § 5(a) of the Maryland Code may violate Art. 46 of the Maryland

Constitution since § 5(a) appears to discriminate against men. The Constitution is cited as authority for the invalidity of the statute.

In addition to citing two statutes and a constitutional provision, the husband relies on a previous court opinion: *Frontiero v. Richardson.* Rarely will an opinion involve only one type of authority. Most opinions will cite and interrelate several kinds of authority.

In the Maryland example it was fairly easy to identify the reference to the constitutional provision since the court provided us with a citation to the precise provision of the state constitution under discussion. This is not always so. Courts will occasionally refer to constitutional provisions by means of verbal shorthand, without ever providing the reader with a complete citation to the relevant provision of the constitution. This is most common in opinions dealing with the first fourteen amendments to the United States Constitution. For example, a court might refer to "the equal protection clause" without specifying that the court means Section One of the Fourteenth Amendment to the United States Constitution.

2. STATUTES AND ORDINANCES

Statutes and ordinances are rules of law enacted by legislatures. When enacted by the federal legislature (i.e., Congress) or by a state legislature (e.g., the California Legislature), they are known as *statutes.* When enacted by a local legislative body such as a city council or county board of supervisors, they are usually called *ordinances.*

You will recall that court opinions are collected in volumes called reporters and are cited by referring to the volume and page number of the reporter in which the case appears (p. —). A different system is used for collecting and citing statutes and ordinances. Most often, statutes are *codified,* i.e., arranged by subject matter in volumes known as "codes." The codes are often broken down into units called *titles* with each title involving a different subject matter. Titles are further subdivided into chapters, sections, and subsections. The statutes are often (but not always) cited by reference to the title number, the name of the code, the section and/or subsection number of the statute being used, and the date of the edition of the code (p. —). The page number on which the statute appears in the code is *not* used in the citation. The popular name of the statute (e.g., the Civil Rights Act) may be included in the citation.

Most federal statutes are found in the United States Code. One such statute is the "All Writs Statute" which might be cited as follows:

The All Writs Statute, 28 U.S.C. § 1651 (1966).

The first number in the citation (28) refers to the title into which this statute is codified, i.e., title 28. The abbreviation U.S.C., of course, stands for the United States Code, the name of the code containing the statute. Immediately after this abbreviation is a symbol (§) followed by the number 1651. The symbol is legal shorthand for the word "section," and the number refers to the section of the Code where the act can be found, section 1651. Thus, the All Writs Statute can be found in title 28 of the United States Code in section

1651; 1966 is the year of the edition of the Code, not necessarily the year this particular statute was enacted.

Not all statutes are printed in codified volumes. Uncodified statutes exist which are printed in a *chronological* rather than a subject-matter order. The volumes containing such statutes are not called codes, but rather *statutes at large, acts, session laws,* etc.

Nor are statutes universally cited in the manner described above, whether codified or uncodified. The order of the information may be changed, with the name of the code or session laws coming first, followed by the numbers for the title and section. The date might also be placed elsewhere than at the end of the citation.

The following hypothetical example from an opinion of the District of Columbia Court of Appeals contains a citation to the All Writs Statute in the U.S.C. and to certain sections of Titles 1 and 11 of the District of Columbia Code. The example illustrates how statutes are sometimes relied upon by courts as authority. Note also the different citation format for a D.C. statute and a U.S.C. statute. As indicated, this kind of diversity is common in the citation of statutes:

> The jurisdiction of this court in the present case is based on D.C.Code 1973, §§ 1-1510 and 11-722, which sections give this court the power to review the orders and decisions of administrative agencies such as the Department of Human Resources. Specifically, D.C.Code 1973, § 1-1510(2), provides that this court can "compel agency action unlawfully withheld or unreasonably delayed". In addition, under the All Writs Statute, 28 U.S.C. § 1651 (1966), this court can issue all writs "necessary or appropriate" in aid of its jurisdiction. Thus there is ample statutory authority conferring on this court responsibility to ensure compliance under this program. There is, however, no explicit statutory authority or direction for the award of costs in such a proceeding.

3. ADMINISTRATIVE REGULATIONS

Administrative regulations are rules of law that are enacted or promulgated by administrative agencies of the federal, state, and local governments. The power to write regulations is generally delegated to the agency by a statute of the legislature and is limited to the area specified in that statute. The regulations will either (1) clarify or explain the meaning of a statute that the agency is charged with enforcing, or (2) establish the procedures that the agency will follow in administering such a statute.

The most extensive source of administrative regulations is the federal government with its numerous agencies. Many of the regulations promulgated by federal agencies are collected and organized by subject matter in a set of volumes called the *Code of Federal Regulations* (abbreviated as C.F.R.). They are cited, like federal statutes, to the title and section number where they appear in these volumes. For example, consider the following hypothetical example from an opinion of a United States District Court which contains citations to several federal administrative regulations as well as to federal statutes:

In this action plaintiff seeks judicial review of defendant's decision that she is not entitled to Widow's Benefits under Title IV of the Federal Coal Mine Health and Safety Act of 1969, 30 U.S.C. § 901 et seq. (1972). The only question is whether the decision that the plaintiff has failed to establish that her deceased husband was totally disabled by pneumoconiosis, or a disease presumed to be pneumoconiosis, at the time of his death is supported by substantial evidence.

First, it is clear that plaintiff has failed to establish her claim under 28 C.F.R. § 410.490 which requires the presentation of medical evidence and none is herein presented.

Next, the permanent criteria are set out in 20 C.F.R. § 410.401.476. Pneumoconiosis is defined therein as a chronic dust disease of the lung arising out of the employment in the Nation's coal mines, or as any other chronic respiratory disease or pulmonary impairment where the conditions for the application of the presumptions described in sections 414(b) or 454(b) are met. The provisions for determining whether a miner was totally disabled due to pneumoconiosis at the time of his death are set out in sections 410–430.

The first rule of law cited in this example is the Federal Coal Mine Health and Safety Act of 1969, in 30 U.S.C. § 901 et seq. This of course, is a citation to a Federal *statute* which can be found in the United States Code, Title 30, section 901 et. seq. (The term et seq. means "and following" and indicates that the statute consists of a number of sections in addition to § 901.) The remaining citations are to administrative regulations promulgated by the federal agency that is charged with administering the Act. The court is relying upon these regulations as authority. The regulations may be found, according to their citations, in Titles 28 and 20 of the Code of Federal Regulations (C.F.R.).

Regulations are also promulgated by *state* agencies. Often, however, there will be no one official collection of state regulations comparable to the Code of Federal Regulations.

4. PROCEDURAL COURT RULES

Procedural court rules are rules of law governing the mechanical aspects of litigation such as how and when various motions can be made, when discovery is available, etc. They are promulgated by the courts, often pursuant to a statute by the legislature or to a provision in the constitution authorizing the court to make such rules. There may also be procedural court rules created exclusively by the legislature.

The federal courts have several sets of rules governing the conduct of various types of litigation. The most common are the *Federal Rules of Civil Procedure* and the *Federal Rules of Criminal Procedure*. These and other federal court rules are cited by reference to the abbreviated name of the compilation and to the number of the rule being cited. The following example, quoting from Rule 6, illustrates how a court rule might be cited and relied upon as authority in an opinion:

Moreover, we believe that it is appropriate, in this case, to adopt the method of computation provided for in F.R.Civ.P. 6(a) which provides:

(a) Computation. In computing any period of time prescribed or allowed by these rules, by the local rules of any district court, by order of court, or by any applicable statute, the day of the act, event, or default from which the designated period of time begins to run shall not be included.

The procedural rules for state and local courts follow the same general pattern as those of the federal courts. It will usually be clear from the context of the opinion that a given citation is referring to such court rules. Consider the following hypothetical example from an opinion of the Appellate Division of the New York Supreme Court:

> The motions are directed to the discretion of the trial court as provided for in Court of Claims Rule 25-a[4][b]. Rule 25-a of the Court of Claims should be strictly construed and enforced unless it is shown that unusual and substantial circumstances would cause undue hardship if not remedied.

Here it is readily apparent that the procedural court rule cited in the opinion is from the New York Court of Claims.

In reading court opinions, therefore, it is crucial that you understand what kind of enacted law the court is discussing and applying, the main ones being constitutions, charters, administrative regulations, and procedural court rules.

Section D. Case Law as Authority

An opinion will often cite other opinions. These other opinions will be interpreting enacted law, common law, equity, or a combination of the three.

1. OPINIONS APPLYING ENACTED LAW

A court frequently has the responsibility of interpreting enacted law—constitutions, statutes, regulations, ordinances, procedural court rules, etc. In doing this, the court will usually seek guidance from other opinions, if any, that have interpreted and applied the same enacted law that is currently before it.

2. OPINIONS APPLYING COMMON LAW

Below you will find four interrelated descriptions of the term *common law*, the last of which will be our primary concern here:

• At the broadest level, common law simply means case law as opposed to statutory law. In this sense, all case law develops and is part of the common law.

• The term common law also refers to the legal system of England, America, and countries adopting or based on this system. Its counterpart is the civil law system of many Western European countries other than England, e.g., France. The origins of civil law include the jurisprudence of the Roman Empire set forth in the Code of Justinian. (Louisiana is unique in that its state law is in large measure based on the civil law—the Code Napoléon—unlike that of the remaining forty-nine common law states.) While there is overlap between the two systems, there is generally a greater reliance on case law in common law systems than in civil law systems. The latter tend to place a greater emphasis on code or statutory law than common law systems.

• More narrowly, common law refers to all of the case law *and* statutory law in England and the American colonies before the American Revolution. The phrase "at common law" will often refer to this colonial period.

• The most prevalant definition of common law is judge-made law in the absence of controlling enacted law. As we shall see, statutes are superior in authority to the common law. Indeed, statutes are often passed with the express purpose of changing the common law in a particular area. Such statutes are referred to as statutes in derogation of the common law. Another meaning of the phrase "at common law," therefore, is the law that existed before it was changed by statute.

Courts are sometimes confronted with disputes for which there is no applicable enacted law, i.e., there are no constitutional provisions, statutes, or regulations governing the dispute. When this occurs, the court will apply—and if necessary, create—common law to resolve the controversy. Here common law is used in the fourth sense given above. That is, it is made by judges to compensate for the lack of enacted law applicable to the case at hand. In creating the common law, the court will rely primarily on the unwritten customs and values of the community from time immemorial. Very often these customs and values will be described and enforced in old opinions which are heavily cited by modern courts in the continuing process of developing the common law.

There was a time when many areas of the law were controlled by the common law, particularly contract and tort law. While statutes in derogation of the common law have considerably altered this influence, the common law still remains a potent force in these and in many other areas of the law.

3. OPINIONS APPLYING EQUITY

Historically, equity represents a separate branch of law that developed years ago in England at a time when the common law had become inflexible. During this period, only specific and highly formalized causes of action were recognized in the courts that applied common law (referred to as "courts of law" or common law courts), and the remedies available there were even more limited. As a result, many disputes went unresolved by the courts of law, and in some of the cases that were resolved, only an inadequate remedy was available. The phrase "inadequate remedy at law" refers to the weak remedies available in the courts of law. This situation led eventually to the establishment of a separate court system known as the courts of equity or the *chancery courts*. The equity courts tended to be more flexible than the courts of law in seeing that justice was done. They recognized causes of action, defenses, and remedies that the courts of law ignored. Figure 3–2 lists some of the more significant features that distinguished the two court systems:

Some Distinguishing Features of Courts of Law and Courts of Equity	
Courts of Law	**Courts of Equity**
1. Cases could be tried by a jury; the jury would resolve the questions of fact.	1. There was no jury; the judge decided both the legal questions and the factual questions.
2. The plaintiff's recovery was usually limited to a money award, called a "judgment for damages."	2. The plaintiff could obtain "specific" relief not involving a money or damage award, e.g., could force the defendant to complete his or her contract, or could obtain an injunction prohibiting the defendant from doing something. A major reason why the equity court would grant this kind of relief was that the remedy at law, i.e., the money judgment, would not be adequate to do justice to the plaintiff for the injury suffered.
3. Cases were often decided on the basis of a rigorous reading of the letter of the law; technicalities were very important.	3. Cases were often decided on the basis of fairness or the "equities" of the matter even though following the letter of the law might have led to a different result.
4. A court of law exercised "legal" powers.	4. A court of equity exercised "equitable" powers.

FIGURE 3–2..
Courts of Law and
Courts of Equity.

As you can see, the courts of equity filled an important gap that existed in the law. For example, suppose that two parties enter into an agreement for the sale of a parcel of land. They later finalize the transaction by executing a deed that is legally valid in all respects. Subsequently, however, they discover that, due to a clerical error, the deed failed to mention part of the land that was covered in the original agreement. If the buyer sues the seller in a *court of law* in an attempt to obtain the portion of the property left out of the deed, the buyer would probably lose because all of the technical formalities for a deed were in order. Such a result, however, does not seem fair or equitable in spite of its compliance with the letter of the law on the execution of deeds. A *court of equity*, on the other hand, would probably give the buyer relief because of the unfairness of having to pay for something that is not conveyed in the deed even though it was originally bargained for. For a court to decide otherwise might be "legal," but it would hardly be equitable.

Or suppose that Smith enters a valid contract with Jones under which the latter is to build a special structure on Smith's land. Jones breaches the contract and refuses to build the structure. In a *court of law*, Smith would be limited to an award of damages, i.e., to money. If, however, Smith is not able to find another builder who has the ability to erect the same kind of structure, then an award of damages will not be an adequate remedy, since Smith will be unable to have the structure built. A *court of equity,* on the other hand, might grant the equitable relief of "specific performance," which would force Jones to perform the original contract.

Hence courts of equity were often available to a litigant who needed relief from a "legal" but unfair result or who needed a *form* of relief that was not available in a court of law.

Although the courts of equity met an urgent need, the dual system of courts was often unnecessarily confusing and expensive. It was sometimes difficult to know in which court a case should be brought. Some parties were forced to litigate their dispute in *both* courts. Around 1840, states began to abolish the dual system and to replace it with a single court system that could apply *both* law and equity to the cases before it. At the present time, the federal courts, those of England, and nearly all the states have abolished the dual system of law and equity courts. They have combined both law and equity into a single court system.

Equitable principles, however, remain very much a part of our judicial system even after the merger of law and equity. The practical effect of the merger is that equitable defenses such as mistake and equitable remedies such as specific performance need no longer be raised in a separate court system. One and the same court exercises both equitable and legal powers. In an action for breach of contract, for example, if the court determines that a damage award would not be adequate, the court will no longer send the plaintiff to a court of equity; it will simply exercise its equitable powers then and there, e.g., by granting the remedy of specific performance. If, however, that court determined that a money or damage award would fairly compensate the plaintiff, i.e., the remedy at law *was* adequate, then the court could exercise its legal power to limit the award of a successful plaintiff to a damage judgment.

4. OPINIONS APPLYING A COMBINATION OF ENACTED LAW, COMMON LAW, OR EQUITY

Most opinions, as indicated, use many types of authority. In fact, one of the major functions of court opinions is to pull together *all* of the law governing a particular issue and to interrelate these various kinds of authority, explaining or reconciling possible inconsistencies, determining which provision governs where two or more conflict, etc. For example, in deciding a dispute about the validity of an administrative regulation, a court may discuss in its opinion not only the regulation itself, but also (1) the statute that authorized the regulation, (2) the common law doctrine that this statute changed, (3) the constitutional provision that may have been violated by the statute or the regulation, and (4) any prior court opinions that interpret the constitution, the statute, the regulation, common law doctrine, etc.

Note on Secondary Authority Used in Court Opinions

Thus far we have discussed the various kinds and combinations of *laws* that an opinion can apply. As we shall see in Chapter 16, when the authority being applied by a court is a law, e.g., a statute or a common law doctrine, it is called *primary authority*. *Secondary authority*, on the other hand, is anything else that the court could rely on to reach its conclusion, e.g., a law review article, a legal encyclopedia, a treatise written by a scholar on some topic (p. 203).

Later, we shall cover the proper *use* of both kinds of authority (primary and secondary) in your legal writing.

Assignment #7

In each of the following opinions, identify the kind of authority mentioned by the court.

a. People v. Sohn, p. 299.

b. Stephens v. Dept. of State Police, p. 302.

c. Nicholson v. Conn. Half-way House, Inc., p. 307.

List each authority found in these opinions once, regardless of how often it is cited in the opinion. Also include any citations found in the footnotes. Next to each item on your list, indicate the nature of the authority, using one of the following:

[C]   a consitutional provision or charter

[S]   a statute or ordinance

[R]   an administrative regulation

[PCT]   a procedural court rule

[AD]   an administrative decision

[OAG]   an opinion of the attorney general (or corporation counsel)

[E]   an encyclopedia

[T]   a treatise (e.g., hornbook, manual, formbook)

[LP]   legal periodical literature (e.g., a law review article)

[OTJ]   an opinion written by a court that is part of the same judicial system as the court citing the opinion (OTJ means an Opinion written by a court in This Jurisdiction).

[OOJ]   an opinion written by a court that is not part of the same judicial system as the court citing the opinion (OOJ means an Opinion written by a court from some Other Jurisdiction).

[O]   other kind of authority

When you complete the assignment, compare your answer to the Suggested Response, p. 367.

PART TWO

How to Brief an Opinion

Chapter Four

Introduction to Briefing

Section A. The Psychology of Reading Court Opinions

The message of this section can be simply stated: be prepared for a difficult road ahead as you launch into the skill of case analysis. There are a number of reasons for this difficulty:

1. JUDGES ASSUME A GREAT DEAL ABOUT THE READERS OF THEIR OPINIONS

Most often the judge writes his or her opinion on the assumption that the reader already knows a great deal about the law and the legal system. A new student is therefore at a disadvantage. The judge does not spell out everything. A great deal is left to implication. The reader must be constantly reading between the lines while at the same time giving full deference to *every* word in the lines.

2. THE SKILL OF CASE ANALYSIS WILL TAKE YEARS TO DEVELOP

Unfortunately, many students are *very* impatient. They have trouble understanding why they have not mastered the skill of case analysis a month or two after they begin the effort. They find themselves reading opinion after opinion without comprehending much beyond the surface. The biggest mistake made by such students is their impatience. Case analysis cannot be learned quickly. It is an art that must be refined over the span of one's entire career.

3. MANY OPINIONS ARE POORLY WRITTEN

Judges often do an inadequate job in writing their opinions. The organization of the opinion may be loose; sentence and paragraph structure may be very difficult to follow; the writing may be rambling, elliptic, and internally inconsistent.

It should be some comfort to you to know that the difficulty you will experience when beginning to read opinions will not always be your own fault. This does not mean that you can put an opinion aside simply because it is difficult to read due to the poor quality of the judge's writing. Such opinions simply require that you work much harder at trying to understand them.

The following excerpt from an article by D. W. Stevenson contains a very good summary of the criticisms often made about opinion writing.

Stevenson, D. W., "Writing Effective Opinions," 59 *Judicature* 134 (No. 3, October, 1975).

People—judges among them—write in order to say something to someone. Any communication situation involves three components: a writer, his message, and an audience. Too often, however, judges write as if only the writer counted. Too often they write as if to themselves and as if their purpose were to provide a documentary history of having made a judgment. Instead, they must realize that the purpose of an opinion is to make a judgment credible to a diverse audience of readers.

Readers of opinions have long complained that a great many published opinions are ineffectively written and therefore difficult to use. Over the years a number of law review articles—some very good ones—have asserted that opinions are too long, that they are filled with unnecessary detail, that they are overloaded with footnotes, that they are couched in jargon unclear to many of their readers, that they are poorly arranged and carelessly worded. According to [Herbert A.] Gregory, many opinions require of their readers "the labor of casting aside the brushwood in order to get at the real law which the court has applied to a particular case."*

Nor is this negative view of much opinion writing held only by the readers of opinions and by legal scholars. It is held by an astonishing number of opinion writers themselves. Recently, at a Regional Appellate Judicial Conference, I asked a room full of judges to write a sentence or two telling me what they thought about the opinions written by their colleagues, if not by themselves, and their comments were as strongly critical of opinion writing as anything in the journals. "Opinions are too long and contain too many citations," they said. "Opinions fail to express a principle of law applied in such a way that the principle can be stated and applied in another case." "They tend to ramble rather than clearly define and discuss the issues." "They frequently summarize previous opinions rather than stating a conclusion from them." "They conceal the issues." "They fail to speak in plain words." "They are filled with 'legalese'."

Why is it that judges who are fully aware of the complaints about opinion writing and who voice those same complaints themselves continue to write ineffective opinions? Is there something inherent in judicial discourse, some strange habit of language acquired with judicial robes? Are judges inadequately trained in English composition? Do opinion writers, pressed for time by crowded court calendars, necessarily rush too quickly from rough draft to final copy? Is it because of "dictaphone writing"?

---

* Herbert B. Gregory, *Shorter Judicial Opinions*, 34 Virginia Law Review, 369 (1948).

I believe that the root cause of much ineffective opinion writing is none of these—though unquestionably some of these contribute. Rather, I believe the real cause of ineffective opinion writing is that too often judges give little thought either to the purposes of their opinions or to the audiences whom they address. They may "know" that opinions potentially have complex audiences: the litigants, the attorneys representing them, the bench and bar, the legislature, the news media, the community. But if that knowledge is not translated into specific behavior, opinions will continue to be poorly written.

4. MANY OPINIONS INVOLVE DIFFICULT POINTS OF LAW

Not all opinions, of course, are poorly written. Some are carefully drafted and well organized—yet are still very difficult to read and understand simply because they involve difficult and complex points of law. Generally, the "easier" cases never go to court but instead are settled by the parties out of court.

Given the obstacles that you face in comprehending opinions, what should you do? The chart in Figure 4–1 presents a number of guidelines (some of which were discussed in Chapter 2) that should assist you in acquiring a realistic frame of mind as you begin to develop the skill of case analysis.

The task of becoming skillful in case analysis is indeed difficult and time consuming. It may take hours to comprehend a single opinion. If you apply yourself diligently, however, and if you have a realistic outlook of what must be done, you will find that the time needed to handle opinions will tend to decrease. What will increase from this approach will be your satisfaction in being able to use case law effectively in the resolution of legal problems.

Section B. An Eleven-Part Brief

The word "brief" can refer to three different kinds of documents:

- an appellate brief,
- a trial brief, and
- a case brief.

An appellate brief is a party's formal written argument to a court of appeals on why a lower court's decision should be affirmed, modified, or reversed. A trial brief is an attorney's set of notes on how he or she proposes to conduct an upcoming trial. It is sometimes called a trial manual or trial book. A case brief, our primary concern here, is an *analytical summary of an opinion*.

To "brief a case" means to identify the essential components of an opinion. This brief serves two functions:

a. to help you clarify your thinking on what the opinion "really" means, and

b. to provide you with a set of notes on the opinion to which you can refer later without having to reread the entire opinion every time you need to use it.

Rarely will you be reading an opinion simply for enjoyment. The objective of case analysis is to determine whether the "law" in an opinion applies to the facts of the client's problem on which you are currently working. Before you

FIGURE 4–1..
Case Reading
Guidelines.

Guidelines for Developing the Skill of Case Analysis

1. When reading an opinion, expect the unknown; expect the unexpected.

2. Have a legal dictionary at your side. Know how to use it; know how to avoid abusing it (p. 28). Dictionary definitions can be no more than starting points for you. Remain skeptical about whether the court intended the definition you found in the dictionary. Initially you may use the dictionary frequently. You will find, however, that you will need the dictionary less and less if you use it diligently and properly during this early stage of your opinion-reading career.

3. Be prepared to go to a hornbook, a legal encyclopedia, or a law review article to gain a *background* understanding of the law being discussed in the opinion. This can sometimes be time-consuming. But if it is needed in order to make sense out of the opinion, it must be done.

4. Be prepared to do at least some research into the judicial system of the court that wrote the opinion you are analyzing. This will not only help you understand the court's description of the prior proceedings but will also help you anticipate what further proceedings may have occurred in the case *after* this opinion was written.

5. Be prepared to read some opinions that are poorly written and that will require more effort than usual to understand.

6. Be prepared to read opinions in sequence. Often an opinion will be only one in a series of opinions which together have developed a particular point in the law. Your understanding of the opinion you are trying to analyze will be increased if you read this opinion in the context of related opinions on the same legal topic.

7. Be prepared for the reality that there will almost always be more than one interpretation of what an opinion says and of how it applies to new fact situations.

8. Be prepared to read, reread, and reread again every opinion that you are trying to analyze. It is almost impossible to understand an opinion fully after one reading.

9. For important opinions, find out what others have written about the opinion. For example, has the opinion been commented upon in law reviews? To find out, check the tables of cases in the *Index to Legal Periodicals*, the *Current Law Index*, and the *Legal Resource Index* (p. 173). Do this, however, only after you have tried to brief the opinion on your own.

10. Do not study in isolation. Seek out a colleague or a fellow student with whom to compare notes on the opinions you are studying. *After* each of you thoroughly briefs the opinion on your own, meet to discuss it. Compare briefs. Compare your analysis on the application of the opinion to a new set of facts. Debate your views as a way of gaining further insight and feedback. If you have many opinions to study, select a few of the major ones for this kind of dialogue.

---

can apply an opinion, however, you must be able to read it, to understand what it has said. This is done by briefing the opinion.

Any given opinion can consist of several opinions: the *majority* opinion (where a majority of the judges agree on the result and the reasoning behind the result); *concurring* opinions (where the judges agree on the result but not on the reasoning); and *dissenting* opinions (where the judges do not agree on the result). A *plurality* opinion is also possible. If a majority of justices cannot agree on a result, the largest number who do agree will constitute a plurality and will write their opinion together. There will be no majority opinion. Judges who disagree with the plurality can write either concurring or dissenting opinions. When you brief an opinion, you will be briefing the majority opinion (or the plurality opinion if no majority existed).

There are many styles of briefing, and the same person may, in fact, employ several different styles of briefing for different purposes. The process, however, is the same regardless of the format used. The task of briefing consists of carefully reading and analyzing the opinion, of breaking down the information contained in the opinion into categories, and of organizing this data into a structured outline. In this text we have adopted a briefing format consisting of eleven components, each of which will be considered in detail in the following chapters of Part II.

In Chapter 12, there is a model brief that conforms to the eleven-part briefing format outlined in Figure 4–2. Flip through the pages of Chapter 12 now in order to obtain a feel for the structure of this kind of brief (p. 175).

A brief that conforms to this eleven-part structure is a *comprehensive brief*. In Chapter 12, you will find such a brief as well as a "thumbnail brief" of the same opinion. The latter is a much shorter version of a comprehensive brief. This early in your career, however, you should concentrate on preparing comprehensive briefs. Eventually, you will find yourself moving toward the shorter version. The danger is that you will move in this direction too quickly. Learn how to do a thorough job before relying too heavily on the shorthand-and-shortcut approach.

The skill of briefing is designed to equip you for another skill—*applying* opinions to the facts of client cases. The latter skill will be covered in Parts III and IV of the book. Part II will be a preparation for this broader skill.

The Eleven Components of a Brief
1. The *Citation*
Where the opinion can be found (pp. 25, 175)
2. The *Parties*
Names, relationship, litigation status (p. 81)
3. The *Objectives* of the Parties
What each side is seeking (p. 87)
4. The *Theory of the Litigation*
The cause of action and the defense (p. 90)
5. The *Prior Proceedings*
What happened below (p. 97)
6. The *Facts*
Those facts that were key to the holdings (p. 103)
7. The *Issue(s)*
The questions of law (p. 137)
8. The *Holding(s)*
The answers to the issues (p. 145)
9. The *Reasoning*
Why the court answered the issues the way it did (p. 149)
10. The *Disposition*
What order was entered by the court as a result of its holdings (p. 168)
11. *Commentary* on opinion
Concurring and dissenting opinions, personal views, counter brief (narrower or broader interpretations), history of the case, the case in sequence, case notes in law reviews (p. 171).

FIGURE 4–2..
Format of a Brief.

Chapter Five

Identifying the Parties
in an Opinion

Opinions grow out of litigation. The litigants or *parties* are the persons, groups, corporations, governments, etc., who are directly involved in the litigation, i.e., those who are suing or being sued, prosecuting or being prosecuted. Identifying these parties and their relationship to each other is an important step in understanding the opinion.

Identification of Parties: Guideline #1

There are three components to the identification of the parties in an opinion:
(1) the names of the lead parties
(2) one or more categorizations for each party or group of parties; and
(3) the litigation status of each party or group of parties.

The following is an example of how the element of parties might be stated in a brief of an opinion involving only two parties:

PARTIES:
> International Paper Co./employer of McGoogan/defendant below/
> appellant here
> v.
> McGoogan/employee of International Paper Co./plaintiff below/
> appellee here

Note that the description of each party contains all three of the components stated in Guideline #1: (a) the names of each party (International Paper Co./

McGoogan), (b) a categorization of the identity of each (employer/ employee), and (c) the litigation status of each (defendant/plaintiff; appellant/appellee).

1. IDENTIFYING THE NAMES OF THE LEAD PARTIES

The text of the opinion will not always give the *names* of the parties. The court may simply refer to the parties as "plaintiff," "appellant," etc. If so, check the caption of the opinion at the very beginning. For example, in our illustration above, we described two parties in the opinion of *International Paper Co. v. McGoogan*. Here is the caption for this opinion:

INTERNATIONAL PAPER COMPANY,
Appellant,
v.
Michael B. McGOOGAN, Appellee.
No. 73–220.
Supreme Court of Arkansas.
Feb. 4, 1974.

This opinion involved only two parties. It is not unusual, however, to find multiple parties involved on each side of a lawsuit. For example, consider the following caption:

> **Gil DYE and Joanne Dye, his wife, Thomas Bischoff and Judy Bischoff, his wife, Derek Longstaff and Marilyn Longstaff, his wife, Reed Perkins and Carol Perkins, his wife, Appellants,**
>
> **v.**
>
> **CITY OF PHOENIX, a Municipal Corporation; John D. Driggs, Mayor of the City of Phoenix, Ed Korrick, Henry E. Brodersen, Armando de Leon, Calvin C. Goode, Margaret T. Hance and John T. Katsenes, Council Members of the City of Phoenix, A.I. Marshall, Jr., and Jack Ingerbritson, and La Espanada, a limited partnership, Appellees.**
>
>
>
> **No. 1 CA-CIV 2678.**
> Court of Appeals of Arizona,
> Division 1,
> Department A.
> Nov. 13, 1975.
>
>

A total of nineteen parties are identified in this caption. It is *not* necessary to list each of these parties in your brief. To do so would be unwieldy and would serve no useful purpose. Instead, follow Guideline #2.

Identification of Parties: Guideline #2

In identifying the parties in an opinion, it is usually sufficient to give only the *lead* parties. The lead parties are those listed first on each side of the dispute in the caption of the opinion. If there are additional parties, indicate this fact with the phrase "et al." or "and others."

Following this Guideline, we would identify the names of the parties in the *Dye* opinion simply as:

Dye and others/
v.
City of Phoenix and others/

The captions of some opinions begin with the expression "In re" or "In the Matter of" (e.g., In re Clovis Green, Jr., Petitioner; In the Matter of Disbarment of Sidney Fenton). The caption may give you the names of the two *main* opposing parties. If not, the beginning of the opinion itself will usually provide these names. In the following example, the names we need are found within the caption:

**In the Matter of the ESTATE of Floyd
H. CROZIER, Deceased.
Byron D. CROZIER, Appellee,
v.
Inez DOYLE et al., Appellants.
No. 56894.**
Supreme Court of Iowa.
Aug. 29, 1975.

In your brief, the parties should be listed as follows:

Crozier, B./
v.
Doyle and others/

Note that we have included the first initial of Crozier. This is to help distinguish Byron Crozier from the deceased, Floyd. You should use flexibility in applying any of the Guidelines provided in these chapters. There is no problem in slightly modifying the Guidelines in order to achieve greater clarity or to cover an unusual situation such as a caption that is out of the ordinary.

2. IDENTIFYING ONE OR MORE CATEGORIZATIONS OF EACH PARTY OR GROUP OF PARTIES

It is extremely important that you quickly develop the habit of classifying the parties in an opinion into descriptive categories. For example:

NAME OF PARTY	CATEGORY
1. John Doe	private citizen
2. Human Service Commission	city agency
3. May Smith	minor
4. Joan Davidson	governor
5. Peterson and Berstein	accounting firm
6. Joe Mortson	federal prisoner

There may well be other categories into which each party fits. John Doe is also a man, a human being, a citizen of a particular city, etc. Do you include every conceivable category that comes to your mind about a particular party? No. The following Guideline applies:

Identification of Parties: Guideline #3

In categorizing each party or group of parties, select the descriptive category that best describes the party's *relationship* to the other party or the role in which the party came into conflict with the other party.

How do you determine what the most relevant category is? You must look to the opinion. Read it carefully and try to identify what the dispute between the parties is about. What is their relationship? What incident, transaction, or complaint brought them into conflict? Once you have identified the nature of the dispute, try to characterize the role each party played in it. Your characterization of this role should provide you with the most relevant categorization of the party. If, for example, the dispute involves a contract to sell an automobile, the most relevant category for one party may be "seller" or "dealer," while the other party may best be characterized as a "buyer" or "consumer." If the dispute involves a divorce, the relevant categories will probably be "husband" and "wife."

Why is it important to develop the skill of categorizing the parties? Because of its relationship to the application process:

**Relationship between the Categorization of Parties
and the Application of Opinions:**

When comparing the facts of an opinion with the facts of a client's case in order to determine whether the opinion applies to the client's case, it is often critical to compare the *fact categories* in the opinion with the *fact categories* in the client's case. (See p. 107.)

The skill of determining whether the opinion applies to a client will be examined in Part III of this text. However, you should be aware at this point that the application process often involves not only the comparison of individual facts, but also the comparison of various *categorizations* of facts in the opinion with *categorizations* of facts in the client's case. One such categorization that is almost always significant is the categorization of the parties in relationship to each other.

3. IDENTIFYING THE LITIGATION STATUS OF THE PARTIES

The litigation status of a party is the *procedural* position that each party has had in the litigation. This position is designated by terms such as "plaintiff," "defendant," "appellant," "appellee," "petitioner," "respondent," etc. (As we saw earlier, the appellant is the party who brings the appeal. The appellee or respondent is the party against whom the appeal is brought.)

Identification of Parties: Guideline #4

In identifying the litigation status of the parties, look first to the caption of the opinion. If the litigation status is not stated in the caption, it will usually be described in the first few paragraphs of the opinion. State the original litigation status of the parties in the first proceeding of the case as well as their status at the time the opinion was written.

**Ross WANGSGARD, Plaintiff and
Appellant,
Peggy FITZPATRICK et al., Defendants
and Respondents.
No. 13890.**
Supreme Court of Utah.
Nov. 3, 1975.

Here the caption tells us that the parties are Wangsgard, Fitzpatrick and others (et al.). Wangsgard was originally the plaintiff and is *now* the appellant. Fitzpatrick and others were originally the defendants. At the writing of *this* opinion, they are the respondents. Hence the parties in this opinion would be designated as follows in your brief:

Wangsgard/plaintiff below/appellant here
v.
Fitzpatrick and others/defendants below/respondents here

Note our use of the terms "below" and "here" in the foregoing example to distinguish between (a) the original litigation status of each party and (b) that party's litigation status at the time the opinion was written.

Note on the Relationship Between the Parties and the Facts of the Opinion

When you have identified the three components of the parties (names, categorizations, and litigation status), you have also begun to identify the *facts* of the opinion. Who the parties are, what their relationship is to each other, and what their litigation status is—all are facts.

Assignment #8

Identify the parties in the following opinions, giving all three components for each party:

a. People v. Sohn, p. 299.

b. Brown v. Southall Realty Co., p. 300.

c. Stephens v. Dept. of State Police, p. 302.

d. Nicholson v. Conn. Half-Way House, Inc., p. 307.

e. Conn. v. Menillo, p. 309.

Check your answers with the Suggested Responses beginning on p. 370.

Assignment #9

Identify the parties in the following opinions, giving all three components for each party:

a. Mumma v. Mumma, p. 311.

b. Owen v. Ill. Baking Corp., p. 315.

c. Thompson v. Royall, p. 316.

d. MacPherson v. Buick Motor Co., p. 319.

e. Goldberg v. Kelly, p. 330.

Chapter Six

Identifying the Objectives and the Theories of the Parties

Section A. The Objectives of the Parties

The next component of the brief consists of the parties' *objectives*. Parties enter into or defend against litigation because they want to accomplish specific, concrete objectives. In general, the plaintiff will be seeking to obtain something from the defendant or will be trying to stop the defendant from doing something; the defendant's objective will usually be simply to prevent the plaintiff from obtaining that end. Occasionally the defendant will go further and seek not only to defeat the plaintiff's claim but to assert his or her own claim against the plaintiff. There is a great variety of objectives that the parties might be seeking. Some of these are illustrated in Figure 6–1.

Identification of Party Objectives: Guideline #1

The information describing the parties' objectives will often be found within the first few paragraphs of the opinion.

Identification of Party Objectives: Guideline #2

If there is no clear indication in the opinion as to what the objectives of the parties are, infer the objectives from the nature of the dispute and from any other clues you may find in the opinion.

FIGURE 6–1.
Examples of Party
Objectives.

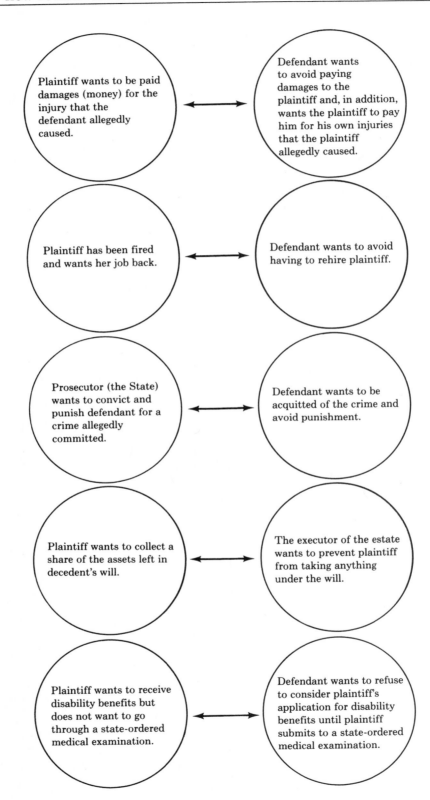

Identification of Party Objectives: Guideline #3

If the opinion describes the plaintiff's objective but does not indicate what the defendant's objective is, assume that the defendant's only objective is to prevent the plaintiff from obtaining his or her objective.

As Guideline #2 indicates, it is sometimes possible to infer the objectives of the parties from the nature of the dispute or from other clues provided in the opinion. For example, in a criminal case it is usually safe to assume that the government (the prosecutor) is seeking to convict and punish the defendant and that the defendant is seeking to be acquitted. Similarly, in a dispute involving negligence, where the plaintiff has allegedly been injured by the defendant, the plaintiff will normally be seeking money (damages) from the defendant as compensation for those injuries.

Opinions will sometimes provide you with potentially misleading statements as to the parties' objectives. Consider the following three statements, for example:

"appellant seeks a review of the lower court's determination that the evidence was inadmissible..."

"plaintiff is asking this court to require defendant to answer certain interrogatories..."

"defendant is seeking a new trial..."

What these statements have in common is that each describes a *procedural* objective of the party, not the objective the party was trying to accomplish in bringing the suit. Consider the first statement. The appellant certainly did not become involved in litigation *for the purpose* of having certain evidence admitted at trial. The admission of the evidence is simply a *means* of obtaining the ultimate objective: winning the litigation and having the court order the relief that caused the appellant to come to court in the first place. This is equally true of the other two statements listed above. Requiring interrogatories to be answered or obtaining a new trial are only *means* to achieving the ultimate or final objective—the objective which you must identify.

Identification of Party Objectives: Guideline #4

In identifying the objectives of each party, look for that party's *ultimate* objective: what is the *end* result that the party hopes to achieve once all administrative and judicial proceedings are over? In most opinions this question can best be answered by viewing the party's objectives from the point at which the litigation began—at an administrative agency or, if no agency was involved, at the trial court. Do not confuse ultimate objectives with procedural objectives.

There are exceptions to guideline #4, although they are not common. Assume that a state agency sues a city agency to prevent the latter from proceeding with a construction project until it files an environmental impact statement pursuant to a state statute requiring such a statement. The objective of the state may not be to stop the project, but simply to force the city to comply with the requirement of an impact statement. In this example, the ultimate objective of the state *is* procedural—to obtain compliance with a statute that lays out certain steps (i.e., procedures) that must be followed before a construction project is undertaken. Again, such situations are infrequent; procedural objectives are rarely ultimate objectives.

Section B. Identifying the Theories of the Parties: The Cause of Action and the Defense

We turn now to a closely related topic: the *theories of the parties*. By this term we mean a brief statement of the legal grounds upon which each party bases the right to obtain the objective it is seeking. The emphasis is on *legal* grounds; litigation must be based on more than bruised feelings.

There are two types of theories present in all litigation: the *cause of action* and the *defense*.

A cause of action is a legally acceptable reason for suing. It is legally acceptable when it is based on a rule of law (e.g., negligence, a statute), the commission or violation of which entitles the aggrieved party to sue. The cause of action is an *offensive* legal theory in that it is used to initiate a claim against an opposing party. Since a plaintiff, by definition, is the party initiating the lawsuit and raising a claim against the defendant, he or she must always state a cause of action in support of that claim. There may be more than one cause of action in the same lawsuit. The plaintiff may advance several different legal theories. Moreover, it is possible for the defendant in a lawsuit to raise a claim against the plaintiff. This new claim, called a *counterclaim*, must also be supported by a cause of action.

The second type of legal theory found in every lawsuit is the defense. A defense is a legal theory that is raised in response to and that attempts to defeat the plaintiff's cause of action. Unlike a counterclaim, a defense does not state a new claim against the opposing party. Its only effect, if successful, is to defeat the other party's cause of action and thus prevent the latter from obtaining its objective.

Just as the cause of action is normally raised by the plaintiff, the defense is normally raised by the defendant. However, a plaintiff may also have occasion to raise a defense. If, for example, the defendant states a counterclaim against the plaintiff, the latter must in turn raise any defenses that it may have to that counterclaim.

The most common defense is a *denial* of one or more facts necessary to support the cause of action. This denial is based on a different view of the same rule of law raised by the opponent. The party asserting the denial is saying that the rule of law (e.g., negligence, a statute) that is the foundation of the cause of action cannot be established because of a failure to prove an essential element of that rule of law. Thus the theory asserted in a simple denial is the legal insufficiency of the opponent's theory.

There is a more sophisticated defense, often called an *affirmative defense.* This defense requires the party to affirmatively allege *new* facts in addition to those alleged by the plaintiff. For example, suppose Smith contracts to buy a ring from Jones for $500. Smith later backs out of the deal, and the only other offer Jones can obtain for the ring is $200. After selling the ring for $200, Jones decides to sue Smith for the difference. His *objective* is to force Smith to pay *damages* in the amount of $300. His *theory* or *cause of action* is *breach of contract.* Smith's objective is to avoid having to pay the damages. If, for his defense, he simply asserts that there never was a contract because an essential element of a contract is missing, the defense would be a *denial.* Suppose, however, that Smith raises a defense of *fraud,* alleging that Jones had represented the ring to be a diamond ring when in fact it was only cut glass. This latter defense would be an affirmative defense because it involves new facts (e.g., the fact that the stone was only cut glass) that were not raised by the plaintiff. An affirmative defense is a rule of law or legal theory that, like a denial, is asserted to defeat the cause of action. Generally, the party asserting the affirmative defense (Smith in our example) would have the obligation of alleging (i.e., of pleading) and of proving the facts supporting this defense.

Identification of the Theories of the Parties: Guideline #1

A party's theory, whether it is a cause of action or a defense, must be based upon one or more rules of law.

The most common legal theory discussed in opinions is one based on statute. For example, examine the following hypothetical statute:

84–1111. The practice of optometry by any unregistered or unlicensed optometrist is hereby declared to be a menace and a nuisance, dangerous to the public health and safety, and the Board of Examiners in Optometry shall promptly abate such practice by writ of injunction filed in the county in which such practice is conducted.

This is a hypothetical statute from Georgia's state code on Professions, Businesses and Trades. Suppose that Smith, a client of your office, is working as a full time *assistant* to a licensed optometrist. The Board of Examiners in Optometry believes that Smith's activities constitute the "practice of optometry" by an "unregistered or unlicensed optometrist," and the Board goes to court to obtain an injunction requiring him to stop his activities. The plaintiff in the litigation is the Board. The cause of action in this litigation would be *violation of section 84–1111.* This is the legal reason given by the Board for its objective of preventing Smith from practicing optometry without a license. Smith is the defendant in this litigation. His objective will be to prevent the Board from interfering with the type of work he does. In order to accomplish this objective, he might raise one or several defense theories. For example, he might argue that:

- he does in fact have a license; or
- § 84–1111 was not intended to apply to people like himself who work only as assistants under the supervision of a licensed optometrist; or
- § 84–1111 is in conflict with another statute of the state code that permits him to do what he does; or
- § 84–1111 is invalid because it violates a provision of the state constitution; or
- § 84–1111 is invalid because it violates a provision of the United States Constitution.

Each of these legal theories, including both the cause of action and the five defense theories, is based upon one or more rules of law. The cause of action, of course, is based upon § 84–1111. The five defenses listed above are based upon the same statute, although the last three defenses are based upon other rules of law in addition to § 84–1111.

Statutes often form the basis of legal theories in both civil and criminal litigation. Consider, for example, the following statute from the criminal code of the state of Tennessee:

> **39–2018.** If any person vend, or attempt to vend, directly or indirectly, any lottery ticket, in any scheme to be drawn in this or any other state or county, he is guilty of a misdemeanor, and, on conviction, shall be fined five hundred dollars ($500), and imprisoned one (1) month in the county jail.

Suppose that a Tennessee prosecutor brings a criminal charge against Rev. Jones for vending lottery tickets in the churchyard. The state's *objective* is to convict and punish Rev. Jones for the commission of a crime. The state's cause of action[1] is *violation of § 39–2018*. Rev. Jones's *objective* is to avoid conviction and punishment. He may seek to achieve this objective by raising as his defense the theory that

- he never had anything to do with lottery tickets; or
- while he admits to having possessed lottery tickets, he never attempted to "vend" these tickets within the meaning of § 39–2018; or
- § 39–2018 was never intended by the legislature to be applied to lotteries held by churches or religious groups; or
- § 39-2018 is invalid because it violates a provision of the Tennessee Constitution; or
- § 39-2018 is invalid because it violates a provision of the United States Constitution.

As in the preceding example involving Smith and the Board of Examiners in Optometry, each of these defense theories is based upon a statute, here § 39–2018. The first three theories are denials by the Rev. Jones that he in fact vio-

---

1. Although the phrase "cause of action" is mainly used for the legal theory in *civil* litigation, there is no reason why we cannot speak of a *criminal* cause of action in referring to the prosecutor's legal theory for bringing a criminal prosecution against a defendant. While technically correct, however, the phrase "cause of action" is not often used in criminal law litigation.

lated the statute. The fourth and fifth defenses incorporate constitutional rules of law vis-à-vis § 39–2018. The prosecutor's theory is, of course, also based upon the statute and its alleged violation by Rev. Jones.

Causes of action are also frequently based on the common law, which, as we have seen, is judge-made law in the absence of controlling enacted law. The most widely used common law causes of action are *breach of contract* and *torts* such as negligence and libel.

With this general introduction on what we mean by theories of the parties, we turn now to their identification in opinions for purposes of the brief.

Identification of the Theories of the Parties: Guideline #2

The information needed to identify the *cause of action* will usually be found within the first few paragraphs of the opinion where the court describes the type of action or area of law involved in the litigation.

Early in the opinion you will often find statements such as

> This is an action for libel brought by . . . .
>
> Plaintiff in this libel case contends that . . . .
>
> Appellant sued for libel, alleging that . . . .

The opinion may be as clear in stating the *response* or *defense* of the other side. If not, follow Guideline #3:

Identification of the Theories of the Parties: Guideline #3

In identifying the *defense* or *response* to a cause of action, if the court does not clearly state the nature of the defense, you should carefully read the entire opinion and attempt to infer the defense from whatever information is given concerning the position of the opponent; where there is no basis for such an inference, assume that the defense is a simple denial of the cause of action.

Even where the court clearly identifies the cause of action or the defense theory of a party, you may find that you are still uncertain about the actual nature of that theory. For example, suppose that the opinion simply states, "This is an action for violation of § 505 of the Licensing Code" or "This is an action for nuisance." In the first example, the cause of action is based upon a statute. The court may include in its opinion a brief quotation from that statute, but suppose that it does not do so. How are you to know what the statute says? In the second example we have only the word "nuisance" to describe the cause of action. Are you familiar with this term? In either of these two situations, unless you are already familiar with the rules of law stated by the court, you may be unable to understand the cause of action or the defense raised in the opinion. Hence, Guideline #4:

Identification of the Theories of the Parties: Guideline #4

In identifying the theories of the parties, particularly in an opinion involving an unfamiliar area of law, be prepared to go to additional research sources in order to increase your understanding of the theories raised by the parties in the opinion. (See p. 28.)

For example, if you were reading the opinion on an "action for nuisance," you might wish to look that term up in a legal encyclopedia, such as *Corpus Juris Secundum* or *American Jurisprudence, 2d,* or in a hornbook or treatise such as *Prosser on Torts* to obtain a general overview of the law of nuisance. Once you have this background and return to your examination of the opinion, the discussion of the cause of action in the opinion may make a little more sense to you. Be careful, however, not to confuse the opinion with the material in the treatise or encyclopedia. The law in the opinion may be somewhat different from the statements made in the treatise or encyclopedia. Hence, as indicated earlier (p. 28), you should use these sources only to obtain a *general* picture of the relevant area of law. For the precise statement of what the law is and of how it applies in a particular state, you must rely on the opinion itself and on other opinions from the same jurisdiction.

The following Guideline provides one final word of caution:

Identification of the Theories of the Parties: Guideline #5

When identifying the theories of the parties in an opinion, be careful not to confuse the causes of action and defenses in that opinion with the causes of action and defenses raised by the parties *in other opinions* cited and discussed in the opinion you are reading.

Guideline #5 is a reminder that in the process of examining an opinion, you will often find that the court mentions other court opinions. We shall refer to these as *internal opinions,* meaning any discussion of or excerpts from opinions within the opinion you are briefing. The court may describe the causes of action and defenses raised by the parties in an internal opinion. For example, read the excerpt in Figure 6-2 from the opinion of *People v. Anderson.* As you can see, the *Anderson* opinion cites three other opinions:

- People v. McCombs
- People v. Perry
- People v. Soznowski

The legal theory of the prosecution in *Anderson,* indicated in the first sentence, is *attempted burglary.* The defense theory is described in the second sentence of the excerpt; the defendant claims that the state failed to prove a necessary element (i.e., intent) of the crime of burglary. This is a simple defense, a *denial* of the state's theory.

The balance of the excerpt consists primarily of the *Anderson* court's discussion of two other opinions, *McCombs* and *Perry.* (*Soznowski* is also cited

After a bench trial, Anderson was found guilty of the crime of attempted burglary and sentenced to a term of two years and one day. On appeal, he asserts that the state failed to prove intent beyond a reasonable doubt.

In People v. McCombs, 94 Ill.App.2d 308, 236 ◄———— The *McCombs* opinion
N.E.2d 569, the court reversed a burglary conviction, holding that the evidence established only an inference that when defendant secretly entered a home at night, he intended to resume a previously defined relationship with the daughter of the homeowner, thus raising sufficient and consistent circumstances to negate any inference that defendant had the intent to commit a felony sufficient to sustain the burglary conviction.

Similarly, in People v. Perry, supra, the court ◄———— The *Perry* opinion
held that inconsistent circumstances and other proof negated any inference that defendant intended to commit the crime of theft when he was discovered at the door of complainant's bedroom. There, defendant had visited the complainant late at night on other occasions, thereby raising a reasonable inference of an inconsistent motive for his presence, leaving serious doubt of an intent to commit the crime of theft. See also, People v. ◄———— The *Soznowski* opinion
Soznowski, 22 Ill.2d 540, 177 N.E.2d 146....

FIGURE 6–2.
Excerpt from *People v. Anderson.*

but is not discussed.) Note that in discussing these two opinions, the *Anderson* court mentions the theories in each. The theory in *McComb* is *burglary,* and in *Perry* it is *theft.* The differences between attempted burglary, burglary, and theft may or may not be significant. The point is that you should not confuse the internal opinions with the opinion you are briefing. You want to state the legal theory in *Anderson:* attempted burglary.

As we shall see later, internal opinions can be invaluable in helping you understand and apply the opinion you are briefing. Be careful, however, to note any differences between the latter and the internal opinions. Do not gloss over either the differences or the similarities.

Assignment #10

In each of the following opinions, identify (i) the objectives of the parties, (ii) the causes of action, and (iii) the defenses:

a. People v. Sohn, p. 299.

b. Brown v. Southall Realty Co., p. 300.

c. Stephens v. Dept. of State Police, p. 302.

d. Nicholson v. Conn. Half-Way House, Inc., p. 307.

e. Conn. v. Menillo, p. 309.

Check you answers with the Suggested Responses, p. 371.

Assignment #11

In each of the following opinions, identify (i) the objectives of the parties, (ii) the causes of action, and (iii) the defenses:

a. Mumma v. Mumma, p. 311.

b. Owen v. Ill. Baking Co., p. 315.

c. Thompson v. Royall, p. 316.

d. MacPherson v. Buick Motor Co., p. 319.

e. Goldberg v. Kelly, p. 330.

Chapter Seven

Identifying Prior Proceedings in Opinions

Most litigation is made up of a series of stages, e.g., trial, middle appeals, final appeal. A court opinion represents a decision at only one of these stages. Prior to the time it was written, a number of other stages of litigation may already have taken place. For example, suppose you are reading the opinion of *State Workers' Compensation Board v. Smith*, decided in 1951 by a State Court of Appeals. In the following hypothetical sequence of proceedings, seven litigation events happened before this opinion was written at stage 8:

PRIOR PROCEEDINGS:

1. *Administrative Hearing I:* Plaintiff (Smith) sought worker's compensation benefits from the State Workers' Compensation Board. RESULT: Claim denied (1943).

2. *Appeal I:* Plaintiff challenged the Board's decision in the State District Court (a state trial court) on the ground that he had been denied constitutional due process at the hearing. RESULT: For the Board; administrative decision affirmed (1943).

3. *Appeal II:* Plaintiff appealed to the State Court of Appeals (a state middle appeals court). RESULT: For the Board; trial court decision affirmed (1944).

4. *Appeal III:* Plaintiff appealed to the State Supreme Court. RESULT: For the Board; decision of the Court of Appeals affirmed (1946).

5. *Appeal IV:* Plaintiff appealed to the United States District Court (a federal trial court). RESULT: For plaintiff; due process violations existed in the way that the agency hearing was conducted; judgment below reversed, new hearing ordered (1948).

6. *Administrative Hearing II:* The Board held a new hearing, this time avoiding the due process violations. RESULT: Compensation was denied (1949).

7. *Appeal V:* Second appeal to the State District Court. RESULT: For plaintiff; administrative decision reversed (1950).

PRESENT PROCEEDING:

8. *Appeal VI:* Board appealed to the State Court of Appeals. RESULT: For plaintiff; affirming State District Court judgment below (1951).

The 1951 opinion written at stage 8 was *State Workers' Compensation Board v. Smith.* Within this opinion, probably in the first three or four paragraphs, the prior proceedings would be summarized, although they would not be outlined in the manner presented above.

You will sometimes see prior proceedings referred to as the *proceedings below.* To the extent that the word "below" means lower in the judicial hierarchy, the phase "proceedings below" may not always be accurate. At the time the State Court of Appeals wrote its opinion in 1951, there had been not only proceedings *below* (before the Workers' Compensation Board and the State District Court), but also proceedings *above* (in the State Supreme Court) as well as a proceeding at the *same level* (the first appeal to the State Court of Appeals). Hence the term "prior proceedings" is preferred since it includes proceedings that have occurred at any level. Note also that, as indicated by the appeal to the United States District Court in the hypothetical, the prior proceedings in an opinion may include both state and federal proceedings in the same litigation.

Although this chapter is primarily about *prior* proceedings, it should be mentioned that there can also be *later* proceedings in the litigation. In our hypothetical above, for example, it is possible that after losing its appeal to the State Court of Appeals in 1951, the Workers' Compensation Board appealed further to the State Supreme Court. The State Supreme Court might have decided to reverse the appellate court's decision and might have returned the dispute to the agency for a third hearing. Obviously, these later proceedings could not possibly be summarized in the 1951 Court of Appeals opinion since they would not yet have occurred at the time this opinion was written. Yet it could be crucial for you to know about these subsequent proceedings if you were reading the 1951 opinion. There is nothing more frustrating than to spend hours laboring over an opinion that was subsequently reversed or overruled. Fortunately, a technique exists for discovering whether there have been any *subsequent* proceedings in the same litigation. This technique, called *shepardizing,* involves consulting a set of books known as *Shepard's Citations.* These volumes (called citators) list the citations to most of the reported opinions published in the country. Below each citation, the citator gives references to subsequent opinions in the same litigation (known as the history of the case), as well as references to subsequent opinions in other litigation which have cited the opinion you are reading, and indicates whether these subsequent opinions have affected the validity of the earlier opinion. Thus, by consulting the Shepard's citator, you can learn whether the opinion you are reading has been reversed, overruled, modified, quoted from, or simply mentioned by a subsequent opinion. The information found in a Shepard's citator is not part of the prior proceedings. Its value lies in:

1. telling you whether the opinion is still valid and thus worth briefing at all;

2. helping you assess how much "weight" you should accord the opinion in a legal memorandum; and

3. helping you locate other similar opinions that you may want to consider using in your legal memorandum.

We will return to shepardizing when we cover key facts (p. 122) and the final component of the brief, the commentary (p. 172).

Back to prior proceedings. Not all opinions have prior proceedings as complex as those listed in the workers' compensation opinion example presented at the beginning of this chapter. Trial court opinions may have *no* prior proceedings or perhaps only one prior proceeding at an adminstrative agency.

Also, it may not be possible to identify *all* the proceedings that have occurred in the litigation. The court may simply omit any reference to prior proceedings or may provide only a short and perhaps cryptic description of the proceedings that it does mention. In most instances, this is an indication that the prior proceedings are relatively unimportant to an understanding of the opinion.

In briefing, you should read the opinion carefully and attempt to identify as many of the prior proceedings as possible. The following Guidelines state the kind of information you should look for and the manner in which you should organize this information in your brief.

Identification of Prior Proceedings: Guideline #1

To the extent that the information is provided in the opinion, your description of the prior proceedings should include the following information about both the prior and the present proceedings:

(a) For each *prior* proceeding, identify
    (1) the nature of the proceeding;
    (2) the party initiating the proceeding;
    (3) the name of the court or agency involved; and
    (4) the result of the proceeding, stated briefly.

(b) For the *present* proceeding, identify
    (1) the nature of the proceeding;
    (2) the party initiating the proceeding; and
    (3) the name of the court or agency involved.

Identification of Prior Proceedings: Guideline #2

State the prior proceedings chronologically, starting with the first proceeding in the litigation and concluding with the present proceeding.

Note that for each prior proceeding, you are asked to identify the *result* of that proceeding. What we mean by this term is a brief statement of the outcome of the proceedings. Do not confuse "result" with the word "holding" which means the court's answer to a specific issue or question of law. The identification of holdings in opinions will be discussed later in this book.

To illustrate the operation of these Guidelines, consider a hypothetical example from an opinion of the Michigan Supreme Court in *Triplett v. Chrysler Corporation*. Like the hypothetical with which we started this chapter, this is a worker's compensation case. The following excerpt presents the court's description of the prior proceedings:

> In April, 1971, Triplett, the plaintiff filed a petition for hearing before the Workers' Compensation Bureau. He sought disability benefits for total and permanent loss of industrial use of both his lower extremities alleging emphysema as the cause of this disability. The Hearing Referee denied the claim, but the Workers' Compensation Appeal Board reversed the referee's decision and awarded plaintiff permanent and total disability benefits. The Michigan Court of Appeals denied Chrysler Corporation leave to appeal on April 1, 1975. Application was then filed with this Court.
>
> On order of the Court, application for leave to appeal is considered and the same is hereby granted. Pursuant to GCR 1963, 865.1(7), we hereby reverse the decision of the Workers' Compensation Appeal Board.

Applying Guidelines #1 and #2 to this excerpt, we would describe the prior proceedings in this opinion as follows:

PRIOR PROCEEDINGS:

1. *Administrative Hearing:* Plaintiff (Triplett) sought disability benefits in a hearing before the Worker's Compensation Bureau. RESULT: Claim denied.

2. *Administrative Appeal:* Plaintiff appealed the denial of compensation to the Workers' Compensation Appeal Board. RESULT: Hearing Referee's decision reversed and benefits awarded.

3. *Appeal I:* Chrysler Corporation applied for leave (permission) to appeal the award to the Michigan Court of Appeals. RESULT: Application denied.

PRESENT PROCEEDING:

4. *Appeal II:* Chrysler now applies for leave to appeal to the Michigan Supreme Court.

Note that we have *not* included the *result* of the present proceeding in our description above. We know from the portion of the opinion given above what the result or decision of the Michigan Supreme Court was in the present proceeding: the Court granted leave to appeal and reversed the decision of the Workers' Compensation Appeals Board. However, it is not necessary to include this information at this point in the brief. If you were to brief the *Triplett* opinion in its entirety, the result of the present proceeding would appear elsewhere in the brief.

Identification of Prior Proceedings: Guideline #3

The first step in identifying prior proceedings is to identify the court that wrote the opinion you are briefing.

Start with the caption which will print the name of the court that wrote the opinion. Simply by looking at the court's name, you should obtain at least a general sense of the judicial system of which this court is a part. (See the overview of judicial systems in Chapter 1.) Is it the highest court in its system? The trial court? Eventually these will be relatively easy questions for you to answer—at least for today's federal courts, the courts of your state, and the highest courts of every other state. With this background information, you will be in a better position to understand the court's description of the prior proceedings.

Identification of Prior Proceedings: Guideline #4

Information on prior proceedings will usually be found in the early paragraphs of the opinion. At times, however, in order to obtain a complete picture of all the prior proceedings, you will have to read the entire opinion.

For many opinions, the court's description of the prior proceedings will enable you to infer the hierarchical interrelationship among the various agencies and courts mentioned. If not, don't remain in the dark. Ask your teachers and fellow students for help. If necessary, a small amount of legal research on the judicial system can be well worth your time (p. 29).

Identification of Prior Proceedings: Guideline #5

Do not remain confused about the relationship between the court that wrote the opinion and the other agencies and courts mentioned by the court in its prior proceedings. Ask for help and be prepared to do some background legal research on the judicial system into which the court fits.

Assignment #12

Identify the prior proceedings in the following opinions:

a. People v. Sohn, p. 299.

b. Brown v. Southall Realty Co., p. 300.

c. Stephens v. Dept. of State Police, p. 302.

d. Nicholson v. Conn. Half-Way House, Inc., p. 307.

e. Conn. v. Menillo, p. 309.

Check your answers with the Suggested Responses, p. 373.

Assignment #13

Identify the prior proceedings in the following opinions:

a. Mumma v. Mumma, p. 311.

b. Owen v. Ill. Baking Corp., p. 315.

c. Thompson v. Royall, p. 316.

d. MacPherson v. Buick Motor Co., p. 319.

e. Goldberg v. Kelly, p. 330.

Chapter Eight

The Identification
of Key Facts

In this chapter we cover the skill of identifying key facts. Then we move to issues, holdings, and reasoning. In a sense, however, the identification of all four of these components (facts, issues, holdings, and reasoning) must take place simultaneously. Although we will discuss each separately, they are all closely interrelated, as we shall see.

Section A. Facts, Rules of Law, and Conclusions of Law

> There is no aspect of case analysis that is more abused by so many people so many times than fact analysis.

When you are trying to solve a legal problem, your initial concern is often, "What's the law?" As you become more deeply involved in the study of law, however, you will learn that the more appropriate question to ask is, "What are the facts?" While the two questions are closely related, students often give minimal attention to the facts with the unfortunate result that they begin talking about law in a vacuum. A fundamental principle of our legal system is that a "law" has little meaning outside the context of a particular set of facts to which it has been applied or is now being applied. Without this context, the statement of the law is a mere generality. For example, examine the following law:

> Divorce can be granted on the ground of cruelty.

We cannot go very far with this statement. It is a good starting point, but nothing more. What does "cruelty" mean? Is psychological as well as physical violence covered? Can one incident of cruelty be enough, or must there be a pattern of cruel behavior over a period of time? A major way to try to obtain answers to such questions is to turn to case law. We read cases in order to determine the various *factual contexts* in which the law has been applied. Again, without this context, we are left with a generality. Case analysis is one of the tools that will enable us to go beyond this point.

First, some definitions as we explore the role of facts in greater depth:

- A *fact* is information describing a thing, occurrence, or event.

- A *rule of law* is an enforceable pronouncement of government, e.g., a statute, regulation, or constitutional provision, that directly or indirectly establishes a standard of conduct.

- A *conclusion of law* is the determination of whether or in what manner a specific rule of law applies to a specific set of facts.

The following statements illustrate each of these concepts:

1. At 3:00 P.M. on August 25, 1975, Tom Smith drove his car at 40 m.p.h. down a city street that was posted with a 25 m.p.h. speed limit.

2. Title 16, § 215(b) of the state statutory code provides: "All persons exceeding the posted speed limit on any city street by 15 m.p.h. or more shall be guilty of a misdemeanor punishable by a fine of not more than $1,000."

3. When Smith drove his car at 40 m.p.h. on a city street posted at 25 m.p.h., he violated § 215(b), which makes it a misdemeanor to exceed the "posted speed limit" by "15 m.p.h."

The first statement in this example is a statement of *fact;* it is information describing an occurrence or event, telling us *what* happened, to *whom* it happened, *when* and *where* it happened, etc. The second statement is a statement of a *rule of law;* it is an enforceable norm or standard of conduct created by a valid governmental authority (the state legislature). The third statement is a *conclusion of law;* it describes how the specific rule of law in statement two applies to the specific facts contained in statement one (see Figure 8–1).

A conclusion of law reached by a court in an opinion is called a *holding.* It is binding on the parties to the litigation and can be used as *precedent* for similar disputes in future litigation. The holding or conclusion of law is one of the essential components that must be identified when briefing an opinion. The techniques for doing so will be considered in the next chapter. Our major concern here is to emphasize the crucial role that facts play in determining the holding. Without a *particular* set of facts, there would be no holding. Furthermore, even a slight change in the facts can sometimes produce a totally different conclusion of law or holding.

FIGURE 8–1.
Reaching a Conclusion of Law.

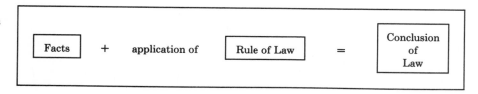

Suppose, for example, that Tom Smith in our illustration above had been driving his car at 39 m.p.h. instead of 40 m.p.h. The rule of law in the second statement would obviously no longer be applicable since he would not have exceeded the speed limit "by 15 m.p.h. or more." Or suppose that Tom Smith was a police officer traveling 40 m.p.h. while responding to a call. It may not be as clear that § 215(b) was violated in this situation. What if Tom was going 40 m.p.h. because he was rushing his child to the hospital? It may be that the statute was not intended to apply to such emergency conditions. As you can see, changes in the facts can have considerable impact on the conclusion of law involved.

Our example involved a statute, yet the same sensitivity to facts must exist when the rule of law is a constitutional provision such as the due process clause.

> What due process requires in one situation may not be required in another, and this, of course, because the least change of circumstances may provide or eliminate fundamental fairness. *Crooker v. California,* 357 U.S. 441, n. 6 (1958)

Later in this chapter, we will discuss the techniques for identifying the *key* facts of an opinion—how to weed out some of the facts stated in the opinion until you are left with a tight summary of the essential facts upon which the court's decision is based. You must not let this weeding process mislead you. The question is not *whether* the facts of an opinion are important. (They are.) Rather, the question is which of the facts are *most* important. Which facts are so key that if they were changed, the holding in the opinion would have changed?

Section B. What Is a Key Fact?

Key facts are sometimes called essential facts, material facts, operative facts, etc. As used in this book, the definition of such a fact is as follows:

> A fact in an opinion is a key fact when a holding of the court would have been different if that fact had been different or had not been in the opinion.

There is no mathematical formula that will enable you to determine what facts were key to a court's holding. There is, however, a method that can be helpful in your search for key facts. But there is no absolute guide.

The first step in the search is to recognize that the facts in an opinion have varying degrees of relevance and importance; a court will almost always tell us much more than we need to know. A given fact could fall anywhere on the fact spectrum (see Figure 8–2).

Irrelevant Facts	Background Facts	Important Facts	Key Facts

FIGURE 8–2. A Fact Spectrum: The Role of Facts in a Holding Reached by a Court.

Admittedly, it will sometimes be very difficult to place a certain fact within the spectrum. The boundary line between the various categories will often be very thin. Different readers of the same opinion may reach diametrically opposite conclusions on the significance of given facts. Indeed, these differences are at the heart of *advocacy* in the interpretation of opinions. When two sides in litigation do battle over the applicability of an opinion to a current case, a major component of their disagreement will often be their differing views as to which facts were key to the court's holding.

The concept of a key fact is not unique to court opinions. There are key facts involved in *every* decision, including your own. As we shall see, the key facts of any decision will be individual facts that you considered as well as categorizations of such individual facts.

Suppose that you are about to decide which word processor to purchase for your computer: the ABC Word Processor ($200) or the XYZ Word Processor ($220). While there are some differences in the features of the two products, both will perform equally well for your purposes. Only XYZ, however, provides free phone support through an 800 number. ABC has everything on one diskette, while two diskettes must be used for XYZ. Finally, XYZ is slightly more difficult to learn to operate than ABC. Weighing all of these facts, you buy the XYZ Word Processor. As with many decisions, there are facts that could support either decision. *What were the key facts in the decision to buy the XYZ product?*

Step one in answering this question is to review the facts that were before you:

- The two products will serve your purposes equally well;
- XYZ is $20 more expensive than ABC;
- XYZ has free home support through an 800 number;
- XYZ consists of two diskettes while ABC has everything on one diskette;
- XYZ is slightly more difficult to learn to operate than ABC.

Which of these facts were key? A common sense test is to speculate whether the purchase decision would have been different if any of these facts did not exist or were changed, assuming all the other facts remained the same. Suppose XYZ was $100 more expensive? Suppose the phone support was not free? Suppose one of the products would serve your needs significantly better than the other? It is through this kind of probing that we attempt to arrive at the key facts. If changing any of the above facts would have changed the decision, then those facts were probably key.

This probing is essentially a game of WHAT IF:

- *What if* XYZ were more than $20 above the cost of ABC? Would this have changed the decision to buy XYZ?
- *What if* the phone support were not free? Would this have changed the decision to buy XYZ?
- Etc.

Whenever you can safely speculate that the decision would have been different if a certain fact were different, that fact was probably a key fact in the decision. For example, the free home support number was a key fact if you speculate that you would have bought the ABC system if phone support (for XYZ) were not free.

Conversely, whenever you can safely speculate that the decision would *not* have been different if a certain fact were different, that fact was *not* a key fact in the decision. The extra $20 for XYZ, for example, would not be a key fact if you can safely speculate that you still would have bought the XYZ product if it were $30 more expensive, or indeed $20 *cheaper* than ABC. There obviously was nothing magic about XYZ being $20 more expensive than ABC because we got the same result without this fact.

Whenever actual facts and changed facts produce the same result, we must ask whether there is a *fact categorization* that was key rather than any individual fact.

Note that we have concluded that the following facts or fact changes would have produced the same result:

• XYZ is $20 more expensive than ABC;

• XYZ is $30 more expensive than ABC;

• XYZ is $20 cheaper than ABC.

There is nothing about these *individual* facts that are key since none of them is essential to the decision. Any one of them would lead to the same decision. What are some of the fact categorizations that apply to each of the above individual facts? Here are some possibilities:

• At this price, it was affordable to you;

• You deemed the price differential between the two products to be insignificant;

• You felt that the price was reasonable.

Each one of these statements is a *fact categorization,* which simply means that the statement applies to all the individual facts under examination.

Now we ask: were any of the fact categorizations key to your decision to buy the XYZ product? We answer this question the same way that we answered the question about whether any of the individual facts were key. If we changed the fact categorization, would the decision have been different? If so, then that fact categorization was a key fact. Regarding the first fact categorization listed above, we ask: would you have bought the XYZ product if its higher cost rendered it *un*affordable to you? The answer is undoubtedly no; therefore, the fact that it was within your budget, i.e., was affordable (even though it was $20 more expensive) was a key fact categorization in your decision to buy XYZ. The same question is asked about each of the fact categorizations that you have identified.

Summary: The Search for Key Facts

1. State the decision that was made.

2. Lay out all the facts that were considered in making the decision. The goal is to determine which individual facts and which fact categorizations were key to the decision.

3. For each individual fact, speculate on whether the decision would have been different if that individual fact had not been present or had been different.

(a) If the decision would have been different, then the individual fact was a key fact.

(b) If the decision would not have been different, then the individual fact was not a key fact.

5. Determine whether fact categorizations were key rather than (or in addition to) individual facts.

(a) Start with an individual fact. Change it several different ways and speculate on the effect each change would have had on the decision.

(b) Determine what fact categorizations cover or describe every fact and every fact change that you speculate would lead to the same result.

(c) Assess whether each fact categorization is key by speculating what the decision would have been if that fact categorization had not been present.

————

Given the importance of the fact categorizations, we need to examine them more closely. To categorize a fact simply means to identify broader classifications into which that fact fits or might fit. These classifications can take different shapes. Some may be broader generic groupings. Others may be simple adjectives. It is as much a fact categorization to say that Mr. Jones, Mr. Smith, and Mr. Davis are "human beings" as to say that they are "professionals" or "meticulous."

How many fact categorizations can you think of for the following statement:

A blue 1967 Ford Falcon

Many of the responses below would be acceptable by everyone; others are more debatable. Include both. To develop your skill of viewing individual facts in broader categories, identify any fact categorizations that are plausible.

A blue 1967 Ford Falcon

a 1967 Ford Falcon

a 1967 Ford automobile

a Ford automobile

an American automobile

an automobile

a necessity rather than a luxury

a motor vehicle

a vehicle

a moving object

a familiar sight

a middle-class product

a consumer product

personal property

an expensive item

a product that is within the budget of the general public

something that requires skill to operate

something that requires a license to operate legally

something that is regulated by the government

something that is potentially dangerous

a product that the general public can operate with only minimal understanding of how it works mechanically

a product so common that the general public has expectations as to what it should be able to do

etc.

Assignment #14

Identify as many fact categorizations as you can for the following statements:

(a) A 1988 General Motors school bus.

(b) A college sophomore majoring in history.

(c) A secluded dirt road in the country.

(d) A Smith & Wesson .32 caliber handgun.

(e) Mrs. Jones threw a brick directly at her husband.

Assignment #15

Below you will find several facts found within some of the opinions in Appendix A. List any fact categorizations mentioned by the court with respect to the facts in *italics:*

(a) In Brown v. Southall Realty, p. 300, the code violations pertained to Mrs. Brown's *basement.* Check your response with the Suggested Response, p. 375.

(b) In Stephens v. Department of State Police, p. 302, the plaintiff was a *trooper* in the Oregon State Police.

(c) In Nicholson v. Connecticut Halfway House, p. 307, the defendant owned *10–12 Irving St.*

(d) In Connecticut v. Menillo, p. 309, Menillo was *not a physician.*

(e) In Mumma v. Mumma, p. 311, the wife performed *sporadic clerical services for an undetermined period when her husband was beginning his practice.*

(f) In MacPherson v. Buick, p. 319, the plaintiff purchased a *Buick.*

(g) In Goldberg v. Kelly, p. 330, the plaintiffs received *AFDC.*

Later we will examine whether any of these fact categorizations were key to the holdings in these opinions.

In reading court opinions, you will be examining conclusions or holdings such as the following:

- the defendant's conduct constituted price fixing;
- the defendant did not commit burglary;
- the defendant is not in compliance with § 43 of the environmental code.

How do we determine what facts were key to these results? There may be individual facts in the opinion that were key, or there may be fact categorizations of one or more individual facts that were key. To find out, we go through the same "what if" process that we used to determine the facts that were key to the purchase of the XYZ word processor.

To illustrate, let's look at the opinion of *People v. Sohn* on p. 299 of this text. Re-read this short opinion now. The question before the *Sohn* court was whether the evidence justified a finding of guilt beyond a reasonable doubt. The conclusion of the court was that guilt had *not* been established to meet this standard. Our question is: what facts were the key facts in the mind of the court when it reached this holding? We start our search by examining the individual facts in the opinion:

- Sohn and his co-defendants called the police.
- Sohn and his co-defendants remained on the scene until the police arrived.
- The complainant (i.e., the victim, the person bringing the complaint against Sohn and his co-defendants) pled guilty to possession of a pistol during the same incident.

Which of these facts were key to the court's holding that Sohn's guilt had not been established beyond a reasonable doubt? Recall the test that is based on our definition of a key fact:

Test to Determine Whether a Fact Was Key to a Holding

To determine whether a fact in an opinion was key to the court's holding, we isolate the fact and ask ourselves if the holding would have been different if that fact had been changed in the opinion (assuming all the other facts in the opinion had remained the same). The change can occur by eliminating that fact or by altering it.

Before we study the techniques that will allow us to carry out this test, we will use the test in the *Sohn* opinion in order to provide an overview of the analytical process. Half the battle is learning how to structure the question of whether a fact is key.

1. WE COULD ELIMINATE A FACT AND ASK OURSELVES WHETHER THE DECISION WOULD HAVE BEEN THE SAME IN SPITE OF THE ELIMINATION

Example: Take out the fact in *Sohn* that the complainant pled guilty to possession of a pistol during the same incident.

Question: If all the facts in the opinion were the same except that the complainant did *not* plead guilty to possession of a pistol, would the court still have decided that guilt had not been established beyond a reasonable doubt?

Analysis: (a) If you conclude that the court would still have found that guilt had *not* been established beyond a reasonable doubt even though the complainant had not pled guilty to possession of a pistol, then the fact that the complainant *did* plead guilty was *not* a key fact in the opinion. This is so because it is your assessment that the decision would be the same whether or not the complainant pled guilty to possession of a pistol. The elimination of this fact would have made no difference to the result of the opinion. Pleading guilty may have been a relevant fact; it may even have been an important fact. But it was *not* a key fact.

(b) If, on the other hand, you conclude that the court would have found that guilt *had* been established beyond a reasonable doubt when we eliminate the fact that the complainant pled guilty to possession of a pistol, then the latter *was* a key fact. This is so because it is your assessment that the holding would not be the same if the complainant had not pled guilty to possession of a pistol.

How do you support your conclusion that a fact is or is not key? How do you resolve any unclarity in your mind as to whether a fact is key? You use the techniques of identifying key facts that will be discussed in section F of this chapter (p. 118).

2. WE COULD CHANGE A FACT AND ASK OURSELVES WHETHER THE DECISION WOULD HAVE BEEN THE SAME IN SPITE OF THIS ALTERNATION

Example: Change the fact that Sohn remained on the scene until the police arrived. The changed facts now read that Sohn called the police but left the scene immediately after the call.

Question: If all the facts of the opinion were the same except that Sohn did not remain on the scene after he called the police, would the court still have held that guilt had not been established beyond a reasonable doubt?

Analysis: (a) If you conclude that the court would have found that guilt had still *not* been established beyond a reasonable doubt even though Sohn fled the scene after he called the police, then it was *not* a key fact in the opinion that Sohn remained on the scene. This is so because it is your assessment that the decision would be the same whether or not Sohn fled. It would have made no difference to the result of the opinion. Staying on the scene may have been a relevant fact; it may even have been an important fact. But it was *not* a key fact.

(b) If, on the other hand, you conclude that the court *would* have found that guilt had been established beyond a reasonable doubt if Sohn had fled from the scene, then the fact that he did not flee *was* a key fact in the opinion. This is so because it is your assessment that the holding would not be the same if Sohn had fled from the scene.

You obtain support for your conclusion and you resolve any doubts in your mind about whether a fact is key by using the techniques of identifying key facts to be treated in section F of this chapter (p. 118).

3. WE EXAMINE ALL FACT CATEGORIZATIONS AND ASK OURSELVES WHETHER THE DECISION WOULD HAVE BEEN THE SAME IF ANY OF THE FACT CATEGORIZATIONS WERE NOT PRESENT OR WERE DIFFERENT.

Thus far we have been considering individual facts in the *Sohn* opinion. What about fact categorizations? Do any exist? If so, we must assess whether they were key to the holding.

The court uses an adjective to describe the evidence on how the incident began. This evidence was:

"extremely equivocal"

This is a fact categorization. It is a broader category that covers individual facts. To determine whether this fact categorization was a key fact in the court's holding, we subject it to the same "what if" process.

What if the evidence was *not* "extremely equivocal"? What if it was clear how the incident began? Would this have made a difference in the holding? Answering such questions—through the techniques of section F—will help us decide whether this fact categorization was key.

Assignment #16

Examine the opinion of *Brown v. Southall Realty Co.*, p. 300. Below you will find two facts from a client's case that differ from the facts in *Brown:*

a. The commode functioned properly.

b. All housing code violations occurred after the lease agreement was signed.

For each fact difference, formulate the *question* of whether *Brown* would apply to the client's case in spite of the difference. Assume that all other facts in the client's case are the same as those in *Brown*. Do not answer the question, simply phrase it. Check your response with the Suggested Response, p. 376.

Assignment #17

Examine the opinion of *Nicholson v. Conn. Half-Way House, Inc.*, p. 307. Below you will find three facts from a client's case that differ from the facts in *Nicholson:*

a. At the opposite end of Irving Street, there was a vacant lot rather than a factory.

b. The defendant's property was a single-family dwelling.

c. In a similar neighborhood where defendant operates another halfway house, there have been three muggings in the past two years, all of which have been traced to residents of this other halfway house.

For each fact difference, formulate the *question* of whether *Nicholson* would apply to the client's case in spite of the difference. Assume that all other facts in the client's case are the same as those in *Nicholson*. Do not answer the question, simply phrase it.

As we have seen, one of the ways that we test the "keyness" of a fact is by changing that fact and then asking ourselves what effect the change would have on the holding. Where do these fact changes come from? Since fact changes are potentially infinite in number, how do you decide what changes to make? To answer this question, we need to recall the main reason that we brief opinions. Briefing is a device used to increase our understanding of an opinion that we want to *apply* to a new set of facts. The new facts are the facts of a client's case (or of a teacher's hypothetical question). The fact changes that we make in our search for key facts in an opinion are directly tied to and are based upon the facts in the client's case.

Suppose that you are briefing the opinion of *X v. Y*, and that you are trying to apply this opinion to a client's case. Assume the following facts involved in each:

Facts of *X v. Y:*
Opinion

A sister severely injures her brother with a bat. The brother sues the sister for battery. The court holds that such suits should not be allowed in the courts. The suit is dismissed.

Facts of Client's Case:

A brother hits his sister in an auto accident. The sister wants to sue her brother for negligence.

As we try to apply the opinion of *X v. Y* to the facts of the client's case, we must determine what were the key facts in this opinion. One way to do this is to change facts in the opinion and assess the effect of this change on the holding. Again our question: what facts should we change and what should the changes be? The answer depends on the fact differences between the client's case and the opinion.

One of the fact differences is that *X v. Y* involved a brother suing a sister, whereas in the client's case the sister seeks to sue her brother. We know what happened in *X v. Y*; the court held that the suit could not be brought. We now want to know whether it was a key fact in *X v. Y* that the plaintiff was the brother of the defendant. One way to find out is to *change* this fact and to assess the change on the holding.

WHAT IF it was the *sister* who sued the brother for battery in *X v. Y*? Would the court still have held that the suit could not be brought? If the answer is yes, then it was *not* a key fact in *X v. Y* that the plaintiff was the sister. Perhaps the key fact was the *fact categorization* of close family relationship, i.e., the court will bar suits between close family members.

Note that we made fact changes in the opinion based on the facts in the client's case. We changed the facts in the opinion to conform to the facts in the client's case and then asked ourselves what effect this would have on the holding in the opinion. Once we identified a fact difference in the client's case, we asked ourself WHAT IF the opinion contained that fact difference.

The analytical process is diagrammed in Figure 8-3. We will return to it in greater detail later.

Section C. The Totality of Facts as Key

The chart in Figure 8-3 suggests that you can always treat one fact at a time in an opinion. This is not necessarily so. In some opinions, no one fact viewed in isolation is a key fact. Only when most or all of the facts are viewed together do you begin to obtain an idea of what was key.

In our discussion of *Sohn* above, we began by examining one fact at a time. There is another way to analyze this opinion:

• examined in isolation, it is not a key fact that Sohn called the police;

• examined in isolation, it is not a key fact that Sohn waited until the police arrived;

• examined in isolation, it is not a key fact that the complainant was also convicted of a crime;

• etc.;

• what is key is the *totality* of these facts; the court reached the conclusion it did because of the peculiar combination of these facts viewed together.

FIGURE 8–3.
The Analytical Process
for Applying Opinions
via Key Facts.

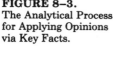

If this is so, then the *Sohn* opinion cannot apply to a client's case unless the sum total of the client's facts are the same or very similar to the combination of facts in *Sohn*.

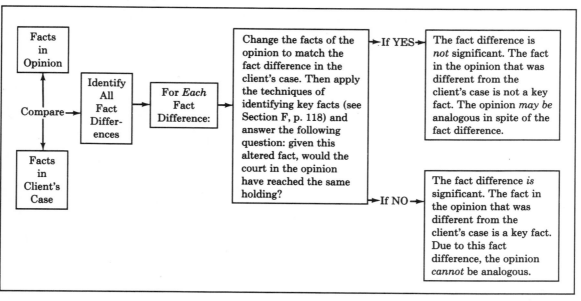

If this type of case analysis is carried too far, however, the application of opinions to new fact situations would be virtually impossible. It will be rare indeed to find a client's case containing the same totality of facts as that found in an opinion. Nevertheless, the advocate who does *not* want an opinion to apply will often try to argue that what is key in the opinion is the *totality* of the facts and that this same totality does not exist in the client's case on whose behalf the advocate is working.

While you should be aware of the totality argument and should be prepared to use it, if necessary, in your own advocacy, care must be exercised in doing so. The totality argument is easy to make, but it will seldom be successful before a court or administrative agency because if the argument were carried to the extreme, very few opinions would ever constitute precedent for subsequent cases.

A wiser, more sophisticated, and more productive form of case analysis is to examine one fact at a time or one small cluster of facts at a time in your pursuit of what is or is not key. Keep your eye on the totality, but thoroughly analyze the pieces.

Section D. Introduction to the Techniques of Identifying Key Facts

Thus far we have established the analytical structure for determining what facts in an opinion were key to holding(s) in the opinion. That structure is the fact-modification process that we explored above. Up to now, we used this process simply to *ask* the key-fact question. We are ready to try to *answer* the question. We now turn to those techniques that can be helpful in answering the question of whether a given fact in the opinion was key to its holding. The rest of this chapter will explore all these techniques except one—which will be covered in Chapter 10. At the outset, a number of important points must be made about the techniques:

1. The techniques are guides only. They will not guarantee definitive conclusions about which facts were key.

2. Not all techniques will be useful or relevant in every opinion. While you should explore every technique, it may be that some will not be very productive in a given opinion.

3. Do not rely on any technique in isolation from the others. Explore them all. Your use of one technique may lead you to the conclusion that a certain fact was key. Be prepared, however, to change your conclusion if the other techniques point the other way. Conversely, your use of one technique may lead you to the conclusion that a certain fact was *not* key. Be open to the possibility, however, that the other techniques will convince you otherwise.

4. Since you rarely, if ever, will achieve certainty in the identification of key facts, you should expect some disagreement among readers of the opinion as to what facts were key. The positions you take on the key facts are *advocacy arguments*. Hence, as you search for the facts that *you* think were key, you should also try to anticipate what *others* will claim to be key. Which of the techniques will *they* use to support their analysis of the key facts? This point will be critical when we later study the *application* of opinions in an interoffice *memorandum of law.*

5. The process of identifying key facts is almost a mind-reading exercise. You are trying to get into the "head" of the court at the time it wrote the opinion. When the language of the opinion is not clear or when it appears contradictory, you must speculate about the thinking process of the court. What was the court trying to do? Isn't this statement of the court inconsistent with the statement it made earlier? Is the *result* of the opinion consistent with positions taken by the court in the opinion? Why would the court go out of its way to make that point? Etc. These are the kinds of probing questions that will often be needed to understand the court's analysis in the opinion. Such questions will be essential in your search for key facts.

6. Keep in mind that you examine the keyness of facts from the perspective of the court, not from the perspective of the parties in the opinion. To the parties litigating the case that resulted in the opinion, *every* fact was probably important or key. But the parties did not write the opinion. You want to know what facts were key *to the decision maker*—the court.

7. As we shall see, there is often more than one legal issue or question in an opinion. The court's answer to a legal issue is its *holding.* Each legal issue and holding has its own key facts. While the same facts might sometimes be key for more than one issue and holding, you should start your search for key facts (a) by isolating each individual issue in the opinion, and (b) by asking what facts were key to the court's holding for that issue.

8. The search for key facts through the techniques will be time consuming, particularly in view of point 5 made above. It is true that it will be relatively easy to identify some facts in the opinion as key or as non-key. For most of the facts in the opinion, however, your conclusion on keyness or non-keyness will be much more difficult and painful to reach. The advocacy as to the applicability of the opinion will often center on these facts.

9. You cannot tell in advance how many facts were key to a holding. Usually, there will be several facts that will be key for each holding, and these facts will often be fact categorizations (p. 107).

Section E. Spotting the Obvious

There are at least two situations in which you should have no difficulty reaching conclusions about the keyness of facts:

a. Facts that are obviously *not* key

b. Facts that obviously *are* key

(a) Common sense will tell you that there will usually be some facts in an opinion that could not possibly be key. Suppose, for example, that the opinion was about a divorce granted to Helen Johnson against her husband, Peter Johnson. It is highly unlikely that the court would have reached a different result if Helen's husband were named *Paul* Johnson. The name of the spouses would be irrelevant to whether grounds for divorce existed. Using our test for the keyness of a fact, if we changed Peter's name to Paul, we can safely predict that the court would not have reached a different result. The defendant's first name was not key to the decision, assuming all the other facts remained the same. So, too, in a negligence action by George against the ABC Company for an injury to George's right arm, if the opinion found the Company liable, the same result would probably have been reached if George's *left* arm had been injured, again assuming that all the other facts remained the same. The location of the injury was probably irrelevant.

Hence you can use common sense as a guide in identifying facts that were clearly *not* key. Caution, however, is needed in using this guide. There *are* opinions whose results turn on extremely narrow facts. If there is any doubt in your mind as to the role that a given fact had in the court's decision, you will need to go through all the techniques to be discussed below.

(b) There will be times when it will be obvious that certain facts *are* key. Refer again to the opinion mentioned above in which the court granted a divorce to Helen Johnson against her husband, Peter Johnson. It should be clear that one key fact in this opinion is that the parties were spouses. The court would not have granted a divorce if the parties were not married! The result of the opinion *would* have been different if we changed the fact that Helen and Peter were each other's spouses. Two unmarried neighbors, for example, cannot be divorced from each other. Again, common sense is a guide.

Sometimes the language of the court is also a clear guide. Suppose you are reading an opinion in which the court found fraud in a particular transaction. In the opinion you find the following language:

> Liability in this case depends on the thoroughness with which the falsehood is communicated.

Liability *depends* on thoroughness. Here is a gift from court. The court is obviously telling us that one of the key facts in the opinion is the thoroughness of the falsehood that was committed. If we changed this fact (e.g., by substituting a vague or incomplete falsehood), we can safely predict that a different result would have been reached. In another example, suppose that a court tells us that it is "fatal" to the plaintiff's claim for relief that he did not give notice of the sale to the defendant. Again, the fairly dramatic language by the court helps us identify a key fact. The failure to give notice was *fatal.* It seems obvious that this failure was a key fact.

Pay particular attention to "when" or "if" clauses in which the court conditions conclusions on certain facts. Example:

> When an automobile buyer knows of the defect in the automobile, he cannot later complain that he did not get what he bargained for from the seller.

Another gift. *Knowledge* of the defect is key. It appears clear that this court would reach a different result if the buyer was ignorant of the defect. A stated condition of the court's conclusion that the buyer cannot complain is the latter's knowledge of the defect. Always take advantage of this kind of clarity in a court opinion.

Identification of Key Facts: Guideline #1

(a) Common sense can be a guide in identifying facts that are obviously *not* key because they clearly had no impact on the holding of the court.

(b) Common sense can also be a guide in identifying certain facts as key. Also, watch for sentences in which the court appears to condition a conclusion on certain facts. Such facts are usually key.

Caution, however, is needed in applying this guideline. To say that something is obviously key is not to say that it is conclusively so. So very little is certain in case analysis. Try to spot what appears to be obvious, but don't be surprised if what is obvious to you is not so obvious to your opponent. A preeminent sign of a skillful reader of court opinions is the ability to gauge how the other side is going to respond to your interpretation of the key facts.

Section F. Ten Techniques for Identifying Key Facts

Ten techniques for identifying key facts are summarized below. The first one, reasoning, will be examined in greater detail in Chapter 10. The techniques are listed in the *approximate* order of their *potential* usefulness. It is highly likely, for example, that the first technique in the list will aid you in identifying the key facts in an opinion. Those techniques presented toward the end of the list are less likely to be helpful for most opinions that you will be reading. This is not to say that any of the techniques can be ignored. It may be that for some opinions a technique toward the end of the list will be crucial in helping find the key facts. The likelihood, however, is that the most productive techniques will be those at the top of the list. The others, while sometimes very helpful, will mainly serve to bolster whatever conclusions you reach when employing the earlier techniques in the list. The ten techniques are not mutually exclusive; there is overlap among them. In using one of the techniques, you may find yourself simultaneously using some of the others. This should not concern you. The list is a guide only, not an end in itself.

Techniques for Identifying Key Facts

1. Reasoning
2. Fact categorizations used by the court
3. The court's response to a party's position on the importance of certain facts
4. Sheparidizing
5. The court's discussion of the facts of internal opinions
6. The court's response to facts deemed important or unimportant by a lower court or agency in the same litigation
7. Adjectives
8. Repetition
9. Facts mentioned early in the opinion
10. Totality of the facts

1. REASONING

The reasoning in an opinion tells us why the court reached the result it did or, more technically, why a legal issue led to a particular holding. The key facts for a holding must be consistent with and be based upon this reasoning. Hence, a major guide in the identification of key facts will be the identification of reasoning. An examination of reasoning will be found in Chapter 10 after we study legal issues.

2. FACT CATEGORIZATIONS USED BY THE COURT

As we have stressed a number of times, you should give careful attention to *individual* facts stated by the court (e.g., four families lived on the east end of Johnson Street), and express or implied *fact categorizations* of these individual facts (e.g., Johnson street was a residential area). The use of such fact categorizations *by the court* is a strong, but not necessarily conclusive, indication that it is the broader categorization that is key rather than the individual facts.

Fact categorizations are at the heart of the briefing process (how to *read* an opinion) and of the application process (how to *apply* a holding in an opinion to the facts of a client's case). A major debate between advocates will center on how broadly or narrowly the key facts of a holding can be stated:

• The advocate who wants the holding of an opinion to apply to the facts of the client's case will usually try to phrase the key facts of the holding as *broadly* as possible.

• The advocate who does not want the holding of an opinion to apply to the facts of the client's case will usually try to phrase the key facts as *narrowly* as possible.

When we examine reasoning, one of our concerns will be whether the reasoning supports a narrower or a broader statement of the facts as key. Hence, there is a great deal at stake in the distinction between individual facts (narrow) and fact categorizations (broad).

Suppose that you are reading an opinion involving a group of inmates in solitary confinement who are claiming that their living conditions in confinement constitute cruel and unusual punishment in violation of the Constitution. The court may give the facts in great detail for each inmate, such as:

• the size of the cell;

• the kind of clothing given the inmate;

• the temperature in the cell;

• the temperature outside (depending on the season of the year);

• sleeping facilities in the cell;

• toilet facilities in the cell;

• the kind and amount of light and ventilation in the cell at different times during the day;

• the health of the inmate before and during confinement in the cell;

- the kind and amount of food;
- rodents in the cell;
- etc.

It is quite possible for such an opinion to have thousands of facts. While it is conceivable that all these facts are key, it is unlikely. As always, each of the techniques of identifying key facts must be used. One such technique is to identify categorizations used by the court to describe the individual facts.

As you read page after page of facts in the opinion, the court may occasionally provide you with certain categorizing words and phrases. For example, the court may refer to a group of facts on the condition of the cell as:

- "unsanitary," *or*
- "dangerous to health," *or*
- "excessive."

Categorizations such as these can be significant. It may be that what is key in the opinion is the fact categorization rather than the individual facts that are the foundation for the categorization. Be sensitive to such categorizations when they are provided by the judge, especially when they are repeated or otherwise emphasized in the opinion.

Again, the word "categorization" simply means a *broader* classification or description of a fact or group of facts (see Figure 8–4).

There are many different kinds of opinions that involve large numbers of facts. For example:

- employment discrimination opinions in which the court provides many facts on the employment policies and practices of an employer;
- divorce opinions in which the court provides many facts on the marriage relationship that existed between the husband and wife over the years;
- contract opinions in which the court provides many facts on the written and verbal transactions that took place between buyer and seller;
- antitrust opinions in which the court provides many facts on the business ventures of a company;
- etc.

While it is true that in *all* opinions you must identify the fact categorizations provided by the court, it is particularly important to do so in lengthy opinions containing numerous facts.

In opinions with many facts, the court may not say that any individual facts are conclusive or dispositive, but that "taken on the whole," or "given all these circumstances," or "viewed in their entirety," the facts lead the court to a particular conclusion. Here again, it is extremely important to determine whether the judge provides you with any fact categorizations. When the facts are viewed "on the whole" or "on balance," does the judge express or imply any fact categorizations? For example, in a union opinion with numerous facts, the court may say or imply that its assessment of the composite facts leads

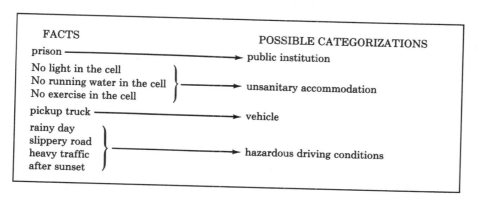

FIGURE 8–4.
Examples of Fact
Categorizations.

it to conclude that the employer's activities in response to the union organizing activities of the employees were "knowingly hostile." It may be that it is this fact categorization that is key.

———

A note of caution is needed in using this technique of identifying key facts. It is sometimes difficult to distinguish between a fact categorization and a rule of law or a portion of a rule of law. Indeed, the same concept may be commonly thought of as *both* a fact and a rule of law.

Assume that you are reading a negligence opinion. The rule of law being applied in the opinion is the common law of negligence. The court first goes through many individual facts in the opinion (e.g., a witness saw the defendant's car speed toward the plaintiff's car, a crash was heard soon after, the dent on the plaintiff's car contained some paint chips that matched the defendant's car, etc.), and then the court concludes with the observation that the defendant "caused" the accident. Causation is a fact. Indeed, it is a fact categorization in that it is a composite description or conclusion with respect to other facts. But causation is also a rule of law. It is part of the definition of negligence, i.e., it is one of the elements (p. 150) of negligence. Our concern is whether something that is both a rule of law and a fact can be a key fact. Could causation be a key fact in the above example if the issue in the opinion was whether the defendant caused the accident?

No. If causation is part of the rule of law *in contention*, then it would beg the question to refer to it as a key fact. If the court's holding was that causation existed, it would make no sense to refer to causation as a key fact for this holding. The argument would be circular. You need to find out what facts were key to the court's holding that there was causation. Similarly, if the court was interpreting the phrase "unreasonable noise" in § 32 of a statute, it would be circular to say that unreasonable noise was a key fact. We want to know what *other* facts were key to the court's holding that there was or was not "unreasonable noise" under the statute.

3. THE COURT'S RESPONSE TO A PARTY'S POSITION ON THE IMPORTANCE OF CERTAIN FACTS

Earlier we said that we want to identify the key facts from the perspective of the court, not of the parties in the opinion. Yet we can sometimes use the perspective of a party to help us understand the perspective of the court. The opinion will do one of the following:

a. provide a statement of the facts *without* any indication of what facts either of the opposing parties felt were important;

b. provide a statement of the facts *plus* some indication of what facts either of the opposing parties felt were important.

The second situation may provide a helpful clue to what facts were key to the court. The clue comes from carefully examining the court's express or implied *response* to a party's position on the importance of certain facts. Does the court agree? Disagree? In the process of giving this response, the court will either clearly tell us what facts are *not* key or will provide helpful guidance on what facts it feels *are* key.

In the following hypothetical example from an opinion, you can see this technique at work.

> We recognize, of course, that Prudential stresses that "responsibility for and control of all significant decisions affecting the office and clerical staff is centralized in the Regional Home Office through various devices." The Regional Home Office doubtless does have ultimate authority over every district office. Since, however, its authority encompasses 48 district offices in seven states, it would be an extraordinary feat to exercise that control on a day-by-day basis.

In this example, the court tells us that one of the parties (Prudential) feels that it is important that a great deal of centralized authority exists in the Regional Home Office. The court *responds* as follows: while there may be ultimate authority in the Regional Home Office, it is unlikely that the authority can be exercised on a "day-by-day basis." The court may be saying that what is key is not so much the existence of a central office with authority, but the *unlikelihood that this office can control decisions on a day-to-day basis.* Here, then, is a court's *response* to what someone else says is an important fact, and within this response, we have a clue to what the court felt was a key fact.

4. SHEPARDIZATION

This technique involves what is called "reading cases in sequence." You find out if any other opinions have discussed the opinion you are briefing. If so, these discussions may help you assess the key facts of the latter opinion. The major process by which you locate such other opinions, if any, is *shepardizing*. To shepardize a case means to use the volumes of *Shepard's Citations* to determine, among other things, whether any subsequent opinions have cited the opinion you are shepardizing (and briefing).

Assume that you are briefing the opinion of *State v. Ray,* a 1975 case decided by the Supreme Court of Texas. There are many facts in the *Ray* opinion leading to the court's holding that the defendant committed a burglary, e.g., Ray is a twenty-three-year-old male with four prior felony convictions; on March 13, 1973, he opened an unlocked door of a neighbor's car, took valuables from the glove compartment, and fled. You are trying to identify the key facts of the court's holding that there was a burglary. Specifically, you are focusing on whether it was key that he entered a *car*. In addition to using the other techniques for identifying key facts, you shepardize *State v. Ray*. In the library, you use the volumes of *Shepard's Citations* that cover opinions of the Texas courts. Assume that these volumes tell you that *State v. Ray* has been cited by four other opinions:

- *State v. Roberts* (1976)
- *Renwick Co. v. Florene* (1977)
- *State v. Granger* (1978)
- *State v. Doran* (1980)

In the library, you now go to the reporters containing each of these opinions. You want to know what they said about *State v. Ray*. You start with *State v. Roberts*. As you read this opinion, you find that it does cite *State v. Ray*, but there is no discussion of the *Ray* opinion. The cite to *Ray* is buried in the middle of a long footnote. Hence, the *Roberts* case is not very helpful in acquiring a deeper understanding of *State v. Ray*. Next, you read *Renwick Co. v. Florene*. It contains the following statement:

> The Texas courts have not been reluctant in the past to confront difficult cases. State v. Ray. . . .

Again, not very helpful. There is no discussion of *Ray*. The third case you examine is *State v. Granger*. In reading this opinion, you find the following:

> In State v. Ray, the defendant was convicted of burglarizing a car.

This is all we are told about *State v. Ray*—no further discussion. So far, we are not doing very well. *State v. Granger* sheds little light on what was important in *State v. Ray*. The *Granger* case simply repeats a few of the facts of *Ray*. No discussion, hence no enlightenment. Finally, you read *State v. Doran*. This opinion does discuss *Ray*:

> Texas has never limited the crime of burglary to breaking and entering homes and offices where people live or work. In State v. Ray, for example, the Supreme Court of Texas agreed that burglary was committed when the defendant entered a car. What was critical in the case was the entering of an enclosed structure whether or not people lived or worked regularly therein.

The *Doran* opinion does shed some light on the opinion you are briefing, *State v. Ray*. The *Doran* opinion is telling us that what was key in *Ray* was the fact that an *enclosed structure* was entered. This certainly supports the view that car was *not* a key fact in *State v. Ray* and that what *was* key was the broader fact categorization of enclosed structure.

As you can see, it takes some time and work to use the "shepardizing" technique of identifying key facts. It is quite common for *Shepard's Citations* to lead you to many opinions that will *not* be helpful in your quest for the key facts in the opinion you are briefing. It may be that none of them will be helpful. Yet the technique should still be tried.

Later, we will examine other functions that shepardizing can play in case analysis (p. 172).

5. THE COURT'S DISCUSSION OF THE FACTS OF INTERNAL OPINIONS

In the fourth technique above, we tried to use *subsequent* opinions to help us identify key facts in the opinion we are briefing. In this fifth technique, we will seek the same help through an examination of *prior* opinions. The prior opinions are those cited *within* the opinion you are briefing and will be referred to here as *internal opinions*. Our concern is how internal opinions can help us identify the key facts of the opinion you are briefing.

Three kinds of internal opinions need to be distinguished:

• Internal opinions that are part of the same litigation as the opinion you are briefing;

• Internal opinions that are cited but not discussed by the opinion you are briefing;

• Internal opinions that are cited and also discussed by the opinion you are briefing.

(a) Same Litigation In this fifth technique, we are *not* referring to internal opinions that are part of the same litigation. Such opinions will be examined in the sixth technique later.

(b) Internal Opinions That Are Cited But Not Discussed The opinion you are briefing may cite numerous internal opinions. For most of these opinions, the court will provide little or no discussion. For example, the following hypothetical excerpt is from the opinion of *Winters v. Lansberry:*

> The doctrine of equitable estoppel is a cornerstone of our jurisprudence. Tribble v. Jackson, 34 Mass. 354, 230 N.E.2d 190 (1975); Harrison v. United States, 34 F.Supp. 462 (E.D.Pa.1976); Butter Cup Co. v. Nickle Plate Ltd., 401 F.2d 45 (5th Cir. 1980).

In our search for the key facts of *Winters v. Lansberry,* we are given very little help by the court's citations to the opinions of *Tribble, Harrison,* and *Butter Cup Co.* We are not given any of their facts. We cannot, therefore, compare any of their facts with those of the *Winters* opinion. Without being able to make this comparison, the internal opinions cannot help guide us to the key facts of *Winters.*

(c) Internal Opinions That Are Discussed When the court *does* discuss an internal opinion, two things are required for the discussion to be helpful in identifying key facts: we must be given at least some of the facts of the internal opinion; and the court, expressly or impliedly, must compare these facts with one or more of the facts of the opinion you are briefing.

Assume that you are briefing the opinion of *Ellis v. Ellis* in which Bob Ellis sued his sister Diane Ellis for damaging his home computer. Diane raised the defense of intrafamily tort immunity, arguing that siblings cannot sue each other in tort. The court denies the defense and rules in favor of Bob.

We now want to determine what facts were key to this holding of the court. In the *Ellis* opinion, we find the following:

> We believe that Richardson v. Richardson properly states the principles that govern the case before us. In *Richardson,* the court ruled that a son could sue his father for theft of the son's trust account since no intrafamily tort immunity attaches to property suits among family members. This clearly would cover a suit between siblings for damage to a computer.

Here the court gives us some of the facts of an internal opinion, *Richardson v. Richardson,* and compares these facts to those before the court. What does this comparison tell us the key facts in *Ellis v. Ellis* probably were? First, siblings is not key; the broader fact categorization of family member is key. Second, computer damage is not key; the broader fact categorization of property damage or interference is key. The *Ellis* court's reliance on *Richardson* supports these conclusions.

Another example. Assume that you are briefing the opinion of *Adams v. Viking Construction Co.* Adams was injured from a blasting accident when the explosives being transported by Viking suddenly ignited. Viking is a private company that has total discretion on the jobs that it will and will not take. Adams argued that Viking should be absolutely liable, meaning that it is liable even if it was not negligent. Viking countered by saying that its liability, if any, must be based on a showing that it was negligent in transporting the explosives. The court held that negligence did not have to be proved; absolute liability applied because Viking was engaged in an inherently dangerous activity. What were the key facts for this holding? In the opinion, we find the following:

> Viking relies on the case of *Baltimore RR v. Innis* in which the court held that the plaintiff had to prove that the railroad was negligent in transporting poisonous gases which leaked out, causing injury. But in that case, the railroad was *required* to transport the substance by the government as a condition of its right to operate the railroad. No such requirement exists here.

This excerpt strongly suggests that one of the key facts in *Adams v. Viking Construction Co.* was the fact that Viking had full discretion on the work that it would contract to do—it was not required by the government to transport the explosives. If this requirement did exist, then the holding in *Adams* would probably have been different—the court would have required a showing of negligence and would not have imposed absolute liability.

A final example. Assume you are briefing the opinion of *Zakrajshek v. Shuster.* The following is an excerpt from the *Zakrajshek* opinion, which cites *Annala v. Bergman.* In the first paragraph of this excerpt, the court provides some of the facts in *Zakrajshek.* In the remainder of the excerpt, the court compares these facts with the facts in *Annala.* The court distinguishes *Annala* from the facts currently before it, finding that *Annala* is not applicable. As you read this excerpt, pay particular attention to the fact comparison:

> In a letter dated February 11, 1972, Employers Insurance advised Shuster that it had on February 7 received from him a check for $1,377, the amount due on his account. But it also advised that the policy could not be reinstated because it had

been cancelled prior to his injury due to nonpayment of premiums. The letter went on to propose writing instead a new policy effective as of the date the check was received, which apparently was done.

The plaintiff argues that under the rule stated in Annala v. Bergman, 213 Minn. 173, 6 N.W.2d 37 (1942), this reinstatement of coverage related back to and became effective as of the date of cancellation. In *Annala* the insurance policy had been canceled before the employee's accident on February 3, 1940. Upon receipt of the delinquent premium payment, the insurer reinstated the same policy of insurance, effective February 5. We said in that case that the statutory scheme of the Workers' Compensation Act mandated continuous coverage and that when an insurer cancels a policy and then reinstates the same policy the reinstatement must be as of the cancellation date.

The present case is distinguishable from *Annala* in that the insurer in *Annala* reinstated the very same policy while Employers Insurance in this case wrote an entirely new policy.

In *Zakrajshek,* the insurance company wrote an entirely new policy. In *Annala,* the insurance company reinstated the old policy. It is probably a key fact in *Zakrajshek* that a new policy was written. We reach this conclusion by carefully examining how the court treats *Annala.* The court uses the fact of the issuance of a new policy as significant in its analysis of the applicability of *Annala.* When a court identifies facts in this way, it is highly likely that those facts are key.

———

In each of the above three examples, we saw one court referring to or discussing an internal opinion (see Figure 8–5). The court in the column on the left had to determine whether an internal opinion was precedent or authority (p. 203) for the case before it. It is extremely important that you become sensitive to the various ways in which courts handle internal opinions. A number of options exist:

How Courts Handle Internal Opinions

1. If the court agrees with the holding, reasoning, or other position of the internal opinion, the court is *following* the internal opinion as precedent.

2. If the facts of the internal opinion are the same as or substantially the same as the facts of the case before the court, and the court agrees with the holding of the opinion, the court is following an opinion that is *on all fours* with the case before the court.

3. If the court is following an internal opinion whose facts are similar but still somewhat different from the facts before the court, the latter is *extending* the internal opinion. It is a precedent that is being followed and extended.

FIGURE 8–5.
Internal Opinions.

OPINION YOU ARE BRIEFING	INTERNAL OPINION DISCUSSED
Ellis v. Ellis — — — — — — — — — →	Richardson v. Richardson
Adams v. Viking Construction Co. — — — — →	Baltimore RR v. Innis
Zakrajshek v. Shuster — — — — — — →	Annala v. Bergman

4. If the court refuses to follow an internal opinion because its facts are different from the facts before the court or because of some other reason, the court is *distinguishing* the internal opinion. It is possible, however, for a court to accept some aspect of the opinion and to reject other aspects. Such an opinion is being followed in part and distinguished in part.

5. If the court refuses to follow or extend an internal opinion written by the same court even though the facts of the opinion are substantially the same as the facts before the court, the latter is *overruling* the internal opinion.

6. Occasionally, a court will reject or refuse to follow an internal opinion even though the court neither distinguishes it on the facts nor overrules it. The court simply disagrees with the internal opinion. When this occurs, the internal opinion is usually one that is written by a court within another judicial system.

Note on Opinions Within Opinions Within Opinions

When one court quotes from another opinion, the quoted opinion may be citing or even quoting from still another opinion. This situation involves one opinion citing another opinion that in turn is citing another opinion; it is an opinion within an opinion within an opinion. For example, here is an excerpt from *Thomas v. Thomas:*

> The doctrine has never been part of our system. For example, we recently held in Phillips v. Smith, 53 So.2d 908, 912 (1970) that "a waiver will not be valid without evidence that the waiver was intelligently made and according to Buckley v. Simpson, the waiver must be 'in writing' and signed. 14 So.2d 38, 42 (1951)."

In this excerpt, the *Thomas* opinion is citing the *Phillips* opinion that in turn is citing the *Buckley* opinion. More specifically, the *Thomas* opinion is following the *Phillips* opinion, which in turn is following the *Buckley* opinion.

Assignment #18

For each of the opinions mentioned below in 1–9,

> **(a)** List all internal opinions, if any, that were *followed* by the court.
>
> **(b)** List all internal opinions, if any, that were *extended* by the court.
>
> **(c)** List all internal opinions, if any, that were *distinguished* by the court.
>
> **(d)** List all internal opinions, if any, that were *overruled* by the court.
>
> **(e)** List all internal opinions, if any, that the court disagreed with or rejected for any other reason.
>
> **(d)** List all internal opinions, if any, whose use by the court is unclear because of how little the court says about them.

1. *Brown v. Southall Realty,* p. 300. Check your response with the Suggested Response, p. 376.

2. *Stephens v. Department of State Police,* p. 302. Do not include opinions of the attorney general in your answers.

3. *Nicholson v. Conn. Half-way House, Inc.*, p. 307.

4. *Connecticut v. Menillo*, p. 309.

5. *Mumma v. Mumma*, p. 311.

6. *Owen v. Illinois Baking Corp.*, p. 315.

7. *Thompson v. Royall*, p. 316.

8. *MacPherson v. Buick Motor Co.*, p. 319. (Answer the above questions for Cardozo's majority opinion only.)

9. *Goldberg v. Kelly*, p. 330. (Answer the above questions for Brennan's majority opinion only.)

6. THE COURT'S RESPONSE TO FACTS DEEMED IMPORTANT OR UNIMPORTANT BY A LOWER COURT OR AGENCY IN THE SAME LITIGATION

We saw earlier that most opinions have prior proceedings, p. 97. Assume that you are briefing the opinion of *Coronado Park v. Ohio* decided by the United States Supreme Court. Before this case came to the U.S. Supreme Court, there may have been a number of prior opinions in the same litigation, e.g., in an Ohio state middle appeals court, in the Ohio Supreme Court, in a U.S. District Court, and in a U.S. Court of Appeals. These prior opinions are part of the same litigation even though the order in which the names of the parties are given will not always be the same. For example, *Coronado Park v. Ohio* may have been called *Ohio v. Coronado Park* in one of the earlier opinions. Furthermore, the names of the parties will not always stay the same as the case is appealed through all the prior proceedings. One of the opinions in the appendix of this book is *Goldberg v. Kelly* decided by the U.S. Supreme Court (p. 330). When this case was in the U.S. District Court, it was called *Kelly v. Wyman*. Such changes can be due to a number of reasons, e.g., in a case that initially had multiple parties, one of the named parties may drop out of the litigation and be substituted by one of the other multiple parties as the case goes through the various appeals.

Not all opinions have prior proceedings. The major example of an opinion with no such proceedings is a trial court opinion that did not begin in an administrative agency. Furthermore, an opinion with prior proceedings may say very little about what happened "below," other than who won and who is appealing. In either situation the sixth technique for identifying key facts cannot be used.

This technique requires the following:

• The opinion you are briefing has prior proceedings.

• The opinion *discusses* what happened below in addition to telling us who won and who is now appealing.

• The opinion tells us what facts were considered important or unimportant by the lower court or agency in reaching its decision.

• The opinion tells us whether it agrees or disagrees with the assessment of the facts made by the lower court or agency.

What is crucial is the court's *response* to the fact assessment made below in the other tribunals. If, for example, the appellate court in the opinion you are briefing tells us that it agrees with the trial court's view that the plaintiff should win "because" the plaintiff was the first party to file the notice in the clerk's office, then being first to file is probably a key fact. If, on the other hand, a court tells us that it disagrees with the agency's determination that the mother's open cohabitation with her male friend disqualifies her for custody of her children, then we are equally safe in concluding that open cohabitation is *not* a key fact in the court's holding on custody.

7. ADJECTIVES

The opinion you are briefing may use certain adjectives for some of the facts in the opinion, e.g., "important," "telling," "noteworthy," "irrelevant," "of minor significance." The use of such adjectives can be useful guides in your search for what is and is not a key fact. Indeed, the adjectives may be so emphatic that your conclusion on keyness should be obvious (p. 116).

8. REPETITION

Some facts are repeated over and over in the opinion. You must carefully note the context in which this repetition occurs. A court might be repeating a fact simply because of sloppy opinion writing. On the other hand, the repetition may signal a certain significance of the fact in the mind of the judge writing the opinion. Depending on how the fact is used by the judge, its repetition may suggest that it was key or that it was not key to the result reached.

9. FACTS MENTIONED EARLY IN THE OPINION

A court will sometimes begin an opinion (or begin the discussion of individual issues within an opinion) with facts that are important in the case. On the other hand, such facts may be merely introductory in nature without any particular significance. As with all the techniques, care must be used in applying them. No technique, particularly those at the bottom of the list of the ten, should be used in isolation.

10. TOTALITY OF THE FACTS

As we have already seen, the totality argument is relatively easy to state: no individual facts or fact categorizations are key in themselves since it is the totality of all the facts together that is key (p. 114). As indicated, this approach to an opinion tends to be overly simplistic. It can be overdone. Rarely can it be said that the combination of facts in an opinion is so unique that *only* that combination could have produced the result reached. As an advocate, you may occasionally want to try this argument, but you should be aware that the totality argument is only infrequently successful.

Section G. Using the Techniques

The following outline presents the analytical steps that you should go through as you search for key facts in an opinion by using the ten techniques. Some of the steps will be covered in greater detail later. For now, it is important that you obtain a general overview of the entire process so that you can see how the various pieces will eventually fit together.

Assume that you are briefing the opinion of *Smith v. Jones,* a 1975 decision of the Supreme Court of Alabama. The opinion is five pages long with no concurring or dissenting opinions. Among the many facts in the opinion we are told that Jones is a six-year-old boy who was injured while playing in a yard owned by Smith in Birmingham, Alabama. Smith had a four-foot fence around the yard, but it was in disrepair, and seldom kept out unwanted intruders. A faded sign on the fence read "No Trespassing." Inside the yard, Smith kept an old car. Smith knew that the lock on the door was broken. One day Jones climbed over the fence, got into the car, and accidently released the emergency brake. The car was on an incline and rolled into a wall. Jones suffered a dislocated shoulder. He then sued Smith for negligence. At the trial court, Smith raised the defense of contributory negligence by Jones. The trial court held that Smith was negligent and that Jones was not contributorily negligent. Smith then appealed to the Supreme Court of Alabama. In the five page opinion of *Smith v. Jones,* the court affirmed the decision below. The court also held that Smith was negligent and that Jones was not contributorily negligent.

You now want to identify the key facts in the opinion of *Smith v. Jones.* The steps you take are as follows:

ANALYTICAL STEPS FOR THE IDENTIFICATION OF
KEY FACTS:

Step 1: Read through the entire opinion quickly in order to obtain an overview of what it is about.

Step 2: Use a legal dictionary for words and phrases that are new to you. If needed, also consult a treatise or legal encyclopedia to obtain a general understanding of the area of the law treated in the opinion. In *Smith v. Jones,* for example, if you are not sure what contributory negligence is and the opinion does not explain it, spend a few moments with a treatise such as *Prosser on Torts* or a legal encyclopedia such as *Am Jur 2d* to acquire the information that the opinion assumes the reader already has (pp. 210, 211).

Step 3: Be sure that you have identified the other components of the brief discussed earlier: parties (p. 81), objectives (p. 87), theories (p. 90), and prior proceedings (p. 97). In the process of doing this, you have already identified facts (e.g., the relationship between the parties), some of which you may eventually conclude are key facts.

Step 4: Make a preliminary determination of how many legal issues exist in the opinion. (Issue identification will be examined in greater depth later, p. 137). In *Smith v. Jones,* there are two issues: one involving negligence and one involving contributory negligence.

Step 5: Give a *shorthand* statement of each legal issue in the opinion. For example: Was § 34(d) violated? Is the employee entitled to workers' compensation? Is the regulation constitutional? Etc. For *Smith v. Jones,* a shorthand statement of the legal issues would be:

- Was the defendant negligent?
- Was the plaintiff contributorily negligent?

Step 6: Give a *shorthand* statement of the answer provided by the court for each issue. This can usually be provided in a simple yes/no format. In *Smith v. Jones,* the shorthand answer to the first issue is yes, and to the second issue, no. (As we have seen, the technical term for the answer to a legal issue is *holding,* p. 4.)

Step 7: Now examine one issue at a time. Organize your search for key facts around each individual issue. You want to know what facts were key to the court's answer (holding) for each issue. In *Smith v. Jones,* we want to know:

- What were the key facts in the court's conclusion that the defendant was negligent?
- What were the key facts in the court's conclusion that the plaintiff was not contributorily negligent?

Examine each question separately even though, as indicated earlier, you may ultimately conclude that some facts were key to more than one issue.

Step 8: Begin with what you feel is the main issue in the opinion. This will usually be the issue that the court spends the most time discussing.

Step 9: In your mind or on a sheet of paper, make a note of *every* fact that the court mentions in connection with the issue you are tackling. You might want to label them, Fact #1, Fact #2, Fact #3, etc.

Step 10: Recall the key-fact formula: a fact is key if the result in the opinion would have changed if that fact had been different or had not been in the opinion (p. 105). More technically:

> A fact is key if a *holding* in the opinion would have changed if that fact had been different or had not been in the opinion.

Ask this question for each fact you listed in Step 9. One of the facts in the *Smith v. Jones* opinion is that the fence was four feet high. Assume that we have labeled this as Fact #4 for the main negligence issue. We then ask:

> Was it a key fact to the court's holding of negligence that the fence was four feet high? *Or,*
> Would the court have still found the defendant negligent if the fence was not four feet high?

Don't worry yet about trying to answer this question. Half the battle is won if you can discipline your mind (a) to focus on facts, and (b) to ask yourself what role they played in the holding.

Step 11: Now ask the key-fact question by altering the fact under examination. Let's change Fact #4:

> Would the court have still found the defendant negligent if the fence was three feet, eleven inches?

If, by using the techniques described below, our answer to this question is yes, then it is NOT a key fact that the fence was four feet high. The court would have reached the same holding without this fact. There is nothing magic about the figure "four" in terms of the holding. If, however, by using the techniques described below, our answer to this question is no, then it MAY BE a key fact that the fence was four feet high. Why? Because when we took this fact out of the opinion, our assessment is that the court would have reached a different holding—it would *not* have found the defendant negligent.

Step 12: Keep challenging the same fact under examination—again and again—through the altering process.

> Would the court have still found the defendant negligent if the fence was nine feet high?

If the answer is yes, then again it is NOT a key fact that the fence was four feet. If the answer is no, then it MAY BE that four feet is key *unless we already eliminated four feet as key by an earlier assessment,* e.g., by determining that the same result (holding) would have been reached if the fence was three feet, eleven inches.

Step 13: Now make two lists. In the first list place every fact you assessed in Steps 11 and 12 that you think would produce the same holding. In the second list place every fact you assessed in these steps that you think would produce a different holding. For our Fact #4, assume that our lists would be as follows:

First List	Second List
(Each of the following facts would produce the same holding—that the defendant was negligent)	(Each of the following facts would produce a different holding— that the defendant was not negligent)
• four feet	• nine feet
• three feet, eleven inches	• eight feet
• two feet	• seven feet
• one foot	• etc.
• no fence at all	
• etc.	

Step 14: Ask yourself what are the common characteristics of each list. What is similar about each list? What *fact categorization* encompasses all the items in each list? What is it about everything in the first list that kept drawing us to the conclusion that the court would have reached the same holding if each one of these items had been in the opinion? What is it about everything in the second list that kept drawing us to the conclusion that the court would have reached a different holding if any of these items had been in the opinion? One possibility is as follows:

Fact Categorization Common to the Items in the First List:	Fact Categorization Common to the Items in the Second List:
• The yard is somewhat accessible	• The yard is somewhat inaccessible

Step 15: Ask yourself whether Step 14 led you to a *fact categorization that was key* to the court's holding that the defendant was negligent. By using the techniques described below, we want to know whether the court found the defendant negligent at least in part *because* the yard was somewhat accessible. Would the court have reached a different result (holding) if the yard was somewhat inaccessible in view of the size of the fence?

Step 16: We are now ready to apply the techniques for identifying key facts in order to try to answer the questions that have been raised in the above steps. We have before us nothing more than *candidates* for key facts: (a) individual facts: four feet; three feet, eleven inches; nine feet, etc., and (b) fact categorizations: accessibility/inaccessibility of the yard. We now need to find something concrete in the opinion on whether any of the individual facts or any of the fact categorizations (our candidates) are key or are not key. Again, we do so by using the ten techniques.

Step 17: For each of the facts in the opinion that you have numbered, be sure to identify whatever might be obvious as a matter of common sense or because of emphatic language used by the court. What about the fact that the yard was in Birmingham? If it is highly unlikely, as a matter of common sense, that the court would have reached a different result if the yard was located in any other city of Alabama, then there is no need to waste time worrying about whether it was a key fact that the yard was in Birmingham. Also, as you read the opinion, be alert to the use by the judge of emphatic language that appears to condition the holding on certain facts. Pay particular attention to "when" and "if" clauses that might serve this function.

Step 18: For every individual fact and for every fact categorization, go through each of the ten techniques. As indicated earlier, there may be some overlap in the techniques, and some may not be very helpful in a given opinion. Also, some of the techniques may simply reinforce conclusions you reached in Step 17 as to facts you feel are obviously not key or are obviously key. Finally, remember that all the techniques may not point to the same conclusion as to whether a fact is key. Two techniques, for example, may suggest that a certain fact (or fact categorization) is key, while three other techniques may point to a different conclusion. Don't block out such apparent inconsistencies. Make note of them. It is a sign of sophistication for a student to have enough self-confidence to be able to say, "I think that fact 'x' is key because of.... However, there is a possibility that it is not key because of...."

Back to our assessment of the fact on the height of the fence:

1. *Reasoning* Identify the reasoning of the court for the holding to the issue on which you are concentrating (p. 149). Does this reasoning support the view that four feet was key to the conclusion that the defendant was negligent? Or is a broader fact categorization more consistent with this reasoning? How broad is the reasoning? (We will discuss reasoning in Chapter 10.)

2. *Fact categorizations* What fact categorizations, if any, are used by the court itself? Are they similar to those we identified in Step 14 above? Any time a court expressly or impliedly uses a fact categorization, we must be alert to the good possibility that the fact categorization is key.

3. *The court's response to a party's position on facts* In the *Smith v. Jones* opinion, assume that the judge tells us that Smith thinks he should not be liable because he took pains to erect a fence around his yard. Pay particular attention to the court's response to this position of a party on the facts. This response may tell us what facts the court thinks are key.

4. *Shepardization* In the library we go to the set of *Shepard's Citations* that will enable us to shepardize the *Smith v. Jones* opinion. We want to use *Shepard's* to tell us what other opinions have said about *Smith v. Jones. Shepard's* will give us the citations to these other opinions, if any exist. We then read these opinions in the reporters to see what they said about *Smith v. Jones.* Do they discuss the facts of *Smith v. Jones?* If so, what facts do they say (or imply) were important in *Smith v. Jones?* Assume that *Shepard's* leads you to the 1982 opinion of *International Trucking Co. v. Richardson,* which does discuss *Smith v. Jones.* In the *International Trucking Co.* case, you find the following statement: "In *Smith,* what was critical was the failure of the defendant to take those precautions which a prudent landowner would take to discourage young children from entering an area where a potentially dangerous object exists." Such a statement is clearly strong support that a key fact categorization in *Smith v. Jones* was the fact that the yard was relatively accessible to children. And it reinforces the point that it is not the height of the fence in itself that was key, but rather it is the degree of the yard's accessibility that was key.

5. *The court's discussion of the facts of other opinions* One opinion will usually cite other opinions within its own opinion (p. 94). Make note of every internal opinion cited within *Smith v. Jones.* In particular, concentrate on those opinions, if any, whose facts are discussed by the court that wrote *Smith v. Jones.* Does the court compare any of the facts of *Smith v. Jones* with the facts of one of these internal opinions? If so, the comparison may provide clues to what the court in *Smith v. Jones* feels are the key facts.

6. *The court's response to facts deemed important or unimportant by a lower court or agency in the same litigation* There was no agency involved in the *Smith v. Jones* litigation. But there was a lower trial court decision. We are briefing the appellate opinion that grew out of this trial decision. In the appellate opinion, does the court mention any facts that the trial court felt were important or unimportant? If so, how does the appellate court respond to this position of the trial court on the facts? Again, this response is sometimes a good lead to what facts the appellate court thinks are key.

7. *Adjectives* Does the court in *Smith v. Jones* use adjectives that describe the relative importance of any of the facts in the case? If so, special note should be made of them. Of course, certain *strong* adjectives can be close to conclusive on the keyness or non-keyness of a certain fact, e.g., "crucial," "irrelevant." Such adjectives might lead us to conclude that the fact is obviously key or obviously not key.

8. *Repetition* Does the opinion keep repeating certain facts? If so it may simply mean that the judge is redundant. On the other hand, it may mean that the fact was important to the holding reached by the court.

9. *Facts mentioned early in the opinion* Pay particular attention to the facts mentioned in the first two or three paragraphs of the opinion. A court will often begin an opinion with the facts that it deems to be important. As with repetition, however, caution is needed in using this technique. A court may mention facts early in the opinion simply to lay the foundation for what is to come later where the "really" important facts will be provided.

10. *Totality of the facts* Can it be said that *every* fact in the opinion is key? If *any* facts in the opinion were changed, would a different holding have resulted?

Step 19: In Step 9 above, we recommended that you number every fact in the opinion mentioned in connection with an issue. For the negligence issue in *Smith v. Jones,* your list of facts might consist of the following:

#1 six-year-old
#2 boy
#3 playing in yard
#4 four-foot fence around yard
#5 fence in disrepair
#6 seldom kept out intruders
#7 "No Trespassing" sign
#8 sign was faded
#9 old car in yard
#10 lock on door of car is
    broken

#11 Smith knows it is broken
#12 Jones climbs over fence
#13 Jones gets into car
#14 accidently releases
    emergency brake
#15 car is on incline
#16 car rolls into wall
#17 Jones dislocates shoulder
#18 yard is in Birmingham, etc.

Thus far we have concentrated on Fact #4—the four-foot-fence around the yard. Steps 10 to 18 above mainly concerned Fact #4. It is now necessary to go through Steps 10 to 18 for *every* fact listed above in connection with the negligence issue. These facts and/or fact categorizations that grow out of them are all candidates for being key facts. They must all be put through the same analytical process. So too for the other issue in *Smith v. Jones*—contributory negligence. Every one of the above facts (and any others) that are discussed by the court in reference to the issue of contributory negligence must be put through Steps 10 to 18. If a certain fact is discussed by the court in reference to both issues in *Smith v. Jones*, then you must go through Steps 10 to 18 for that fact *twice* since you are assessing the impact of that fact on two separate holdings.

Identification of Key Facts: Guideline # 2

(a) Isolate all the legal issues in the opinion. Examine one issue at a time.

(b) List every fact mentioned by the court in connection with an issue. Examine one fact at a time.

(c) Phrase the key-fact question for the fact under examination.

(d) Formulate fact categorizations out of every fact that would appear to have resulted in the same holding.

(e) For every individual fact and every fact categorization that you have isolated, apply the ten techniques for identifying key facts.

At the beginning of this chapter, we said that "no aspect of case analysis . . . is more abused by so many people so many times than fact analysis." You should now have a feel for why so many people are "abusive" in the handling of facts in an opinion. You should also have a feel for why we called case analysis an "art" in Chapter 1. An opinion must be handled with great delicacy. *You cannot adequately analyze it simply by highlighting certain language in the opinion with a felt pen!* It takes time and work to study an opinion. Many people shy away from the task and resort to the felt pen (and to what we will later call "crane analysis," p. 182). If, however, the task is worth doing, then it is worth doing correctly.

Chapter Nine

Identifying Issues
and Holdings

Section A. The Interdependence of Key
Facts, Issues, Holdings, and Reasoning

In Chapters 5 to 7 we examined the four components of a brief listed in column "A" below. The next four components are listed in column "B," the first of which we have already begun studing.

"A"	"B"
Parties	Facts
Objectives	Issues
Theories	Holdings
Prior Proceedings	Reasoning

The four components of column "B" are intimately related to each other. Indeed, they should all be studied simultaneously since the identification of any one of these components will often be dependent on the identification of the other three.

While we will continue to cover the components of a brief one by one, you should keep in mind the interdependence of the four components of column "B." Once we finish our examination of all four components, you will be asked to identify the key facts and to give complete statements of the issues in the opinions we have been briefing.

Section B. Introduction to Issues and Holdings

Our specific goal in this chapter is to address the following themes:

• The structure of a legal issue (shorthand and complete statements of a legal issue);

• The methods of identifying legal issues in opinions (general guidelines and the four tests);

• The structure of a holding (shorthand and complete statements of a holding);

• The identification of holdings in opinions.

This chapter *begins* our study of issue identification. As indicated above, issue identification is closely connected with key-fact identification. Hence, we will be returning to the skill of issue identification in later chapters as we continue to explore the concept of key facts.

Section C. The Structure of a Legal Issue

There are two kinds of legal issues or questions:

(1) A question about how one or more rules of law apply to a given set of facts. When a court answers this kind of question, it does so in the form of a *holding.*

(2) A question about what happened (e.g., who did what to whom). When a court answers this kind of question, it often does so in the form of a *finding.*

At a *trial,* both kinds of issues are present, particularly the second. On *appeal,* the first kind of issue predominates. Our primary concern in this chapter is the first kind—one involving the application of rule(s) of law to facts.

Legal issues are often phrased in one of two ways:

• shorthand statement of a legal issue;

• complete statement of a legal issue.

(i) Shorthand Statement A shorthand statement consists mainly of a rule of law along with one or two facts:

• Was the driver *negligent?*

• Does *§ 98* require disclosure?

• Can an eight-year-old child commit a *burglary?*

• Should the *summary judgment* have been granted?

• What *standard of care* applies to a chiropractor?

The rule of law in question in each of the above statements has been italicized. In Chapter 3 (p. 61), we examined the various kinds of laws that can exist, e.g., constitutional provision, statute, regulation, common law doctrine. A legal issue in an opinion will involve the interpretation and application of one or more of these kinds of law.

Shorthand statements of legal issues serve important functions in the law. In Chapter 8, for example, we saw that one of the first steps in the process of identifying key facts is to state—in shorthand—each of the legal issues in the opinion you are briefing (p. 131). Also, in a law office, your oral communication with supervisors and fellow employees will often be in shorthand. More elaborate statements of legal issues usually come later in written communication.

The danger in using shorthand, however, is that you might forget that it is *shorthand* and, as such, is incomplete. Use it solely as a starting point. Your goal should be to learn to phrase legal issues in their *complete* form.

(ii) Complete statement A complete statement of a legal issue always has at least two parts:

1. The rule of law being interpreted and applied, including a reference to the particular language or portion of the rule that is the focus of the controversy, and

2. The key facts that concretely raise this controversy.
   For example:

> Did a county merchant violate § 38, which prohibits "illuminated signs after 2 A.M. in the county" when the merchant kept on several night lights after 2 A.M. in front of the store after closing?

This issue cites the rule of law being interpreted and applied (§ 38) and gives a brief quote from the rule, focusing on the language that is directly relevant to the controversy ("illuminated signs after 2 A.M. in the county"). The key facts raising this controversy are also included (merchant used night lights, in county, after 2 A.M., etc.). Assume that these are the facts that (after using the techniques for identifying key facts) you can demonstrate were key to the court's answer or holding for this issue.

In addition to a rule of law and key facts, legal issues sometimes contain a third part: *context facts*. These are non-key facts that are added either for background purposes or because someone in the litigation vigorously argued that they were key facts. The italicized portions of the following restatement of the above issue are context facts:

> Did a *drugstore* merchant in the county violate § 38, which prohibits "illuminated signs after 2 A.M. in the county" when the merchant kept on several night lights after 2 A.M. in front of the store after closing *even though no neighbors complained about the lights?*

The fact that the defendant was a drugstore may have been irrelevant to the court. The same result would probably have been reached if the store was a supermarket or a beauty parlor. What was key was the fact that the defendant was a merchant. So too, the presence or absence of complaints from the neighbors may have been irrelevant to the result. The violation of the statute (§ 38) may not be dependent on such complaints. The defendant probably claimed that the statute was not violated because the neighbors did not complain about his night lights, i.e., the defendant felt that it was key that such complaints did not exist. Such factual claims are often phrased in an "even though" format toward the end of an issue, as in the above example.

You can include context facts so long as you do not confuse them in your own mind with key facts and so long as they do not needlessly clutter up the statement of the issue.

Section D. Issues That Interpret and Apply More Than One Rule of Law

In the above examples of legal issues, only one rule of law was involved, e.g., one section of a statute in the drugstore case. It is not uncommon, however, to find an issue that interprets and applies more than one rule of law, e.g., two statutes; a statute and a constitutional provision; a statute and a common law doctrine. Furthermore, the rules of law may be from the same or from different legal systems or jurisdictions.

Here are some examples (stated in shorthand):

Do § 15 (c) of the Motor Vehicle Code and § 178 of the Licensing Code require a hearing on the suspension? (two statutes)

Can the XYZ Agency impose penalties under § 35 of the Administrative Code in view of the statutory restrictions on punishment in § 199 of the Penal Code? (a regulation and a statute)

Do the compulsory blood tests under § 45 of the Paternity Code violate the Due Process Clause of the Fourteenth Amendment? (a statute and a constitutional provision)

Section E. Methods of Identifying Legal Issues in Opinions

Now that we know the basic structure of a legal issue, our next concern is finding issues in the opinion you are briefing. Students often have difficulty determining how many issues there are in an opinion and what they are. The following points should be helpful in confronting this difficulty:

1. There will usually be several issues in an opinion. It may be, however, that you are reading an edited version of the opinion (e.g., in a school casebook) from which the editor has cut out portions of the opinion that cover certain issues.

2. The issues will fall roughly into one of two categories: substantive and procedural. Procedural issues deal with the technicalities of bringing or defending the litigation, e.g., the format of the complaint, the jurisdiction of the court, the admissibility of evidence. Everything else is a substantive issue, e.g., the pollution of a river, the breach of a contract, the commission of a crime. Substantive issues cover nonprocedural rights and obligations. There are some opinions that contain only procedural issues. While there are some opinions that contain only substantive issues, most have a mixture of both.

3. It is not unusual for an opinion to have five or six issues. One or two of them, however, will often be the main ones that are given the most attention and space by the court.

4. The end of the opinion is often the "clean up" section of the opinion in which the court treats most of the minor issues of the opinion. Each such issue may be given a paragraph or two of space—or less.

5. Some judges structure their opinions by headings (Sufficiency of Pleading, Due Process of Law, Damages, etc.), by numbers (I, II, III, etc., or 1, 2, 3, etc.), or by letters (A, B, C, etc.). Within each of these units, the judge will often treat one legal issue. Such well-organized opinions facilitate the job of issue identification. Most opinions, however, are not this well structured. The judge may ramble and discuss several issues simultaneously.

6. When a court states issues, it will usually provide only *shorthand* statements of those issues, e.g., "the question is whether two unmarried persons who are living together can sue each other in contract," or "we turn now to the problem of whether the statute applies," or "is § 3(a)(i) constitutional?" Rarely will a court include all the key facts in the statement of its issues. Our goal, however, in briefing the opinion is a *complete* statement of the issues.

7. There are times when the court will not even provide a clear shorthand statement of an issue it discusses, particularly the minor issues. We must *infer* what the issue is from the court's discussion. For example, suppose the court says, "In this state, contributory negligence is not applicable to a products liability case." You may not find the word "issue" or "question" anywhere in the discussion. The court may not use a question mark. It may not say "the question is" or "the issue is" or "the problem is whether contributory negligence in this state applies to a products liability case." We must infer that this is the issue being examined. Care must be used, however, in making this inference. Every statement of a legal principle made by a court cannot be translated into a legal issue. The four tests for a legal issue, to be discussed below (in guideline #11), must be used before you can make the inference.

8. If there are concurring or dissenting opinions (p. 51), determine what they say about the legal issues in the case. Of course, the concurring or dissenting judges may differ with the judges in the majority as to what the issues are. Yet, this discussion of the difference can sometimes help you sort out what you think the issues are in the majority opinion.

9. Some opinions will tell you (usually in footnotes or at the very beginning or end of the opinion) what issues are *not* in the case or what issues the court will *not* discuss. For example, "We find it unnecessary to determine whether the new rule requiring counsel to be present is to be applied retroactively" or "This decision will address the reach of the statute, not its constitutionalty." Read these statements carefully. They should be of at least some help in avoiding confusion as to what are the issues.

10. Pay particular attention to what the parties say the issues are. For example, "Appellant claims that section 45 does not apply," or "Peterson says that his wife is not entitled to one half of the house," or "Defendant asserts that this court lacks jurisdiction." Here again we have shorthand statements of legal issues, this time from the perspective of the parties. Very often these statements will accurately lead you to the issues in the opinion, *unless the court explicitly tells you otherwise.*

Examine the following passage from an opinion: "The plaintiff contends that the regulation does not cover his conduct. Since, however, we conclude that this regulation is not validly based on its governing statute, there is no need to determine whether the regulation applies to his activities." Here the plaintiff is saying that the issue is the applicability of the regulation. The court, however, tells us that the party has *not* stated the issue properly. Hence, watch for what the parties claim are the issues, and note the court's response to such claims. In most situations, you will find that the party has accurately stated the issue (in shorthand). If not, the court will say so and lead you to what the proper issue is.

11. The above general guidelines should enable you to identify the number of legal issues in an opinion and to begin the process of identifying them. To be sure that you have not gone astray, the following four specific tests should be applied. A legal issue must meet all four tests.

The tests are slightly different depending on whether the opinion you are reading has prior proceedings (p. 97). Prior proceedings are those events that have occurred in the litigation thus far—either in an administrative agency or in a court. An example of an opinion with *no* prior proceedings is a trial court opinion in which nothing happened earlier in an agency or in a court.

The critical component of each test below has been italicized:

The Four Tests for a Legal Issue in an Appellate Court Opinion or in a Trial Court Opinion with Prior Proceedings:	**The Four Tests for a Legal Issue in a Trial Court Opinion with No Prior Proceedings:**
(a) The *parties,* expressly or impliedly, are in *disagreement,*	(a) The *parties,* expressly or impliedly, are in *disagreement,*
(b) Over the meaning or application of one or more *rules of law* in contention,	(b) Over the meaning or application of one or more *rules of law* in contention,
(c) Based on the *facts* of *their* litigation, and	(c) Based on the *facts* of *their* litigation, and
(d) Based on an *alleged error* made *earlier* in the same litigation by an agency or lower court in connection with the rule(s) of law.	(d) Based on an *alleged error* made during the *pretrial* or *trial* stage of the litigation in connection with the rule(s) of law.

(a) Parties in Disagreement Suppose you are reading an opinion in which the court makes the following statement: "Trial courts must not allow a plaintiff's counsel to ask defendants about the amount of insurance the latter might carry." In guideline #7 above, we said that you will often have to *infer* a legal issue from what the court says, particularly when the court does not clearly state the legal issue. From the above statement about insurance, it is very tempting to *infer* that one of the legal issues in the opinion is whether plaintiff's counsel has the right to ask defendants about the amount of insurance the latter might carry. Resist this temptation until you ask yourself whether there is any *disagreement between the parties* about the statement.

If not, then you cannot infer a legal issue on the basis of the statement. It may be that the court is simply stating general legal principles (about which both sides will agree) leading up to other principles (about which the parties do not agree). An opinion will often contain numerous legal principles, sometimes referred to as "black letter" laws. Most of them will be background principles that are the foundation for the central conclusions of the court. These preliminary principles should not be confused with issues or with holdings. The best way to avoid this confusion is, again, to ask yourself whether there is any indication that the parties are in disagreement about the principles.

Note that this first test for a legal issue says the parties "expressly or impliedly" are in disagreement. No problem exists when the disagreement is expressly stated in the opinion. Suppose, for example that the court tells us that "the defendant argues that § 34 applies while the plaintiff takes strong exception to this interpretation of the statute." It is obvious from such language that the parties are in disagreement. You will often find, however, that the court will give the position of only one of the parties, e.g., "the appellant claims that proximate cause has not been established." We may *not* be explicitly told the appellee's position on proximate cause. Disagreement, however, can usually be determined by implication. When we are given the position of only one party (plus considerable discussion of this position), the likelihood is that the court is impliedly telling us that the other party disagrees.

At times, the implication of disagreement may be based solely on the fact that one of the parties appealed. After the court describes what happened below (in a case with prior proceedings), we may be told that "the plaintiff appealed" without any indication of what the defendant thinks. Again, we are fairly safe in assuming that the court is impliedly telling us that the nonappealing party (appellee) will disagree with whatever basis the other party (appellant) will assert in bringing the appeal. We should be able to support this assumption by relying on our earlier determination of the objectives of the parties in the litigation (p. 87).

Whether the disagreement or contention is express or implied, it must exist. By definition, a legal issue cannot be based on agreement. Many students fall into the trap of formulating issues on matters about which the parties are in agreement. The trap is wider than you think.

Occasionally a court will tell us that the parties agree that a certain issue exists. This is not the kind of agreement that disqualifies something from being a legal issue. For example: "Plaintiff and defendant acknowledge that this court must rule on the constitutionality of the regulation, the plaintiff taking the position that it is constitutional, while the defendant asserts that it is not." Here the parties agree on what the issue is, but they do not agree on the interpretation or application of the rule of law involved. In this example, sufficient disagreement does exist to meet the first test of a legal issue. The contention is over the meaning or application of rule(s) of law, which leads us to the second test.

(b) Meaning or Application of a Rule of Law Every legal issue must center on the meaning or application of one or more rules of law. The basis of the parties' disagreement *is* this meaning or application. There are ten main kinds of rules of law. They are listed below in the approximate order in which they are most frequently found in opinions as the basis of legal issues:

1. a statute	**6.** a (procedural) court rule
2. a common law doctrine	**7.** an ordinance
3. a regulation	**8.** an executive order
4. a constitutional provision	**9.** a charter provision
5. an equitable doctrine	**10.** a treaty

In Chapter 3 there is an overview of many of these kinds of law (p. 61).

Most legal issues in an opinion will center on the meaning or application of only one rule of law, e.g., the interpretation of a particular statute. More complex issues, as we have seen, involve the interrelationship of more than one rule of law:

• Is one statute consistent with another statute?
Example: Does § 32 impose a different requirement than § 36?

• Is a regulation validly based on its governing statute? (All regulations must be so based.)
Example: Does § 6(b) of the statutory code authorize the agency, in § 45 of its regulations, to conduct in-house searches every three months?

• Did the statute change the common law? (A statute is always superior in authority to a common law doctrine.)
Example: Did the legislature in § 10 of the statutory code intend to abolish the tort defense of charitable immunity?

• Is the rule of law constitutional?
Example: Does the statute violate the Equal Protection clause of the Constitution?

(c) Based on the Facts of Their Litigation   This test is needed in order to be sure that you are focusing on the facts of the particular litigation before the court in the opinion. The court may refer to *other* facts, e.g., the facts of opinions (which we have called internal opinions) that the court discusses. This discussion can be very important for purposes of identifying key facts (p. 124), but do not confuse the facts of the internal opinions with the facts actually before the court.

(d) Alleged Error   Most of the opinions you will be briefing will have prior proceedings (p. 97). In such opinions, a party will be claiming that an error was made during the prior proceedings. You need to identify this error. For example:

• the trial court erred in concluding that guilt was established beyond a reasonable doubt;

• the trial court did not properly apply the statute on the distribution of assets;

• the middle appeals court erred in abolishing the defense;

• the trial court should not have declared the regulation unconstitutional;

• the trial court should not have allowed the jury to reach an excessive damage award;

• the administrative agency did not use the correct definition of "medical disability" required by the statute.

Each such alleged error will almost always be the foundation for a separate legal issue in the opinion you are briefing.

In most opinions, the court will be fairly clear as to what the alleged errors are. Sometimes, however, you are simply told that a certain party appealed, and you must infer what errors that party is probably alleging on appeal based on what happened below and on what the objectives of that party were in the litigation (p. 87).

There is a major exception to the requirement that a legal issue must be based on an alleged error that occurred during prior proceedings. This exception relates to the appealability of the case. Often the very first issue before the appellate court is whether the court should hear the appeal. This issue is *not* always dependent on an alleged error below. The appellee (the party against whom the appeal is brought) may be arguing that the appellate court has no subject-matter jurisdiction (p. 145) to hear the appeal. This issue is not based on any alleged errors below. It is based on the interpretation of the statute or constitutional provision that tells the appellate court what kinds of cases it can hear. Another example of an appealability issue that is not dependent on any alleged errors below would be whether an appellant (the party bringing the appeal) who has failed to file a notice of appeal can still have the case heard on appeal. This issue is dependent on an interpretation of the filing requirement, not on any alleged errors that occurred during the prior proceedings. Appealability issues, therefore, which often involve the jurisdiction of the court, are usually not based on alleged errors that occurred earlier in the litigation.

One final point before moving to the topic of holdings. The tests for a legal issue listed earlier are the same for opinions with or without prior proceedings except for the fourth test. If you are briefing a trial court opinion with no prior proceedings, then, of course, nothing happened below. The alleged error occurred *during* the pretrial or trial stage in the same court that wrote the opinion you are briefing. The errors involved, however, are the same kind as those listed above, e.g., errors on the interpretation of a statute, on the sufficiency of a complaint, on the constitutionality of a regulation, on the admissibility of evidence, etc.

Section F. Holdings

Your task of identifying a holding is 99 percent complete if you have successfully identified the legal issue to which the holding is the answer. As with legal issues, holdings can be phrased in one of two ways:

• complete statement of a holding
• shorthand statement of a holding

(i) Complete statement A complete statement of a holding must contain the same two essential parts as a legal issue: the rules of law being applied and

the key facts. The only difference is that the holding is not phrased as a question. It is phrased as an affirmative statement that answers the question one way or another (see Figure 9–1). A *complete* statement of the holding simply recasts all the components of a *complete* statement of a legal issue in the form of an answer.

(ii) Shorthand statement A shorthand statement of a holding is a simple yes or no answer. It is preferable to give a shorthand statement of the holdings in your brief of an opinion *if you have phrased the legal issues completely.* A yes/no answer avoids needless repetition.

In the following assignments, you will be asked to provide *shorthand* statements of the legal issues and holdings in the opinions printed in Appendix A of this book. You will not be asked to give *complete* statements of these legal issues until the end of Chapter 10 when we have finished our study of identifying key facts.

Assignment #19

Give a shorthand statement of every legal issue and a shorthand statement of every holding in the following opinions:

a. *People v. Sohn*, p. 299.

b. *Brown v. Southall Realty*, p. 300.

c. *Stephens v. Dept. of State Police*, p. 302.

d. *Nicholson v. Conn. Half-Way House, Inc.*, p. 307.

e. *Conn. v. Menillo*, p. 309.

Check your answers with the Suggested Responses, p. 377.

FIGURE 9–1.
Example of Alternate
Holding Possibilities.
(complete statements)

LEGAL ISSUE

In a disability case, is the agency required to inquire into the availability of work for a claimant with psychological problems in order to determine whether the claimant is "unavailable for work for medical reasons" under § 3?

HOLDING POSSIBILITIES

OR

In a disability case, the agency is required to inquire into the availability of work for a claimant with psychological problems in order to determine whether the claimant is "unavailable for work for medical reasons" under section 3.

In a disability case, the agency is not required to inquire into the availability of work for a claimant with psychological problems in order to determine whether the claimant is "unavailable for work for medical reasons" under section 3.

Assignment #20

Give a shorthand statement of every legal issue and a shorthand statement of every holding in the following opinions:

a. *Mumma v. Mumma,* p. 311.

b. *Owen v. Ill. Baking Corp.,* p. 315.

c. *Thompson v. Royall,* p. 316.

d. *MacPherson v. Buick Motor Co.,* p. 319.

e. *Goldberg v. Kelly,* p. 330.

Chapter Ten

Identifying the Reasoning in an Opinion

In this chapter, we have two objectives:

a. developing the skill of identifying the reasoning in an opinion;

b. exploring the relationship between reasoning and key facts (how reasoning can assist you in identifying key facts).

Section A. The Reasoning Process

From the broadest perspective, the reason a court reaches a particular result is that this result is deemed necessary to achieve justice. This truism, however, is not very helpful in understanding the analytical process that a court goes through in its effort to arrive at justice. To understand this process, we need a more focused definition of reasoning. Simply stated, reasoning is the explanation why a court reached a particular answer or holding for a particular issue. Every issue in an opinion will have its own holding, the reasoning for which will be expressed or implied. Our task is to examine the kinds of explanations you are likely to find for holdings.

Courts go through the following steps to resolve each individual issue in an opinion:

THE PROCESS OF ISSUE RESOLUTION IN OPINIONS:

    1. The court targets the rule of law (or rules of law) to be applied.

    2. For each rule of law, the court identifies what is in contention.

Three interrelated possibilities exist:

(i) Contention over the meaning or definition of the rule of law or of its element(s).

(ii) Contention over whether the facts fit within the rule of law or its element(s).

(iii) Contention over whether one rule of law is consistent with another rule of law.

3. The court explains (expressly or impliedly) how it resolves the contention. *This explanation is the court's reasoning.*

The starting point is to focus on the rule of law that must be applied, e.g., a statute, a regulation, a constitutional provision, a common law doctrine. Each rule can be broken down into components or *elements* (p. 47). The focus of the court may be on the entire rule of law or on one of its elements. This is so for every rule of law that must be applied in the opinion.

The next step is to determine what kind of dispute exists on the rule of law or element, i.e., what is the nature of the contention over the rule or element? Three kinds of contention are listed in the above overview. The court's reasoning is found in the way that it handles and explains its resolution of the contention.

To explore these steps in greater detail, we need to examine each of the three kinds of contention that can exist:

(i) What is the definition?

(ii) Do the facts fit?

(iii) Is there consistency?

It will not always be easy to determine what kind of contention exists for a given rule of law that the court is applying. Nor is this determination always necessary to understand the court's reasoning. The categories are not ends in themselves. They simply provide an analytical framework within which to focus our study of reasoning.

(i) Contention Over the Meaning or Definition of the Rule of Law or of Its Element(s): What is the Definition? The word definition, as used here, does not mean Webster's explanation of language. *A definition of a rule of law (or of an element within a rule of law) refers to the court's interpretation of the rule in the light of (a) the purpose or policy behind the rule, and (b) the facts that are before the court.* As we shall see, definitions are not mechanically picked out of dictionaries and are not examined in a vacuum.

Some examples of definitional issues are shown on page 151. Before examining the reasoning that a court will use in resolving such an issue, a number of points should be made about this kind of issue.

The dispute over definition will almost always be whether the rule of law (or an element within it) should be defined narrowly or broadly. Indeed, one of the great themes of legal analysis is the tension between the broad and the narrow interpretation.

In the first example at the top of page 151 the broad definition of confinement is "any restriction of movement." The narrower definition adds a qualifier—the plaintiff must be "conscious" of the restriction. Assume that while the plaintiff is in his room, the defendant locks the door of the room but

Rule of Law (The element to be defined in each rule of law is in quotation marks.)	Contending Definitions
(a) "Confinement" in the tort of false imprisonment (common law doctrine).	• Does it mean *any* restriction of the plaintiff's movement? • Does it mean any restriction of movement of which the plaintiff was *conscious?*
(b) A court is authorized to "divide property" (§ 15–204 of statutory code) (statute)	• Does property mean only *real* property? • Does it mean *any* property?
(c) "Official activity" (§ 75 of administrative code) (regulation)	• Does it mean activity by *paid* government employees? • Does it mean anyone acting on behalf of the government whether for compensation or as a *volunteer?*
(d) "Religion" in the First Amendment of the U.S. Constitution (constitutional provision)	• Is religion activity on behalf of *organized churches?* • Is religion activity pursuant to a *belief in a supernatural power or an ethical commitment?*

the plaintiff is unaware of this. Sometime before the plaintiff decides to leave, the defendant unlocks the door. Later, the plaintiff finds out that for a period of time he was locked in his room, and sues the defendant for the tort of false imprisonment. One of the issues is: Was there "confinement"? The answer depends on whether the court adopts the broad or narrow definition of this element.

When reading opinions, it is not always easy to determine whether contention exists between the parties over a definition. Two situations need to be examined. First, an opinion in which the court gives only one definition, and second, when the court gives no definition at all.

A court may spend a good deal of time defining something, but not make clear whether the parties have conflicting views of what the definition should be. Only one definition is provided by the court. Unless the court is expressly or impliedly examining more than one definition of the rule, the dispute is probably *not* over the definition in spite of how much attention the court gives to it. Rather, the dispute will be over whether the facts fit within the rule. In this section we are limiting our discussion to those issues within opinions where you *can* articulate more than one definition.

Of course, a fairly clear sign that there is no definitional issue in an opinion is when the court gives no definitions at all. The court does not bother to give a definition of a rule of law or element because the definition is not in issue, and the court assumes that the reader already knows what the definition is. Again, in such an opinion the issue will probably be whether the facts fit within the rule. We will discuss the latter kind of contention later.

We turn now to the reasoning that a court will use in resolving a true definitional issue. Our examination will focus on two of the major kinds of rules of law: statutes and common law doctrines. The discussion on statutes, however, will also be relevant to other kinds of enacted law, e.g., constitutional provisions, regulations, charters, ordinances, etc. Similarly, the discussion of the common law will be relevant to equitable doctrines.

(a) Statutes Statutes are written by the legislature. When a court is interpreting a statute, it should be carrying out the meaning *intended* by the legislature. If this were not so, the court would be acting like a legislature. Indeed, it would be usurping the powers of the legislature. *A court must not rewrite the statute under the guise of interpreting it.* Yet courts are frequently charged with doing precisely this.

The court may violently disagree with the *wisdom* of a particular statute; it may feel that the legislature was foolish in enacting it. Yet it is not the institutional function of the court to second-guess the legislature. When there is a dispute as to the meaning or definition of a statute, the court in theory has a very limited function: to determine what the legislature *intended*.

At this point, we are not talking about the *validity* of the statute. The question of validity is essentially a question of consistency: is the statute consistent with other rules of law that are superior in authority to a statute? We will examine consistency later. For now our focus is the definition of a statute that is not being subjected to a consistency or validity challenge.

Legislative intent is a complicated subject. How does one determine the intention of a legislature when it enacts a statute? Clearly, we cannot ask what was the intent of individual legislators of whom there may have been hundreds. Legislators have widely different motives for voting as they do. Many may not closely read the text of what they are voting to enact. Yet the court must still decide what to do with statutory language that is ambiguous and unclear.

The more ambiguous the language, the greater the danger that the court will be reading into the language its own biases, interests, policy preferences, etc. Some have argued that it is physically (or mentally) impossible for a court *not* to do this. There is no such thing as a purely objective uncovering of legislative intent. Interpreters of language inevitably inject themselves into the language. There is considerable truth to this, although courts will rarely, if ever, admit that they are infringing on the legislative domain by writing or rewriting statutes. Dissenting opinions, however, will frequently make this charge against the opinion of the majority. Justice Foley does so in the dissenting opinion of *Stephens v. Dept. of State Police* (p. 306). Similarly, Justice Black in his dissenting opinion in *Goldberg v. Kelly* calls the majority justices to task for using "judicial power for legislative purposes" (p. 340).

Nevertheless, at least the starting point in the court's search for the definition of statutory language is the determination of legislative intent. This principle can guide us in understanding the reasoning of the court so long as we recognize that the search is not a mechanical process. There is an unacknowledged but inevitable writing dimension to the task of interpretation. It is unacknowledged in the sense that a court (or at least the majority opinion of a court) will never admit that it is rewriting the statute that it is interpreting. It is inevitable in the sense that the dynamics of language resist a neat demarcation between author and interpreter.

A court's treatment of legislative intent in resolving contention over the definition of a statute (or of an element of a statute) will either be express or implied:

Express:

The court explicitly mentions legislative intent and uses the various techniques to be described below in determining what it is. We are *expressly* told what definition the legislature intended.

Implied:

The court does not even refer to the phrase legislative intent. It simply provides the definition of the statutory language in question. By *implication,* however, the court is telling us that this definition is what the legislature intended.

The court will do one or the other. In your brief of the opinion, when you are providing the reasoning for an issue that centers on the disputed definition of a statute, you should state whether the court is expressly or impliedly following legislative intent in coming up with the "correct" definition.

How then does the court determine legislative intent? The following are the most commonly used techniques. In your statement of the reasoning, you should indicate which ones the court employed:

1. The plain meaning of the statutory language
2. Definitions statutes
3. Other court opinions within the same jurisdiction
4. Legislative history
5. The policy behind the statute
6. Regulations interpreting the statute
7. Other canons of construction
8. Other statutes within the same jurisdiction
9. Opinions from other jurisdictions

1. *Plain meaning of the statutory language* The legislature used specific language in the statute. Words have meanings. The legislature is presumed to have intended whatever normal or plain meaning these words have, unless it clearly indicates otherwise. A *term of art* is a word or phrase that has a special or technical meaning. If there are indications that any of the words used in the statute are terms of art, then the court will tell us what they mean. If not, then the ordinary meaning of the words will govern.

2. *Definitions statutes* The statute the court is interpreting will usually be part of a cluster of statutes on the same topic. Occasionally, the legislature will provide a definitions statute that will apply to the entire cluster. The court may rely on such a definitions statute to interpret the statute in question. Unfortunately, however, the definitions statute may not be very helpful. The definitions may need definitions!

3. *Other court opinions within the same jurisdiction* Has this statute ever been interpreted before? Prior court opinions within the same jurisdiction (or legal system) are often relied upon by a judge. Earlier we referred to these as "internal opinions" (p. 124). If such opinions exist interpreting the same statute, they will usually have a large role in the judge's reasoning on the case currently before the court.

4. *Legislative history* Later we will look in greater detail at the role of legislative history in legal analysis (p. 215). Judges sometimes make use of legislative history as an aid in determining legislative intent. (See, for example, *Stephens v. Dept. of State Police*, p. 304.) What happened in the legislature before this statute was enacted? What was the language in the original draft of the bill? Was this language changed before the bill became law? Why was the change made? Questions such as these can sometimes provide insight into what the legislature intended by particular language in the statute.

5. *The policy behind the statute* This is the most important part of a court's reasoning in interpreting statutory language. Indeed, policy considerations permeate and dominate all the other techniques for identifying legislative intent. The court will attempt to determine why the statute was passed. What policy was the legislature trying to implement when it passed the statute? What evil or problem was it trying to correct? Answers to such questions (which often come out of an inquiry into legislative history) will often be helpful to a court in attempting to interpret a statute. A court, for example, may select a broader or narrower definition of statutory language depending upon the policy that prompted the legislature to produce the statute. (This was part of the court's reasoning in voiding the lease in *Brown v. Southall Realty Co.*, p. 300.)

6. *Regulations interpreting the statute* Some statutes are carried out by agencies. The latter will often write regulations that interpret the statute, including regulations that define important terms in the statute. A court might rely on such regulations unless the court determines that the agency has misread the statute through these regulations.

7. *Other canons of construction* There are a number of guidelines or rules (called canons) that courts often use in intepreting statutes that are ambiguous. The plain meaning rule referred to above in item #1 is an example of such a guideline. Others include *expressio unius est exclusio alterius, ejusdem generis*, etc. They are usually explained by the court as they are applied.

8. *Other statutes within the same jurisdiction* Assume the court is trying to define the word "minor" in the *tax* code. Suppose that the same word is used and defined in the *probate* code of the same state. Technically, the court cannot say that the definition the legislature used in one statute was the same definition it intended for that word in another statute on a different subject. Nevertheless, courts will often look to such definitions for guidance, particularly when the two statutes using the same word are on relatively similar subjects. We will come back to this point later in Chapter 14, p. 189.

9. *Opinions from other jurisdictions* Here the court must use even greater caution. Assume you are reading a California opinion where the court is interpreting the word "minor" in the California tax code. Can the court rely on a *New York* opinion interpreting the same word in a New York statute?

Again, the answer is technically no. How can a New York opinion be used to understand what the California legislature intended? The two state legislatures may have had different definitions in mind for the same word. Yet such opinions are sometimes relied upon, particularly when there is great similarity between the language and purpose of the two statutes. (See for example, the Virginia court's reliance in *Thompson v. Royall* on opinions interpreting similar statutes of other states, p. 319.)

(b) Common Law Doctrines Common law is judge-made law in the absence of controlling enacted law (p. 10). Many aspects of the law of torts, contracts, and criminal law, for example, are governed by common law doctrines. When a court is creating common law, it is acting like a legislature, but there is no problem of the usurpation of legislative powers because the common law operates in areas where there is no controlling statutory law.

How does the court resolve a dispute over the scope, meaning, or definition of a common law doctrine? How does it arrive at the "correct" definition? Since the legislature did not write the common law doctrine, the court obviously cannot seek the legislative intent of the doctrine. Two interrelated approaches are taken by the court:

• An examination of prior opinions interpreting the common law doctrine;

• An examination of the policy that prompted the creation of the common law doctrine.

A common law doctrine usually develops out of thousands of opinions over a very long period of time. Many of the doctrines were brought from England during our colonial era. Today when a court must interpret the common law, it logically looks to prior opinions for guidance. It will *also* pay careful attention to the policy behind the doctrine in question. Whom was it trying to protect? What problems was it trying to remedy? Answers to such policy questions can provide guidance to meaning.

The policy examination has another dimension. In addition to providing guidance on the current meaning of a common law doctrine, the study of policy can also prompt the court to re-examine the need for the doctrine itself. It may be time for the court to change or abolish the doctrine. For example, the common law doctrine of charitable immunity severely restricts the right of a citizen to sue a charity for the torts that a charitable organization commits. The original policy behind the doctrine was the need to preserve the limited resources of this socially beneficial entity; one or two lawsuits could wipe out the charity. Today, however, some courts have questioned the relevance or need for the doctrine, particularly in view of the fact that the charity can protect itself by purchasing liability insurance. A re-examination of the policy has led to a change in the doctrine itself in some states.

When you are briefing an opinion that is wrestling over contending definitions of a common law doctrine, your identification of the court's reasoning should incorporate the essence of this kind of policy analysis.

(ii) Contention Over Whether the Facts Fit Within the Rule of Law or Its Element(s): Do the Facts Fit? We now turn to the second major kind of contention that can exist, summarized by the question, "Do the facts fit?" Here, there is no visible dispute over the definition of the rule of law, or over a particular element of the rule of law. The dispute is over whether the facts fit within the rule or element.

For example, assume you are reading a negligence opinion in which the issue is whether the defendant *caused* the plaintiff's head injury. The rule of law involved is the common law of negligence. The focus is on one of the elements of this rule of law, namely, causation. There may be no dispute between the parties on the definition of causation—whatever is a substantial factor in bringing something about—but intense disagreement may exist on whether the defendant was a substantial factor in bringing about the head injury. In short, the contention is over whether the facts fit within the definition. A number of facts may be examined by the court, e.g., evidence of a prior head injury, evidence that the plaintiff's own conduct helped produce the injury, evidence of third-party involvement, evidence that an act of God intervened. Given all these facts, the court must decide whether the defendant was a substantial factor in bringing about the head injury. Do the facts fit?

Another example: Assume that you are reading a divorce opinion in which the issue is whether an antenuptial agreement signed by the wife before the marriage was *fair*. The rule of law involved is a statute, § 1102, that states that antenuptial agreements shall be enforced if they are "fair." Again, there may be no dispute between the parties on the definition of the element of fairness. Indeed, the court may state no definition at all. The contention between the parties is whether the facts of the case fit within the statutory element of fairness. The court's discussion is based upon a meaning or definition of fairness, *but we are not told what it is*. The court may assume that the reader already knows the definition, and, since there is no contention between the parties over the definition, the court feels it unnecessary to provide one. In the opinion, the court lays out a myriad of facts relevant to the issue of fairness, e.g., the wife was inexperienced in financial matters when she signed the agreement, but she asked her accountant to read the agreement before she signed it; the husband did not disclose all his assets at the time; the husband asked the wife whether she wanted to consult her own attorney before she signed, but she declined. Given all these facts, the court must decide whether the agreement was "fair" under § 1102. Do the facts fit?

In such cases, what reasoning does a court go through in deciding whether the facts fit within a rule or element?

If a definition is provided, the court's reasoning will usually consist of the *logical connections* that the court sees between the facts and the definition. In the first example above on causation, the court may focus on the logical and common sense links between the facts surrounding the head injury and the definition of causation in order to assess whether the defendant was a substantial factor in producing the injury. As we read the opinion, we should ask ourselves the following kinds of questions: What facts suggest that the defendant was a substantial factor according to the court? *Why* does the court think so? What facts suggest that he was not a substantial factor according to the court? *Why* does the court think so? The court's express or implied answers to these "why" questions are the logical connections that should help guide us to its reasoning. The answers explain the court's position on whether the facts do or do not fit within the rule.

What about an opinion in which the court gives us no explicit definition of the rule or element? In such opinions, we cannot say that there is no definition. All we can say is the court is not explicitly telling *us* what it is. In such instances, our task is to try to *infer* the definition that the court is using. In the divorce case on antenuptial agreements, perhaps we can infer that the definition of fairness used by the court is as follows: that which would be deemed equitable by a reasonable person. If so, then the court's reasoning will consist of the same kind of discussion on logical connections referred to above in the negligence-causation example when a definition was expressly provided.

What if you cannot infer the meaning or definition used by the court? You will have to seek help outside the opinion, e.g., consult a section of a treatise or legal encyclopedia (p. 28) that gives some background instruction on the rule of law that the court is not defining for us. *If you remain in the dark about certain basic rules of law, it will be impossible for you to identify the court's reasoning or indeed to understand the opinion at all.*

Of course, the less a court says about the logical connections between rules and the facts, the more difficult it is to identify reasoning. Suppose the fairness case above was written by an appellate court that affirmed the conclusion of the trial court that the antenuptial agreement was fair. There is very little discussion of the facts. We are told that trial courts have considerable discretion in determining what is and is not "fair." Or we are simply told that "there was sufficient evidence to warrant the trial court's holding." Even if we can infer the definition of fairness that the appellate court used, we are going to have trouble identifying this court's reasoning. We simply don't know what the logical connections are because we are not told. Fortunately, this does not happen often. When it does occur, the court will usually be covering one of the subsidiary or minor issues in the opinion.

———

Finally, we need to look at a different kind of issue where the court's minimal discussion of the issue can make it difficult to identify reasoning.

Earlier we said that there are two major kinds of legal issues (p. 138). First, an issue about whether a rule of law applies to a set of facts (leading to a holding); and second, an issue about what happened (leading to a finding). The former can be called an *application issue*, the latter a *factual issue.* Examples:

> A statute (§ 23) imposes a use tax on "all motor vehicles" operated for business. The defendant denies that the statute was intended to cover the small plane that she owns. She argues that the statute means "motor vehicles" that operate on the ground. Furthermore, she denies that the plane is ever used in her business. She says that she uses it solely for personal weekend vacation trips.
>
> *Application Issue:* Is a plane a "motor vehicle" under § 23?
>
> *Factual issue:* Does the defendant use the plane solely for personal purposes?

In a factual issue, the question is: what are the facts? In an application issue the question is: what are the legal consequences of the facts? Our main concern thus far has been the first kind of issue. The causation and fairness examples above were application issues. We did not focus on whether the actual facts (what happened) were in dispute. The question was whether the legal concepts of causation and fairness applied to the facts. We need to say a word about the reasoning that a court will use in resolving the second kind of issue, i.e., the what-happened issue.

Most of the opinions you will be briefing will be written by appellate courts in which the court is reviewing decisions of trial courts and agencies. It is important to remember that an appellate court is not a fact-finding tribunal. It does not take testimony; it does not examine new evidence. It simply examines the record made by the lower tribunal and reviews this record for errors (p. 14). The lower tribunal (agency or trial court) will have made findings of fact. On appeal, one of the issues may be whether these findings were supported by the evidence. You will find this issue phrased in different ways:

- Is the finding supported by a sufficiency of the evidence?

- Was the court rational in making this finding?

- Should the court have allowed the question to go to the jury? (Was the evidence so clear one way that the court should have resolved the factual question on its own without letting the jury resolve it?)

- Did the court abuse its discretion in making this finding?

- Etc.

The dispute *on appeal* is NOT whether the appellate court would have reached a different finding of fact if the appellate court were the fact finder. The appellate court did not sit through the trial. It did not listen to the testimony. It did not observe the facial expressions of the witnesses as they testified. Hence, considerable deference is given by the appellate court to the factual conclusions reached by the lower tribunal. The appellate court will not second-guess the fact findings made below (or it is not supposed to do so). In trying to identify the reasoning of the appellate court on this kind of issue, we need to keep this perspective in mind.

Assume that the trial court had before it the question of whether the defendant, Jones, shot and killed Smith. At the *trial*, the following evidence was considered by the court:

- Smith was shot with a gun that he owned while he was in a parked car. The gun was kept in the glove compartment.

- Jones had been sitting in the car with Smith. Several minutes before the shooting, a person unknown to Jones came over to the car and began arguing with Smith over a gambling debt. This person has since disappeared.

- An hour after the shooting, Jones was picked up by the police. He was running away from the scene of the crime with Smith's wallet in his possession.

- Jones claims that this third person shot Smith. There were no fingerprints on the gun. Jones offered no explanation why he had Smith's wallet.

The trial court reached the conclusion that Jones shot Smith. This is the trial court's resolution of the factual (what-happened) issue. Jones now appeals and claims that this finding was in error. What reasoning will the *appellate* court use on this factual dispute?

The appellate court might take a number of approaches:

i. State whether it accepts or rejects the fact finding made below. Provide an elaborate discussion of the *logical connections* that exist or that do not exist between the *evidence* and the *fact finding* reached below.

ii. State whether it accepts or rejects the fact finding made below with no discussion as to why.

iii. Do something in between (i) and (ii) above, e.g., state its conclusion with at least a minimal discussion as to why.

Most courts will adopt the third approach (iii). The court may say, for example, that although the evidence was conflicting, there was sufficient evidence to justify a finding that Jones shot Smith. It will then point out that Jones was caught fleeing from the scene soon after the shooting. By implication, the court is saying that innocent persons do not usually run away from the scene of a crime. Or, the court might explicitly make this observation about human nature. The reasoning of the court will consist of such express or implied *logical connections* between the evidence and the factual conclusion in question.

Unfortunately, you will also find many opinions adopting the second approach above (ii). The court, for example, simply says, "There was sufficient evidence to warrant the finding reached below." Or, "The court did not abuse its discretion in reaching this determination." No discussion. No analysis of the facts by the appellate court. When this occurs, it is close to impossible to identify the reasoning of the court. We can try as best we can to infer what logical connections the appellate court felt were present or absent, but, again, the less the court says, the more difficult is our task of identifying the reasoning.

(iii) Contention Over Whether One Rule of Law is Consistent with Another Rule of Law: Is There Consistency? A dispute over consistency arises when more than one rule of law is being interpreted in the same issue. The question is whether one rule violates or contradicts another. For example:

Rules of Law Being Interpreted in the Same Issue	The Question of Consistency
[a] • § 7 says that service of process must be made during the daytime from sunrise to sunset. • § 1533 says that service of process can be made up to 10 P.M.	Is § 7 consistent with § 1533? Do they contradict each other?
[b] • § 42(j) requires female teachers to take a six-month leave during pregnancy. • The Fourteenth Amendment of the U.S. Constitution guarantees "equal protection of the laws."	Is § 42(j) consistent with the Fourteenth Amendment? Does § 42(j) violate the Fourteenth Amendment?

[c] • § 46 of the state legislative code requires the social services agency to investigate all allegations of paternity in order to force fathers to fulfill their support obligations. • § 45.907 of the agency's administrative code provides that mothers who do not cooperate in establishing the paternity of their children will be denied financial aid. • The Fourteenth Amendment of the U.S. Constitution guarantees "due process of law."	First: Is § 45.907 validly based on § 46? Is the regulation consistent with the statute? Does the statute authorize the agency to *condition* aid on cooperation in paternity proceedings? Second: If the regulation is validly based on the statute, does the condition violate the Fourteenth Amendment? Are the regulation and the statute consistent with the Fourteenth Amendment?

A consistency dispute will arise because of an alleged violation of one or more of the following principles:

• Statutes, regulations, common law doctrines, etc., must not conflict with constitutional provisions.

• Agency regulations must be validly based on statutes.

• Common law doctrines must not conflict with statutes.

Phrased another way:

• Constitutional provisions are superior in authority to statutes, regulations, common law doctrines, etc.

• Statutes are superior in authority to regulations.

• Statutes are superior in authority to common law doctrines.

The situation becomes more complex when different legal systems or jurisdictions are involved: state and federal. The above principles still apply, but they do not answer the question of when *state* rules of law must be consistent with *federal* rules of law. The following principle is needed:

> On matters within the power of the federal government, (a) state statutes, state agency regulations, state common law doctrines, etc., must be consistent with (b) the U.S. (federal) Constitution, federal statutes, and federal agency regulations.

Phrased another way:

> On matters within the powers of the federal government, (a) the federal Constitution, federal statutes, and federal agency regulations are superior in authority to (b) state statutes, state regulations, state common law doctrines, etc.

What reasoning process does the court use to resolve a consistency dispute? First of all, the court will either expressly or impliedly tell us which rules of law are allegedly in conflict and what the hierarchy is among these rules of law in terms of authority. The court, for example, may tell us that the petitioner challenges the constitutionality of the statute. As the court discusses constitutionality, it is, of course, impliedly saying that statutes are not valid unless they are consistent with the Constitution.

Next the court will explore the question of whether the rules of law are reconcilable: does the statute violate the Constitution, does the regulation go beyond what the statute authorizes, etc.? The answer depends upon the *meaning* of the rules of law involved. Definitions again become critical. The consistency dispute, therefore, is treated as a *definitional* dispute in the manner described earlier. For statutes, the question of legislative intent becomes important. For constitutional provisions, the question is what meaning was intended by the authors of the provisions, and how this "original intent" can be interpreted in the context of modern society. Consistency does or does not exist depending on the scope and meaning of the rules of law involved.

Assume that a workers' compensation statute is being challenged because it has been interpreted by the agency as not allowing attorneys to represent claimants at compensation hearings. Does the statute violate the claimant's constitutional right to due process of law? We have a consistency problem: is the statute consistent with the Due Process Clause of the Constitution? The answer depends in part on the meaning of the constitutional provision. What is the definition or test for due process of law? Is it broad enough to include a right to counsel at an agency hearing of this type?

In another example, assume that an agency regulation requires a certain license and this requirement is being challenged because the regulation allegedly violates the statute the agency is supposed to be implementing. We have a consistency problem: is the regulation consistent with the statute? The answer depends in part on the meaning of the statute. What is the definition for the relevant language in the statute? Is it broad enough to authorize the agency to pass a regulation requiring the license? The answer to these questions depends on legislative intent in enacting the statute. See the nine techniques outlined above on how the court goes about uncovering legislative intent (p. 153).

———

This concludes our discussion of the three main kinds of contention that can exist in legal issues. While the discussion isolated the three, it should be noted that all three can exist in the same opinion. There may be contention over what a rule of law means (what is the definition?), over whether the facts fit within whatever definition the court comes up with (do the facts fit?), and over whether that rule of law conflicts with another rule of law (is there consistency?).

Assignment #21

In the following opinions, state the rule(s) of law being applied. If an element of a rule of law is at the center of the controversy, state that element. Finally, identify which of the following kinds of contention exist with respect to those rules and/or elements:

(i) What is the definition?

(ii) Do the facts fit?

(iii) Is there consistency?

If you have difficulty answering any of these questions for any of the opinions, describe the difficulty as best you can.

For questions (a) to (e), check your answers with the Suggested Responses that begin on p. 380.

(a) *People v. Sohn*, p. 299.

(b) *Brown v. Southall Realty*, p. 300.

(c) *Stephens v. Department of State Police*, p. 302.

(d) *Nicholson v. Conn. Half-way House, Inc.*, p. 307.

(e) *Connecticut v. Menillo*, p. 309.

(f) *Mumma v. Mumma*, p. 311.

(g) *Owen v. Illinois Baking Corp.*, p. 315.

(h) *Thompson v. Royall*, p. 316.

(i) *MacPherson v. Buick Motor Co.*, p. 319.

(j) *Goldberg v. Kelly*, p. 330.

Section B. Reasoning and Key Facts

Reasoning is one of the most important techniques of identifying key facts (p. 119). The general principle of the technique can be simply stated: *While a court is presenting its reasoning for a particular holding, it will simultaneously be telling us what the key facts are, or it will be giving us very strong clues as to what they might be.* No fact can be key to a holding unless that fact is compatible with and is based upon the reasoning of the court for that holding.

To demonstrate how reasoning can help you identify key facts, we will examine the hypothetical opinion of *Jackson v. Gavin:*

Jackson v. Gavin
First District Court of Appeals, 1988

DAVIDSON, Judge.

In November, Sam Gavin purchased a used Chevrolet from Mary Jackson, a housewife who is Sam's neighbor. The price was $2,300, paid in cash. The day after Gavin brought the car home, he discovered that the rear windshield wiper did not work. Jackson, who never mentioned the wiper before the sale, refused to repair it. Gavin then instituted this action in the County Trial Court, alleging that Jackson violated § 160(g) of the State Code Annotated, which provides in pertinent part: "a defect in a used car must be disclosed by the seller to the buyer, and the failure to do so will entitle the buyer to recover from the seller the cost of repairing the defect." The parties stipulated that the cost of repairing the wiper was $127.67. Gavin's suit was to recover this amount. Following a judgment for Gavin, Jackson appealed to this court.

Jackson alleges two errors, first that the Trial Court failed to rule that she is not a "seller" under § 160(g) because she is not in the business of selling used cars, and second, in finding that the car was defective under the statute. Finally, Jackson has asked this court to rule that § 160(g) is unconstitutional as an impairment of the obligation of contracts.

It must be pointed out that on its face, § 160(g) covers any seller and not just those in the business of selling used cars. Yet this interpretation of the statute is troublesome in the light of its legislative history. When § 160(g) was being considered by the legislature, a Conference Committee report stated that "the disclosure law was needed because of the imbalance in the bargaining posture between buyers of used cars and dealers." On the floor of the Senate, the chair of the Consumer Protection Committee said "over 12,000 used cars a year are sold in our capital city alone; consumers are complaining of being ripped off by large sales organizations that have a far greater expertise in the mechanics of cars than the average consumer, and therefore are in a better position to take advantage of the vulnerable consumer." All this suggests that the legislature was thinking about the *business* of selling used cars. The purpose of the statute is to protect buyers from those sellers who have vastly more knowledge than buyers. This disadvantage is less likely to exist in isolated sales between neighbors who can be expected to be on relatively equal footing. In any event, we do not think that § 160(g) was intended to cover such isolated sales.

Furthermore, even if Jackson was a seller under § 160(g), we do not feel that a "defect" existed that she was under an obligation to disclose. It is true that Jackson failed to inform Gavin about the faulty rear windshield wiper, but is this the kind of "defect" that § 160(g) was designed to have disclosed? We think not. It has long been held in this jurisdiction that "defect" refers to those flaws that affect the capacity of the car to be driven. See Hamilton v. Seeger, 289 A.2d 91; Georgetown v. Bastion Cable, 337 A. 1105; and Pennsylvania v. Richardson, 402 A.2d 245.

This much is conceded. Jackson and Gavin disagree, however, over whether a flawed rear windshield wiper affects the capacity of the car to be driven. Gavin points out that in inclement weather, the wiper can be critical. The car, however, can still be operated in spite of the condition of the wiper. A driver has alternative ways of finding out what is going on behind him, e.g., he can use the mirror on the outside of the driver's door, and can extend his head out the driver's window in order to see when backing up. Furthermore, many cars do not have rear wipers and yet can still be operated. We conclude, therefore, that the malfunctioning wiper is not a "defect" under the statute that must be disclosed.

In view of our analysis of the statute, there is no need to decide whether § 160(g) unconstitutionally impaired the obligation of contracts. When a case can be resolved on a statutory basis, courts are reluctant to address a constitutional issue that might be involved. Hence we express no opinion on this issue.

Judgment below is reversed.

Assume you are briefing *Jackson v. Gavin*. There are two, and potentially three, issues in this opinion. Stated in shorthand, they are:

ISSUE I: Is Jackson a "seller" under § 160(g)?
HOLDING I: NO

ISSUE II: Was there a "defect" under § 160(g) that must be disclosed?
HOLDING II: NO

ISSUE III: Is § 160(g) unconstitutional as an impairment of the obligation of contracts?
"HOLDING" III: No holding because the court does not reach this question.

Issue I is a definitional issue. The parties disagreed about the meaning of "seller." Does it mean any seller (broad) or a seller who is in the business of selling (narrow)? Did the legislature intend a broad or a narrow statute? What is the definition?

Issue II is not a definitional issue since everyone agreed on the definition of defect (flaws that affect the capacity of the car to be driven). The disagreement was over whether the facts fit within the definition. Do the facts fit? From another perspective, however, it might be said that issue II *is* a definitional issue since there was a need to define the word "flaws." In effect, we need a definition of the definition. But the court does not proceed in this fashion. It starts from the premise of an agreed-upon definition and then focuses its attention on the problem of applying the definition to the facts. Hence, we have treated issue II as an application (do-the-facts-fit) issue. How we label the issue, however, is less important than our ability to understand the court's reasoning in resolving it.

Issue III is a consistency issue. Does the statute violate the Constitution on the obligation of contracts? Is there consistency?

There are holdings for issues I and II. We need to determine how the court's reasoning for these holdings can help us identify the key facts for the holdings.

Issue I. As we saw earlier, when a court is interpreting the meaning of a statute, the starting point of its reasoning is to attempt to determine the legislative intent of the statute through techniques such as the plain meaning rule, identifying the policy or purpose of the statute, etc. (p. 153). Judge Davidson did this in the opinion and came to the conclusion that the legislature intended to limit the disclosure requirement of § 160(g) to sellers in the business of selling used cars. The court's reasoning is the legislative intent and the process that the court used in determining what this intent was.

In the light of the court's reasoning, we can safely conclude that one of the key facts for holding I was that Jackson was a neighbor engaged in an isolated sale. Or perhaps it is more accurate to say that the key fact was the fact categorization that Jackson was a nonmerchant. Apply the test for a key fact: change the facts and ask what effect it would have on the holding (p. 110). If we altered the facts so that now we have Jackson selling cars commercially, it is fairly obvious that the court would have reached a different holding on Issue I. Hence, the identification of the court's reasoning for a holding has simultaneously lead us to a key fact for that holding.

In Issue II, the fight is over whether the car had a "defect" under § 160(g). Gavin's complaint was that the rear window wiper did not function properly. Jackson denied that this was the kind of defect that § 160(g) was meant to cover. There was no dispute between the parties over the meaning of "defect" in the statute. We are told that the definition is clear; it means those flaws that affect the capacity of the car to be driven. The question before the court on this issue is whether a faulty rear windshield wiper fits within this definition. Do the facts fit?

In the court's discussion of this issue, it emphasizes a number of facts. First of all, not all cars are equipped with rear window wipers and yet they can be operated. Furthermore, a driver has alternatives available when a rear window wiper is not operating. The driver can use the mirror on the outside of the driver's door, and can extend his or her head out the driver's window in order to see when backing up. Therefore, the court concludes, a malfunctioning rear window wiper does not affect the capacity of the car to be driven. This is the reasoning of the court in holding that there was no defect under § 160(g).

Note that the court has made a number of *logical connections* between the facts and the definition of "defect." These logical connections are excellent clues to the key facts for holding II. The key facts for issue II are as follows: the car could be driven in spite of the malfunction, and alternatives were available to compensate for the malfunction. These key facts naturally flow out of and are intimately based on the court's reasoning for holding II.

While issue III—the consistency issue—was not addressed by the court, we would use the same steps to find its key facts via reasoning if the issue had been discussed. First we would identify the court's reasoning for its resolution of the conflict, e.g., through its interpretation of the meaning of the relevant statutory and constitutional provisions, and then determine what key facts grow out of and are dependent on that reasoning.

———

The first set of assignments below will ask you to identify the reasoning for the opinions in the appendix of the book. Reasoning is also the last technique for identifying key facts that we will study. Having now covered all of the ten techniques (p. 118), we are ready to identify the key facts in these opinions as well as complete statements of the issues within them.

Assignment #22

For each holding in the following opinions, identify the court's reasoning:

a. *People v. Sohn*, p. 299.

b. *Brown v. Southall Realty Co.*, p. 300.

c. *Stephens v. Dept. of State Police*, p. 302.

d. *Nicholson v. Conn. Half-Way House, Inc.*, p. 307.

e. *Conn. v. Menillo*, p. 309.

Check your answers with the Suggested Responses, p. 382.

Assignment #23

For each holding in the following opinions, identify the court's reasoning:

a. *Mumma v. Mumma*, p. 311.

b. *Owen v. Ill. Baking Corp.*, p. 315.

c. *Thompson v. Royall*, p. 316.

d. *MacPherson v. Buick Motor Co*, p. 319.

e. *Goldberg v. Kelly*, p. 330.

Assignment #24

For each of the following opinions, (i) identify all the key facts for each holding, (ii) give a complete statement of each issue, and (iii) give a shorthand statement of each holding. [Be sure to coordinate your answers to the responses you gave to Assignments #19 (p. 146), #21 (p. 161), and #22 above.]

a. *People v. Sohn*, p. 299.

b. *Brown v. Southall Realty Co.*, p. 300.

c. *Stephens v. Dept. of State Police*, p. 302.

d. *Nicholson v. Conn. Half-Way House, Inc.*, p. 307.

e. *Conn. v. Menillo*, p. 309.

Check your answers with the Suggested Responses, p. 386.

Assignment #25

For each of the following opinions, (i) identify all the key facts for each holding, (ii) give a complete statement of each issue, and (iii) give a shorthand statement of each holding. [Be sure to coordinate your answers to the responses you gave to Assignments #20 (p. 147), #21 (p. 161), and #23 above.]

a. *Mumma v. Mumma*, p. 311.

b. *Owen v. Ill. Baking Corp.*, p. 315.

c. *Thompson v. Royall*, p. 316.

d. *MacPherson v. Buick Motor Co.*, p. 319.

e. *Goldberg v. Kelly*, p. 330.

Chapter Eleven

Dictum, Disposition, and Commentary

Section A. Dictum

The word "dictum" means remark or observation. (The plural of dictum is dicta.) In the law, the word is used as an abbreviation of the phrase, "obiter dictum," which means a gratuitous or unnecessary remark or observation. When we say that there is dictum in an opinion, we are referring to a comment made by the judge that was not necessary to resolve the specific issues before the court.

Suppose that the facts before the court raise the question of the constitutionality of a search conducted by police investigators where the defendant consented to the search. The concern of the court is whether the consent was valid. The court concludes that the consent was valid and that the search was constitutional. It then adds the following comment:

> Even if the defendant had not consented to the search, it still would have been constitutional.

This statement constitutes blatant dictum, and the court just about acknowledges it as such by the use of the highly speculative "even if" language to introduce the conclusion. The court did not have to decide whether a search is constitutional if no consent is given. These were *not* the facts of the opinion: the defendant *did* consent. The court is saying something that it did not have to say, something based upon facts that are different from the actual facts of the opinion.

Another example. In an opinion that involves the liability of the defendant for civil negligence, the court says:

> We have no doubt that the defendant may be prosecuted for criminal negligence as well.

The conclusion is obviously dictum; there was no need for the court to comment on the law of *criminal* negligence in a *civil* negligence litigation.

Sometimes a court will preface a statement with a remark that inevitably signals dictum:

> Although the question is not now before this court, we think it appropriate to say. . . .

Dictum in an opinion is not binding or mandatory authority (p. 204). It can never be part of the holding of an opinion. If a passage from an opinion contains dictum, it does not mean that the passage is wrong or that it cannot be used. It simply means that to the extent that it is dictum, it is not part of the holding of the opinion. The opinion does not *stand* for any principle found in the dictum. The dictum can only be persuasive authority (p. 207).

Section B. Disposition: What Happens as a Result of the Court's Holdings in the Opinion

A *judgment* is the court's resolution of the dispute in which there is a statement of the rights and duties of the parties. The *disposition* is whatever must happen in the litigation as a result of the holdings that the court made in the opinion.

If you are reading a trial court opinion in which there are no prior proceedings, the disposition will normally consist of a statement of who wins the judgment. For example, "Judgment for plaintiff."

At times, the disposition is couched in terms of a decision on the particular procedural motion or petition raised by one of the parties, e.g., an application or petition for a writ of habeas corpus or a motion for summary judgment (p. 41). Here are two examples of this type of disposition:

> Accordingly, petitioner's application for a writ of habeas corpus will denied.

> For the reasons stated above, the motion of summary judgment filed by plaintiff John E. Kinney will be denied, and summary judgment will be entered in favor of defendant Penn Central.

You will note from the above excerpts that the focus is on the *result* of the opinion and not on the reasons why the court reaches this result or on the holdings that constitute the law of the opinion. The reasoning of the opinion and the holdings are to be stated elsewhere in your brief of the opinion. Limit your identification of the disposition to a statement of who won and what the court did procedurally as a result of the decision. Sometimes, however, you will find that while the court is stating the disposition, it includes partial statements of the holding and/or of the reasoning as in the following excerpt:

For the reasons indicated above, the court concludes that plaintiff, Abbott, was given neither express nor implied warranties in its favor upon which this action for breach of warranty can be based. Defendant's motion for summary judgment is, therefore, granted by separate order.

The court's determination that neither express nor implied warranties existed is probably part of the holding in the litigation. Do *not* state this as part of the disposition. Limit yourself as follows for purposes of the brief:

Disposition: Motion for summary judgment granted to the defendant.

In most opinions that you will be briefing, there will be prior proceedings. Something happened earlier in the same litigation. For example, there may have been a prior administrative decision that one or more of the parties is seeking to have reviewed by a court. The basis of the appeal will be that the administrative agency did something wrong that must be reviewed and corrected on appeal. There may also have been lower court decisions within the same litigation. The disposition of the appellate court will be expressed in terms of what was done "below." Several possibilities exist:

Reverse:
> to change the result reached below.

Reverse and remand:
> to change the result reached below and to send the case back (remand it) to the lower tribunals for further proceedings based upon the holdings in the appellate court opinion.

Modify:
> to partially change the result reached below.

Some opinions can have relatively complicated prior proceedings. Suppose that all of the following occurred below:

1. Trial court sustains defendant's motion for a directed verdict (p. 46) and awards the judgment to the defendant. Plaintiff appeals.

2. Court of Appeals reverses and awards the judgment to the plaintiff. Defendant applies to the Supreme Court for a writ of certiorari (p. 52).

Now the Supreme Court enters the picture. Here is the disposition that it reaches:

> Having concluded that plaintiff was entitled to have defendant's motion for a directed verdict overruled, we grant certiorari, affirm the decision of the Court of Appeals as herein modified, reverse the trial court's order sustaining defendant's motion for a directed verdict and its judgment in accord therewith, and remand this case to that court, directing it to order a new trial.

Note that within this disposition the Supreme Court unravels what occurred below in accordance with whatever holdings the Supreme Court reached. Step by step, the court travels back "down" through the prior proceedings to undo (reverse), affirm, or modify what occurred within each step of those proceedings. If there are prior proceedings in the litigation, therefore, your identification of each of these prior proceedings (separately stated elsewhere in your brief of the opinion) will frequently be of great assistance to you in identifying the disposition since, to a large extent, the disposition will be a response to what happened below.

Normally, but not always, the information on the disposition will be found within the last paragraph of the opinion.

Assignment #26

In the following opinions, state the disposition of the court:

a. *People v. Sohn*, p. 299.

b. *Brown v. Southall Realty Co.*, p. 300.

c. *Stephens v. Dept. of State Police*, p. 302.

d. *Nicholson v. Conn., Half-Way House, Inc.*, p. 307.

e. *Conn. v. Menillo*, p. 309.

Check your answers with the Suggested Responses, p. 391.

Assignment #27

In the following opinions, state the disposition of the court:

a. *Mumma v. Mumma*, p. 311.

b. *Owen v. Ill. Baking Corp.*, p. 315.

c. *Thompson v. Royall*, p. 316.

d. *MacPherson v. Buick Motor Co.*, p. 319.

e. *Goldberg v. Kelly*, p. 330.

Section C. Commentary on the Opinion

At the end of your brief, you should include a set of notes to yourself. The comprehensiveness of the notes will depend on the importance of the opinion and the time that you have available. While no particular order or structure is required for these notes, you might consider collecting your thoughts under the following headings:

1. Concurring and dissenting opinions

2. Personal views

3. Counter brief (narrower/broader interpretations)

4. History of the case

5. The case in sequence

6. Case notes in law reviews

1. CONCURRING AND DISSENTING OPINIONS

A concurring opinion agrees with the result or disposition of the majority, but for different reasons. A dissenting opinion disagrees with the result or disposition of the majority. Some opinions may concur in part and dissent in part with the majority. If there are concurring and/or dissenting opinions, or any other separate opinions, take notes on them. Why did the judges refuse to join the majority? Did they disagree with the way the majority phrased the issues? Did they think that the majority misinterpreted the important (key) facts?

If you are briefing an appellate court opinion, be sure that you know how many judges heard the case, e.g., nine for the U.S. Supreme Court, seven for many state supreme courts. What was the vote on this case? How close was the vote? If the vote was close, then the concurring and dissenting opinions become all the more important. The views expressed in these opinions might become majority views in later cases on the same or similar issues. The retirement of one or two members of the court may be all that is needed.

2. PERSONAL VIEWS

Give your views on the case at two levels: visceral and intellectual.

(a) Visceral Think back to the time when you first read the facts of the case. For the moment, divorce yourself from legalisms and technicalities and ask yourself: who should win? At the "gut" level, which party is "in the right?" How would someone unschooled in the law decide this case? Why? If you were a high school senior and the facts were plainly laid before you—without any flowery language or jurisprudence—how would you decide the case? Why?

(b) Intellectual Now give your intellectual response to the case, and compare it with your visceral response. Was the opinion well reasoned? Did it make unwarranted assumptions? Did the opinion persuade you? Was the concurring or dissenting opinion, if any, more persuasive? Why? To what extent is your intellectual response different from your visceral response?

3. COUNTER BRIEF (NARROWER/BROADER INTERPRETATIONS)

In your brief of the case you took certain positions as to what the key facts were for each holding. You probably expressed some of these facts narrowly and some broadly (p. 119). Now look at the opinion from a different perspective. How would *someone else* interpret the key facts of the opinion? Would someone else phrase the issues even more broadly than you did? Would someone else express them even more narrowly? Recall the ten techniques used to support conclusions on the keyness of facts (p. 118). Show how some of these techniques might be used to reach different conclusions from yours on which facts were key. In short, challenge your own interpretation of the case. Give counter positions. Assume that someone is reading the opinion who feels differently (at the visceral and/or intellectual level) about the correctness of the result in the opinion. How would this other person brief the opinion?

4. HISTORY OF THE CASE

Were there further appeals in this case? What happened to the parties after the opinion you are briefing? Shepardize the case. One kind of information that *Shepard's Citations* gives you about a case is the subsequent history of the same litigation. Was the case reversed on appeal? Affirmed? Is the case still good law? To the extent that there is such history, *Shepard's* will give it to you.

5. THE CASE IN SEQUENCE

Other litigation, involving other parties, may have occurred on the same or similar issues after the case you are briefing was decided. You need to find out what other cases have said about these issues, particularly from courts in the same jurisdiction. There are three main ways to see the case in sequence with other cases on the same or similar issues: *Shepard's*, the digests of West, and the ALRs.

(a) Shepard's In addition to giving you the history of a case, *Shepard's* will also give you the *treatment* of the case. A case is treated whenever another case mentions it. We have already seen how this works when we covered the fourth technique of identifying a key fact (p. 122). *Shepard's* will tell you if other cases have discussed your case. When you read these other cases, you will find out if they reached the same conclusion. Was the case followed by later cases? Was there disagreement? Did other cases distinguish the facts before them as justification for reaching a different result?

(b) Digests of West Almost every opinion that you will be briefing will be printed in one of the West reporters (p. 22). Find your opinion in a West reporter (using a parallel cite if necessary, p. 241). At the beginning of every opinion in a West reporter, there are headnotes that summarize a portion of the opinion. Each headnote has two numbers: a consecutive number and a key number that goes with a key topic (p. 24). Jot down this key topic and number for any headnote that summarizes those portions of the opinion in which you are primarily interested. Take this key topic and number to any digest of West, e.g., the *American Digest System*, the most comprehensive digest in existence. In the digest, look up your key topic and number. Cases summarized by West under this key topic and number should cover issues that are the same or similar to those in the case you are briefing. This then is another way to locate other case law so that you can see your case in context with other cases.

As indicated, each headnote also has a consecutive number. This number can be of assistance to you in using *Shepard's*. As you examine each headnote, select the ones that you feel are the most important: those that summarize the heart of the opinion. Jot down each number that appears at the very beginning of the headnote (not the key number, but the consecutive number). When you are sheparding this case, look for small raised numbers in the columns of *Shepard's*. These elevated numbers correspond to the consecutive numbers in the headnotes of the case you are sheparding. Make note of any case in the columns of *Shepard's* that has the elevated number you jotted down. Such cases should be checked first. They will probably be directly relevant to the issues you are most anxious to view in sequence.

(c) ALRs Go to the *American Law Reports*. This set of books has five parts: ALR, ALR2d, ALR3d, ALR4th, ALR Fed. Each part has its own index system, e.g., a Quick Index. In the index, try to find a reference to a research paper (called an annotation) on the same or similar issues that were covered in the case you are briefing. Once you find such an annotation, you will be given extensive citations to cases on these issues. You will then see how other cases have resolved these issues.

6. CASE NOTES IN LAW REVIEWS

There are many law reviews or legal periodicals, e.g., *Maine Law Review, Columbia Law Review*. One section of most law reviews is devoted to "Case Notes." These notes consist of summaries and commentary on selected opinions. You should consider comparing your analysis of the case you are briefing with the analysis of the author of a case note on the same case. You may find this comparison to be quite helpful.

How do you determine whether your case has been "noted" in a law review? There are three indexes to use: *Index to Legal Periodicals, Current Law Index*, and *Legal Resource Index*. Each of these indexes has a section covering case notes (sometimes referred to as the Table of Cases). In this section, see if the case you are briefing is listed. If so, you will be given citations to legal periodical literature containing case notes on your case.

Chapter Twelve

A Composite Brief

Thus far we have covered the eleven components of a *comprehensive* brief of an opinion (p. 79). Each of the components have been examined individually. In this chapter we will bring the pieces together in composite form. We will also look at a much shorter version of a brief: the *thumbnail* brief.

Section A. Comprehensive Brief

In the assignments in this book, one of the opinions under examination has been *Brown v. Southall Realty Co.* The brief of this opinion will be presented below. You will note that an additional element has been added to this brief: the identification of the pages in the book where the opinion is found. If you are briefing an opinion directly out of a reporter, all you will need is the citation of the opinion—the first component of the brief. If, however, you are briefing an opinion that has been reprinted in a textbook (such as the one you are now reading) or in a course casebook, you should also include the page numbers where the opinion is found in the textbook or casebook.

One final introductory point about the brief. One of the components of a brief is the facts of the case. Throughout the book thus far we have stressed the importance of *key facts*. In the main, your statement of the facts should be limited to the key facts. In Chapter 9, p. 139, we discussed *context* facts: those non-key facts that are added either for background purposes or because someone in the litigation vigorously tried to argue that they were key facts. In your statement of the facts for the brief, you can include some context facts along with the key facts.

A Comprehensive Brief	
CITATION:	Brown v. Southall Realty Co. Inc. 237 A.2d 834 (D.C.1968)
PAGES IN TEXT:	300–302
PARTIES:	Brown/tenant/defendant below/appellant here vs. Southall Realty/landlord/plaintiff below/appellee here
OBJECTIVES:	Southall wants to evict Brown and regain possession of the rented premises. Brown initially wanted to avoid being evicted and now wants to avoid having to pay rent.
CAUSE OF ACTION:	Southall: Brown breached her duty under the lease to pay rent.
DEFENSE:	Brown: The lease is illegal and no rent need be paid under it because of a violation of §§ 2304 and 2501 of the D.C. Housing Regulations.
PRIOR PROCEEDINGS:	(1) TRIAL. Southall sued Brown for possession of its rented premises for nonpayment of rent. RESULT: Judgment for Southall, awarding it possession of the rented premises.
PRESENT PROCEEDING:	(2) APPEAL. Brown now appeals the judgment of the lower court to the D.C. Court of Appeals.
FACTS:	Tenant leases housing from landlord. At the time of the lease, there are Code violations in the premises that render it unsafe and unsanitary. The landlord knew of these violations before entering into the lease. Later, the landlord sues the tenant for possession due to nonpayment of rent. Landlord wins. Tenant appeals even though at the time of the appeal the tenant had moved from the premises and did not wish to return.
ISSUE I:	Can a tenant appeal a judgment awarding possession to the landlord when the judgment would be res judicata on matters such as whether rent is due even though the tenant no longer wants possession of the premises?
HOLDING I:	YES
REASONING I:	The court allowed this appeal because of the consequences of the doctrine of res judicata. If the appeal were not allowed, the trial court decision on the issue of rent would be final. The issue of *possession* may now be moot since the tenant no longer wants possession. But the *rent* issue is still alive. If it is not resolved now, then res judicata will prevent the tenant from later claiming that she does not owe rent in the event that the landlord later sues for rent.
ISSUE II:	Is a lease void when the landlord knows before entering the lease that there are unsafe and unsanitary conditions in the rented premises in violation of §§ 2304 and 2501 of the D.C. Housing Code?

HOLDING II:	YES
REASONING II:	It was the intent of the Commissioners (who wrote the Housing Code) to have a lease declared void when the landlord enters it knowing that there are unsafe and unsanitary conditions that make the rented premises uninhabitable. To infer any other intent would contradict the purpose of §§ 2304 and 2501, which is to insure that housing is livable.
DISPOSITION:	Judgment for landlord is reversed.
COMMENTARY:	See pp. 170ff. on what should be included here.

Section B. Thumbnail Brief

A thumbnail brief is, in effect, a brief of a brief! It is a shorthand version of the comprehensive brief. By definition, therefore, you must know how to do a comprehensive brief before you try a shorthand one. Many students fall into the trap of doing *only* shorthand briefs. It is true that students of law and practitioners often have a great deal of work. It takes considerable time to write a comprehensive brief. It is highly recommended, however, that early in your career you develop the habit and skill of preparing briefs comprehensively. Without this foundation, your shorthand briefs will be visibly superficial.

A Thumbnail Brief	
CITATION:	Brown v. Southall Realty v. Brown, 237 A.2d 834 (D.C.1968)
PAGES IN TEXT:	300–302.
FACTS:	Landlord leases premises knowing Code violations exist. Unsafe and unsanitary. Landlord wins possession action for nonpayment of rent. Tenant moves out and appeals.
ISSUE I:	Does res judicata require this court to hear the appeal?
HOLDING I:	YES
REASONING I:	If the appeal is not allowed, res judicata will bar the tenant from later denying that rent is due.
ISSUE II:	Is the lease void because of a violation of §§ 2304 and 2501?
HOLDING II:	YES
REASONING II:	If the lease were not declared void, the purpose of the regulations (to provide livable housing) would be defeated.
DISPOSITION:	Judgment for landlord is reversed.

PART THREE

The Application of Court Opinions

Introduction

In Part III of this book, our goal is to explore the *process* of applying case law. What are the analytical steps that are required? In Part IV, our theme will be *writing* that contains this analysis, e.g., a memorandum of law, a letter, an appellate brief. Before we discuss the skills of writing, we will cover the skills of analysis in the application of case law. It is true that analysis and writing often occur simultaneously. Yet considerable thinking should take place *before* you write. In Part III, we will study the nature of this preliminary thinking.

Our guiding principle in the application of case law is *stare decisis:*

Similar cases should be decided in the same way unless there is good reason for a court to do otherwise.

A primary theme of our judicial system is the achievement of continuity by following and building upon *precedent.* When a dispute in a new case comes before a court, one of the major concerns will be: how have earlier cases resolved this kind of dispute? This

does not mean that the court will slavishly follow what other courts have done. Precedents can be changed and rejected. The starting point in the analysis, however, is an assessment of whether there are prior court opinions that could become precedents for the case currently before the court. A judge will feel and appear intellectually incomplete if this assessment is not made.

This preoccupation with precedent has been frequently criticized, as we saw in Jonathan Swift's comment at the beginning of this book. Yet what is the alternative? Suppose judges rarely or never considered prior opinions as possible guides to the cases before them. Every court would make up its own mind based on its own sense of justice and fair play. Chaos could result. There would probably be substantial inconsistency in the way that courts resolve the same kinds of cases, even within the same court system. The public would receive little or no guidance on whether its conduct might be declared illegal. Every dispute might have to end up in court. The system would break down. Stare decisis, therefore, acts as a stabilizing force within the courts and in society as a whole. If there are precedents, courts should follow them or explain to us why it is not appropriate to do so.

What do we mean by a precedent? When is a prior court opinion a precedent? For our purposes:

> A precedent is a prior court opinion that interpreted and applied a rule of law to a set of facts that is similar to the rule of law and facts currently before the court.

For example, assume that the litigation currently before the court involves a dispute between two corporations over the interpretation of "fraud" in § 45.8 of the state code covering commercial sales contracts. Five years ago, a court in the same state decided *Gregory Lane Co. v. Washington Construction Inc.*, an opinion that applied § 45.8 to a fraud dispute that arose out of a commercial sales contract between two corporations. *Gregory Lane Co. v. Washington Construction Inc.* is a precedent. It applied the same rule of law (§ 45.8) to the same set of facts that is currently before the court.

To be a precedent, however, it is *not* necessary that the prior opinion be exactly or overwhelmingly the same as the case currently before the court. Such an opinion is said to be "on all fours" with the current case. An opinion that does not meet this standard of similarity can still be a precedent so long as there is "sufficient" similarity in the facts and rule of law being interpreted. In the following chapters, we will explore the process of comparison and the nature of this sufficiency.

Chapter Thirteen

Fact Comparison in the Application of Case Law: Fact Similarities: Fact Dissimilarities, and Fact Gaps

Section A. Overview of the Application Process

Assume that you are reading an opinion with one issue. As we have seen, an issue has two main components (p. 139):

a. a rule of law (e.g., a statute, a common law doctrine);

b. key facts.

In order for the court's holding on this issue to be a precedent and to apply to our client's case, we must compare *both* of the above to:

a. a rule of law that must be interpreted in the client's case (e.g., a statute, a common law doctrine); and

b. the facts of the client's case.

In Chapter 14, we will cover (a): the rule-of-law comparison. In this chapter, we will cover (b): fact comparison.

The essence of sophisticated case analysis is sophisticated fact analysis. The starting point in fact analysis is fact comparison (see Figure 13-1).

It is not enough to be able to show a similarity between the facts of the client's case and some of the facts of the opinion. You must be able to show that there is a sufficient similarity between the facts of the client's case and ALL of the KEY facts that led to the court's holding on a particular issue.

181

FIGURE 13–1.
Fact Comparison.

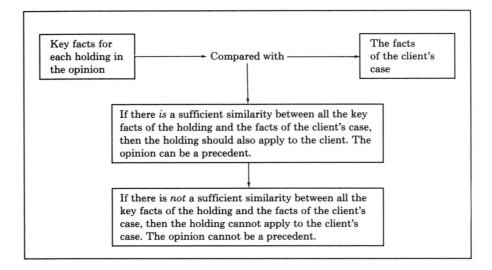

Section B. "Crane Analysis"

First a word about the enemy. What is the *opposite* of the kind of case analysis covered in this and in the next chapter? What should you avoid early in your legal career? We have called the enemy "crane analysis." This method of applying opinions to new facts consists of simply *lifting* language out of the opinion and quoting it in your memorandum or appellate brief. Like a crane excavating land, you reach down into the opinion, find the "juicy" quote, lift it out, and drop it into whatever you are writing. That's it. No commentary, no statement of the issue in the opinion you are applying, no identification of the key facts in this opinion, no fact comparison. Just the quote. In short, crane analysis comes very close to being no analysis at all. Any quotation taken out of context is inherently suspect. Crane analysis is the use of quotes out of context.

Practically everybody uses crane analysis at one time or another—judges, lawyers, paralegals, students, etc. As you begin doing a lot of reading, you will discover that you are surrounded by it!

Crane analysis is a kind of shorthand analysis. There is, of course, nothing wrong with quoting from an opinion. Furthermore, it is *not* necessary to provide the *full* context of every quote that you use. Experienced and highly skilled writers do use shorthand: they will sometimes use quotes from opinions without giving the full context of issues, key facts, etc. But they will rarely do so for important opinions. If the opinion is critical to the argument, it will usually be given a much fuller treatment.

As we have stressed a number of times in this book, it is too early in your career to begin writing in shorthand. Hence, avoid crane analysis.

Section C. Similarities, Dissimilarities, and Gaps

Our ultimate goal, as you saw in Figure 13-1, is to compare key facts for a holding with the facts of the client's case. Our starting point, however, is *every* fact in the opinion and *every* fact in the client's case. In comparing these two sets of facts, you should come up with three categories: similarities, dissimilarities, and gaps.

Example:

Facts in the Client's Case	Facts in the Opinion
Frank Peters is a prisoner. He has been in prison for four years, ten months following a conviction for burglary. The prison wants to transfer him to a mental hospital because it feels that he is mentally ill. The prison does so without providing him with a hearing as to whether the transfer is proper. You work in a law office that represents Peters. You want to challenge the legality of the transfer because of the absence of a hearing.	In *Upsaw v. Wyoming*, Mary Upsaw was an involuntarily committed mental patient. After being institutionalized, the hospital staff diagnosed her as untreatable. The staff wants to transfer her to a prison. She requests a hearing. The request is denied by the prison, and the transfer takes place. She then asks a court to rule that the transfer was invalid. The court does so in *Upsaw v. Wyoming*, holding that a pretransfer hearing was required.

Similarities between the client's case and *Upsaw v. Wyoming:*

• Both Peters and Upsaw are in institutions.

• They are both there against their will.

• Both are being transferred to a different kind of institution from the one where they are presently kept.

• Both are deemed to be mentally ill at the time of the transfer.

• Both were not given hearings before the transfer.

Dissimilarities between the client's case and *Upsaw v. Wyoming:*

• Peters is male; Upsaw is female.

• Peters is in prison; Upsaw is in a mental hospital.

• Peters is being transferred to a mental hospital; Upsaw is being transferred to a prison.

Gaps between the client's case and *Upsaw v. Wyoming:*

• We know that Peters has been institutionalized for four years, ten months. The opinion does not tell us how long Upsaw has been institutionalized.

• We know that Upsaw *requested* a hearing before the transfer. We are not told in the facts of the client's case whether Peters made a request for a hearing before he was transferred.

• We can assume from the opinion that Upsaw was mentally ill at the time she was institutionalized. We are not told in the facts of the client's case whether Peters was mentally ill at the time he was initially institutionalized in the prison.

Note carefully the structure of the above analysis thus far. You lay out the facts of the client's case and the facts of the opinion. In comparing them, you make three lists: similarities, dissimilarities, and gaps. This is how you should approach *every* opinion that you are considering as a possible precedent. Next we move to assessing the implications of these lists.

The client of your office is Frank Peters. The client wants the holding of *Upsaw v. Wyoming* to apply since the court held that a pretransfer hearing is necessary. The prison where Peters is held does not want it to apply. How will the advocates for both sides argue the applicability or nonapplicability of the *Upsaw* holding? The *structure* of their argument will be as follows:

ADVOCACY PRINCIPLES IN
APPLYING HOLDINGS IN OPINIONS:
Assessing the Implications of Fact Similarities,
Fact Dissimilarities, and Fact Gaps

Let us assume that after your initial fact comparison between (i) all the facts relevant to a particular holding in an opinion, with (ii) all the facts of the client's case, you find that there are fact similarities, dissimilarities, and gaps. What do you do with them? The answer depends on whether you want the holding to apply to the client's case or whether you are trying to avoid the holding. The following advocacy principles apply:

(1) You Want the Holding to Apply

    (a) *Fact Similarities.* You argue that the facts of the client's case are substantially similar to all the key facts for that holding.

    (b) *Fact Dissimilarities.* You acknowledge that there are some differences between the facts of your client's case and the facts discussed by the court in reference to the holding. But you argue that the differences are not with any of the key facts for that holding. In effect, you argue that the differences are irrelevant.

    (c) *Fact Gaps.* You acknowledge that there are some fact gaps between the facts of your client's case and the facts discussed by the court in reference to the holding. But you argue that there are no fact gaps as to any of the key facts for that holding. In effect, you argue that the fact gaps are irrelevant.

(2) You Do Not Want the Holding to Apply

    (a) *Fact Similarities.* You acknowledge that there are some similarities between the facts of your client's case and the facts discussed by the court in reference to the holding. You argue, however, that the similarities are not with all the key facts for that holding. There is still a substantial dissimilarity between the facts of the client's case and one or more of the key facts for the holding.

    (b) *Fact Dissimilarities.* You emphasize the fact differences between the facts of your client's case and the facts discussed by the court in reference to the holding. You argue that the differences are with one or more of the key facts for the holding.

(c) *Fact Gaps.* You argue that the fact gaps are critical. The fact gaps make it impossible for the other side to show that there is a substantial similarity with all the key facts for the holding.

While both sides will vigorously argue their respective positions, each may have to concede certain points, e.g., that there are similarities between the facts of the client's case and the facts of an opinion whose holding you want to avoid, or that there are fact differences pertaining to a holding that you want applied. Rarely will you enjoy a 100% favorable comparison.

Back to our example of Frank Peters and the opinion of *Upsaw v. Wyoming.* The following analysis will concentrate on some of the fact dissimilarities, although the same process will govern all the dissimilarities, similarities, and gaps. Recall that Peters wants the holding of *Upsaw* to apply, i.e., that a pretransfer hearing should be held, while the prison wants to avoid this holding. In our initial fact comparison, a number of fact dissimilarities were identified.

First, Peters is a man and Upsaw is a woman. Peters will, of course, acknowledge that this is a difference, but he will argue that it is an irrelevant difference: it was *not* a key fact in *Upsaw v. Wyoming* that Upsaw was a woman. The court would still have held that a pretransfer hearing was necessary even if Upsaw had been a man. Since the other side will probably concede this point, Peters will not have to waste time using any of the ten techniques for identifying key facts (p. 118).

The next fact difference is that Peters is a prisoner, while Upsaw was a mental patient. Again, the same process of analysis takes place. Peters must argue that the court in *Upsaw v. Wyoming* would have reached the same holding if Mary Upsaw had been a prisoner about to be transferred to a very different environment. The fact that she was a mental patient was not a *key* fact. According to Peters, the broader *fact categorization* of institutionalization was key in *Upsaw v. Wyoming,* and there *is* a similarity on this point between the Peters case and the opinion. The other side will probably try to argue that it was key that she was a mental patient. Both sides will use as many of the ten techniques as possible to support their positions. In so doing, careful references will be made to the entire opinion.

This kind of analysis will occur for all the fact similarities and dissimilarities that we initially listed. As indicated, for some of the facts, there may be no dispute. For example, both sides may agree that it was a key fact in *Upsaw v. Wyoming* that no transfer hearing was held. Remember, for the holding to apply, *all* the key facts for that holding must be similar to the facts of the client's case. If any one of the key facts is not similar, then the entire holding cannot apply. Hence, the side that does not want a holding to apply can afford to concede that there is a similarity between the facts of the client's case and *some* of the key facts of the holding. This side need only establish that at least one of the key facts is not similar. The side that wants the holding to apply must show a similarity with *all* the key facts.

What about the fact gaps? There are two kinds of fact gaps: those that exist because of missing facts in the client's case, and those that exist because of missing facts in the opinion.

(a) Missing Facts in the Client's Case It is not uncommon for you to need more facts about the client's case. No matter how comprehensive your initial client interview was, there may still be questions that you failed to ask. As pointed out in Chapter 1, one of the purposes of case analysis is to give you some direction on the facts that you should try to obtain (p. 11). In our example above, we listed as a fact gap that we did not know whether Peters ever asked for a hearing before he was transferred. Having found and read *Upsaw v. Wyoming,* you now know that this is a fact that you need to inquire into since such a request was made in the opinion you want to use as a precedent. This fact gap can be easily closed—you simply ask the client, Peters.

Suppose for some reason that you cannot close the fact gap in this way, e.g., Peters is too sick to know and the records fail to disclose whether he made the request. Or suppose that you *can* find out, but you learn that Peters did *not* make the request for the hearing before the transfer. What, then, do you do?

You must argue that it was *not* a key fact in *Upsaw v. Wyoming* that Mary Upsaw requested the hearing. You must be able to show that the court's holding requiring a pretransfer hearing was *not* dependent on a request made by the person transferred; the court held that the hearing was required whether or not it was requested. To support this view, you again use as many of the ten techniques as are helpful. The other side, of course, may try to show that the request was key to the holding in *Upshaw.*

(b) Missing Facts in the Opinion Some fact gaps can never be closed. In our example, we know how long Peters was institutionalized, but we do not know how long Mary Upsaw was institutionalized. Assume that the opinion simply does not tell us. Hence, we will never know. If you want the opinion to apply, you obviously argue that since the court did not tell us how long she was institutionalized, this fact cannot have been important to the holding. Therefore, we need not bother about it. At the very most, you may have to show that there is nothing about this fact that would have changed the court's holding. It would have required the hearing whether Mary Upsaw was institutionalized one day, four years and ten months, or ten years.

Assignment #28

Make a list of the similarities, dissimilarities, and gaps in the *W v. H* opinion and Jane's case below. Assume that you work for an office that represents Jane.

> Facts in the client's case: Jane wants to sue her husband for divorce on the ground of abandonment. She claims that he is very moody to the point of abnormality. In the last six months, he has refused to talk with her because of his disagreement with the way she handles the household expenses. Out of total frustration, Jane left him last week. She went to live with her mother.

> Facts in the *W v. H* opinion: W (wife) sues H (husband) for a divorce on the ground of abandonment. When H told W that he had received a job offer in another country, W refused to go with him. He took the job anyway and moved out. The court held that there had been an abandonment and granted W the divorce.

Assignment #29

Read *People v. Sohn,* p. 299. Compare it to the facts of Thompson's case below. Assume that the office for which you work represents Thompson:

Thompson was convicted of assault in the first degree in New York and is now appealing. At the trial, it was established that Thompson sued the complainant (the assault victim) in a prior civil action for trespass arising out of the same incident that led to the assault charge. The judgment in the civil action was for Thompson. At the scene of the alleged assault, the victim called the police. Thompson knew this but waited until the police arrived.

Make a list of all similarities, dissimilarities, and gaps between the facts in *Sohn* and the facts in Thompson's case.

Assignment #30

Your supervisor has asked you to work on the Parker case. Parker is a client of the office. He is a single-parent father of two small children. You are asked to determine the effect of *Brown v. Southall Realty Co.,* p. 300, on the Parker case. The facts in the Parker case are as follows:

Smith Realty Corp. is suing Parker, a District of Columbia resident, for nonpayment of rent. Parker has not paid his last month's rent and does not wish to do so. The lease agreement between Parker and Smith Realty Corp. contained a number of clauses, several of which are noteworthy:

Paragraph 17:   "Landlord need not provide any refrigeration facilities. If the Tenant desires a refrigerator, he must furnish his own."

Paragraph 24:   "In the event Landlord commences proceedings for any breach by Tenant of the provisions of this agreement, Tenant hereby waives trial by jury in such proceedings."

In view of Paragraph 17, Parker had no refrigerator. He kept all perishables on the ledge outside the window or on the porch.

Prior legal research has already led you to conclude that Paragraph 17 violates § 100 of the District of Columbia Housing Regulations, which "requires landlords to furnish refrigerators to tenants," and that Paragraph 24 violates § 195(b) of the Regulations, which prohibits "any landlord from asking a tenant to waive the tenant's right to a jury trial as a condition to entering the lease."

Identify similarities, dissimilarities, and gaps. Then assess the implications of what you have identified from the perspective of each side. The structure of your arguments for Parker and for Smith Realty should be based on the "Advocacy Principles in Applying Holdings in Opinions" on p. 184. Although rule-of-law comparison will not be covered until the next chapter, try to include comparisons between the rules of law that were applied in *Brown* and the rules of law that must be examined in the Parker case.

Chapter Fourteen

Rule of Law Comparison

It is highly unlikely that a bankruptcy opinion can be a precedent for a murder case that is currently before the court. The rules of law involved in both situations are substantially different. The bankruptcy opinion interpreted the bankruptcy statute. In the murder case, the court must interpret the murder statute or perhaps the common law of homicide. No matter how similar the facts, if there is no similarity between the rule of law applied in the opinion and the rule of law to be applied in the case, the opinion cannot be used as a precedent.

We saw earlier that there are ten major kinds of rules of law that are interpreted and applied in opinions (p. 144):

1. a statute
2. a common law doctrine
3. a regulation
4. a constitutional provision
5. an equitable doctrine
6. a (procedural) court rule
7. an ordinance
8. an executive order
9. a charter provision
10. a treaty

We also saw that in some opinions the issue involves the interrelationship between more than one law, e.g., whether one statute is consistent with another statute, whether a regulation is validly based on a statute, whether a state statute violates a federal constitutional provision.

Assume that you are working on a client's case that involves the interpretation of one of the above rules of law or a combination of them. You are looking for precedents. You know that an opinion cannot be a precedent unless it interprets and applies a rule of law (or rule-of-law combination) that is similar to what must be interpreted in the client's case. The question is: how similar must they be?

In the best of all worlds, they will be *exactly the same*. For example:

• Your client's case involves the interpretation of § 790 of the Ohio Probate Code. In your search for precedents, you hope to find opinions that interpret § 790 of the Ohio Probate Code.

• Your client's case raises the issue of whether § 12 of a federal regulation violates the First Amendment of the United States Constitution. In your search for precedents, you hope to find opinions that interpret the constitutional validity (under the First Amendment) of § 12 of the federal regulation.

Obviously, the rule-of-law comparison is quite easy in such situations. You can concentrate all your attention on the problem of fact comparison (p. 181) since it is clear in these examples that there is sufficient similarity between the rule or rules of law interpreted in the opinion and those that must be interpreted in the client's case—they are exactly the same.

Now we come to a more troublesome question. Can an opinion be a precedent if the rule of law (or rule-of-law combination) that it interprets is *different* from the rule of law (or rule-of-law combination) that must be interpreted in the client's case? For example:

• Your client's case involves the interpretation of § 790 of the Ohio Probate Code. Can an opinion that interprets § 14(b) of the Ohio Tax Code be a precedent for your case?

• Your client's case raises the issue of whether § 12 of a federal regulation violates the First Amendment of the United States Constitution. Can an opinion be a precedent for your case if the opinion interprets the constitutional validity (under the First Amendment) of § 52 of a federal statute?

The general answer is no—but there are exceptions. Great care must be used whenever you try to use an opinion as precedent that does not interpret and apply the *exact same* rule of law (or rule-of-law combination) that is involved in the client's case. You run the risk of being charged with comparing apples and oranges. While there are circumstances, as explained below, when the comparison *is* proper, you should understand that these circumstances are quite limited. Caution is needed whenever you try to deviate from the norm of exact similarity in the rule-of-law comparison. The exceptions will be explored under the following headings:

1. Statutes

2. Common law

3. Statutes and regulations

1. STATUTES

Assume that a client's case in your office presents the following problem:

• The client is an eighteen-year-old who wants to run for the City Council of Boston.

• The Massachusetts Elections Code provides in § 4(b) that no person can be a candidate for the City Council unless he or she has "reached the age of majority." You want to know whether the client—an eighteen-year-old—has "reached the age of majority" under § 4(b). Assume that the statute does not define this phrase, the legislative history of § 4(b) is not helpful, and that there are no administrative regulations interpreting it.

• In your search for precedents, you try to find opinions that have interpreted § 4(b) of the Massachusetts Elections Code. You find none. But you do find *Smith v. Jones*, an opinion that interprets and applies a different statute.

• In *Smith v. Jones:* the court interpreted and applied § 115.4 of the Massachusetts Elections Code, which says that in order to vote in the general election, you must be of "majority age." This phrase was not defined in the statute. The court in *Smith v. Jones*, however, held that the phrase means "over seventeen."

Can *Smith v. Jones* be a precedent for your client's case?

Note that the statute interpreted and applied in the *Smith* opinion is *not* exactly the same as the statute that is at issue in the client's case. Section 4(b) is different from § 115.4. Different rules of law are involved. In the client's case, we want to know what the Massachusetts legislature meant by the phrase "reached the age of majority" in § 4(b). In *Smith v. Jones,* the court told us what the Massachusetts legislature meant by the phrase "majority age" in § 115.4. It is quite possible that the legislature meant something different when it wrote § 4(b).

Yet there is similarity in the *language* of the two statutes and in their *function*. The relevant language in both statutes is very similar:

> § 4(b): "age of majority"
>
> § 115.4: "majority age"

There is also a similarity in the function served by both rules of law. Both statutes cover qualifications for participation in the political process through elections. To be sure, the functions are not the same. The qualification to *be* an elected official may be different from the qualification to *vote* for elected officials. Yet the similarity, nevertheless, exists.

When you have a similarity of statutory language *and* a similarity in the functions or purposes served by the statutes, you can then make an argument that the opinion can be a precedent. The argument is never ironclad since you are dealing with two different statutes. You cannot say that "age of majority" in § 4(b) means "over seventeen" because *Smith v. Jones* said that "majority age" in § 115.4 means "over seventeen." You must be much more discreet in how you state the argument:

> In our case, we want to interpret § 4(b) on who can be a candidate for the City Council. The statute says that the person must have "reached the age of majority." The phrase "age of majority" has not been defined in the statute, and there are no opinions interpreting it. Section 115.4, however, says that to vote in the general election, you must be of "majority age." *Smith v. Jones* held that this phrase meant "over seventeen." Both statutes have very similar language, and both cover qualifications to participate in the political process. One can argue, therefore, that when the Massachusetts legislature used the word "majority" in both statutes, it had the same group of people in mind—those over seventeen.

Note that there is no definitiveness in this argument. You must recognize that you are always on shaky ground when you argue that an opinion interpreting a statute is a precedent for a client's case when a different statute must be interpreted. Nevertheless, the argument can be made so long as the following three conditions are met:

a. You show a similarity in the language of the two statutes.

b. You show a similarity in the functions or purposes served by the two statutes.

c. There is no direct authority on the meaning of the statute involved in the client's case.

The last condition is very important. As we looked for the meaning of § 4(b) in our example, we said the phrase was not defined elsewhere in the Code, no opinions existed interpreting § 4(b), its legislative history was not helpful, and there were no administrative regulations on the statute. If any of this authority did exist on the meaning of the phrase "age of majority" in § 4(b), we would *not* try to rely on an opinion that interpreted a different statute. We would not need to. Use such an opinion *only* when there is no better alternative to finding a definition.

Of course, there may be considerable debate among advocates as to whether all three conditions have been met. For example, the other side may disagree that § 4(b) and § 115.4 serve similar functions. Section 4(b) covers qualifications for holding public office. One might argue that the legislature intended a higher age for this purpose than for the purpose of voting, given the much greater responsibility and maturity involved in being an elected official. Hence, *Smith v. Jones* is not a precedent since it had nothing to do with being a public official. You will try to argue the other way. Both sides will put forward their best arguments covering each of the three conditions.

Thus far we have been assuming that the two statutes (in the opinion and in the client's case) have been written by the *same* legislature. In our example § 4(b) and § 115.4 were both written by the Massachusetts legislature. Suppose, however, that the statutes were written by two different legislatures: § 4(b) was written by the Massachusetts legislature and § 115.4 was written by the Florida legislature. Assume further that *Smith v. Jones* is a Florida opinion interpreting § 115.4. Can *Smith v. Jones* be a precedent for a client's case in Massachusetts where we have the problem of interpreting a Massachusetts statute? The answer is yes, *so long as the above three conditions are met*. Recognize, however, the difficulties involved. The *Smith* opinion interpreted the intent of the Florida legislature. In the client's case, we are trying to interpret the intent of the Massachusetts legislature. Is it possible that our understanding of what the Florida legislature intended can help us determine the intent of the Massachusetts legislature? Yes, although strict adherence to the three conditions is necessary. We must show similarity of language and purpose, and most important, we must demonstrate that there is no clear answer to our problem within Massachusetts law before we try to go outside the state for a possible precedent.

The first two conditions are often met if both legislatures have passed what are called "uniform laws," e.g., the Uniform Commercial Code, the Uniform Reciprocal Enforcement of Support Act, the Uniform Child Custody

Jurisdiction Act. These statutes are proposed in every state in order to try to achieve some uniformity in subject areas where this is deemed necessary. The legislatures are free to adopt, modify, or reject these proposals. The more popular uniform acts, such as those mentioned above, are often adopted by most of the states without significant change. When this is so, you obviously have considerable help in establishing the first two conditions for using an opinion that interprets a statute of another state—similarity in language and function. Yet this similarity is not automatic. You must carefully assess whether all three conditions are met in each individual case where you want to use an out-of-state precedent in a case involving statutory law.

2. COMMON LAW

Common law is judge-made law in the absence of controlling enacted law (p. 10). Suppose that you have a common law issue in your client's case, e.g., whether the element of intent has been established in a cause of action for *battery.* In your search for precedents you nataurally look for opinions that have interpreted this same rule of law. You want opinions that have interpreted the intent needed for a battery. Suppose none exist, but that there are opinions in your state interpreting the intent needed for *other* common law causes of actions, e.g., intent in assault, intent in trespass. Can these opinions be used as precedents for your battery case? The rules of law are different. Common law battery is different from common law assault or common law trespass. The opinions, however, *can* be precedents if you go through the same kind of analysis described above for using opinions that interpret different statutes:

a. You must show a similarity in the language of the element in the two common law causes of action.

b. You must show a similarity in the function or purpose of (sometimes referred to as the policy behind) the element in the two common law causes of action.

c. There must be no direct authority that interprets the element in the common law cause of action involved in the client's case.

Our battery example involved the use of an opinion on a different rule of law, but within the same state. What about using a common law opinion from another state? This is frequently done when the out-of-state opinion involves the *same* rule of law, i.e., the same common law doctrine—so long as the facts are sufficiently similar, as discussed in Chapter 13. It is much rarer to use an out-of-state opinion on a common law that is different from the common law involved in the client's case.

3. STATUTES AND REGULATIONS

We said earlier that regulations of administrative agencies are not valid unless they are based on the statutes of the legislature (p. 160). Assume that you are working on a client's case involving the following rules of law:

Statute (§ 39): "No compensation can be received unless the applicant is available for work"

Regulation (§ 2.680): "An applicant is not available for work if he or she refuses to accept any employment including work that is substantially different from previous jobs."

The client of your office is a former police officer who is claiming benefits under § 39. The officer says that she is "available for work" under this statute. The administrative agency charged with carrying out this statute, however, denies the benefits because the officer has refused to accept employment as a dishwasher. The client challenges this denial. She believes that "available for work" means available for the kind of work in which the applicant was most recently employed. In her case, this means employment as a police officer; she has never been a dishwasher. The agency disagrees. The regulation (§ 2.680) says that "any" employment must be accepted.

Hence our issue is as follows: is § 2.680 validly based on § 39? Did the agency misinterpret the statute (§ 39) when it wrote its regulation (§ 2.680)? The regulation is supposed to carry out the statute, not change it, add to it, or modify it in any way. Does § 2.680 modify § 39, or does it simply incorporate a detail that is consistent with the legislature's purpose in enacting § 39? We have a consistency issue (p. 159).

We now go looking for precedents. We want to try to find a court opinion that interpreted and applied these same rules of law. We want an opinion that decided whether § 2.680 is validly based on § 39. Suppose, however, that no such opinions exist. Yet you do find the opinion of *Shapiro v. Johnson* in which the court had before it the question of whether a different regulation (§ 23.972) of the same agency was validly based on our statute (§ 39). It held that it was not. Can the *Shapiro* opinion be a precedent for us? Note that the opinion and the client's case involve the same statute, but different regulations. Yet the same basic issue is involved: is the regulation consistent with the statute?

The opinion *may* be a precedent. We need to know how similar the two regulations are. More important, we need to examine the meaning and purpose of the statute. If the opinion helps us in the latter objective, it may be a very useful precedent. The more similar the two regulations and the more discussion in the opinion about the legislative intent of the statute, the greater the likelihood that the opinion can be a precedent—even though it does not directly discuss the regulation in the client's case.

In our example, we carefully read why *Shapiro v. Johnson* held that § 23.972 was not validly based on § 39. Undoubtedly the opinion discussed the meaning and purpose of the legislature in enacting § 39. We must determine whether this discussion is relevant to our regulation, § 2.680. Does the meaning and purpose of § 39, as presented in *Shapiro*, also apply to § 2.680? Is the reasoning of *Shapiro* broad enough to cover our regulation?

These are the kinds of questions that we must ask ourselves in trying to determine whether an opinion interpreting a different regulation but the same statute can be a precedent.

Assignment #31

This assignment will involve the same problem discussed above. An ex-police officer is challenging a regulation (§ 2.680) that requires her to accept a job "that is substantially different from" her previous jobs. She claims that this regulation is invalidly based on § 39, the governing statute. There are no opinions interpreting § 39 and § 2.680. *Shapiro v. Johnson*, however, interprets § 39 and §23.972, a different regulation.

Section 23.972 provides as follows: "No application for compensation shall be acted upon until the applicant has been out of work for at least three months." *Shapiro v. Johnson* held that this regulation was invalidly based on § 39. It added a condition to § 39 that the legislature did not intend. The court said that the purpose of § 39 was to provide relief to unemployed individuals and that the legislature intended the statute to be construed liberally in favor of applicants who are out of work.

Make an argument that *Shapiro v. Johnson* can be a precedent in the ex-police officer's case involving § 2.680.

Note

In this chapter and in the preceding chapter we have been examining when an opinion can be a precedent. A separate question is whether the opinion is a *binding* precedent. The latter topic will be covered in Chapter 16 on mandatory and persuasive authority (p. 205). You do not get to the question of whether an opinion is a binding precedent until you first decide whether it can be a precedent at all. This has been our concern up to this point.

PART FOUR

Authority and Case Analysis in Legal Writing

"...there is no such thing as good writing. There is only good rewriting."

Justice Louis D. Brandeis

Thus far we have covered the briefing of an opinion (Part II) and the process of applying a holding in an opinion to a client's case (Part III). Occasionally we have made reference to the memorandum of law, the appellate brief, and other kinds of legal writing involved in the practice of law. In the chapters of Part IV our concern will be the ways in which case law can be used in these kinds of legal writing. Oral advocacy will also be covered.

Chapter Fifteen

Factors Determining the Length and Comprehensiveness of Case Analysis

Section A. Introduction

Case analysis in legal writing tends to fall into one of four categories:

(1) Incomplete/Confusing Case Analysis in Writing

The opinion is cited in a manner that does not clearly indicate whether the writer thinks the opinion applies or that does not clearly indicate what the opinion stands for—what it held.

Example: We must avoid permitting any of the employees from using the facilities during company time. Robins v. Jackson, 84 Mass. 307, 39 N.E.2d 1072 (1970). If we do not do so, we are open to the claim that by implication we have authorized them to do so. U.S. v. Alabama, 310 U.S. 48, 39 S.Ct. 107, 16 L.Ed. 409 (1950); Peters v. Jones, 39 F.Supp. 602 (W.D.Cal.1968).

This excerpt from a legal memorandum leaves a lot to be desired. Three opinions are cited. At best, the reader is forced to guess what the opinions were about or what their holdings were. The writer provides no analysis. The reader is told, in effect, to go read these opinions and figure out for him or herself how they apply to the problem being discussed. A more extreme example would be a statement followed by nothing more than seven or eight citations to court opinions. This is known as a "string cite."

(2) Conclusory Case Analysis in Legal Writing

In this kind of case analysis, it is clear that the writer thinks the opinion applies or that it does not apply. However, very little argument is provided other than the conclusion of the writer.

Example: Jones v. Smith, 75 F.Supp. 310 (D.Vt.1975) held that an "undue concentration of the retail market could amount to a monopoly." *Jones* applies since Peterson Tire Company has amassed an undue concentration of the retail tire market.

(3) Demonstrative Case Analysis in Writing

The writer provides a statement of the conclusion on whether the opinion applies plus *several* of the major steps taken to reach that conclusion. A clear statement of the holding is provided.

(4) Exhaustive Case Analysis in Writing

The writer provides a statement of the conclusion on whether the opinion applies plus *all or most* of the steps taken to reach that conclusion. A clear statement of the holding is provided.

Section B. Length and Comprehensiveness

What kind of case analysis is most effective? How comprehensive should your analysis of an opinion be? Five *pages?* Five *lines?* A number of factors must be considered:

1. The time that you have available.

2. The tolerance and sophistication of your reader(s).

3. The dictates of advocacy and the importance of the opinion to the objective of the party.

1. THE TIME THAT YOU HAVE AVAILABLE

As indicated earlier, the process of briefing and applying opinions can be very time consuming. It could take hours to do a careful job of understanding an opinion and presenting the arguments on why it is or is not applicable. You are somewhat in the position of the king who had to be told that "there is no royal road to geometry." So too, there is no royal (easy) road to using opinions. If you are writing a memorandum or appellate brief in which you must discuss numerous opinions, the time required to do this well can be substantial.

Many students waste a good deal of time due to faulty technique in briefing and in applying cases. This is the reason why so much attention was given to these skills in Parts II and III of this book. While good technique can shorten the time that you need, there is no way to avoid the reality that opinions are often extremely difficult to understand and to use, and that a quality work product in handling them in your legal writing is going to take time.

2. THE TOLERANCE AND SOPHISTICATION OF YOUR READER(S)

Even if you feel that you need to use a lot of space explaining the applicability of an opinion, it will do you no good to do so if the reader of your writing will either refuse to read it, or be irritated by the length of your argument. Some teachers, supervisors, hearing officers, and judges take the firm position that, "If you can't say it in a page or two, it's probably not worth reading." Obviously, such readers of your writing are primarily interested in the *conclusion* of your argument with perhaps a *summary* of several points of the argument. They do *not* want to read a detailed step-by-step analysis (e.g., identifying all factual similarities, dissimilarities, gaps; comparing these with all the facts in the client's case; providing lengthy justifications for the facts you feel are key, etc.). This is not to say that you are relieved of your responsibility of going through all these steps. Unless you go through the steps *at least mentally*, you run the risk of faulty analysis. The writing, however, that you eventually submit to the teacher, supervisor, hearing officer, or judge will rarely contain *all* the steps that you went through to reach your conclusion.

Many readers of your writing may want at least a *demonstrative* argument in which you show or demonstrate support for your conclusion on whether the holding in the opinion applies. They will want to know at least some of the major steps that led you to your conclusion.

Suppose that the opinion you are writing about, e.g., in an appellate brief, is very familiar to the judge(s) for whom you are writing. The opinion may be frequently used in the area. Such a judge may well be bored or even insulted and angered by an exhaustive analysis of such an opinion—unless you are suggesting that the opinion should be given an interpretation that is different from the commonly accepted interpretation.

Suppose that you are writing a letter to an agency official or business person who is not an attorney. In this letter you want to talk about the implications of one or more opinions. What kind of analysis do you use? If the reader is not familiar with case law, then an exhaustive analysis and perhaps even a demonstrative analysis may be inappropriate. The reader may not be able to understand it. A conclusory analysis written in nontechnical language may be more appropriate. You will be asked to write this kind of letter in Chapter 19.

Ask your supervisor to show you examples of legal writing from the office files that do an effective job of case analysis. Ask questions about these examples. Try to determine how the nature of the audience influenced the way in which case law was used.

3. THE DICTATES OF ADVOCACY

Advocacy is the presentation of an argument in the light most favorable to the client on whose behalf you are arguing. The advocacy technique just discussed warns us not to irritate by providing an exhaustive analysis when the reader wants nothing more than the headlines—a conclusory analysis. There are, of course, other advocacy techniques of case analysis, the most important of which deal with how you handle similarities and dissimilarities between the facts in the opinion and the facts in the client's case.

In most legal memoranda or appellate briefs, there are one or two major opinions that will be at the heart of the argument being made. Obviously, these opinions will require the full treatment—at least demonstrative analysis. Then there may be five or six minor opinions that you use to bolster the arguments made through the major ones. Conclusory analysis will probably be sufficient for the minor opinions. It is essential that opinions be prioritized in this way so that maximum attention is given to those that are most important to the controversy. The dictates of advocacy require this to be done.

You must also anticipate what the arguments of the other side will be. What are the major opinions on which your opponents will rely? Advocacy usually requires that you give considerable attention to these opinions if you have not already done so. Often the most persuasive writing gives the appearance of balance and perspective. You vigorously argue for your position, but you do not insult the intelligence of the reader by suggesting that there is only one position, and that the reader would have to be insane, unjust, or callous to even consider any other position. Good writers are not afraid of stating what the position of the opposition is. But when this is done, they quickly provide reasoned arguments as to why this other position should not be adopted.

Chapter Sixteen

Primary Authority and Secondary Authority: Their Use and Abuse in Legal Writing

Section A. Definitions

1. AUTHORITY

Authority is anything that a court *could* rely on in reaching its conclusion.

Primary Authority and Secondary Authority:
    Primary authority is any *law* that the court could rely on in reaching its conclusion. Examples include: statutes, regulations, constitutional provisions, ordinances, treaties, common law and equitable doctrines, other court opinions (see Chapter 3, p. 61).

    Secondary authority is any *nonlaw* that the court could rely on in reaching its conclusion. Examples include legal and nonlegal periodical literature, legal and nonlegal encyclopedias, legal and nonlegal dictionaries, legal and nonlegal treatises (texts on various subjects), annotations (research papers in ALR, ALR 2d, ALR 3d, ALR 4th, ALR Fed.).

Mandatory Authority and Persuasive Authority:
    Mandatory authority is whatever the court *must* rely on in reaching its conclusion. Only primary authority can be mandatory authority, e.g., another court opinion, a statute, a constitutional provision. A court is never required to rely on secondary authority, e.g., a law review article or legal encyclopedia. Secondary authority cannot be mandatory authority.

Persuasive authority is whatever the court relies on when it is not required to do so. There are two main kinds of persuasive authority: (a) a prior court opinion that the court is not required to follow but does so because it finds the opinion persuasive, and (b) any secondary authority that the court is not required to follow but does so because it finds the secondary authority persuasive.

2. NONAUTHORITY

Nonauthority is (a) any primary or secondary authority that is not "on point" since it does not cover the facts of the client's case, (b) any invalid primary authority, e.g., an unconstitutional statute, or (c) any book that is solely a finding aid, e.g., *Shepard's Citations*, digests (p. 122).

Section B. Mandatory Authority

Courts *must* follow mandatory authority. There are two broad categories of mandatory authority: (a) enacted law (p. 62), e.g., a statute, a constitutional provision, an ordinance, a regulation; and (b) other court opinions. These categories will be considered separately.

1. ENACTED LAW AS MANDATORY AUTHORITY

An enacted law is mandatory authority and must be followed if the following two tests are met:

a. It was the intention of the authors of the enacted law (e.g., the legislature that wrote the statute) to cover the facts or the kind of facts that are currently before the court; and

b. The application of this enacted law to these facts does not violate some other law that is superior in authority (e.g., the statute does not violate the Constitution).

Suppose that Smith is arrested for burglarizing a house. Section 14 of the state code provides, "It shall be a felony to break and enter a dwelling for the purpose of stealing property therein." Section 14 is mandatory authority for the court so long as it is clear that the statute was intended to cover this kind of situation and the statute is not unconstitutional. Suppose, however, that Smith was arrested for breaking into a car. Is a car a "dwelling" for purposes of § 14? Did the legislature intend to include motor vehicles within the meaning of "dwellings"? Would it depend on whether the owner ever slept in the car? These are questions of legislative intent (p. 152). If the statute was not intended to cover these facts, it is not applicable; it cannot be mandatory authority.

Even if the enacted law was intended to cover the facts before the court, it is not mandatory authority if it violates some higher law. The authors of a regulation may intend to cover a particular individual's activities, for example, but if this regulation is inconsistent with the statute that the regulation is supposed to be carrying out, the regulation is not mandatory authority; it is invalid (p. 160). Similarly, a statute may clearly cover a given set of facts but be invalid because the statute is unconstitutional. For example, a statute that prohibits marriage between the races is clearly intended to prevent whites from marrying blacks, but the statute is not mandatory authority because it is in violation of the Constitution.

Federal enacted law can sometimes be mandatory authority in *state* courts. The United States Constitution is the highest authority in the country. If a provision of this Constitution applies, it controls over any state law to the contrary. Federal statutes and the regulations of federal agencies are also superior in authority to state laws in those areas entrusted to the federal government by the United States Constitution, e.g., regulation of interstate commerce, patents, bankruptcy, foreign affairs. Federal statutes and regulations in these areas are mandatory authority in state courts.

Can the enacted law of one state ever be mandatory authority in another state? Generally no, with two exceptions involving the principles of conflict of law and full faith and credit. We will consider these principles when we examine court opinions as mandatory authority.

2. COURT OPINIONS AS MANDATORY AUTHORITY

When is a court *required* to follow the holding of an opinion? We have already considered when an opinion is analogous or when it can be a precedent. There must be a sufficient similarity (a) between the key facts of the opinion and the facts of the current case (p. 181), and (b) between the rule of law that was interpreted and applied in the opinion and the rule of law that must be interpreted and applied in the current case (p. 189). We are now considering when an opinion is a *binding* precedent. This is another way of asking when it is mandatory authority. If the opinion is not on point, if it is not analogous because the similarity listed above does not exist, then the opinion cannot be mandatory authority; it is nonauthority.

To determine when an analogous opinion is binding, we must examine the relationship between the court that wrote the opinion and the court that is currently considering that opinion. Five variations will be briefly covered:

1. The highest court in the judicial system is considering an opinion written by a lower court in the same judicial system.

2. A court is considering an opinion written in the past by the same court.

3. A court in one state is considering an opinion written by a court from another state.

4. A state court is considering an opinion written by a federal court.

5. A federal court is considering an opinion written by a state court.

In each of these five situations a court is attempting to determine whether a prior opinion is binding in the litigation currently before the court. Assume that each opinion *is* analogous, i.e., the facts currently before the court are similar to the key facts in the opinion under consideration, and the rules of law are also similar.

1. *Lower Court Opinion Being Considered by a Higher Court in Same Judicial System.* A higher court is never required to follow an opinion written by a lower court in the same judicial system, whether or not the opinion is analogous. If the opinion is analogous, it can only be persuasive authority; the higher court can follow it if it chooses to do so.

2. *A Court Opinion Being Considered by the Same Court That Wrote the Opinion.* Does a court have to follow its *own* prior opinions? If for example, the Florida Supreme Court wrote an opinion in 1970, is that opinion mandatory authority for the Florida Supreme Court in 1988 if the facts before the court in 1988 are similar to the key facts in the 1970 opinion and the rules of law are similar? No. A court is always free to *overrule* its own prior opinions.

Suppose that the opinion was written by an intermediate or middle appeals court. Does that same court have to follow this opinion later if the opinion is analogous? No. *Any* court can later overrule itself and reach a holding that differs from the holding it reached in the earlier opinion so long as there is no opinion in existence written by a higher court that is contrary to the holding the middle appeals court now wants to reach.

3. *One State Court Considering an Opinion Written by Another State Court.* One state court, generally, does not have to follow an opinion written by another state court no matter how similar the opinion is. An Idaho court, for example, does not have to follow an opinion written by a Massachusetts court.

There are two main exceptions to the principle that an opinion of one state is not mandatory authority in another state. The first involves conflicts of law and the second, full faith and credit.

(a) Conflicts of Law Suppose that an accident occurs in New York, but the negligence suit based on this accident is brought in an Ohio state court. Assume that the Ohio court has subject-matter jurisdiction over the dispute and personal jurisdiction over the parties (p. 12). What negligence law does the Ohio court apply? Ohio negligence law or New York negligence law? The negligence law of the two states may differ in significant respects. This is a conflicts-of-law problem. Under the principles of the conflicts of law, a court of one state may be required to apply the law of another state. It may be, for example, that the law to be applied will be the law of the state where the injury occurred or the law of the state that is at the center of the dispute. If this state is deemed to be New York, then the Ohio court will apply New York negligence law. Analogous opinions of New York courts on the law of negligence will be mandatory authority in the Ohio court.

(b) Full Faith and Credit The United States Constitution provides that "Full Faith and Credit shall be given in each State to the public Acts, Records, and judicial Proceedings of every other State." Art. IV, § 1. Suppose that Richards sues Davis for breach of contract in Delaware. Davis wins. Richards cannot go to another state and bring a breach-of-contract suit against Davis in the other state arising out of the same facts. If the Delaware court had proper jurisdiction when it rendered its judgment, the Delaware opinion must be

given full faith and credit in every other state. The case cannot be relitigated. The Delaware opinion is mandatory authority in every other state.

4 and 5. *State Court Considering an Opinion Written by a Federal Court and Vice Versa.* The general rule is that state courts are the final arbiters of what the state law is, and federal courts are the final arbiters of what the federal law is. State courts do *not* have to follow opinions written by federal courts *unless* the issue before the state court involves a federal question—one arising out of the United States Constitution or out of a statute of Congress, e.g., does a state statute violate a provision of the United States Constitution? Federal courts do not have to follow state court opinions *except to the extent that* the federal court is determining what the state law is on a given topic.

Section C. Court Opinions as Persuasive Authority

When a court does not *have* to follow an opinion because it is not mandatory authority, it might still decide to follow it as persuasive authority.

A court could even adopt *dictum* in an opinion as persuasive authority. Recall that dictum is unnecessary commentary in an opinion on facts or laws that are not before the court that wrote the opinion, p. 168. Another court is certainly never required to follow dictum, but it is free to adopt the dictum if it finds it persuasive.

Sometimes a court is faced with a great deal of persuasive case authority from which to choose. How does a court decide which persuasive authority to select?

A number of factors go into a court's determination of whether a position taken in a prior opinion is persuasive enough to adopt. A judge will usually be interested in knowing how many other courts have adopted this position. Is there a "majority rule" or school of thought that has developed around the position? Has the opinion been frequently cited with approval? How well reasoned is the opinion? These considerations will help a judge decide whether to adopt an opinion as persuasive. Finally, it is human nature for judges to gravitate toward those opinions that are most in tune with their personal philosophies and biases—although preferences on this basis are never acknowledged.

Section D. Secondary Authority as Persuasive Authority

As we have seen, secondary authority is not the law itself. It was *not* written by the legislature, a court, an agency, a city council, etc. Secondary authority can never be mandatory authority; it can only be persuasive. In the following chart, there is an overview of the major kinds of secondary authority that a court could decide to rely upon in reaching its conclusion.

Summary of Secondary Authority		
Kind	**Contents**	**Examples**
1. Legal Encyclopedia	Summaries of the law, particularly case law, organized by topic.	*Corpus Juris Secundum* *American Jurisprudence 2d*
2. Nonlegal Encyclopedias	Summaries of many topics on science, the arts, history, etc.	*Encyclopaedia Britannica*
3. Legal Dictionaries	Definitions of legal terms taken almost exclusively from court opinions.	*Words and Phrases*
4. Legal Dictionaries	Definitions of legal terms that come from a variety of sources.	*Black's Law Dictionary* *Ballentine's Law Dictionary* West's *Legal Thesaurus/Dictionary*
5. Nonlegal Dictionaries	Definitions of all words in general use.	*Webster's Dictionary*
6. Legal Periodicals (general)	Phamphlets (later bound) containing articles written on a variety of legal topics.	*Harvard Law Review* *American Bar Association Journal*
7. Legal Periodicals (specialized)	Pamphlets (later bound) containing articals written on a specialized area of the law or subject matter.	*Journal of Family Law* *Journal of Legal Education*
8. Nonlegal Periodicals	Pamphlets on general topics.	*Newsweek* *Foreign Affairs*
9. Legal Treatises	Summaries of and commentaries on areas of the law.	*McCormick on Evidence* Johnstone and Hopson, *Lawyers and Their Work* *Restatement of the Law of Torts*
10. Nonlegal Treatises	Perspectives on a variety of topics.	Samuelson, *Economics*
11. Loose-Leaf Services	Collections of materials in three-ring binders covering current law in designated areas.	*Abortion Law Reporter* *Prison Law Reporter* Commerce Clearing House, *Products Liability Reporter*
12. Form Books, Manuals, Practice Books	Same as legal treatises with a greater emphasis on the "how-to-do-it" practical dimensions of the law.	Dellheim, *Massachusetts Practice* Moore's *Federal Practice* *American Jurisprudence, Pleading and Practice Forms Annotated*

13. Legal Newspapers	Daily or weekly compilations of information relevant to practice.	*Daily Washington Law Reporter* *National Law Journal*
14. Nonlegal Newspapers	General circulation newspapers.	*New York Times* *Detroit Free Press*

Some of these secondary authorities quote from the law itself, i.e., they quote primary authority. As a general rule, *you should never use someone else's quotation of the law.* Quote directly from the primary authority. Use the secondary authority to bolster your arguments on the interpretation of the primary authority. This is the main function of such secondary authority: to help you persuade a court to adopt a certain interpretation of primary authority. You are on very dangerous ground when you use secondary authority as a substitute for primary authority.

Secondary authority will frequently paraphrase primary authority, e.g., a treatise or legal encyclopedia will summarize the law of a particular state on a topic. You will be *very* tempted to use such summaries in your own legal writing. Before examining the dangers of such use, we will look at two excerpts, one from a treatise (*Prosser on Torts*, see Figure 16-1) and one from a legal encyclopedia (*Corpus Juris Secundum* see Figure 16-2). As you read these excerpts, note the following characteristics of each:

1. Each excerpt is clearly written.

2. Each excerpt is very quotable; it is very tempting to use parts of these excerpts in your own legal writing.

3. The footnotes in each excerpt contain many references (citations) to court opinions that are used to support the positions stated in the text. (These footnotes are excellent leads to case law.)

4. None of the opinions cited in the footnotes are analyzed in any depth; little attention is given to the issues or key facts in these opinions.

5. The opinions cited in the footnotes are from both federal and various state judicial systems.

6. While the excerpts do contain some specifics, in the main they consist of general statements about the law.

7. Both excerpts contain references to clusters of opinions: "early decisions," "some cases." The excerpts discuss several opinions as a group.

8. The authors of both excerpts write with an authoritative tone; they appear to have done their research and know what they are talking about.

––––––––

What is wrong, you might ask, with using quotes from such excerpts in your own legal memorandum, appellate brief, or other writing? While they can be used and sometimes *should* be used (with proper citation to avoid the charge of plagiarism), the difficulties with using quotes from such excerpts are as follows:

The privilege of necessity, whose basis has been said to be "a mixture of charity, the maintenance of the public good and self-protection," [91] has been recognized in a comparatively small number of cases which have dealt with the problem. It appeared very early in a decision permitting the Crown to enter private land and dig for saltpeter to make gunpowder,[92] and one allowing goods to be jettisoned from a boat during a storm in order to save the passengers.[93] Later cases permitted a traveler on a public highway to turn out to avoid a temporary obstruction, and pass over the adjoining land.[94] But the privilege was not recognized where the way was a private one, and the interest in having it open did not extend to the public.[95]

Out of these early decisions, two lines of cases have developed, involving so-called "public" and "private" necessity. Where the danger affects the entire community, or so many people that the public interest is involved,[96] that interest serves as a complete justification to the defendant who acts to avert the peril to all. Thus one who dynamites a house to stop the spread of a conflagration that threatens a town,[97] or shoots a mad dog in the street,[98] or burns clothing infected with smallpox germs,[1] or, in time of war, destroys property which should not be allowed to fall into the hands of the enemy[2] is not liable to the owner, so long as the emergency is great enough, and he has acted reasonably under the circumstances.

---

91. Winfield, Law of Torts, 1937, 62.

92. King's Prerogative in Saltpetre, 1607, 12 Co. Rep. 12, 77 Eng.Rep. 1294. Even earlier is Maleverer v. Spinke, 1538, 1 Dyer 35b, 73 Eng.Rep. 79.

93. Mouse's Case, 1609, 12 Co.Rep. 63, 77 Eng.Rep. 1341.

94. Taylor v. Whitehead, 1781, 2 Dougl. 745, 99 Eng.Rep. 475; Campbell v. Race, 1851, 7 Cush., Mass., 408; Morey v. Fitzgerald, 1884, 56 Vt. 487; Shriver v. Marion County Court, 1910, 66 W.Va 685, 66 S.E. 1062. Cf. Chicago & A. R. Co. V. Mayer, 1904, 112 Ill.App. 149 (defendant blocking highway); Dodwell v. Missouri Pac. R. Co., Mo.1964, 384 S. W.2d 643 (same).

95. Williams v. Safford, 1849, 7 Barb., N.Y., 309; Bullard v. Harrison, 1815, 4 M. & S. 387, 105 Eng.Rep. 877. But cf. Haley v. Colcord, 1879, 59 N.H. 7; Kent v. Judkins, 1865, 53 Me. 160.

96. The act must be for the purpose of protecting the public. A private benefit to the actor is not sufficient. Newcomb v.

Tisdale, 1881, 62 Cal. 575; Whalley v. Lancashire R. Co., 1884, 13 Q.B.D. 131; Grant v. Allen, 1874, 41 Conn. 156.

97. Surocco v. Geary, 1853, 3 Cal. 69; Conwell v. Emrie, 1850, 2 Ind. 35; Russell v. Mayor of New York, 1845, 2 Denio, N.Y., 461; American Print Works v. Lawrence, 1837, 23 N.J.L. 9, 590; Stocking v. Johnson Flying Service, 1963, 143 Mont. 61, 387 P.2d 312 (fighting forest fire).

98. Putnam v. Payne, 1816, 13 Johns., N.Y., 312.

1. Seavey v. Preble, 1874, 64 Me. 120; State v. Mayor of Knoxville, 1883, 80 Tenn. (12 Lea) 146. Cf. McGuire v. Amyx, 1927, 317 No. 1061, 297 S.W. 968 (committing suspected smallpox patient to pesthouse).

2. Harrison v. Wisdom, 1872, 7 Heisk., 54 Tenn., 99 (liquor); United States v. Caltex, Inc., 1952, 344 U.S. 149, rehearing denied, 344 U.S. 919 (stored petroleum and refinery). Cf. Juragua Iron Co. v. United States, 1909, 212 U.S. 297.

FIGURE 16–1. Excerpt from a Treatise. Source: William L. Prosser, *Handbook of the Law of Torts*, 4th ed. (St. Paul, Minn.: West Publishing Co., 1971), 125, § 24.

1. The excerpts are secondary authority, and the goal of your writing is to use primary authority to support your arguments.

2. The excerpts consist mainly of summaries of court opinions; these opinions should be *individually* analyzed before you use any of them in your writing. A student memo is on shaky ground when it discusses opinions as a group without analyzing the important ones. An experienced reader of such a memo will often suspect that the student is overly relying on a secondary authority even if the student does not cite the secondary authority being used.

3. The excerpts are based upon opinions from a variety of jurisdictions, and your legal writing must focus on the law of the jurisdiction in which the client is litigating the case.

In short, too much reliance upon such excerpts represents laziness in legal research and case analysis. It is sometimes not easy to find and apply case law. If someone else at least appears to have done all the work for you, why not use the secondary authority? The answers to this question are found in the three difficulties mentioned above.

§ 546(98). —— —— Treatment

A medical expert may testify as to the proper treatment to be administered or as to whether certain treatment was proper, necessary, or usual, although according to some decisions he cannot testify whether a practitioner in a particular case exercised ordinary skill or care.

Library References

Evidence ⬤⟞ 512.

A medical expert may testify to the proper treatment to be administered, or the probable effect of a lack thereof, or the probable result of a delay.

The witness may state whether he is familiar with the degree of care and skill of physicians and surgeons in good standing in the county during the time in question, and testify as to the usual and ordinary practice among physicans in the locality in treating a given injury, and whether certain treatment was proper, or whether the treatment under consideration was necessary, usual, or sanctioned by medical usage in the same locality.[7]

According to some cases, however, the medical witness cannot testify as to whether the treatment used was the usual and ordinary practice of the profession at the place and time. The witness can testify as to what constitutes skill in the profession in such a way. . . .

7. **U.S.**—Corpus Juris quoted at length in Corrigan v. U. S., C.C.A.Idaho, 82 F.2d 106, 108.

Ala.—Torrance v. Wells, 122 So. 322, 219 Ala. 384.

Ariz.—Butler v. Rule, 242 P. 436, 29 Ariz. 405.

Cal.—Gist v. French, 288 P.2d 1003, 136 C.A.2d 247.

Conn.—Green v. Stone, 176 A. 123, 119 Conn. 300.

Ga.—Pennsylvania Threshermen & Farmers Mut. Cas Ins. Co. v. Gilliam, 76 S.E.2d 834, 88 Ga.App. 451—Autry v. General Motors BOP Assembly Plant, 69 S.E.2d 697, 85 Ga.App. 500—Mayo v. McClung, 64 S.E.2d 330, 83 Ga.App. 548.

Ind.—Huber v. Protestant Deaconess Hospital Ass'n of Evansville, 133 N.E.2d 864, 127 Ind.App. 565.

Iowa.—Lowman v. Kuecker, 71 N.W.2d 586, 246 Iowa 1227—McGulpin v. Bessmer, 43 N.W.2d 121, 241 Iowa 1119.

Kan.—Flentie v. Townsend, 30 P.2d 132, 139 Kan. 82—James v. Grigsby, 220 P. 267, 114 Kan. 627—Corpus Juris quoted in Foreman v. Surber, 213 P. 667, 113 Kan. 42.

Md.—Galusca v. Dodd, 57 A.2d 313, 189 Md. 666.

Mich.—Winchester v. Chabut, 32 N.W.2d 358, 321 Mich. 114.

Mo.—Wojciechowski v. Coryell, App., 217 S.W. 638.

N.Y.—Burch v. Greenwald, 286 N.Y.S. 661, 247 App.Div. 471.

N.C.—Dickson v. Queen City Coach Co., 63 S.E.2d 297, 233 N.C. 167.

Or.—Darling v. Semler, 27 P.2d 886, 145 Or. 259—Hamilton v. Kelsey, 268 P. 750, 126 Or. 26 . . .

Before covering the *proper* use of secondary authority in your legal writing, the value of secondary authority and nonauthority *as a research tool* should be re-emphasized. Often the most valuable parts of these texts are the footnotes. The citations in the footnotes to court opinions (and to other authority) can be invaluable to you as you pursue your search for opinions "on point," i.e., for opinions that are analogous. Whether or not you quote directly from the secondary authority in your legal writing, if the secondary authority has led you to opinions that you eventually use in your writing (after proper legal analysis), the secondary authority will have been of tremendous service to you.

There is another service that secondary authority can provide, independent of whether you use the authority in your writing. As mentioned earlier, you will often be reading court opinions and doing legal research in areas of the law that are new to you. You may need help in trying to make sense out of what might appear to be quite formidable and esoteric areas of the law— with or without the inevitable Latin phrases. One approach is to read a chapter in a treatise or a section in a legal encyclopedia in order to:

- obtain an overview of the law under consideration in the opinion;
- obtain some of the basic definitions in the area.

Armed with this general understanding, you will be better equipped to resume your research and analysis in the unfamiliar area of law.

FIGURE 16–2.
Excerpt from a Legal Encyclopedia. Source: *32 Corpus Juris Secundum, Evidence* (St. Paul, Minn.: West Publishing Co., 1964), § 546(98).

Suppose that you want to *use* a quote from the secondary authority *in your legal writing*. What steps must you take in order to do so properly? What is the proper *foundation* for the use of secondary authority in legal writing? The following chart presents the steps that provide this foundation. The secondary authority mentioned in the chart is a treatise, although the steps apply equally to *any* type of secondary authority that you are thinking about using in your legal writing as possible persuasive authority.

**The Foundation for the Use of Secondary Authority in
Legal Writing as Possible Persuasive Authority**

1. You must satisfy yourself through independent legal research that the quote from the treatise that you want to use does not contradict any law (opinion, statute, constitutional provision, etc.) that exists in the jurisdiction where the client is litigating the case. Stated more simply: there must be no contrary mandatory authority.

2. If the quote from the treatise *does* contradict any such law, you cannot use the quote *unless* you satisfy yourself:

    (a) that the court before which the client is litigating the case has the power to change the law that contradicts what the treatise says and, in effect, adopt the treatise's statement as new law in the jurisdiction; and

    (b) that there is a reasonable likelihood that a court with such power is inclined to change the law.

You cannot avoid extensive legal research and painful case analysis simply by quoting from secondary authority—no matter how tempting the latter appears to be. Unless you have conducted exhaustive research and analysis of the relevant *mandatory* authority, you will be unable to establish the necessary foundation to use *secondary* authority.

Many well-written and comprehensively researched legal memoranda and appellate briefs will make very few references to secondary authority. Experienced advocates know that judges are suspicious of secondary authority. It is true that some secondary authorities are highly respected (e.g., *Prosser on Torts*, any of the *Restatements* of the American Law Institute). Yet even these must be used with caution. The preoccupation of a court is on primary authority. Before you use secondary authority in your writing, you must be sure that (a) the secondary authority is not used as a substitute for the primary authority, (b) the secondary authority is not unduly repetitive of the primary authority, (c) the secondary authority will be helpful to the court in adopting an interpretation of primary authority, particularly when there is not a great deal of primary authority on point, (d) you discuss the secondary authority after you have presented the primary authority, and (e) the foundation for the use of secondary authority (see above chart) can be demonstrated if needed.

Suppose that you find something in a treatise that does not contradict any law within the jurisdiction where the client is litigating the case but that concisely states the law that does exist. The treatise quote in such an example is, in effect, an accurate summary of the law. While you are on much safer ground in using such a quote, you should provide some indication in your legal writing that there is such a parallel between the law and the treatise quote. At the very least, you should state in your writing that the quote from the secondary authority is consistent with the law of the jurisdiction and be prepared to back up this statement if it is later challenged or questioned by anyone.

Finally, you may find statements in secondary authority that neither contradict nor summarize the law of your jurisdiction. The issue being discussed in the secondary authority may simply have never arisen in your jurisdiction. Such issues are usually called issues of "first impression." Again, you are on relatively safe ground in using such discussions in your legal writing. In fact, the use of secondary authority is usually most effective when it treats issues that have not yet been resolved in your jurisdiction. Courts are often quite receptive to adopting secondary authority as persuasive authority when novel questions or issues are involved.

Chapter Seventeen

Using and Abusing
Legislative History
in Legal Writing

What is legislative history? It is the record of everything that took place in the legislature prior to the enactment of a statute. The chart below contains the sequence of events of a hypothetical bill in Congress before it became law (a statute). In the left-hand column, the event is listed. In the right-hand column is the name of the document that will record and describe the event. The sum total of these documents constitutes the legislative history of the statute.

The theory of legislative history can be simply stated: if you know what occurred in the legislature before the statute became law, you might be aided in attempting to interpret the language that the legislature eventually used in the statute it enacted.

Legislative History of a Federal Statute (Hypothetical Sequence)	
Event	**Some of the Documents Describing the Event (The documents of legislative history)**
1. Member of Congress introduces a bill.	Statement of the Member on the need for legislation Printed Bill Congressional Record
2. House of Representatives Committee holds hearings on the bill.	Hearing transcripts

3. The bill is amended in Committee.	Printed amendment
4. The Committee writes its recommendations to the full House on the bill.	Committee Report
5. Debate on the House floor.	Congressional Record
6. House amends the bill.	Printed amendment Congressional Record
7. House passes the bill as amended.	Congressional Record
8. Senate Committee holds hearings on the bill.	Hearing transcripts
9. Committee adopts amendment to the bill.	Printed amendment
10. Committee amends the bill again.	Printed amendment
11. Committee writes its recommendations to the full Senate on the bill.	Committee Report
12. Debate on the Senate floor.	Congressional Record
13. Amendment to the bill is proposed.	Printed amendment Congressional Record
14. Senate rejects the amendment and passes the bill without the amendment.	Congressional Record
15. Conference Committee (consisting of House and Senate members) seeks a compromise on the House and Senate versions of the bill and makes its recommendations to the full Congress.	Conference Committee Report
16. Debate on House floor over the conference committee recommendations and final vote of the House.	Congressional Record
17. Debate on Senate floor over the Conference Committee recommendations and final vote of the Senate.	Congressional Record

In addition to the documents and books listed in the second column of the chart, the following sets of books will often also describe the events listed in the first column:

- U.S. Code Congressional & Administrative News
- CCH Congressional Index
- Congressional Information Service
- Information Handling Service (legislative histories on microfiche)
- Senate Journal; House Journal

- Digest of Public General Bills

- Etc.

As indicated in the chart, the sequence of events concerned a federal statute—one passed by Congress. The documents listed are available in most large law libraries. For state statutes, however, the picture is quite different. Although the legislative process may be very similar, the documents describing that process within state legislatures are often incomplete and difficult to obtain. For city councils and county boards of supervisors, the situation is even worse; it is almost impossible to trace the legislative history of an ordinance, particularly an old one.

The chart outlined the legislative history of a *new* statute covering a topic that had no prior legislation. Let us call this statute § 10. Suppose that five years after § 10 was enacted, the legislature amends it. (Note the difference between this kind of an amendment and the amendments treated in the chart above. The chart described amendments to a *bill* before it became law; here we are referring to an amendment of a *law*.) Just as the original § 10 has a legislative history, so too the amendment to § 10 will have its own legislative history since amendments to statutes must go through the same legislative process as the original statutes.

Of course, not all statutes have as extensive a legislative history as § 10. Not every bill is subjected to hearings, committee reports, etc. There are three factors that usually determine the extensiveness of the legislative history of a statute: the originality or novelty of the idea embodied in the statute, the number of people affected, and the cost of implementing the statute. There tends to be very little legislative history if the statute is not novel, if few people are affected, and if little money is involved.

How can legislative history assist you in interpreting a statute? The following four excerpts are from typical documents of legislative history. Note the emphasis in these excerpts on purpose and intent.

Excerpt from Statement of the
Legislator Who Introduced
a Bill to Amend a Statute

MR. BEALL. This amendment applies to page 74, line b. In that section of the bill, section 311, our objective is to require the Secretary of Health, Education and Welfare to conduct a study of the need for the label declaration of the common and usual name of every spice and flavoring used in the fabrication of a food for human consumption.

Excerpt from Debate on Senate Floor
Concerning a Senator's Understanding
of a Proposed Law (S.641, which is
the 641st bill considered by the Senate)

Mr. DOLE. The Senator believes that S. 641, the Consumer Food Act of 1976, will improve the regulation of food processing, and lead to increased consumer awareness of food content through more accurate labeling requirements.

The food surveillance sections of the bill will give FDA the authority to oversee safety procedures as established and practiced by the food processors. When substandard practices are discovered, FDA can demand improvement by setting safety assurance standards.

Excerpt from a Senate Committee Report

The Energy Reorganization Act of 1974, S. 2744, will consolidate the Federal Government's fragmented and uncoordinated energy research and development functions and, at the same time, upgrade the regulation of nuclear power.

To accomplish the first purpose, the act establishes the Energy Research and Development Administration (ERDA). It will be headed by a single Administrator who will exercise broad functions to explore and develop all possible sources of energy. The primary mission of ERDA is to develop the energy technologies that are necessary to give the Nation the capability to attain energy self-sufficiency by as early as 1984.

Excerpt from a Conference Committee Report

The U.S. Parole Commission shall consider the following information, if available and relevant, in parole release determinations: (1) reports and recommendations of prison staff; (2) prior criminal record; (3) presentence investigation reports; (4) recommendations of the sentencing judge; (5) reports of physical, mental, or psychiatric examination; and (6) such other additional relevant information as is available, including information submitted by the prisoner.

It is also the intent of the Conferees that availability and relevance act as limitations on the Commission's responsibility to consider this material. In terms of availability, for example, if a judge has not commented on the sentence or parole of the offender, the Commission is under no duty to solicit such commentary.

———

Once you have a statute before you, your major concern is: what does the statute mean in the context of the facts of the client's case? What is the legislative intent? What is the legislative purpose of the statute (p. 154)? You first attempt to determine what the statute means to you: what do *you* think the legislature intended by the language in the statute? What is the "plain meaning" of this language? You then attempt to determine whether your interpretation has any judicial support by locating any opinions that have interpreted the statute. Next, you do research on the legislative history of the statute to determine if it can aid you in interpreting the statute.

In the documents of legislative history, there may be statements on why the bill was introduced, on what prompted the legislature to enact the statute, on the evil or problem the legislature was trying to solve by the statute, etc. In your legal writing you can quote such statements to support a particular interpretation of the statute.

Suppose that you are trying to interpret the word "training" in § 85 of a statute that authorized public money to be spent "for the training and rehabilitation of veterans of foreign wars." The client of your office is a veteran who is seeking a payment under § 85 for on-the-job training at a mechanic's shop. The question of legislative intent is whether the word "training" in § 85 means formal academic (classroom) training at an educational institution or whether it can include on-the-job training.

As you trace the legislative history of § 85, it would obviously be helpful if you could find statements among the documents such as:

The purpose of this bill is to provide monies that will encourage a *variety of mechanisms* that will insure the training and rehabilitation of veterans. [Emphasis added]

Mr. SMITH. Would I be correct in concluding that the Senator from North Dakota feels that the passage of this bill would mean that *private industry could receive funds* for assisting veterans? [Emphasis added]

Mr. JONES: The Senator from South Carolina is correct.

In your legal memorandum or appellate brief, you would want to quote the above passage in support of the position that when the legislature passed § 85, it did *not* intend to limit training to formal classroom training.

There are a number of difficulties, however, in using legislative history.

1. STUDENTS SOMETIMES CONFUSE LEGISLATIVE HISTORY WITH THE LAW

The documents of legislative history constitute no more than *possible evidence* of what the legislature had in mind when it enacted the statute. These documents are not the law itself.

2. IT IS EXTREMELY DIFFICULT TO DETERMINE THE COLLECTIVE INTENT OF HUNDREDS OF LEGISLATORS WHO VOTED FOR THE STATUTE

Different legislators may vote for statutes for different reasons. There is no guarantee that any document in the legislative history of a statute or any particular quote within such a document will accurately reflect what the entire legislature intended.

3. SOME LEGISLATORS PURPOSELY "PUMP" THE DOCUMENTS WITH POSITIONS AND COMMENTS IN THE HOPE OF INFLUENCING THOSE OF US WHO WILL BE RESEARCHING THESE DOCUMENTS

There is an old saying among legislators that if you can't win the statute, try to win the legislative history. Suppose that a legislator wants to have a statute phrased in a certain way. The legislator, however, does not have the votes to support this version of the statute. He or she then fills or "pumps" the record (i.e., the documents of legislative history) with statements, reports, studies, etc., that would tend to support a particular interpretation of the language of the statute. What could not be achieved directly is tried indirectly. Legislators know that researchers (lawyers, judges, paralegals, students, etc.) will be combing the legislative history for clues to interpretation. It's fair game, according to many legislators, to "plant" material in this history to influence our conclusions on interpretation.

If different legislators taking different positions on the meaning of a statute all attempt to "pump" the record in this way, there may not be much hope of obtaining a coherent picture of legislative intent through the documents of legislative history.

———

In spite of all these difficulties and qualifications, however, the pursuit of legislative history is well worth your time. In fact, the failure to pursue it is often the sign of a poor researcher.

How you use legislative history in your legal writing depends in part upon your audience. If you are writing an external memorandum of law (p. 11) or an appellate brief, you will obviously what to pick and choose among what you find in the documents of legislative history to support the interpretation of the statute that is most favorable to the client of your office. In an interoffice memorandum of law (p. 10), you will do the same, except that you will be much more frank and open about anything in these documents that is *not* favorable to the client.

Chapter Eighteen

Writing the Memorandum of Law

Overview of Chapter:

A. Kinds of legal memoranda

B. The structure of a "simple" interoffice memorandum of law

C. The structure of a "complex" interoffice memorandum of law

D. The structure of an external memorandum of law

E. Model interoffice or internal memorandum of law

F. Common mistakes made in legal writing

G. Memorandum assignments

Section A. Kinds of Legal Memoranda

A memorandum of law is a written analysis of a legal problem. There are two main kinds of memoranda: (1) an internal or interoffice memorandum, and (2) an external or advocacy memorandum. The major difference between the two is their audience.

1. INTEROFFICE MEMORANDUM OF LAW

The main audience of your interoffice memo is your supervisor; the memo is an internal document. Your goal in the memo is to analyze the law in order to make a *prediction* of how a court or other tribunal will resolve the dispute in the client's case. It is extremely important that this memo present the strengths *and weaknesses* of your client's case. The supervisor must make strategy decisions based in part on what you say in the memo. Hence the supervisor must have a realistic picture of what the law is.

2. EXTERNAL OR ADVOCACY MEMORANDUM OF LAW

The main audience of your external memo is someone outside the office, usually a judge or official in an administrative agency. Your goal in this memo is to try to convince the reader to take a certain action in the client's case. Hence, the memo is an *advocacy* document. You will be highlighting the strengths of the client's case and the weaknesses of the opponent's case.

Different terminology is sometimes used for this kind of memo:

• *Points and Authorities Memorandum:* an external memorandum submitted to a trial or appellate court;

• *Trial Memorandum:* an external memorandum submitted to a trial court;

• *Hearing Memorandum:* an external memorandum submitted to a hearing officer or Administrative Law Judge within an administrative agency.

When the document is submitted to an appellate court, it is called an *appellate brief.* The structure of the appellate brief will be considered in Chapter 21.

———

Most of the discussion that follows will be on the internal-interoffice memo. The external-advocacy memo will be mentioned only when there are significant differences.

Section B. The Structure of a "Simple" Interoffice Memorandum of Law

By "simple" memo we mean a relatively short document (under fifteen pages) in which no more than two client issues are discussed.

What is the format or structure of such a memo? The cardinal rule is: find out what format your supervisor prefers. There may be office memos in old files that can be used as models. If your supervisor does not express a preference, consider using the following format:

1. Heading
2. Statement of the assignment
3. Issue(s)
4. Facts
5. Analysis

6. Conclusion

7. Recommendations

1. HEADING

The heading of the memo contains basic information about you and the nature of the memo:

a. A caption centered at the top of the page stating the kind of document it is (Interoffice Memorandum of Law)

b. The name of the person to whom the memo is addressed (usually your supervisor)

c. Your name

d. The date your memo was completed and submitted

e. The name of the case (client's name and opponent, if any)

f. The office file number (usually keyed to the office filing system)

g. The court docket number (if the suit has already been filed and the clerk of the court has assigned a docket number)

h. The subject matter of the memo following the notation "RE:" meaning "in the matter of" or "concerning."

The following example illustrates how this information might be set forth in a memo written on behalf of the client Brown who is suing Miller:

```
                    INTEROFFICE MEMORANDUM OF LAW
    TO:     Jane Patterson
    FROM:   Paul Jackson
    DATE:   March 13, 1984              RE:   Whether substituted
    CASE:   Brown v. Miller                   service is allowed
    OFFICE FILE NUMBER:  84-1168              under Civil Code
    DOCKET NUMBER C-34552-84                  § 34-403(g)
```

Note that the subject-matter description (RE) in this example briefly indicates the nature of the question that will be treated in the memorandum. This information is needed for at least two reasons. First, the average law office case file will contain a large number of documents, often including several legal memoranda. A heading that at least briefly indicates the nature of the subject of each memorandum makes it easier to locate the memorandum in the client's file. Secondly, it is unlikely that the usefulness of your memorandum will end when the client's case is closed. Many law offices maintain fairly extensive libraries of old office memoranda, catalogued and filed by subject matter for reference in future cases. This avoids unnecessary and costly duplication of research time in the event that a similar question arises in a future client's case. The subject-matter heading on your memorandum facilitates the cataloguing and filing of your memorandum in such a library.

The inclusion of the date on which the memorandum was completed and submitted is important for similar reasons. While your analysis and conclusions may have been accurate at the time the memorandum was written, subsequent changes in the law may have occurred by the time the memorandum is referred to by you or by someone else in the office. When the reader sees the date of the memorandum, he or she will know from what date subsequent legal research will be needed.

2. STATEMENT OF THE ASSIGNMENT

Soon after you are given an interoffice memorandum assignment, you should write out what you are asked to do. State the parameters of the assignment. If limitations or restrictions were imposed, e.g., not to cover a particular issue, include them in your written statement. If you have any difficulty writing the statement, consult with your supervisor immediately. The time to clarify what you are to do—and what you are not to do—is before you start spending extensive amounts of time researching, analyzing, and writing. For example:

> Statement of Assignment
>
> You have asked me to prepare a memorandum of law limited to the question of whether our client, Joan Davis, is required to return the overpayment she received from the Department of Revenue and Disbursements. You asked me to discuss Ohio law only.

Should you include this statement of the assignment in your memorandum? The answer is yes *if* this statement does not simply repeat what was summarized in the subject-matter or RE notation of the heading.

3. STATEMENT OF THE ISSUE(S)

Earlier in this text we covered the statement of issues in *court opinions* that you are briefing (p. 137). These issues, of course, grew out of the litigation that led to the opinion. We now turn to the statement of issues in a current *client case:*

a. The structure of client issues

b. Translating client objectives into client issues

c. Advocacy in phrasing client issues

d. Contingency client issues

e. The reformulation of client issues.

(a) The Structure of Client Issues Client issues (like those found in court opinions) can be phrased in two formats: shorthand and complete. A shorthand statement of the issue consists primarily of a reference to the rule of law being interpreted, e.g., "Did Jones violate § 46 by failing to file the application?" "Has the plaintiff established proximate cause?" A complete statement of the client issue consists of:

- A reference to the rule of law being applied in the client's case (e.g., a statute or common law doctrine);
- A very short quote from the language in this rule of law that is in contention in the client's case;
- A statement of the essential facts from the client's case that raises the question of the applicability of this language in the rule of law.

For example:

> **Issue:** Does water withdrawn from the Sol River used to cool a solar furnace and discharged back into the river constitute "refuse matter" under § 13 of the Rivers and Harbors Act of 1933 that bans dumping such matter into navigable waters?

Your issues in a memorandum of law should be complete statements of issues as in this example. You can use the shorthand statement for the subject-matter portion of the heading of the memo (following the "RE" notation), but for the statement of the issues in the body of the memo itself, provide complete statements.

(b) Translating Client Objectives into Client Issues There is a vast range of objectives that a client can have, e.g., determining the legality of a proposed business transaction, forcing someone to pay for the harm caused the client, avoiding payment for harm that someone has claimed the client has caused, obtaining a divorce, preventing conviction for a crime, obtaining release from prison. The law office begins with these broad objectives or goals of the client.

At this stage, the issues are phrased in very general terms, e.g., is it legal for these two corporations to merge, does the tax have to be paid, has negligence been committed, do the grounds for divorce exist, has a crime been committed? Through client interviews and field investigation, the office collects detailed facts on the case. The search then begins for rules of law that potentially apply to these facts, e.g., statutes, regulations, constitutional provisions, common law doctrines. The office may already be familiar with some of these rules due to prior representation of clients with similar problems. The law library, of course, is the main depository of the rules of law. The facts of the case must be thoroughly researched. Out of this mixture of client objectives, facts, and the products of legal research, the office moves toward a more *narrow* and focused statement of the legal issues in the case.

Based upon the preliminary analysis that the office has done thus far, the following critical question is asked:

> According to the potentially applicable rules of law, what specific things must the client establish in order to achieve the objective sought, and which of these specifics, if any, may present difficulties in being established?

The answer to this question serves a number of important interrelated functions:

- It gives the office further direction in the ongoing process of assisting the client.
- It is the basis for a further narrowing of the legal issues.

• It is the organizational principle around which the entire memorandum of law is structured. Everything in the memo should be geared to answering this question.

For example, suppose that the initial objective of the client is to avoid paying an excise tax. The general issue is: does the tax have to be paid? All the relevant facts are collected by the office through interviews and investigation. Legal research on these facts takes place in the library. Potentially applicable statutes and regulations are examined. Potentially analogous opinions are briefed. You then come to a preliminary analysis as in the following hypothetical example:

> Based upon what we know thus far, the client can avoid paying the excise tax if we can establish that:
> i.   the client is a "taxpayer" within the meaning of § 54.9 of the statutory code;
> ii. the client was incorporated in this state after February 12, 1963;
> iii. the client had "net disposable income" in excess of the "base period" within the meaning of § 54.9(c) of the statutory code.
> We should have no problem establishing the first two items. The third, however, will be our main hurdle.

Now the office has further direction on what must be done. We know that no problem is expected on the first two conditions listed above. Perhaps all that must be done is some paperwork to show that the client is a "taxpayer" and was incorporated in the state after February 12, 1963. Some difficulty, however, *is* anticipated in establishing that there was "net disposable income" in excess of the "base period" under the code. This difficulty becomes the catalyst for a further narrowing of the issue. Initially, we asked: does the tax have to be paid? Now we can formulate a more narrow issue. For example:

> When a corporation has had income within the last five years but has not been able to declare any dividends during this time, does the corporation have "net disposable income" in excess of the "base period" under § 54.9(c) for purposes of being relieved of the duty to pay excise taxes?

This is the issue that will require the greatest attention from the office. Negotiation and perhaps even litigation may center on this issue.

The interoffice memorandum of law that you write will concentrate on this issue. Your memo may also touch upon the other two requirements for avoiding the tax (as to which no difficulties were anticipated), but the heart of your memo will be an analysis of the interpretation of "net disposable income" and "base period" within § 54.9(c).

Note the process that we went through in the identification of the issue to be treated in the memo. We began with the client objectives. We collected all the facts of the case and researched them in the library. We found potentially applicable rules of law. Our preliminary assessment of these rules of law led us to a list of requirements or conditions that must be established in order to achieve the client objective. We divided the list into those requirements that the client will probably have no difficulty establishing and those requirements that may pose difficulties. The legal issues were based upon the latter. Each anticipated difficulty became the basis of a separate issue.

This then is how client objectives are translated into legal issues to be treated in a memorandum of law.

(c) Advocacy in Phrasing Client Issues It is usually possible to state the same issue in several different ways, some of which are more favorable to the client than others. Compare, for example, the following two statements of the same negligence issue involving Smith (the plaintiff) and Johnson (the defendant). Can you tell which side wrote which issue?

Is Johnson the proximate cause of Mrs. Smith's heart attack (her second within two months) that occurred in a panic when she saw Johnson hit a curb and a tree on the opposite side of the street as she rushed to catch a bus?	Is Johnson the proximate cause of Mrs. Smith's heart attack, which she suffered when she thought Johnson's car was going to strike her as she observed him jump a curb and hit a tree in the immediate vicinity of where she was trying to board a bus?

The first version of the issue favors the defendant. It phrases some of the facts differently from the plaintiff and includes some not mentioned by the latter:

• This was her second heart attack within two months, suggesting that she is highly prone to such attacks.

• She "rushed" to catch a bus, suggesting that she may have caused her own heart attack. The plaintiff phrases this fact more innocently: "trying to board a bus."

• The defendant says that Johnson "hit a curb." The plaintiff is more dramatic; "jump a curb."

• The defendant tries to emphasize the distance between the impact and the location of Mrs. Kennedy: the curb and the tree were "on the opposite side of the street" from Mrs. Kennedy. The plaintiff, on the other hand, says that all this happened "in the immediate vicinity of where she was."

• Plaintiff explicitly says that "she thought Johnson's car was going to strike her." The defendant merely implies this fact by saying that she was "in a panic."

The component of the issue that is most susceptible to advocacy "manipulation" is the factual component. It is often possible to obtain a slightly more favorable wording of the issue simply by emphasizing those facts most favorable to the client and downplaying those facts that are most damaging. You should *not,* however, completely ignore damaging facts if they are essential to the issue. You opponent will surely include them in its statement of the issue, making the absence of these facts in your own statement very conspicuous.

One effective means of de-emphasizing an unfavorable fact is to describe it only briefly and in broad general terms. Similarly, if a fact is highly favorable to the client's position, it may be helpful to emphasize that fact be describing it in specific, detailed terms. In a suit brought against a factory by a neighboring homeowner, for example, suppose that the issue is whether emissions from the factory constitute an equitably abatable nuisance. The homeowner, in stating this issue, might describe the emissions as "heavy black substances that often obscure visibility to a distance of twenty feet and that contain lead and other materials dangerous to health." The factory, on the other hand, may describe it simply as "smoke."

Most concepts in the English language can be expressed by more than one word. Often each of these words, while they have the same general meaning, will convey slightly different emotional impacts. If you were describing an automobile collision, for example, you might say that defendant:

- made contact with plaintiff's vehicle
- hit plaintiff's vehicle
- struck plaintiff's vehicle
- collided with plaintiff's vehicle
- rammed plaintiff's vehicle
- smashed into plaintiff's vehicle

Earlier we said that an interoffice memorandum must provide the strengths *and* weaknesses of the client's case. You certainly are emphasizing the strengths when you phrase issues in the most pro-client way possible. Since, however, you must also tell your supervisor about the weaknesses of the client's case, you should consider including a statement of the issues in the way that you anticipate your opponent will phrase them in a light favorable to its client.

Assignment #32

Jones has a swimming pool in his back yard. The pool is intended for use by the Jones family members and their guests when an adult is there to supervise. One hot summer night, a neighbor's child opens an unlocked door of a fence that surrounds the Jones' yard and goes into the pool. (There is no separate fence around a pool.) The child knows that he is not supposed to be there without an adult. No one else is at the pool. The child drowns.

The estate of the deceased child sues Jones under § 10, which provides that "property owners are liable for the foreseeable harm that occurs on their property." The main issue in the case is the forseeability of the death.

(a) Phrase the foreseeability issue in the light most favorable to Jones.

(b) Phrase the foreseeability issue in the light most favorable to the estate of the deceased child.

(c) Phrase the foreseeability issue objectively or in as neutral a fashion as possible.

(d) **Contingency Client Issues** Suppose that there are two issues in the client's case: liability and damages. The liability issue is whether the client is responsible for the harm that was caused. The damage issue is how much the client must pay. The damage issue, of course, does not even arise if the liability issue is resolved in favor of the client; there are no damages if the client is not liable. The damage issue is a *contingency* issue: it comes into play only if a prior issue is resolved in a certain way.

Your memo must discuss contingency issues no matter how confident you are that the prior issues will eventually be resolved in favor of your client. In the above example, you certainly analyze the liability issue. You also analyze the damage issue *on the assumption* that you may ultimately lose the liability issue. At the time you write your memo, you have no way of predicting with certainty how a court might resolve the liability issue. Hence, you must be prepared to discuss those issues that are dependent on the resolution of prior issues.

(e) The Reformulation of Client Issues Be prepared to rewrite and rewrite the client issues. Although the client issues are stated toward the beginning of the memo, they probably should be the *last* item that you write in final draft. The more you analyze a problem, the more you will find yourself reworking the issues. The more legal research you do, the more you will find yourself reworking the issues. As indicated, legal issues should be narrowly stated. Perhaps you will later conclude that your initial draft of the issues was too broad. Perhaps an issue should be subdivided into several smaller issues. New facts may materialize through further investigation into the client's case. This may call for a reformulation of the issues. It is fine to begin your analysis with a *draft* of the issues. Be prepared, however, for redrafting.

4. STATEMENT OF THE FACTS

Your statement of the facts of the client's case is probably the most important component of your memorandum. You should take great pains to see that it is concise, highly accurate, and well organized.

(a) Conciseness. An unduly long fact statement will serve only to frustrate the reader. Try to eliminate any unnecessary facts from the statement. One way of doing this is to carefully review your fact statement *after* you have completed your analysis of the issues. If there are facts in your statement that are not subsequently referred to in your analysis, consider eliminating those facts in your final draft of the memorandum.

(b) Accuracy. The temptation will be to indulge in wishful thinking—to ignore adverse facts and to assume that disputed facts will be resolved in favor of the client. Do not give in to this temptation. In an interoffice memo, you must assess the legal consequences of favorable *and* unfavorable facts.

If a particular fact is presently unknown, put aside your writing, if possible, and investigate to determine what evidence exists to prove the fact one way or the other. If it is not practical to conduct an investigation at the present time, then you should provide an analysis of what law will apply based upon your most reasonable estimate of what an investigation may uncover.

The need for accuracy does not mean that you avoid stating the facts in the light most favorable to the client. It simply means that you must be cautious in doing so to avoid making false or misleading statements of fact. It also means that you analyze the favorable and unfavorable facts.

(c) Organization. A disorganized statement of facts will not only prevent the reader from understanding the events in question, but will also interfere with his or her understanding of your subsequent analysis. In general, it is best to start with a brief, one-or-two-sentence summary of the nature of the case followed by a *chronologically* ordered statement of the detailed facts. Occasional variations from strict chronological order can be effective so long as they do not interfere with the flow of the story.

5. ANALYSIS

At this point in your memo you analyze the primary authority and the secondary authority (p. 203) that you feel will help resolve the client issues that you identified earlier.

Start out by presenting the central rule of law that you need to analyze, e.g., a statute, regulation, constitutional provision, common law doctrine. Quote the pertinent portions of the rule of law relevant to the client's problem. Break the rule down into its major components or elements. For example:

> The first issue to be discussed in this memo is the applicability of § 548, which provides that "no license shall be issued unless a registered applicant has presented sufficient evidence of solvency, and operates in an area designated by the Secretary as in immediate need of development." Three things must be shown:
>
> **(a)** the applicant must be "registered";
>
> **(b)** the applicant must present "sufficient evidence of solvency";
>
> **(c)** the Secretary has "designated" the area as "in immediate need of development."
>
> I will discuss each of these requirements separately.

By breaking the rule of law into elements in this way, you have a useful organizational structure for the memo. The memo is organized under the (a)(b)(c) topics. You spend the most time analyzing those elements that are most likely to be in contention.

Your presentation of case law is integrated into the analysis. If, for example, there are opinions interpreting § 548, you analyze them here. You compare the key facts (p. 181), rules of law (p. 189), etc.

Do this for *every* rule of law that you uncovered in the library through legal research as potentially applicable to the client's case. If the issue involves a combination of rules of law (e.g., whether a regulation is validly based on a statute; whether a statute violates the Constitution), each rule is treated in the same way: break it down into elements, discuss one element at a time (concentrating on the elements most in contention), and integrate any available case law.

Secondary authority (e.g., law review article) is also integrated into the analysis according to the guidelines presented in Chapter 16 (p. 203).

An interoffice memo should include a *counteranalysis*. The memo must not be one-sided. Strengths and weaknesses must be analyzed. What would the other side say about your positions? For every argument you make in the memo, ask yourself this question: is it likely that the *other side* will agree with what I have just written? If you think it would not agree or if you have any doubt about whether it would agree, spend some time analyzing what its response would probably be. Explain why you have doubts about whether the argument would be disputed.

6. CONCLUSION

Here you provide your personal views on which side has the better arguments on the issues. Which side do you think will prevail on each issue? State why you reach these conclusions unless the reasons are clear from the body of the memo.

7. RECOMMENDATIONS

What concretely do you recommend as a result of the analysis and conclusions you have presented? What do you think are the next steps? Should a suit be filed? Should further investigation be undertaken? Further research in the library? Be specific in the recommendations that you feel are appropriate.

———

The following is an outline of the structure of a relatively uncomplicated interoffice memorandum of law.

```
           INTEROFFICE MEMORANDUM OF LAW
  TO:    [name of supervisor]
  FROM:  [your name]
  DATE:  [date memo is submitted]
  CASE:  [client file name]      RE: [subject matter of memo]
  OFFICE FILE NUMBER:
  DOCKET NUMBER:

  STATEMENT OF ASSIGNMENT  [what your supervisor has asked you to do]
  ISSUE(S)
  FACTS
  ANALYSIS  [discussion of primary and secondary authority with
            counteranalysis]
  CONCLUSION
  RECOMMENDATIONS  [next steps]
```

Section C. The Structure of a "Complex" Interoffice Memorandum of Law

By "complex" memo, we mean one that is relatively long (fifteen pages or more) in which three or more issues are discussed. This definition is not absolute. Common sense is the main guide. Use the more involved structure to be discussed here whenever you feel that this structure would increase the readability and appearance of the memo.

The following is an outline of the structure of a more complex memo. The components prefaced by an asterisk (*) are the only ones that will differ from the structure we just examined:

    1. Heading
* 2. Table of Contents
* 3. Table of Authorities
* 4. Summary of Issues and Conclusions
    5. Statement of the Assignment
    6. Facts
    7. Analysis
    8. Conclusions
    9. Recommendations
*10. Appendix

We will examine components 2, 3, 4, and 10. All the other components will be the same in simple and in complex interoffice memos.

1. TABLE OF CONTENTS

The table of contents is placed at the beginning of the memo, just after the heading. In this table, list the major topics to be treated in the memo with the page number where each topic begins in the memo. The statement of the topic should be brief, e.g., a word or two that capsulizes each issue or sub-issue. For example:

```
                        Table of Contents

                                                      Page
     I. Liability of Jones for negligence ...................   4
    II. The defense of contributory negligence .............   7
   III. Damages ............................................   13
    IV. Potential discovery problems .......................   17
     V. Etc.
```

2. TABLE OF AUTHORITIES

After the table of contents, include a *table of authorities* in which you list every primary and secondary authority that you will cover in the analysis of the memo with the page numbers where each authority is discussed. First present all the primary authority. List all the cases together (with citations) in alphabetical order. List all the statutes together (with citations), etc. Then list all the secondary authority, if any, that you use (with citations). For example:

```
                        Table of Authorities
                                                            Page
CASES
    Smith v. Jones, 24 F.2d 445 (5th Cir. 1970) ................2,4,12
    Zale v. Richard, 34 Miss. 650, 65 S. 109 (1930) ............3,9
CONSTITUTIONAL PROVISIONS
    Art. 5, Miss. Constitution ................................12,17
    Art. 7, Miss. Constitution ................................20
STATUTES
    Miss. Code Ann. § 23(b) (1978) ...........................2,8,23
    Miss. Code Ann. § 45 (1978) ..............................7
LAW REVIEW ARTICLES
    Colom, W., ''Sex Discrimination in the 1980s,'' 35 Miss.
        Law Journal 268 (1982) ................................19
Etc.
```

3. SUMMARY OF ISSUES AND CONCLUSIONS

At the beginning of the memo, give a complete statement of every issue that you will discuss in the analysis of the memo plus a brief summary of your personal conclusion as to how you think each issue will probably be resolved. At a glance, the reader will have an overview of all the issues that will be treated in the memo along with your conclusions.

In the body of the analysis, there is no need to repeat each issue as it is discussed unless you think that this repetition will be of assistance to the reader who would otherwise have to flip back to the beginning of the memo for a statement of the next issue to be discussed.

4. APPENDIX

Occasionally you may want to provide certain information that you do not feel should go in the body of the memo, e.g., charts, statistical data, photographs. Include them in an appendix at the end of the memo.

––––––––

The following is an outline of the structure of the complex interoffice memorandum of law (assume that the memo has five issues):

```
                    INTEROFFICE MEMORANDUM OF LAW
TO:       [name of supervisor]
FROM:     [your name]
DATE:     [date memo is submitted]
CASE:     [client file name]         RE:  [subject matter of memo]
OFFICE FILE NUMBER:
DOCKET NUMBER:

TABLE OF CONTENTS  [the main topics to be treated in memo]
TABLE OF AUTHORITIES  [list of primary and secondary authority to be
                            treated in memo]
SUMMARY OF ISSUES AND CONCLUSIONS
          A.  Issue I
              Conclusion I
          B.  Issue II
              Conclusion II
          C.  Issue III
              Conclusion III
          D.  Issue IV
              Conclusion IV
          E.  Issue V
              Conclusion V
STATEMENT OF ASSIGNMENT  [what your supervisor has asked you to do]
FACTS
ANALYSIS  [discussion of primary and secondary authority with
          counteranalysis; each issue is separately treated]
          A.  Issue I
          B.  Issue II
          C.  Issue III
          D.  Issue IV
          E.  Issue V
CONCLUSIONS
RECOMMENDATIONS  [next steps]
APPENDIX
```

Section D. The Structure of an External Memorandum of Law

An external memorandum of law is addressed to someone outside the office, e.g., a judge, an agency hearing officer. This memo will obviously *not* dwell on the weaknesses in the case of the client; it will concentrate on the strengths.

Major differences may also exist in the format of the memo itself. You will have to check with the court or agency where you will be submitting the memo to see if it has any specifications or requirements for the format of the heading, whether a table of authorities must be included, etc.

```
┌─────────────────────────────────────────────────────────┐
│                                                          │
│     SUPERIOR COURT OF THE DISTRICT OF COLUMBIA           │
│                  CIVIL DIVISION                          │
│                                                          │
│   ROBERT G. BARNES                  *                    │
│            Plaintiff                                     │
│                                     *                    │
│                                                          │
│       v.                            *     C-34553-75     │
│                                                          │
│   GEMINI REPAIR SHOP, INC.          *                    │
│            Defendant                *                    │
│                                                          │
│   MEMORANDUM OF DEFENDANT GEMINI REPAIR SHOP, INC.       │
│                                                          │
└─────────────────────────────────────────────────────────┘
```

FIGURE 18–1. Example of a Heading of a Memorandum to be Submitted to a Trial Court.

```
┌───────────────────────────────────────────────┐
│                                                │
│        Claimant's Memorandum of Law            │
│             in the matter of                   │
│             ALFRED R. OWENS                     │
│       before the Hearing Examiner              │
│                  for the                       │
│      Department of Public Assistance           │
│          Respectfully submitted by             │
│            George W. Bynum                     │
│          Attorney for Claimant                 │
│            1609 Hobart St.                      │
│            Flint, Mich. 40585                   │
│            (313) 791-4281                       │
│            December 14, 1976                    │
│                                                │
└───────────────────────────────────────────────┘
```

FIGURE 18–2. Example of a Heading of a Memorandum to Be Submitted to an Administrative Agency.

Figure 18-1 is an example of the heading of a memorandum to be submitted to a trial court. The number to the right is the docket number assigned by the clerk of the court to the case. Every document submitted in the litigation will contain this same docket number.

Figure 18-2 is an example of the heading of a memorandum to be submitted to an administrative agency.

Section E. Model Interoffice or Internal Memorandum of Law

The model memo that begins on page 236 is based on one of the opinions in the appendix of this book—*Stephens v. Dept. of State Police,* p. 302. Before you read the memo, it is recommended that you read or reread the opinion. The model follows the format of a relatively uncomplex memo presented earlier in the chapter (p. 222). Assume that your supervisor, Mr. J. Hill, has asked you to determine whether Gary Crawford was illegally dismissed from his job in Oregon.

Assume further that, after thoroughly researching the law in the state of Oregon, you find that the only relevant authorities are the following:

A. *Oregon Revised Statutes 408.240* (1973):
(1) Whenever any public officer or employee leaves a position after June 24, 1950, whether voluntarily or involuntarily, in order to perform military duty, such office or position shall not become vacant, nor shall the officer or employee be subject to removal as a consequence thereof.

B. *Oregon Revised Statutes 408.210* (1973):
As used in this Act, the term "military duty" shall include training and service performed by an inductee, enlistee or reservist or any entrant into a temporary component of the Armed Forces of the United States...but does not include active duty training as a reservist in the Armed Forces of the United States or as a member of the National Guard of the United States where the call is for a period of 15 days or less.

C. *Oregon Revised Statutes 905.788* (1973):
The Superintendent of the Department of Fish and Game Conservation shall have the power to dismiss any employee for absence without leave or for insubordination....

D. *Stephens v. Dept. of State Police*, p. 302.

INTEROFFICE MEMORANDUM OF LAW

TO: Mr. J. Hill
FROM: [your name]   RE: Validity of dismis-
DATE: March 26, 1988   sal of Crawford from
CASE: Crawford v. Dept.   Dept. of Fish and
        of Fish and Game   Game Conservation
        Conservation   under ORS 408.240,
OFFICE FILE NUMBER: 88-101   408.210, and 905.788
DOCKET NUMBER: 4446-8

STATEMENT OF ASSIGNMENT

You have asked me to write a memorandum on whether Gary Crawford was illegally dismissed from his job.

ISSUES

ISSUE I: Whether a state employee has a statutory right to a leave of absence under ORS 408.240 for ''military duty'' consisting of training not combined with military service so as to preclude a finding that he was absent without leave when he left his job to attend a Marine Reserve Training Course after his supervisor had refused to authorize such leave?

ISSUE II: Can a state employee be fired for ''insubordination'' under ORS 905.788 when he violated a direct order of his supervisor where the order was invalid and arose under circumstances that the employee could not reasonably have anticipated in time to challenge by a method other than the violation of that order?

FACTS

Mr. Gary Crawford is employed as a lab technician by the Oregon Department of Fish and Game Conservation. He is also an enlisted man in the United States Marine Corps Reserve. Several months ago Crawford applied for a three-week training program that the Marine Corps was offering in scuba diving. His application was initially rejected by the Marine Corps due to lack of space. However, he was subsequently notified that a vacancy had occurred and that, consequently, his application had been reconsidered and had been accepted. This notice arrived on Friday, February 19, 1988, in the late afternoon. The program was to begin the following Monday morning.

Mr. Crawford immediately called his supervisor, advised him of the notice, and requested a leave of absence. This was the first time that Crawford had ever made such a request, and to his knowledge, no other employee of the Department had ever made a similar request. His supervisor told him that it would be impossible for the Department to grant the leave on such short notice and instructed him to report for work the following Monday. Mr. Crawford ignored this instruction and instead reported to the training program. When he returned to work three weeks later, his supervisor advised him that he had been terminated on charges of absence without leave and insubordination.

ANALYSIS

ISSUE I

There is no question that Mr. Crawford's termination is valid if it can be shown that he was absent without leave. The relevant statute provides:

> The Superintendent of the Department of Fish and Game Conservation shall have the power to dismiss any employee for absence without leave....Or.Rev.Stat. 905.788 (1973).

Mr. Crawford was admittedly absent from his position. However, this absence was not ''without leave,'' in spite of his supervisor's refusal to authorize the absence. Under the circumstances of this case, the leave was automatically authorized by statute.

Or.Rev.Stat. 408.240(1) (1973) provides that:

> Whenever any public officer or employee leaves a position after June 24, 1950, whether voluntarily or involuntarily, in order to perform military duty, such office or position shall not become vacant, nor shall the officer or employee be subject to removal as a consequence thereof....

The term ''military duty,'' as used in this act, is defined in § 408.210 as:

> ...training and service performed by an inductee, enlistee or reservist or any entrant into a temporary component of the Armed Forces of the United States...but does not include active duty training as a reservist in the Armed Forces of the United States or as a member of the National Guard of the United States where the call is for a period of 15 days or less.

As lab assistant for the State Department of Fish and Game Conservation, Mr. Crawford is clearly a ''public'' employee. He left his position ''after June 24, 1950'' in order to attend a military training program that lasted three weeks, a period in excess of sixteen days. Hence the ''15 days or less'' exclusion in the last part of the statute does not apply. It could be argued that his activities did not constitute ''military duty'' since the scuba diving training was not offered to him as a part of his service, e.g., guard duty, combat, etc. This precise argument, however, was considered and rejected by the Court of Appeals in Stephens v. Dept. of State Police, 526 P.2d 1043 (Or.App., 1974).

Stephens involved a state police trooper who, as an army reservist, had applied for and had been accepted into a training course at the United States Army Infantry School in Fort Benning, Georgia. In that opinion Mr. Stephens was a state employee who sought a leave of absence to attend a training program conducted by the military. These facts are substantially similar to the facts in Crawford's case. Crawford also works for the state (Dept. of Fish and Game Conservation) and sought a leave to go to a military training program (Marine scuba diving). It is not significant that different branches of the service are involved or that Stephens and Crawford are part of different military units going to different kinds of training programs. The same issue is involved in Stephens and Crawford: whether §§ 408.240 and 408.210 authorize a state employee to attend a military training program that did not include military service even though they are both ordered not to go by their supervisors.

In Stephens, the Department of State Police contended that the program did not constitute ''military duty'' under Or.Rev.Stat. 408.240 since it did not involve military service. After thoroughly examining both the plain language and the legislative history of the act, the court concluded that:

> ...under the definition of ''military duty'' as contained in ORS 408.210 there is no distinction between periods of service and periods of training only. 526 P.2d 1043, 1046.

In addition to finding the statute applicable, the court noted that:

> [M]ilitary leave is granted by the statute automatically. There is no discretion on the part of any department official to grant or deny the leave. The statute on its face is unconditional. 526 P.2d 1043, 1045. (Emphasis added.)

Given the clear interpretation of the act by the Stephens court, there is little doubt that the charge of absence without leave against Mr. Crawford is unfounded. Section 408.240(1) says ''any public officer or employee'' (emphasis added) cannot be penalized for performing ''military duty'' as defined in § 408.210. Regardless of the attempt by Crawford's supervisor to deny the leave request, leave was ''granted by the statute automatically.''

ISSUE II

Mr. Crawford has also been charged with ''insubordination,'' presumably on the basis that he violated his supervisor's order to report for work during the week in which the military training program began. The power of the Superintendent to terminate employees for insubordination is established in Or.Rev.Stat. 905.788 which provides:

The Superintendent of the Department of Fish and Game Conservation shall have the power to dismiss any employee for...insubordination.

The statute does not define the term ''insubordination,'' and a search of Oregon case law reveals no opinions construing this statute. The only case that is arguably on point is Stephens, supra.

In Stephens, as here, the employee's request for a leave of absence had not only been denied but had resulted in a direct order to report for work on the day the military training program was to begin. Like Crawford, Stephens ignored this order and reported instead to the training program. After deciding the leave issue (see discussion of Issue I above), the Stephens court went on to consider whether the trooper could be fired for ''insubordination'' under Or.Rev.Stat. 181.290, a statute very similar to the ''insubordination'' statute applicable to Fish and Game employees: § 905.788 (1973). The court held that, even though the order requiring Stephens to report for work was invalid under Or.Rev.Stat. 408.240, Stephens could nevertheless be found to have committed insubordination for deliberately violating that order.

The Department of Fish and Game Conservation will certainly argue that this holding is controlling here. I believe, however, that Stephens is distinguishable on this issue.

It is clear from the court's opinion that the result in Stephens was an exception to the general rule that a charge of insubordination cannot be based upon an invalid order:

> While the general rule appears to be that an officer is not insubordinate for refusing to obey an order that is not legally valid, under the peculiar facts of this case we find an exception to exist. 526 P.2d 1043, 1047.

The court based this exception upon two ''peculiar facts,'' neither of which exists in this case.

First, the court stressed the following fact:

> ...there was ample time for Stephens to have anticipated the order and to have chosen another method of determining the matter. 526 P.2d 1043, 1047.

The court noted that Stephens had made a similar request for leave in the past which had been denied. From this fact the court concluded that Stephens was aware of the Department's position on such requests and could have anticipated the order in time to use a method of challenging the Department's position other than direct refusal to obey the order. Mr. Crawford was in a very different position. He had never made a similar request in the past and knew of no one else in the Department who had. His application for the program had initially been rejected by the Marines due to a lack of space, and he could not possibly have anticipated that this determination would be reversed due to the vacancy that arose. Although the program was to begin on a Monday, Crawford's notice of acceptance did not arrive until late afternoon on the preceding Friday, leaving him virtually no time in which to attempt the alternative strategies that the Stephens court suggested were available to Stephens. Thus it cannot be said that Crawford had ''ample time...to have anticipated the order and to have chosen another method of determining the matter.''

Secondly, the court emphasized that, in denying Stephens's request, the Department had justifiably relied upon an opinion of the Attorney General that construed the military leave statute as being inapplicable to periods of military training only, not combined with military service. Clearly, this is not so here. There is no indication in our facts that Crawford's superior relied on an opinion of an Attorney General. Even if the Department had relied upon the Attorney General's opinion here, such reliance could not be deemed ''justifiable'' since that opinion was effectively invalidated by the first holding in Stephens, which specifically found that the leave statute does apply to periods of training not combined with military service. At the time that Crawford's supervisor ordered Crawford not to go, the Stephens opinion had been decided, and Stephens clearly placed all government officials on notice that the Attorney General's interpretation of the statutes was incorrect.

For these reasons, I believe that we can successfully distinguish Stephens on the issue of insubordination. We would then urge the court to apply the general rule that a charge of insubordination cannot be based upon the refusal to obey an invalid order. The basis for an exception to this rule does not exist here.

The Department, however, may advance one final argument. Given the extremely short notice provided by Mr. Crawford, the Department will very likely take the position that the order to report for work, though invalid, was reasonable under the circumstances of this case. The Department may go further and urge the court to adopt, as a new exception to the general rule, the proposition that violation of an invalid order may be insubordination where the order is reasonable under the circumstances. Suppose, for example, that Crawford was essential to the functioning of the laboratory and that a replacement would be difficult to find and train. Under these circumstances Crawford's departure would have been very disruptive to the organization. Further fact investigation would have to be undertaken in order to determine whether this was so.

Thus far in my legal research, I have found no Oregon case law that would support the view that violation of an invalid order could constitute insubordination if, under the circumstances, the order was otherwise reasonable. Here, as in Stephens, the court may look to the case law of other jurisdictions for guidance in deciding whether to adopt this view as a new exception to the general rule noted above. Thus, if I do further legal research on the Crawford case, I will check to determine whether any persuasive authority exists in other jurisdictions on this point.

How likely is it that an Oregon court will carve out another exception to the general rule against firing for violating an invalid order? In attempting to answer this question, we should keep in mind that a police department is a very different kind of organization from a fish and game organization. Police departments are paramilitary organizations in which discipline is traditionally very important. The existence of discipline is often equated with the very life of the organization, its membership, and its mission. This factor may have been an implied reason why the court in Stephens found insubordination to exist in spite of the general rule against it. It may be that one of the ''peculiar facts'' in Stephens was the importance of following orders (i.e., of discipline) in police departments. Discipline does not appear to be as crucial to an organization such as the Department of Fish and Game Conservation. Hence, it is unlikely that the court would bend over backwards, as it did in Stephens, to find insubordination when there is a violation of an invalid order.

```
                          CONCLUSION
     I have no doubt that the court would rule in favor of Crawford on
the first issue--the leave of absence. The first holding in Stephens
would apply to these facts. The leave was valid. I have more diffi-
culty, however, with the second issue. While I think that Crawford
should win on this issue as well, I am troubled by the willingness of
the Stephens court to find insubordination even though the order was
clearly invalid. My instinct is that the Oregon court simply does
not like public employees flouting authority. In my discussion of
the second issue, I pointed out what I think are good reasons for the
court not to find insubordination in our case. Yet I am still left
with some doubt as to what the court would actually do in our case on
this issue.

                       RECOMMENDATIONS
     Some additional investigation should be done in this case. I
would like to find out the exact nature of Crawford's job at the De-
partment of Fish and Game Conservation. Was his job crucial? Was his
abrupt departure disruptive?
     A letter should be written by our office to the Department of Fish
and Game Conservation on behalf of Crawford. We should advise them
of our interpretation of Stephens and request that they reconsider
the dismissal.
```

See p. 257 for the letter that was drafted on the Crawford case.

Section F. Common Mistakes Made in Legal Writing

This section will attempt to provide examples of writing mistakes that are frequently found in student memoranda. Following each example there will be a brief comment identifying the inadequacy in the writing plus a cross reference to portions of this book where the problem identified has been treated. The cross references will either be to chapters already covered, or to material in an appendix of this book. Each example is from a separate memorandum of law. (All the citations used in the examples are hypothetical.)

Before you read the comments on each example or check any of the page references, try to determine on your own what is wrong with each example.

Example #1

The court in People v. Toni, 245 Ga. 172, held that. . . .

Comment: If a parallel cite exists, the citation is incomplete. The parallel citation should be provided; moreover, the date the opinion was decided should be in parentheses at the end of the citation.

Reference: p. 25.

Example #2

"It is true that in the area of practice and procedure in the courts, an inherent rule-making power in the judiciary must be acknowledged as a practical necessity." State v. Ray, 14 Conn. 72, 353 A.2d 723 (1976).

Comment: The citation is incomplete. The page number on which this quote is found in missing. The *opinion* begins on page 72 of Connecticut Reports, but on what page is the *quote* found? The *opinion* begins on page 723 of Atlantic Reports, Second Series, but on what page is the *quote* found? Assume that the quote was from page 75 of Connecticut Reports and from page 724 of Atlantic Reports, Second Series. The complete citation would be: State v. Ray, 14 Conn. 72, 75, 353 A.2d 723, 724 (1976).

Reference: p. 398.

Example #3

Fla.Stat.Ann. § 377.32

Comment: There is no date given to this statutory cite. The citation is incomplete.

Reference: p. 395.

Example #4

The only article that was located on this aspect of divorce law in Maryland is found at 7 Maryland Law Review 901 (1970).

Comment: The name of the law review should be abbreviated as Md.L.Rev. The author (if given) and the title of the article should be provided. For example, Jones, *Common Law Divorce in Maryland,* 7 Md.L.Rev. 901 (1970).

Reference: p. 399.

Example #5

The court said, "We accept the premise established in the *Donald* decision that "due process is a matter for a case by case resolution." Smith v. Jones, 14 Mass. 22, 26, 195 N.E.2d 740, 747 (1945).

Comment: This is an example of a quote within a quote. For the main quote, double quotation marks (") are needed. For the quote within the quote, single quotation marks are used ('). Hence: "We accept the premise established in the *Donald* decision that 'due process is a matter for a case by case resolution.'"

Reference: p. 403.

Example #6

The court concluded that "all *discriminatory* leases can be challenged under section 99." In re Ford, 44 Okla, 7, 9, 32 P.2d 84, 86 (1960).

Comment: If the word "discriminatory" was not italicized in the opinion, but you wish to italicize or underline the word, you must tell the reader that you have altered the quote in this way. This is done by placing the following parenthesis after the cite to the quote: (emphasis added). This means that the italics or underlining was not in the original quote.

Reference: p. 403.

Example #7

The court concluded that "all discriminatory [two year] leases can be challenged under section 99." In re Ford, 44 Okla, 7, 9, 32 P.2d 84, 86 (1960).

Example #8

"[A]ll discriminatory leases can be challenged under section 99." In re Ford, 44 Okla. 7, 9, 32 P.2d 84, 86 (1960).

Comment: Use brackets when *you* add anything to a quote, when *you* change a lower case letter to a capital letter, or when *you* change a capital letter to a lower case letter. The use of brackets in examples 7 and 8 is correct if the bracketed material was not in the original quote.

Reference: p. 403.

Example #9

An oath is "any form of attestation by which a person signifies that he is bound in conscience to perform an act faithfully and truthfully." *Black's Law Dictionary,* 4th Ed., p. 1220 (1951).

Comment: *Black's Law Dictionary* is a secondary source similar to a treatise. A proper foundation must be laid before you use it.

Reference: p. 212.

Example #10

According to McCormick, "A doctrine often repeated by the courts is that where the facts with regard to an issue lie peculiarly in the knowledge of a party, that party has the burden of proving the issue." *McCormick on Evidence,* 2nd Ed., p. 787 (1972). Therefore in our case, since the defendant would have the knowledge, she would have the burden of proof rather than our client.

Comment: Here the student appears to be placing too great a reliance on secondary authority—the McCormick quote. The writer cites this treatise and then immediately applies it to the facts of the client's case almost as if the quote from the treatise were a law. The proper foundation for the use of secondary sources as persuasive authority has not been laid.

Reference: p. 212.

Example #11

Courts often say that where the facts on an issue are peculiarly in the knowledge of a party, that party has the burden of proving the issue. Therefore, in our case, since the defendant would have the knowledge, she would have the burden of proof rather than our client.

Comment: Reread example #10 and compare it with example #11. Note that the student is paraphrasing the McCormick passage here in example #11 plus using some of the exact language of the passage *without citing McCormick.* This kind of theft is called plagiarism. If you are using someone else's ideas, with or without the use of any of his or her language, you must give a complete citation to your source. We sometimes tend to think that because the law library contains a vast amount of secondary authority, such as treatises, we can pick and choose whatever we want without being obliged to tell our readers that we are relying upon someone else's ideas and/or language. This attitude is totally unethical and improper. Be particularly wary of the "everyone does it" attitude. Don't *you* do it, no matter who else does it and no matter how many other people do it.

At times there is a thin line between your own ideas and the ideas/words that you have relied upon to generate your own ideas. You are urged to adopt a conservative approach: when in doubt about whether to give a citation as the source of your thoughts/words, provide the citation. Not only will you cover yourself on a plagiarism charge, but you will also be of assistance to the reader in suggesting that additional material on the topic can be found through the citation.

Reference: p. 401.

Example #12

The court held that wooden riverboats are a fire hazard. Peterson v. Steamboats Ltd., 42 Ohio 317, 18 N.E.2d 31 (1970).

Comment: The analysis is weak—if this is all we are told about *Peterson.* We do not know what rule of law was involved in *Peterson,* and it is unclear whether the facts stated were key facts in *Peterson.*

Reference: p. 181.

Example #13

The standard of care required of administrators of estates is well established in this jurisdiction:

> "Administrator must exercise such care as prudent men bestow on own affairs, or be liable in damages." U.S. Fidelity & Guaranty Co. v. Greer (1925) 29 Ariz. 203, 240 P. 343.

Comment: The author of this excerpt appears to be quoting, not from an opinion but from a summary of the opinion taken from a digest. This is evident from the manner in which the quotation is worded and from the fact that the date of the opinion is misplaced, a common feature of digest summaries. (The date should come at the end of the citation.) Digest summaries, headnotes at the beginning of the opinion, and similar research aids are *not* authority of any kind and should *never* be quoted or cited. Their purpose is only to lead you to opinions that may be relevant to the client's problem. It is the opinion itself that constitutes the authority. In citing and using the opinion, you must rely on the actual words of the court as they are written in the opinion, not on someone else's summary or paraphrase of these words.

Reference: p. 209.

Example #14

In A v. B, 39 F.Supp. 210 (D.R.I., 1940), the court held that before a federal prisoner can have his parole release date terminated for alleged violations of institutional rules, he must be given a hearing pursuant to the "due process" clause of the United States Constitution. This opinion applies here.

Comment: Assume that nothing else is said about the A v. B opinion in the entire interoffice memo from which the above excerpt is taken. The statement of the holding in A v. B appears to be complete (key facts plus rule of law). The difficulty with the excerpt is twofold. First, the analogization between the A v. B opinion and the client's case is nonexistent. All the writer says is that the "opinion applies here." The analysis is very cursory: no fact comparison, no rule of law comparison. It is recommended that you *not* be this cursory in your case analysis. Second, there is no counteranalysis. What would the other side say about the applicability of A v. B to the case currently in litigation? Would it agree that the "opinion applies"? Case analysis rarely leads to only one interpretation of an opinion. If there are counterarguments on the conclusion you have reached on the application of an opinion, you should anticipate what they will be and respond to them in your interoffice memorandum of law.

Reference: p. 184, p. 231.

Example #15

When our client was arrested for being intoxicated in a public place, he should have been given his warnings by the police, including his right to remain silent. The court in Johnson v. Avon, 72 F.2d 310 (2nd Cir. 1940) made this clear when it held that the warnings should always be given. In *Johnson,* a person was arrested for possession of heroin without being given the required warnings. The court invalidated the conviction because of this.

Comment: The analysis of the *Johnson* opinion is incomplete. What was the holding in *Johnson? Johnson* involved an arrest for a drug offense. The client's case involves an arrest for intoxication. This is an obvious factual difference. Was it a key fact in *Johnson* that the arrest was for a drug offense? Why or why not? If it was key, then the holding in that opinion may not apply to the client's case being analyzed in the memo. If the *Johnson* opinion is important, more of the analogization steps should be included; the implications of factual differences need to be discussed.

Reference: p. 199.

Example #16

The issue in Copper v. Barnes, 340 F.2d 104 (3rd Cir. 1962) was whether the detention was excessive.

Comment: The issue is stated incompletely. Unless there is a valid reason to state issues in shorthand, they should be stated completely, i.e., they should include the key facts plus the rule of law being interpreted in the light of those key facts.

Reference: p. 139.

Example #17

The statute (§ 15.913) provides as follows:

> The university shall be open to all persons resident of this state, without charge of tuition, under the regulations prescribed by the regents; and to all other persons under such regulations and restrictions as the board may prescribe.

Our client therefore should be entitled to attend the university.

Comment: The legislative analysis in this excerpt is very elliptic. You should avoid quoting from any enacted law without identifying ambiguities, identifying legal issues, anticipating opposing arguments on your legislative analysis, responding to those arguments, relating the language of the enacted law to the facts of the client's case, etc. Statutes rarely speak for themselves. They are seldom self-evident. No matter how long your quote from the enacted law is, you should not be asking your readers to do their own analysis. It is *your* job in the memorandum to do the analysis.

Also, for all enacted law, you should determine whether any case law exists interpreting the portions of the enacted law in question. You will seek case law written by courts sitting in the same state that wrote the enacted law. If none exists, you should say so in the memorandum.

Reference: p. 190.

Example #18

The phrase "reasonable notice" in § 85 of Florida Statutes Annotated (1945) has been held to mean notice that under the circumstances is calculated to reach the intended recipient. Paulson v. Kahn, 83 So.2d 320 (Fla.1972).

Comment: The *Paulson* opinion is incompletely analogized. (See comments to similar problems in prior examples.) Also, note that the statute is from the 1945 Florida Code. The *Paulson* opinion was written in 1972. Assuming that § 85 was enacted in 1945 or earlier, we need to know whether any significant changes in the statute occurred between 1945 and 1972 when *Paulson* was written, *and* between 1972 and today. Is the 1972 opinion interpreting the same statute that the writer of the memo is considering? It appears that the answer is yes, but you should be alert to the possibility that amendments to the enacted law occurred *before or after* the opinion interpreting it was written.

Example #19

In *Jackson v. Williams,* the court stated:

> "An agent has the implied authority to accept service of process on behalf of his principal." 81 Va. 383, 386, 27 S.E. 221, 225 (1892).

The court arrived at this conclusion after carefully examining. . . .

Comment: Assume that in Hood v. Adams, 128 Va. 97, 125 S.E.2d 785 (1955), the Virginia Supreme Court expressly overruled this holding in *Jackson.* The writer's error in this excerpt is the failure to shepardize the opinion to determine if it is still valid. Even if the opinion had not been overruled, shepardizing would probably have led the writer to other more recent opinions that might have been useful in the memorandum.

Reference: p. 98.

Example #20

The client has been here in New York for over four years. This period of time is not sufficient to establish domicile without more contacts with the state according to Kinner v. Davis, 62 Cal.2d 32, 14 P.2d 385 (1945). Furthermore, there must be an intent to remain in the jurisdiction indefinitely. Queen Tire Co. v. Alex Finance Co., 32 Tex. 194, 18 P.2d 132 (1920).

Comment: There are a number of difficulties with this excerpt. Assuming that New York law applies to the client, why is there reference to California and Texas opinions? If they are being used as persuasive authority, the foundation for their use must be laid. Furthermore the analogization of the *Kinner* and *Queen Tire Co.* opinions is extremely sketchy. It is highly recommended that you avoid this type of case analysis.

Reference: p. 181; p. 207.

Example #21

A surrender of leased premises may be made to and accepted by a duly authorized agent of the lessor. Bove v. Transcom Inc., 116 R.I. 210, 353 A.2d 613 (1976). See also, Irwin v. Wolff, 529 F.2d 1119 (8th Cir. 1976); Phillips v. Kimwood, 269 Or. 485, 525 P.2d 1033 (1974); Manhattan Bible College v. Stritessky, 192 Kan. 287, 387 P.2d 225 (1970; Trego v. Hunt, 21 Ohio App. 438, 153 N.E. 204 (1960); Edelman v. Edelman, 344 Mich. 646, 75 N.W.2d 29 (1956); Bred v. Smith, 421 U.S. 519, 95 S.Ct. 1779, 44 L.Ed.2d 308 (1975); Dudov v. Shoppers City, Inc., 212 Minn. 322, 164 N.W. 2d 800 (1970).

Comment: The author of this excerpt appears to be trying to impress the reader with all these citations. Perceptive readers are rarely impressed by a "string of citations." Note also the great variety of jurisdictions involved: Rhode Island, the 8th Circuit (U.S. Court of Appeals for the 8th Circuit), Oregon, Kansas, Ohio, etc. What law is being applied in this memo? The indiscriminate use of persuasive authority in this manner should be avoided. This is not the way to analogize opinions. No foundation has been laid for the proper use of persuasive case law.

Reference: p. 207.

Section G. Memorandum Assignments

Assignments 33–42

In each of the following assignments you will be asked to write an interoffice memorandum of law. If there are some facts that you need for the heading, e.g., an office file number for the case, you can make up such facts. In the memos, you will be applying one of the opinions in Appendix A. The first time you cite the opinion, use the citation format that you are given for the opinion in the assignment. For example, *People v. Sohn* is cited in Assignment #34 as People v. Sohn, 43 A.D.2d 716, 350 N.Y.S.2d 198 (1973). This is how you should cite the opinion the first time you use it in the memo. When you need to quote from the opinion in the memo, use a blank line to indicate the page number from which your quote is taken. For example, People v. Sohn, 43 A.D.2d 716 at ___, 350 N.Y.S.2d 198 at ___.

Assignment #33

Your office has agreed to represent Mr. Lawrence McKay at an administrative hearing to be held next week. In September of 1984, Mr. McKay was dismissed from his job as a prison guard with the Oregon Department of Corrections on charges of absence without leave and insubordination. Next week's hearing will determine whether these charges merit his termination. Ms. Brenda Dowd, the attorney who will be handling the hearing, has asked you to prepare for her a memorandum evaluating Mr. McKay's chances at this hearing. She provides you with the following statement of facts that she obtained from Mr. McKay during his initial interview:

Mr. McKay is employed as a prison guard for the Oregon Department of Corrections. He is also an enlisted man in the United States Army Reserve. Each summer McKay is required to attend a two-week army reserve training camp where he participates in various military exercises. It is customary during these summer camp sessions for the reserve units from the various states to compete in a precision drill contest. Each state's reserve unit fields a drill team; the winning team is awarded a trophy that is then displayed at their state headquarters until the following year. The competition for this trophy is extremely fierce, particularly among the older men and officers in McKay's unit.

Despite the fact that participation on the drill team is supposedly voluntary, McKay was heavily pressured to join this year. One officer in particular, Colonel Harris, threatened to have McKay called up on active duty and posted overseas if he refused to join the drill team. Believing that Colonel Harris had the power to carry out this threat, McKay agreed to participate on the drill team.

Approximately one month before the summer camp was scheduled to begin, Colonel Harris ordered McKay and the other drill team members to report the following week for an intensive three-week period of precision drill training. This training was arranged by Colonel Harris and several other officers in the unit; it had no official army sanction or approval. McKay had already requested and had obtained a two-week leave of absence from his job at the prison in order to attend the reserve summer camp. Upon receiving Colonel Harris's instructions to report for the drill training sessions, McKay immediately requested an additional three weeks' leave of absence. This request was denied by the prison warden who ordered McKay to continue to report for regular duty at the prison until the start of the summer camp. Fearing that Colonel Harris would carry out his threat to have him called up on active duty, McKay ignored the warden's order and reported for the drill training session the following week, in July of 1984. When McKay returned to work five weeks later (after having completed both the drill training and the two-week summer camp) he was advised by the warden that he had been dismissed on charges of absence without leave and insubordination. McKay immediately requested a hearing on these charges.

Assume that, after thoroughly researching the law in the state of Oregon, you find that the only relevant authorities are the following:

A. Oregon Revised Statutes 408.240 (1973):
(1) Whenever any public officer or employee leaves a position after June 24, 1950, whether voluntary or involuntary, in order to perform military duty, such office or position shall not become vacant, nor shall the officer or employee be subject to removal as a consequence thereof. . . .

B. Oregon Revised Statutes 408.210 (1973):
As used in this Act, the term "military duty" shall include training and service performed by an inductee, enlistee or reservist or any entrant into a temporary component of the Armed Forces of the United States . . . but does not include active duty training as a reservist in the Armed Forces of the United States or as a member of the National Guard of the United States where the call is for a period of 15 days or less.

C. Oregon Revised Statutes 1226.788 (1973):
The Superintendent of the Department of Corrections shall have the power to dismiss any employee for absence without leave or for insubordination. . . .

D. Stephens v. Dept. of State Police, 526 P.2d 1043 (Or.App. 1974), p. 302.

On the basis of this information, draft an interoffice memorandum of law evaluating Mr. McKay's chances of successfully challenging his termination.

Assignment #34

You work for a prosecutor's office in New York City. The office, as a result of a complaint by Ms. Jeannette Sumter, is currently deciding whether to bring a charge of assault in the second degree against Ms. Ruth Stein based upon an incident that occurred last weekend. The two women were involved in a fight outside a bar late in the evening. Both were heavily intoxicated, and both were armed at the time of the fight. Ms. Sumter, the complainant, was carrying a small handgun in her purse during the fight; she has subsequently been charged with possession of a deadly weapon. Ms. Stein was carrying a small aerosol can of mace, a tear-gas-like substance, in her purse. This substance is legal in New York; consequently, she has not been charged with any offense in connection with its possession. Neither woman removed her weapon from her purse during the fight, and each was apparently unaware that the other was armed.

It is unclear how the fight started. Both women claim that the other provoked the fight, and there were no witnesses who actually saw the fight begin. After several minutes a small crowd gathered to watch the women. One passerby called the police; a second warned the two women of the phone call and advised them to leave before the police arrived. At this point Ms. Stein went back into the bar where she was later found by the police. Ms Sumter was arrested several blocks away when Ms. Stein pointed her out to police officers who searched her, found the gun, and placed her under arrest for possession of a deadly weapon. Ms. Sumter was tried, convicted, and given a three-month sentence that was suspended.

Your supervising attorney has asked you to prepare an interoffice memorandum addressing the question of whether, on the basis of the facts described above, the state could prove beyond a reasonable doubt that Ms. Stein was guilty of assault. Assume that, after thoroughly researching the question, the only relevant authority you are able to find is People v. Sohn, 43 A.D.2d 716, 350 N.Y.S.2d 198 (1973), p. 299.

Assignment #35

You work for a law firm that has agreed to represent Mrs. Eunice Henderson, a landlady in Washington, D.C. Mrs. Henderson in interested in bringing an action for possession against Ms. Linda Ross, a tenant in one of her buildings. Ms. Ross has lived in the apartment for the past eight months. She has a one-year written lease that expires four months from now. For the past three months she has withheld her rent payments on the grounds that:

1. the lock on her mailbox in the lobby has been broken ever since she moved in and, as a result, her mail is often stolen out of the mailbox; and

2. for the last four months there has been no electricity in the bedroom of the apartment.

Mrs. Henderson concedes that these conditions exist but claims that she has been unable to have them repaired. A Housing Inspector visited the apartment last week at the tenant's request and found both conditions to be in violation of the D.C. Housing Code [§ 20 concerning the lock and § 39(b) concerning the electricity].

Your supervising attorney has asked you to prepare an interoffice memorandum evaluating Mrs. Henderson's chances of bringing a successful action for possession against Ms. Ross on the grounds of nonpayment of rent. Assume that, after thoroughly researching the question, the only relevant authorities you find are Brown v. Southall Realty Co., 237 A.2d 834 (D.C. 1968), p. 300, and Sections 2304 and 2501 of the District of Columbia Housing Regulations (as quoted in the *Brown* opinion).

Assignment #36

You are employed by a law firm in Connecticut that has agreed to represent a group of tenants from several apartment buildings on the 600 block of Pine Street in Hartford. The group wants the firm to take legal action to prevent Beacon House, Inc. from opening a center for runaway youths on their block. Beacon House has purchased a six-unit apartment building in the middle of the block that it is currently renovating. When the renovations are completed (sometime next month), Beacon plans to use the building as a center for teenagers who have run away from home. The present plans call for a number of offices for staff and counselors, a recreation room, a cafeteria, and a dormitory to house twenty to sixty youths of both sexes. There will be basketball and handball courts behind the building.

The residents of the 600 block of Pine Street are predominantly working class, and the block is entirely residential. The vast majority of the buildings on the street are three-story apartment buildings containing six to twelve units per building. Of the twelve buildings on the block, nine are occupied; the remaining three buildings, including that purchased by Beacon, have been empty for several years. The nearest commercial district is at the intersection of Pine Street and Georgia Avenue, two blocks west of the block in question.

The tenant group that has retained the law firm is composed of representatives of each of the occupied buildings on the block. They oppose the opening of the center for runaway youths because they are afraid that it will result in an increase of crime in the neighborhood, particularly drug-related offenses. Beacon maintains two similar centers in similar neighborhoods in other New England cities. While one of these centers has resulted in no noticeable increase in crime, the opening of their second center in Boston a year ago was followed by a 30 percent increase in violent crime in the neighborhood. That center was recently closed down when the Boston police discovered that it had become a major distribution center for heroin and other drugs.

The residents also fear that the opening of the center will encourage the trend of general deterioration and neglect in the neighborhood with landlords abandoning more and more of the buildings as the neighborhood goes down. A similar trend was occurring in the area surrounding Beacon's center in Boston.

Your supervising attorney has asked you to prepare an interoffice memorandum assessing whether it would be possible to enjoin Beacon's proposed use of the apartment building on the ground that it constitutes an equitably abatable nuisance. Assume that, after thoroughly researching the law, the only relevant authority you can find is Nicholson v. Conn. Half-way House, 153 Conn. 507, 218 A.2d 383 (1966), p. 307.

Assignment #37

You work for a public defender's office in Pennsylvania that has been assigned to represent Sesu Mboto, M.D., who has been charged with performing an abortion in violation of Penn.Crim.Stats. § 22-2505. Dr. Mboto is a citizen of one of the emerging African nations who moved to the United States six months ago. He received his medical training at a medical school in the United States and then practiced medicine in his own country for ten years before returning to the United States as a permanent resident alien. About one month ago, he took the medical boards examination in Pennsylvania; however, the results of that examination are not yet in, and he has not been admitted to practice medicine in the state.

While waiting for the results of his examination, Dr. Mboto has been working at a hospital as an assistant to Dr. Howard Jensen, an expert gynecologist. Last month he was assisting Dr. Jensen in performing a nontherapeutic abortion (i.e., one not necessary to save the life of the mother or of the child) for a woman who was two months pregnant. Shortly after the operation began, Dr. Jensen was advised that a second patient had been rushed into another operating room, suffering from massive bleeding. No other qualified surgeons were available to handle this emergency. Knowing Dr. Mboto's qualifications and skills, Dr. Jensen asked him to complete the abortion; Dr. Jensen then left to attend the emergency case. Dr. Mboto successfully performed the abortion on the first woman. Shortly thereafter he was charged with violating Penn.Crim.Stats. § 22-2505.

Your supervising attorney has asked you to draft an interoffice memorandum addressing the question of whether Dr. Mboto can constitutionally be convicted under the abortion statute. Assume that, after thoroughly researching the question, the only relevant authorities you are able to find are the following:

A. Penn.Crim.Stats. § 22-2505 (1976):

Any person other than a qualified surgeon licensed to practice medicine in this state, who gives or administers to any woman, or advises or causes her to take or use anything, or uses any means, with intent to procure upon her a miscarriage or abortion, unless the same is necessary to preserve her life or that of her unborn child, shall be fined not more than one thousand dollars or imprisoned in the State Prison not more than five years or both.

B. Connecticut v. Menillo, 423 U.S.9, 96 S.Ct.170, 46 L.Ed.2d 152 (1975), p. 309.

Assignment #38

You work for a law firm in the District of Columbia that has agreed to represent Carole Taylor in a divorce proceeding against her husband, Charles. The couple agreed to separate over a year ago and have been living separately ever since. Grounds for divorce can be established. There are no children. The property that is owned jointly or separately by the couple is as follows:

a. the family home, owned jointly and valued at $35,000;

b. a bank account in Charles's name only, containing $10,000;

c. a small T.V. repair shop, in Charles's name only, valued at $78,000.

The divorce is uncontested on all issues except for the division of some of the property. The couple have agreed that the house should be sold and that the proceeds from the sale should be divided equally between them. However, they are in serious disagreement as to the rest of the property. Mrs. Taylor believes that the bank account and the store should be divided equally, since both were acquired during the marriage. Mr. Taylor, however, feels that both items are rightfully his. He is willing to give his wife $2,000 from the bank account but no interest in the store whatsoever.

Mr. and Mrs. Taylor have been married approximately eight years. At the time they were married, they had virtually no assets between them. Mr. Taylor worked as a TV repairman and supported his wife on his salary. Although Mrs. Taylor had taken several bookkeeping courses during high school and had worked as a bookkeeper's assistant before her marriage, her husband did not want her to work after the marriage. She reluctantly agreed to leave her position and has not held a paying job since their marriage.

After several years of marriage, Mr. Taylor had been able to save enough to start his own repair shop. The business has done well, and he has been able to fully pay off all outstanding notes on both the business and the house. For the past five years, since the repair shop first opened, Mrs. Taylor has done all the bookkeeping and accounting for the shop, working an average of about ten to fifteen hours per week. She received no salary or other compensation from her husband for this work. All profits from the shop were deposited directly into Mr. Taylor's bank account and were used, as necessary, to cover the couple's living expenses.

Your supervising attorney has asked you to prepare an interoffice memorandum evaluating Mrs. Taylor's chances of persuading a court to divide the property more equally. Assume that, after thoroughly researching the law in the District of Columbia, you find that the only relevant authority is Mumma v. Mumma, 280 A.2d 73 (D.C. 1971), p. 311.

Assignment #39

You work for a law firm in Indiana that has agreed to represent Lawrence Cooper in a divorce action against his wife, Brenda, who deserted him over a year ago. Mrs. Cooper does not intend to contest the divorce. The only contested issue in the divorce concerns an award of alimony that Mr. Cooper is seeking from his wife.

Mr. and Mrs. Cooper have been married for approximately ten years. About eight years ago, as a result of an automobile accident, which occurred while they were vacationing in New York, Mr. Cooper was partially paralyzed and has been unable to work. Mrs. Cooper works as a magazine editor and earns $40,000 per year. She has supported him during this time. Although unable to hold a paying job, Mr. Cooper has been able to take care of the house and to prepare meals.

Your supervising attorney has asked you to draft an interoffice memorandum on the question of whether the court can award alimony payments to Mr. Cooper under these circumstances. Assume that the only authorities you are able to locate are the following:

A. Indiana Code § 22–1401 (1964):
When a divorce is granted to the wife, the court may decree her permanent alimony sufficient for her support.

B. Owen v. Illinois Baking Corp., 260 F.Supp.820 (W.D. Mich. 1966), p. 315.

Assignment #40

You work for a law firm in Virginia that has agreed to represent Clarence Wellman in a probate proceeding. Mr. Wellman was a close friend of George M. Schuler, a businessman who recently died leaving a rather sizable estate. Shortly after Mr. Schuler's death, a document purporting to be his last will and testament was discovered among his personal papers. The document consisted of three type-written pages, stapled together at the top. It names Clarence Wellman as the primary beneficiary. Mr. Schuler's relatives, led by Sarah Schuler, a distant cousin, are planning to challenge the will on the ground that Mr. Schuler had revoked it by cancellation shortly before his death. The basis of this claim is a notation that has been typed diagonally across the first page of the will. The notation reads: "I hereby revoke this will and declare it to be void and of no effect." Directly below these words is Mr. Schuler's signature. No other signatures appear on this page and the notation does not appear to have been witnessed or to otherwise comply with the requirements of a valid will or codicil in the state of Virginia. The front page contains only the heading "Last Will and Testament of George M. Schuler" and the date, February 27, 1966. The words of revocation were typed so as to slant across this heading. The actual text of the will begins on page two and continues to page three. Neither of these two pages has been marked in any manner. At the bottom of the third page the will is signed by George M. Schuler and three witnesses. With the exception of the alleged cancellation on page one, the will appears to be valid in all respects.

Your supervising attorney has asked you to prepare an interoffice memorandum addressing the question of whether Mr. Schuler's will has been effectively revoked by the signed notation on the first page. Assume that, after thoroughly researching the question, the only relevant authorities you are able to locate are the following:

A. Virginia code § 5233 (1919):

No will or codicil, or any part thereof, shall be revoked, unless . . . by a subsequent will or codicil, or by some writing declaring an intention to revoke the same and executed in the manner in which a will is required to be executed, or by the testator, or some person in his presence and by his direction, cutting, tearing, burning, obliterating, canceling, or destroying the same, or the signature thereto, with the intent to revoke.

B. Thompson v. Royall, 163 Va.492, 175 S.E. 748 (1934), p. 316.

Assignment #41

You work for the legal department of KTS Industries. KTS makes airplane parts that it sells to airplane manufacturers. One of the parts sold to Airways Manufacturing Co. was carelessly made by KTS; it was defective. Airways sells a plane with the defective part to a dealer who resells it to Smith. Airways did not know that the part was defective. While flying one day, Smith is severely injured when the plane crashes into a barn. The crash was caused by the defective part made by KTS.

Smith sues KTS for negligence. The owner of the barn also sues KTS for negligence in damaging the barn.

Prepare an interoffice memorandum in which you discuss the potential liability of KTS to Smith and to the owner of the barn. Assume that the only relevant authority that applies to the case is MacPherson v. Buick Motor Co., 217 N.Y.382, 111 N.E. 1050 (1916), p. 319.

Assignment #42

You work for a law firm that has agreed to represent Mr. Edward Swann, a street vendor who recently lost his peddler's license.

For the past ten years Mr. Swann has sold flowers from a stand on the sidewalk outside city hall. During the last several months he has also peddled fresh fruit from this stand. Because he is severely handicapped (he is 80 percent blind and is able to walk only with the aid of crutches), Mr. Swann is unable to find other employment; his street sales have been his sole means of support. He refuses to accept any charity or government aid as a matter of his personal dignity.

Like other street vendors in the city, Mr. Swann is required by a city ordinance to obtain a peddler's license from the City Department of Licenses and Inspections. When Mr. Swann's license expired last week, he applied for renewal, expecting it to be granted routinely. He was notified yesterday, however, that his application has been denied. The letter of denial read, in pertinent part, as follows:

A routine inspection by our enforcement division indicates that you are vending fresh fruit from your stand outside city hall. Inasmuch as you are presently licensed to sell only non-food items, the sale of foodstuffs is in violation of your license and constitutes grounds for revocation of that license. Consequently, your application for renewal is being denied.

If you wish to appeal this determination, you should contact the Department at the number listed below and request a hearing. . . .

Mr. Swann immediately called the Department of Licenses and Inspections and requested a hearing. Because of the backlog of cases and a shortage of personnel, the Department was unable to schedule a hearing until almost three months from now. Since it is illegal to peddle merchandise of any kind without a license, this leaves Mr. Swann without any means of support for the next three months while the hearing date is pending.

Your supervising attorney has asked you to prepare an interoffice memorandum addressing the question of whether the procedure followed by the city in revoking Mr. Swann's license is constitutionally valid. Assume that, after thoroughly researching this question, the only relevant authorities that you are able to find are the following:

A. United States Constitution, Amendment XIV, § 1:

. . . nor shall any State deprive any person of life, liberty, or property without due process of law; . . . .

B. Goldberg v. Kelly, 397 U.S.254, 90 S.Ct. 1011, 25 L.Ed.2d 287 (1970), p. 330.

Chapter Nineteen

Letter Writing and
Case Analysis

In this chapter, we will be drafting letters based on the facts in the memorandum assignments in Chapter 18. The letters will be written to nonlawyers. Hence they cannot be drafted with the same degree of technical specificity that is found in the memos. Yet the letters will cite and argue the law. They are *advocacy letters* in that they are trying to convince someone of something; they are not client letters that advise the client of the status of the case, lay out options, and recommend a course of action.

Here is a sample of a letter based on the facts in the model memo of Chapter 18, p. 236, on the Crawford case. Before reading this letter, you should reread the model memo in order to be able to compare the style of writing in the memo and in the letter. Following the letter, there are guidelines on incorporating case law into this kind of letter.

Hill, Davis & Henries
Attorneys at Law
1122 Main Street
Portland, Oregon 97205
503-456-9103

Mary Vanter, Director   RE: Gary Crawford
Department of Fish and
  Game Conservation
P.O. Box 3410   4/20/88
Portland, Oregon 97205

Dear Ms. Vanter:

  Our office represents Mr. Gary Crawford, a lab technician in your Department. On March 14, 1988, Mr. Crawford was terminated because he was allegedly absent without leave and insubordinate. We believe

---

the termination was inappropriate and illegal, and we therefore request that he be reinstated.

Mr. Crawford is an enlisted man in the United States Marine Corps Reserve. When he first applied to the Reserve for a three-week training program in scuba diving, he was turned down due to a lack of space. On February 19, 1988, in the late afternoon, Mr. Crawford was notified that space had suddenly became available for a program scheduled to begin the following Monday, February 22, 1987. He immediately asked his supervisor at the Department of Fish and Game Conservation for permission to go. Permission was denied because of the short notice. Nevertheless, Mr. Crawford attended the program. When he returned on March 14, 1988, he was terminated.

Mr. Crawford was within his rights in attending the training program. Oregon law is quite clear on this. The legislature has enacted a policy designed to encourage public employees to perform military duty without fear of penalty or loss of employment rights. The pertinent statute provides as follows:

> Whenever any public officer or employee leaves a position...in order to perform military duty, such office or position shall not become vacant, nor shall the officer or employee be subject to removal as a consequence thereof. Oregon Revised Statutes, 408.240(1).

Furthermore, "military duty" specifically includes "training" programs; it is not limited to combat service or maneuvers. See Oregon Revised Statutes, 408.210 where this is made clear.

This interpretation of the statutes has been enunciated by the Court of Appeals of Oregon. The Court left no room for doubt on the employee's right:

> "[M]ilitary leave is granted by the statute automatically. There is no discretion on the part of any department official to grant or deny the leave." Stephens v. Dept. of State Police, 526 P.2d 1043 (Or.App. 1974) [emphasis added].

Hence, it was improper for Mr. Crawford's supervisor to refuse the request to attend the Reserve training program.

It is important to repeat that Mr. Crawford found out that he was eligible for the Reserve program in the late afternoon on Friday, and that the program was scheduled to begin the following Monday. Mr. Crawford wasted no time in seeking permission of his supervisor on that Friday. When permission was denied, he had no alternative but to attend anyway. No other way existed for him to exercise his statutory right to a leave of absence. Prior to the request for permission on February 19th, Mr. Crawford had never made a similar request, nor was he aware of any other employee making such a request. Hence, it was a complete surprise to Mr. Crawford to be told that he could not go. Again, he was without alternatives.

It is highly irregular to say that an employee is insubordinate—and subject to dismissal—for exercising his unconditional right to a leave of absence when he did everything within his power to exercise this right in an orderly way. What else could Mr. Crawford do?

We submit that he did everything that could be expected of him, given the time pressures that he was under.

Therefore, we are asking you to rescind the termination order. We would be happy to discuss the matter with you further. It is our hope that it can be resolved without resort to litigation.

I hope to hear from you.

Sincerely,

James J. Hill, Esq.

GUIDELINES ON WRITING ADVOCACY LETTERS TO NONLAWYERS FOR ASSIGNMENTS ##43-52

1. The letters you will be drafting here are advocacy documents. Their purpose will be to convince someone of a particular position. Assume that the addressee of each letter is a nonlawyer.

2. The body of the letter should have six main parts:

- A statement identifying the writer of the letter.
- A statement of what the letter is seeking.
- A brief summary of the facts.
- The arguments that support what the letter is seeking.
- A restatement of what the letter is seeking.
- An indication of the next step the letter writer will take or may take.

3. You can cite any laws that you are given in the assignment. But numerous citations ("string cites") and long quotations from many laws are generally inappropriate. Limit yourself to essential citations and brief quotations.

4. If you state issues, use shorthand statements.

5. Assume that you are drafting the letter for the review and signature of your supervising attorney at the office where you work.

6. For the heading of the letter, follow the format in the above example.

7. Make up the following information: the name, address, and phone number of the office where you work, the name of your supervising attorney, the address of the person to whom the letter will be sent, the name and title of this person if it is not given in the assignment, etc. You may make up any additional facts that you need so long as these facts are consistent with the facts that you are given. Do not add facts that dramatically alter the nature of the dispute in favor of one side or the other.

Assignment #43

(a) Read the facts in Assignment #33 on p. 247. You work for the law firm that is representing Lawrence McKay. Draft a letter to the Director of the Oregon Department of Corrections, Robert Farrell, in which you ask for the reinstatement of Lawrence McKay, a client of the law firm where you work.

(b) Assume that at the prison where McKay works, the supervisors have formed the Corrections Supervisors Association to protect their interests. They have hired a law firm for which you work. On behalf of the Association, draft a letter to the Director of the Oregon Department of Corrections, Robert Farrell, in which you ask that McKay *not* be reinstated.

In drafting these letters, follow the Guidelines on p. 259.

Assignment #44

(a) Read the facts in Assignment #34 on p. 249. You work for the law firm that is defending Ruth Stein in the assault case. Draft a letter to Francis Davis who is Ruth Stein's employer at the Joy Day Care Center where Stein is a counselor. Davis has learned that Stein has been charged with assault and is considering suspending Stein because of this. She does not want to take this drastic step, however, if it is clear that Stein will not be convicted. Your letter should try to convince Davis that it is highly unlikely that Stein will be convicted, and that therefore suspension should not be considered.

(b) Helen Smith is a parent of one of the children who attends the Joy Day Care Center. Smith does not want Stein to keep her job as a counselor. Smith has hired a law firm for which you work. The law firm has made inquiries into the assault charge against Stein. Write a letter to Davis to try to convince her that Stein will probably be convicted.

In drafting these letters, follow the Guidelines on p. 259.

Assignment #45

(a) Read the facts in Assignment #35 on p. 249. You work for the law firm that is representing Eunice Henderson. Draft a letter to Ralph Jefferson, a vice-president and chief loan officer of Equity Bank. Henderson has applied for a loan from the Equity Bank in order to buy other apartment buildings in the neighborhood. As collateral, Henderson wants to use the apartment building where Linda Ross lives. Jefferson has heard that a tenant in the apartment is not paying rent and that the tenant may be arguing that the lease is void. Jefferson will not proceed with the loan application until this matter is cleared up. Your letter should explain the problem that Henderson is having with Ross, and convince him that the lease is not void.

(b) The D.C. Tenants Rights Coalition has been fighting Henderson for years. It is opposed to her acquisition of any other apartment buildings in the neighborhood. You work for the law firm that represents the Coalition. Write a letter to Ralph Jefferson in which you try to convince him that Linda Ross's lease is void.

In drafting these letters, follow the Guidelines on p. 259.

Assignment #46

(a) Read the facts in Assignment #36 on p. 250. You work for the law firm that is representing Beacon House. Draft a letter to the president of the New Life Foundation that is considering a large donation to Beacon House for the center for runaway youths. The president has heard that neighbors are seeking an injunction against the center. Your letter should try to convince the president that Beacon House will be successful in preventing the injunction.

(b) You work for the law firm that is representing the tenants from the 600 block of Pine Street who are trying to stop the runaway center from opening.

Draft a letter to the president of the New Life Foundation urging that the donation not be made to Beacon House because you believe the injunction will be granted so that the center will not be opened as planned.

In drafting these letters, follow the Guidelines on p. 259.

Assignment #47

(a) Read the facts in Assignment #37 on p. 251. You work for the law firm that is representing Dr. Mboto. Draft a letter to the Chairperson of the State Medical Ethics Board that must pass on the character of all applicants for a license to practice medicine in the state. The Board knows about the criminal charge against Dr. Mboto. The letter should try to convince the Board that a conviction would be unconstitutional.

(b) You work for the law firm that represents the Anti-Abortion League. Write a letter to the Chairperson of the State Medical Ethics Board in which you try to convince the Board that the conviction of Dr. Mboto would be constitutional.

In drafting these letters, follow the Guidelines on p. 259.

Assignment #48

(a) Read the facts in Assignment #38 on p. 252. Frank Stanton is exploring investment opportunities. For economic reasons, he must act quickly. Among the options he is considering is the purchase of the Taylor T.V. repair shop. He has met with Charles several times; they are close to negotiating a final price. Stanton knows about the pending divorce and about Carole Taylor's claim to a one-half interest in the shop. He is reluctant to make the purchase. He fears that in the middle of finalizing the sale, a court will decree that Carole owns one-half of the shop, and that Carole may not go along with the deal he has negotiated with Charles. You work for the law firm that is representing Charles. Draft a letter to Stanton in which you try to convince him that there is very little likelihood that a court will grant Carole any interest in the shop.

(b) You work for the law firm that is representing Carole. Write a letter to Stanton in which you try to convince him not to make the purchase unless he negotiates directly with her and Charles because there is a very strong likelihood that a court will award her a one-half interest in the shop.

In drafting these letters, follow the Guidelines on p. 259.

Assignment #49

(a) Read the facts in Assignment #39 on p. 252. Mr. Cooper wants to become a citizen of Canada. Assume that Canada's immigration laws require all applicants for citizenship to demonstrate that they are financially able to care for themselves. In his application, Mr. Cooper lists alimony from Mrs. Cooper as his future source of income. The Canadian Immigration Office wants some assurance that he will be entitled to alimony, at least in the immediate future. The Office contacts Mrs. Cooper, asking her to confirm that she will be paying alimony to Mr. Cooper. You work for the law firm that is representing Mrs. Cooper. Draft a letter to the Canadian Immigration Office in which you try to convince the Office that Mrs. Cooper has no alimony obligation to Mr. Cooper.

(b) You work for the law firm that represents Mr. Cooper. Draft a letter in which you explain to the Office that Mrs. Cooper has an alimony obligation to him.

In drafting this letter, follow the Guidelines on p. 259.

Assignment #50

(a) Read the facts in Assignment #40 on p. 253. Assume that one of the items in George Schuler's will was a valuable painting that George had loaned to Clarence Wellman while George was alive. If the will is valid, Wellman will own the painting outright. If it is revoked, the relatives will receive it. While the controversy over the revocation is pending, Wellman tries to sell the painting to the County Art Museum. You work for the law firm that is representing Sarah Schuler. Draft a letter to the director of the museum, Donald Simpson, in which you try to convince him not to purchase or take possession of the painting because the will purporting to give the painting to Wellman was validly revoked.

(b) You work for the law firm that represents Clarence Wellman. Write a letter to Donald Simpson, director of the museum, in which you explain to him that Wellman will soon be in a position to sell the painting because the will granting it to him is still valid.

In drafting these letters, follow the Guidelines on p. 259.

Assignment #51

(a) Read the facts in Assignment #41 on p. 254. You work for the law firm that is representing Smith. Draft a letter to the president of KTS Industries, Joseph Brent, in which you offer to settle the case for $250,000. The theme of your letter is that KTS owed a duty to Smith. For purposes of Assignment #51(a), assume that KTS does not have its own legal department and is not represented by counsel at this point.

(b) Fidelity Insurance Co. is the liability insurance carrier of KTS Industries. While the case with Smith is pending, Fidelity is contemplating a 400% increase in the premium charged to KTS. The reason for this is the number of claims that Fidelity expects if the courts hold that KTS is liable to the ultimate consumers of every product for which KTS makes a component part. You work for a law firm that KTS has just hired. Write a letter to the president of Fidelity, Jessica Kiley, in which you try to convince her that the proposed increase is unwarranted because the courts will not hold that KTS is liable in such situations.

In drafting these letters, follow the Guidelines on p. 259.

Assignment #52

(a) Read the facts in Assignment #42 on p. 254. You work for the law firm that is representing Edward Swann. Draft a letter to the director the City Department of Licenses and Inspections, Jane Kennedy, in which you try to convince her that a pre-termination evidentiary hearing for Swann is necessary.

(b) You work for the law firm that represents Limit Government Now, a lobbying group that wants drastic cuts in government programs. Draft a letter to Jane Kennedy, Director of the City Department of Licences and Inspections, in which you try to convince her that a pre-termination hearing for Swann is not necessary.

In drafting these letters, follow the Guidelines on p. 259.

Chapter Twenty

Oral Advocacy

Another way to demonstrate the skill of case analysis is on your feet. In this chapter you will have this opportunity on the ten cases that we have been following throughout the book, and on a new set of cases. Our shift to oral advocacy will not take us away from our study of the nature of case analysis and the skills of legal writing. Quite the contrary. The shift is simply one of perspective. Arguing case law on your feet should reinforce the briefing and application principles that we have explored thus far. Furthermore, the organization skills that you must demonstrate in oral advocacy are quite similar to the organization skills that you must demonstrate in your legal writing. Whether you are writing or speaking, our goal continues to be a comprehensive study of case law.

Section A. Oral Advocacy: Applying One Opinion

I. Format of the Class
II. Instructions on Making Oral Presentations
III. Preparing for a Presentation
IV. Role of the Judges

I. FORMAT OF THE CLASS

1. The students will be divided into law firms. The number of students in a firm will depend on the number of students in the class. The teacher will let you know how the division will be made.

2. Each law firm will be assigned a client whose case is on appeal. The firm should meet outside class on its own to discuss the case and to plan strategy for a hearing that is about to be held.

3. The hearing will be conducted during a class session. The two law firms representing the opposing parties will sit at the front of the class.

4. There will be four presentations. Each law firm will make a main presentation on behalf of its client and a rebuttal to the main presentation of the other firm. The sequence will be as follows (unless modified by the teacher):

(i) Main presentation from first law firm—10 minutes

(ii) Main presentation from second law firm—10 minutes

(iii) Rebuttal from first law firm—3 minutes

(iv) Rebuttal from second law firm—3 minutes

5. The rest of the class will act as the appellate court. While representatives from the law firms are making their main presentations and rebuttals, they will be interrupted by questions from the bench, i.e., from students in the class who are not in the law firms.

II. INSTRUCTIONS ON MAKING ORAL PRESENTATIONS

SUMMARY INSTRUCTIONS—OVERVIEW OF THE HEARING

• Attorney from the appellant's law firm comes to the podium in front of the class.

• Introduce yourself, give the name of the case now before the court, and state the side you represent.

• State the judgment below.

• State the issue in the case and tell the court, briefly, what result you want it to reach on this issue.

• One opinion will be the centerpiece of your argument. State the relevant holding in this opinion and tell the court how you plan to use it.

• State the key facts for this holding, and compare them to the facts of the case now before the court. Demonstrate a substantial similarity or dissimilarity depending on whether or not you want the holding to apply. Explain whether the reasoning for the holding is broad enough to cover the facts of the current case.

• Give a brief conclusion. Thank the court and sit down.

• The attorney representing the appellee's law firm will then come forward to make its main presentation in the same manner as listed above.

• There will then be two brief rebuttals, one from each side.

DETAILED INSTRUCTIONS

1. Come to the podium. The appellant will argue first.

2. Begin by saying, "If it please the court." At all times you must be very deferential to the judges on the court. (Every student facing you is on the panel of judges considering your case.) When addressing one of the judges, preface your statement with "Your Honor." Say "Your Honors" when addressing the entire court.

3. Introduce yourself. "My name is . . . , an attorney in the law firm of . . ." (The name of the firm can be the last name of all your colleagues with whom you prepared this case.)

4. Give the name of the case now before the court and identify the side you represent.

5. Briefly state what happened below in the case before the court:

> Your honors, the trial court in this case granted a judgment in favor of . . . and we are asking this court to affirm this judgment.
>
> or
>
> The trial court granted a judgment in favor of . . . and we are asking this court to reverse this judgment."

Do not go into the reasons why the trial court reached its judgment. Simply state what it was.

6. State the issue now before the court. Give a shorthand statement of the issue. For example:

> The issue before this court is whether Ajax Company is entitled to a deduction under § 95 of the Internal Revenue Code.

If more than one issue exists, focus on the central issue and briefly refer to the others.

7. Tell the court what result you want it to reach on this issue.

> We are asking this court to rule that Ajax Company should not be allowed to take a deduction under § 95.

Don't elaborate or give any reasons at this point. Simply let the court know what you hope its ruling will be at the end of this hearing.

8. At *any* time, *any* judge has the right to interrupt you and ask you a question. Do the best you can to answer the question and then go back to the outline of the presentation that you prepared. Never argue with a judge. If you want to disagree with something a judge is saying to you, do so *very* cautiously: "With all due respect, your honor, it is our position that . . . ."

9. Tell the court what opinion you are going to discuss to support the result you asked for in step #7. Briefly state the holding of this opinion, and summarize the relationship between this holding and the argument that you will make later on. In outline fashion, you are telling the court how you propose to handle the opinion.

(i) *If you want this opinion to apply,* say: "The main precedent for our position that the deduction should be allowed is the case of *Smith v. Smith.* This case held that a deduction was allowable on facts that are quite similar to ours, as I shall demonstrate in a moment." (You are asking the court to follow this opinion.)

(ii) *If you do not want this opinion to apply,* say: "An important opinion that this court will want to consider is *Smith v. Smith.* While this case held that a deduction was allowable, we believe that the facts of this case are substantially different from the facts before us now, as I shall demonstrate in a moment. Furthermore the reasoning of *Smith v. Smith* should lead this court to conclude that the deduction should be denied in our case." (You are asking the court to distinguish this opinion even though you may want the court to adopt its reasoning.)

10. Identify the central or key facts for the holding you stated for the opinion in step #9. Compare these key facts to the facts of the case before the court.

The central facts in *Smith v. Smith* were.... These facts are quite similar to the facts now before the court because....

or

The central facts in *Smith v. Smith* were.... These facts are quite different from the facts now before the court because....

Keep in mind the following dynamics of advocacy in comparing facts:

(i) If you want a holding to apply, you try to phrase the key facts for that holding as broadly as possible—unless you are lucky enough to have an opinion on all fours with your facts.

(i) If you do not want a holding to apply, you try to phrase the key facts for that holding as narrowly as possible.

(ii) If you want a holding to apply, you try to show that the facts of your case are substantially similar to *all* the key facts in the opinion; and that if there are any fact differences, they are not with any of the key facts of the opinion.

(ii) If you do not want a holding to apply, you try to show that the facts of your case are substantially different from *one or more* of the key facts in the opinion.

(iii) If you want a holding to apply, you try to phrase the court's reasoning for that holding as broadly as possible in order to show that the reasoning is broad enough to cover the facts of your case.

(iii) If you do not want a holding to apply, you try to phrase the court's reasoning for that holding as narrowly as possible in order to show that the reasoning is not broad enough to cover the facts of your case.

11. After you have completed your fact comparison, briefly repeat the conclusion or result that you stated in step #7.

12. End by saying, "Thank you very much, your honors."

13. Your opponent, the appellee, now gets up for its main presentation by going through steps #1–12 above.

14. A brief rebuttal is allowed the law firm that argued first (for the appellant), followed by a brief rebuttal of the second law firm (for the appellee). The rebuttals should not simply repeat the main presentations. They should be responsive to specific points made by the opposition.

III. PREPARING FOR A PRESENTATION

1. Prepare individually and in conjunction with the other members of your law firm. Arrange to meet with the other members of the law firm in order to discuss strategy. Role play the presentations and rebuttals within your group. Critique each other. You will probably find this interaction very valuable. You cannot, however, totally depend on others. You must prepare as if you are the *only* member of the law firm available to argue the *entire* case in class.

2. Do not do any legal research. Apply only the law that is specified in the assignment.

3. When you come to the front of the room to make a presentation, do not bring a speech with you. Bring one or two small note cards on which you have placed the main arguments that you will use. You want to make eye contact with the judges as often as possible as you speak. You want to appear in command. The judges will be interrupting your presentation with questions. All these realities make reading your argument—line by line—inappropriate.

4. The judges will not be reading anything that you submit before the hearing. You should assume that your case is one of many that the judges will consider on the day of the hearing. Hence, within the limited time frame for your presentation, you must be very clear in laying out the case for the judges.

5. You should anticipate and welcome questions from the judges, even though you may find it frustrating to be constantly interrupted. The skillful advocate is able to interweave his or her previously prepared points into answers to their questions. The job of an advocate is to convince the judges of your position. One of the preconditions of doing this is to be aware of what is bothering them. Their questions will help you find this out.

IV. ROLE OF THE JUDGES (STUDENTS NOT MEMBERS OF LAW FIRMS)

1. If you are not assigned to one of the law firms, you will be one of the judges. Sit in your regular seats during the oral arguments.

2. You need to prepare questions to ask the advocates during their presentations. Read over the facts of the assignment and the opinion that will be the basis of the arguments. Make notes on the questions that you would like to ask.

3. While an advocate is making an argument, you may interrupt at any time with a question. You do not have to raise your hand. Simply ask your question. If the advocate is in the middle of a long point, you can say, "Excuse me, counsel, I want to ask you if. . . ." Do not interrupt a fellow judge who is asking a question. It is perfectly proper, however, to interrupt an advocate at any time.

4. Do not ask any questions about what happened below in the case. A judgment was awarded in a nonjury trial. Assume that there are *no* procedural issues concerning how the case came before the current court.

5. There should be many questions from the judges. If minutes go by in which the only voice heard in the room is the advocate talking, then the judges are not doing their job!

Assignment #53

The case that will be argued is: *Lawrence McKay v. Oregon Department of Corrections.* The facts and the law for this case are the same as in Assignment #33 on p. 247. Assume that there has already been a trial in this case that resulted in a judgment for the Oregon Department of Corrections. It was a nonjury trial. McKay is now appealing to the Court of Appeals of Oregon. McKay is the appellant and the Oregon Department of Corrections is the appellee. The basis of the appeal is the correctness of the trial court's interpretation of the law in favor of the Oregon Department of Corrections. The trial court concluded that McKay was not entitled to a leave of absence and that he could be fired for insubordination. There was no trial court opinion. See Instructions on Making Oral Presentations, p. 266, and Preparing for a Presentation, p. 269.

Assignment #54

The case that will be argued is: *Ruth Stein v. New York City.* The facts and the law for this case are the same as in Assignment #34 on p. 249. Assume that there has already been a trial in this case that resulted in a conviction. It was a nonjury trial. Stein is now appealing her conviction and the judgment based thereon to the New York Supreme Court, Appellate Division, Second Department. Stein is the appellant and New York City (through the prosecutor) is the appellee. The basis of the appeal is the correctness of the trial court's interpretation of the law in favor of the New York City. The trial court concluded that Stein was guilty of assault in the second degree beyond a reasonable doubt. There was no trial court opinion. See Instructions on Making Oral Presentations, p. 266, and Preparing for a Presentation, p. 269.

Assignment #55

The case that will be argued is: *Eunice Henderson v. Linda Ross.* The facts and the law for this case are the same as in Assignment #35 on p. 249. Assume that there has already been a trial in this case that resulted in a judgment for Ross. It was a nonjury trial. Henderson is now appealing to the District of Columbia Court of Appeals. Henderson is the appellant and Ross is the appellee. The basis of the appeal is the correctness of the trial court's interpretation of the law in favor of Ross. The trial court concluded that the lease was void. (No res judicata issue exists.) There was no trial court opinion. See Instructions on Making Oral Presentations, p. 266, and Preparing for a Presentation, p. 269.

Assignment #56

The case that will be argued is: *Pine Street Tenants v. Beacon House.* The facts and the law for this case are the same as in Assignment #36 on p. 250. Assume that there has already been a trial in this case that resulted in a judgment for Beacon House. It was a nonjury trial. Pine Street Tenants are now appealing to the Supreme Court of Connecticut. Pine Street Tenants are the appellants and Beacon House is the appellee. The basis of the appeal is the correctness of the trial court's interpretation of the law in favor of Beacon House. The trial court concluded that there was no nuisance and hence no permanent injunction should be granted. There was no trial court opinion. See Instructions on Making Oral Presentations, p. 266, and Preparing for a Presentation, p. 269.

Assignment #57

The case that will be argued is: *Sesu Mbuto, M.D. v. Pennsylvania.* The facts and the law for this case are the same as in Assignment #37 on p. 251. Assume that there has already been a trial in this case that resulted in a conviction of Dr. Mbuto. It was a nonjury trial. Dr. Mbuto is now appealing his conviction and the judgment based thereon to the Supreme Court of Pennsylvania. Dr. Mbuto is the appellant and the State of Pennsylvania (through the prosecutor) is the appellee. The basis of the appeal is the correctness of the trial court's determination that the conviction was constitutional. There was no trial court opinion. See Instructions on Making Oral Presentations, p. 266, and Preparing for a Presentation, p. 269.

Assignment #58

The case that will be argued is: *Carole Taylor v. Charles Taylor.* The facts and the law for this case are the same as in Assignment #38 on p. 252. Assume that there has already been a trial in this case that resulted in a judgment for Charles. It was a nonjury trial. Carole is now appealing to the District of Columbia Court of Appeals. Carole is the appellant and Charles is the appellee. The basis of the appeal is the correctness of the trial court's interpretation of the law in favor of Charles. The trial court concluded that Charles was entitled to the bank account (except for the $2,000 that he voluntarily decided to give Carole) and 100% of the store. There was no trial court opinion. See Instructions on Making Oral Presentations, p. 266, and Preparing for a Presentation, p. 269.

Assignment #59

The case that will be argued is: *Lawrence Cooper v. Brenda Cooper*. The facts and the law for this case are the same as in Assignment #39 on p. 252. Assume that there has already been a trial in this case that resulted in a judgment for Brenda. It was a nonjury trial. Lawrence is now appealing to the United States Court of Appeals for the Seventh Circuit. Lawrence is the appellant and Brenda is the appellee. The basis of the appeal is the correctness of the trial court's interpretation of the law in favor of Brenda. The trial court concluded that there was no constitutional problem in denying alimony to Lawrence. There was no trial court opinion. See Instructions on Making Oral Presentations, p. 266, and Preparing for a Presentation, p. 269.

Assignment #60

The case that will be argued is: *Relatives of George Schuler v. Clarence Wellman*. The facts and the law for this case are the same as in Assignment #40 on p. 253. Assume that there has already been a trial in this case that resulted in a judgment for Clarence Wellman. It was a nonjury trial. The Relatives of George Schuler are now appealing to the Supreme Court of Appeals of Virginia. The Relatives are the appellants and Clarence Wellman is the appellee. The basis of the appeal is the correctness of the trial court's interpretation of the law in favor of Clarence Wellman. The trial court concluded that the attempted revocation was invalid. There was no trial court opinion. See Instructions on Making Oral Presentations, p. 266, and Preparing for a Presentation, p. 269.

Assignment #61

The case that will be argued is: *Smith v. KTS*. The facts and the law for this case are the same as in Assignment #41 on p. 254. Assume that there has already been a trial in this case that resulted in a judgment for KTS. It was a nonjury trial. Smith is now appealing to the Court of Appeals of New York. Smith is the appellant and KTS is the appellee. The basis of the appeal is the correctness of the trial court's interpretation of the law in favor of KTS. The trial court concluded that KTS owed no duty to Smith. There was no trial court opinion. See Instructions on Making Oral Presentations, p. 266, and Preparing for a Presentation, p. 269.

Assignment #62

The case that will be argued is: *Edward Swann v. New York City Department of Licenses and Inspections*. The facts and the law for this case are the same as in Assignment #42 on p. 254. Assume that there has already been a trial in this case that resulted in a judgment for New York City. It was a nonjury trial. Edward Swann is now appealing to the United States Court of Appeals for the Second Circuit. Edward Swann is the appellant and New York City is the appellee. The basis of the appeal is the correctness of the trial court's interpretation of the law in favor of New York City. The trial court concluded that Swann had no right to an evidentiary hearing before his license was revoked;

a post-revocation hearing was sufficient. There was no trial court opinion. See Instructions on Making Oral Presentations, p. 266, and Preparing for a Presentation, p. 269.

Section B. Oral Advocacy: Applying a Case Cluster

In this section you will find additional oral advocacy exercises. The major difference is that the hearing in these exercises will involve the application of a *case cluster* to a set of facts, unlike the exercises in Assignments #53–62 where the focus of your argument was the application of one opinion. For our purposes, a case cluster is two opinions that rule on a similar issue with different results.

Two case clusters are presented below in Assignments #63 and #64. Before you are given the facts that will be the basis of the oral advocacy exercises in these Assignments, you will find a series of questions about the opinions that you will be applying.

Assignment #63

This assignment is based on two opinions:

> *Brubaker v. Dickson,* p. 343.
>
> *In Re Hawley,* p. 350.

(1) What is the issue in *Brubaker?*

(2) What is the holding in *Brubaker?*

(3) What is the issue in *Hawley?*

(4) What is the holding in *Hawley?*

(5) Assume that the facts of the *Brubaker* case were before the court that wrote *Hawley.* What result would the latter court reach? Justice Peters wrote *Hawley.* What decision would Justice Peters reach if he were the judge trying to decide whether Mr. Brubaker's counsel was incompetent?

(6) Assume that the facts of the *Hawley* case were before the court that wrote *Brubaker.* What result would the latter court reach? Judge Browning wrote *Brubaker.* What decision would Judge Browning reach if he were the judge trying to decide whether Mr. Hawley's counsel was incompetent?

(7) Was *Brubaker* decided incorrectly? The attorney may not have been great, but he clearly made tactical decisions. Didn't he? He may have made the wrong ones. Yet the court says that error of judgment is not the test of competence. Is the court wrong when it concludes that there was "a total failure to present the cause of the accused?"

(8) The *Brubaker* court refers to a "reasonably diligent trial counsel." Is the test of constitutional competence a test of negligence? If your lawyer is unreasonable or negligent, then has your trial been fundamentally and constitutionally unfair?

(9) The *Hawley* court says that counsel must investigate defenses "carefully." Is this the test of constitutional incompetence?

(10) FACTS FOR ORAL ADVOCACY EXERCISE:

John Smith is a criminal attorney with about ten years' experience on many kinds of cases. He lives and practices in the state of New Ionia.

He has been having marital problems with his wife, Jane Smith. They have had very long and bitter arguments. Jane sometimes throws small furniture at John during these altercations.

During a recent fight, Jane accused John of adultery. (John had gone to the theater with his secretary, but there was no affair.) During the fight, both became hysterical. Jane started to rip the phone off the wall. John grabbed Jane's arm as both were screaming. John pushed her away from the phone. She fell and severely injured her head. After a period of hospitalization, Jane went to the police and charged John with criminal assault, a felony in the state of New Ionia. He is indicted and decides to represent himself even though he has never handled a case of criminal assault growing out of a marital dispute.

The state allows self-representation in criminal cases so long as the judge decides that the accused has the emotional and intellectual capacity to represent himself or herself. At the arraignment, the trial judge questions John on why he wants to represent himself. "Because I'm innocent," replies John, "and it would be very easy for me to establish my innocence." The judge knows of John's excellent reputation as an attorney, and agrees to allow him to represent himself.

The bar association has a guideline that an attorney should not take cases in which there is a strong likelihood that the attorney would have to become a witness in the case.

John had evidence that Jane assaulted him on numerous occasions in the past. Hospital records (containing incriminating statements by Jane) were available to establish this.

Two months before the trial, John starts to panic. He feels great guilt over the marital difficulties with Jane. He has trouble sleeping and eating. One day he says to himself, "Maybe I should allow Jane to win this case and get the conviction against me. Let her live with the fact that she ruined my career. These hospital records will tell the truth about what I have been through. Let her win, but the truth must be told."

On the night before the trial, John gets about an hour's sleep. He is about forty-five minutes late and initially goes to the wrong courtroom. In the corridor, he meets an old friend who greets him. John acts as if he doesn't know this person and tells him that he (John) is a court stenographer. The friend leaves, saying to himself, "I guess the strain has really gotten to the old boy."

The judge is angry over John's late arrival. "I apologize," John tells the judge, "I'm very upset, but I'm OK now."

John decides not to testify on his own behalf. The prosecutor places Jane on the stand. She testifies that John beat her with a broom stick and kicked her to the ground as they were arguing near the phone.

As John listens to this testimony, he breaks down into tears. Yet he also feels rage against Jane for lying. He is determined to prove that she is not telling the truth. But the tears keep flowing. He thinks back over the years when he worked sixteen hours a day, seven days a week. He neglected Jane and was unfair to her. "I can't blame her for what she's doing," he tells himself. But then the anger over her testimony returns.

After Jane's testimony, John rises and tells the court that he would like to offer evidence for the court's consideration. While standing, he looks through his briefcase for the hospital records. He feels a great sadness and self-pity as he is looking. ("Why bother with these records," he asks himself, "the jury will just think I'm whining.") He then sits down.

"Do you have evidence to introduce?" asks the judge. "No, your honor," replies John. John also waives cross-examination of Jane, and waives his closing statement to the jury. He offers no evidence.

The jury convicts John. On appeal, John is represented by another attorney who asks that the conviction be overturned on the ground that John was represented by incompetent counsel. A hearing on this issue will take place in class.

Assume that the facts of this case arise in the state of New Ionia and that there is no authority in New Ionia on the issue(s) raised by these facts. The case is one of first impression in this state. The name of the case on appeal is *John Smith v. New Ionia*. The only authority that you can consider are *Brubaker v. Dickson* and *In re Hawley*.

On conducting the hearing, see Format of the Class, p. 265, Instructions on Making Oral Presentations, p. 266, Preparing for a Presentation, p. 269, and the Role of the Judges, p. 269. The only difference is that you will be applying two opinions rather than one. You must argue that one of the opinions should be followed in the *Smith* case, and the other should be distinguished.

Assignment #64

This assignment is based on two opinions:

Iowa Dept. of Social Services v. Iowa Merit Employment Dept., p. 354.
Forts v. Ward, p. 359.

(1) What is the BFOQ issue in *Iowa?*

(2) What is the BFOQ holding in *Iowa?*

(3) To limit the functions of a female CO II "would cause discontent among *male* CO II's." Not to limit the functions of a female CO II would be very upsetting to *male* "inmates [who] have fixed ideas as to female roles." (Emphasis added.) There is no way to keep the males happy if we try to accommodate a female. Is this the essence of the *Iowa* case?

(4) Do you think that Justice Harris, who wrote the *Iowa* opinion, would reach the same conclusion if a woman was applying for the *CO I* position? All we are told about the CO I position is that it involves rotating "through various tasks on a somewhat limited basis." Couldn't this mean seeing unclothed inmates occasionally? Wouldn't there be some security problems? Therefore, would this court find a BFOQ for the CO I position if the issue was before it? Do you think that Justice Harris simply wants women out of male prisons?

(5) The court in *Iowa* (through its reliance on *Long*) conceded that "reasonable adjustments should be made" in order to give equal protection rights to both sexes. Did the court consider any such adjustments for Gunther?

(6) In *Iowa,* if Gunther had been granted what she wanted by the court, would the job of her male co-workers become more dangerous since they would have to perform the contact duties from which she would be exempted? Would this constitute reverse sex discrimination against males?

(7) What is the central issue in *Forts?*

(8) What is the central holding of *Forts?*

(9) Assume that all the facts of the *Forts* case were before the court that wrote the *Iowa* opinion. What result would the latter court reach? Justice Harris wrote *Iowa.* What decision would Justice Harris reach if he were the judge trying to decide whether the prohibition of male guards from performing nighttime duty at a female prison constitutes gender-based employment discrimination in violation of Title VII of the Civil Rights Act? How would Harris feel about imposing a fifteen-minute rule during the nighttime? How would he handle the pajama problem?

(10) Assume that all the facts of the *Iowa* case were before the court that wrote the *Forts* opinion. What result would the latter court reach? Judge Newman wrote *Forts.* What decision would Judge Newman reach if he were trying to decide whether a BFOQ existed for a CO II position, and whether the problem could be resolved by exempting a female CO II from close personal/physical contact and intimate surveillance of male inmates?

(11) In *Iowa,* the court had great difficulty exempting female CO II guards from conducting strip searches of males. In *Forts,* the court had no trouble accepting an exemption of male guards from conducting strip searches of females. Can you explain the difference?

(12) FACTS FOR ORAL ADVOCACY EXERCISE:

Fred Smith is a gay mental health Counselor Aide (CA) assigned to the Bay View State Mental Institution. Patients of Bay View State are involuntarily committed by court orders that declare them to be a danger to themselves or to others. Fred is assigned to Ward 7, which has just opened. It houses patients suffering specific psychiatric disorders. All the patients have committed or have threatened to commit acts of violence against women. The patients in Ward 7 are undergoing a special program involving chemical and nonchemical treatments. The legality of this treatment program is not in question.

There are five patients currently in Ward 7. At full capacity, the Ward can treat eighteen patients. Each of the five patients is male. Dr. Janice Davis, the supervising director of twelve of the twenty wards at Bay View State, has decided to limit the Ward 7 population to male patients during the first five years of its operation. The director has also decided that no staff members at Ward 7 can be female since she is not sure what effect female staff members would have on the population, given their mental problem. At present, Fred is the only CA in Ward 7, but there are two other CA positions open.

The main duty of a CA is to provide general assistance to the professional staff at the institution. The CA is also a co-leader of the group therapy sessions, and occasionally runs these sessions in the absence of the psychologist in charge of therapy.

The CA acts as the eyes and ears of the psychologist in reporting all behavior to the latter. It is important that the CA earn the confidence of the patient in order to fulfill this role. A CA has no direct security responsibility, although the CA is expected to be available to assist the guards who have the primary responsibility for security. Such assistance, however, is seldom needed. (No guards are permanently stationed in Ward 7; the guards patrol a number of different wards. At present all guards who work in the area of Ward 7 are male, although there is no requirement that they be male.)

When a patient awakes in the morning, he is asked to relate anything he remembers about his dreams that night. The CA records this information at bedside and then gives it to the psychologist for use in individual therapy conducted by the latter.

Linda Jones applies for one of the CA openings at Ward 7. Linda agrees that it might be unwise for her to be alone with the patients in view of the danger of violence that they might commit against her. Hence she proposes the following arrangement: She will work in Ward 7, but during her first six months on the job, she will never be alone with a patient. A male CA (e.g., Fred) or other male employee will always be within a moment's reach in case trouble develops. After the six-month period, however, this rule will be removed if the director is satisfied that no treatment concern of the program will be compromised thereby. Dr. Davis denies this request and refuses to hire Linda because she is a woman, even though it is clear that she is otherwise qualified for a CA position.

The parent of one of the patients at Ward 7 discovers that Fred Smith is gay and insists that Dr. Davis either remove him or require that he never be allowed to be alone with a patient. She refuses this request, pointing out that Fred has an excellent record at the institution and has never been charged with any irregularities.

The case now before the court is *Linda Jones v. Dr. Janice Davis,* director of the ward. The trial court below ruled in favor of Dr. Davis. In a one-line opinion, the trial court said, "No constitutional or statutory rights have been violated by Dr. Davis." On appeal, the question is whether this conclusion is correct. A hearing will take place in class.

Assume that the facts of this case arise in the state of New Ionia and that there is no authority in New Ionia on the issue(s) raised by these facts. The case is one of first impression in this state. The only authority that you can consider are *Iowa Dept. of Social Services v. Iowa Merit Employment Dept.,* p. 354, and *Forts v. Ward,* p. 359. New Ionia has a statute (§ 23) that "prohibits employment discrimination on the basis of sex unless based on the nature of the occupation." Of course, Title VII of the Civil Rights Act, a federal statute, applies to New Ionia.

On conducting the hearing, see Format of the Class, p. 265, Instructions on Making Oral Presentations, p. 266, Preparing for a Presentation, p. 269, and the Role of the Judges, p. 269. The only difference is that you will be applying two opinions rather than one. You must argue that one of the opinions should be followed in the Linda Jones case, and the other should be distinguished.

Chapter Twenty-One

The Appellate Brief*

Section A. Introduction

The word "brief" has two meanings in the law: first, a written legal argument submitted to an appellate court, and second, an analytical summary of a single court opinion. Part II of this text was devoted to the skills of identifying the components of an opinion in order to arrive at the latter type of brief. In this chapter we will examine the former, the appellate brief.

An appellate brief is a sophisticated, highly stylized, and often lengthy document that is submitted to an appellate court in an effort to persuade that court that an error has (or has not) been made by a lower court. (Kafka is said to have commented that a lawyer is a person who writes a 10,000 word document and calls it a "brief"!) The predominant characteristic of the appellate brief is advocacy. The structure of the brief, the phrasing of the issues, the organization of the analysis—in short, every aspect and every word of the brief—are dictated by considerations of advocacy.

The art of appellate brief writing is a complex and difficult subject that has been treated extensively by leading scholars, judges, and practitioners. Because of its complexity, we will not attempt to examine every aspect of the brief in detail here. Our goal will be limited to providing a basic introduction to the structure and components of an appellate brief.

Before considering the more technical aspects of drafting an appellate brief it is necessary to understand the procedural context in which brief writing takes place. Consequently, the following section briefly explores the scope and limitations of the appellate process.

---

* Coauthored by Wilbur O. Colom of Colom, Mitchell & Colom, P.A., Columbus, Mississippi.

Section B. The Appellate Process

When a court or administrative agency reaches a final decision in the dispute, at least one of the parties is often unhappy with that decision. If the dissatisfied party believes that the adverse decision is the result of an error of law that the court or agency made, it may be possible for that party to ask a higher court to review the decision in order to correct the alleged error. This process of review is called an appeal. The person bringing the appeal is the appellant; the person against whom it is brought is the appellee or respondent.

Appellate review, however, is not boundless. Certain kinds of appeal are discretionary in that the appellate court may refuse to hear the appeal unless it feels that the issues raised by the appellant merit its attention. Even where the appeal is a matter "of right," with no discretion on the part of the appellate court to refuse to hear it, there are certain well-established limitations on the scope of appeal that are common to most kinds of cases. In general, appellate review (whether it is discretionary or of right) is limited to:

1. the *record* developed below;
2. issues *raised* below;
3. issues of *law;*
4. *material* errors; and
5. *final* orders.

1. THE RECORD BELOW

Appellate courts exist primarily to review the determinations of lower courts and administrative agencies and to correct errors and abuses that occurred within these tribunals. Appellate courts will generally limit their consideration to the *record* of what occurred below, i.e., the case docket, transcripts of the proceedings and testimony, copies of exhibits, motions, pleadings, and other items that were considered by the fact-finding tribunal. With rare exceptions, appellate courts will refuse to consider matters outside this record. For example, an appellate court generally will not take into consideration new evidence that was not presented to the trial court.

2. ISSUES RAISED BELOW

Similarly, appellate courts will not review issues unless those issues were first raised before the lower court or agency. The controlling principle is that the trial court or agency should have had an opportunity to make the correct decision before a party may assert on appeal that the court or agency erred. Thus, if a party on appeal wants to raise the issue of whether a trial court properly admitted a certain document into evidence, the party must have objected to the admission of that document during the trial as the precondition of a consideration of that issue by the appellate court. If the objection was not made during the trial, the right to raise it on appeal is often waived.

3. ISSUES OF LAW

Courts at the *trial* level are empowered to consider and resolve two kinds of issues: (a) factual issues (i.e., what actually happened), and (b) issues of law or application issues (i.e., what rules of law are applicable to these facts and how do these rules apply). In general, appellate courts may consider and decide only the latter type of issue, issues of law.

4. MATERIAL ERRORS

Not every error of law made by a trial court will affect the decision that the court reached. Suppose, for example, that the trial court erroneously rules that certain testimony was admissible when it should have been excluded as hearsay. If there has been additional competent and uncontradicted testimony to the same effect, the court's error will probably be considered *harmless error* because the exclusion of the hearsay would not have altered the result. If, on the other hand, there had been no other evidence to the same effect and if the hearsay testimony arguably influenced the jury's verdict, then the error would be considered *material.* Appellate courts will correct only material errors, i.e., those errors that may have influenced the court's decision, and will disregard what they consider to be harmless error.

5. FINAL ORDERS

With limited exceptions, appellate courts will hear appeals only from final orders of the lower court. Generally, this means that all the proceedings before the lower court must have been completed before an appeal will be allowed. For example, suppose that several weeks before trial, a defendant makes a motion to dismiss that the trial court denies. The defendant generally will not be permitted to appeal this decision until the trial is over and a final order has been entered, i.e., until *all* the proceedings before the trial court have been completed. This rule enables the appellate court to review all the alleged errors made by the lower court at once, rather than allowing the litigation to drag out endlessly with each error being appealed one by one. Moreover, an error committed by the trial court early in the litigation may turn out to be harmless in the light of subsequent developments.

There are exceptions to the final order rule, e.g., interlocutory appeals (p. 32), certification of questions of law to an appellate court. In these exceptions, the appellate court *can* act before there is a final decision below. In some complex federal litigation, there will be a bifurcation of the trial where some issues will be tried separately from others. For example, the court may first try the issue of liability and, if necessary, try the issue of damages at a later date. An appeal may be allowed on the liability issue while the trial court resolves the damage issue.

In addition to these five general limitations on the scope of appeal, there are laws governing many aspects of the appeal such as:

1. posting a bond for costs on appeal (p. 49);

2. the time permitted to file the briefs;

3. notice requirements to the adverse party;

4. method of transmitting the record from the lower court to the appellate court;

5. payment of costs;

6. requirements of special appeals such as mandamus;

7. stays (p. 48) and injunctions pending appeal.

The nature of these requirements may vary a great deal from state to state and to some extent may even differ among courts of appeal within a single judicial system. You should, of course, familiarize yourself with the statutes and procedural court rules applicable in your jurisdiction. Failure to comply with their requirements may result in the dismissal of an otherwise valid appeal.

Section C. Organization, Style, and Content of the Appellate Brief

The form of the appellate brief is usually mandated by court rules. Typical of such rules for *federal* courts is Rule 28 of the Federal Rules of Appellate Procedure, which provides:

(a) BRIEF OF THE APPELLANT. The brief of the appellant shall contain under appropriate headings and in the order here indicated:

(1) A table of contents, with page references, and a table of cases (alphabetically arranged), statutes and other authorities cited, with references to the pages of the brief where they are cited.

(2) A statement of the issues presented for review.

(3) A statement of the case. The statement shall first indicate briefly the nature of the case, the course of the proceedings, and its disposition in the court below. There shall follow a statement of the facts relevant to the issue presented for review, with appropriate references to the record. . . .

(4) An argument. The argument may be preceded by a summary. The argument shall contain the contentions of the appellant with respect to the issues presented and the reasons therefor, with citations to the authorities, statutes and parts of the record relied on.

(5) A short conclusion stating the precise relief sought.

(b) BRIEF OF THE APPELLEE. The brief of the appellee shall conform to the requirements of subdivision (a)(1)–(4), except that a statement of the issues of the case need not be made unless the appellee is dissatisfied with the statement of the appellant.

(c) REPLY BRIEF. The appellant may file a brief in reply to the brief of the appellee, and if the appellee has cross-appealed, the appellee may file a brief in reply to the response of the appellant to the issues presented by the cross appeal. No further briefs may be filed except with leave of court.

. . .

(g) LENGTH OF BRIEFS. Except by permission of the court, or as specified by local rule of the court of appeals, principal briefs shall not exceed 50 pages, and reply briefs shall not exceed 25 pages, exclusive of pages containing the table of contents, table of citations and any addendum containing statutes, rules, regulations, etc.

———

The procedural court rules of some *state* courts on the format of appellate briefs can be equally detailed. Here, for example, is Rule 7(f) of the Mississippi Supreme Court:

The front cover of every brief shall show the style and number of the case and shall designate the brief as "BRIEF FOR APPELLANT", "BRIEF FOR APPELLEE", OR "APPELLANT'S REBUTTAL BRIEF". Each brief shall contain a topic or subject index identifying clearly by a sentence or concise statement the separate points to be urged before the Court. The points so identified shall be numbered consecutively, and under each point shall be an alphabetical list of the cases, statutes, textbooks, and other authorities or materials which the brief maker is relying upon in support of that point, showing the page or pages of the brief where that case or other authority is mentioned. All Mississippi cases shall be cited to both the official Mississippi Reports and the Southern Reporter. (The Southern Reporter is the official report for all decisions published since 1966.) Quotations from cases and authorities appearing in the text of the brief shall be followed by a reference to the book and page(s) where the quotation appears.

———

The following components are often found in many appellate briefs. In the remaining sections of this chapter, we will examine each of these components:

- Cover Page
- Table of Contents
- Table of Authorities or Index
- Jurisdiction Statement
- Questions Presented
- Constitutional Provisions, Statutes, and Regulations Involved
- Statement of the Case
- Argument
- Conclusion
- Appendix

Occasionally you may find appellate briefs that combine some of the above components. The same labels are not always used. Again, you must check the rules for specific appellate courts.

Section D. The Cover, Table of Contents, and Index

1. THE COVER

The cover of the appellate brief is the equivalent of the heading on a memorandum of law (p. 223); its purpose is to identify the document. The cover should include:

a. the name of the appellate court;

b. the names of the parties;

c. the case or docket number assigned to the appeal;

d. the name of the court from which the appeal is being taken;

e. the type of brief (e.g., appellant's, appellee's, reply, etc.);

f. the name and address of counsel submitting the brief.

These six components are readily identifiable in the sample cover taken from the brief submitted to the U.S. Supreme Court by counsel for the petitioners in *Doe v. McMillan* (see Figure 21–1).

2. THE TABLE OF CONTENTS

The Table of Contents is an outline of the major components of the brief, including the various point headings (see discussion on p. 292) and subheadings of the argument, and the pages in the brief on which they are covered. The function of the Table of Contents is to provide the reader with quick and easy access to each individual portion of the brief. Because the exact wording of the point headings and the pages on which they are covered will not be known until the brief is completed, the Table of Contents will be one of the last sections of the brief to be written. The following excerpt from the respondents' brief in Doe v. McMillan illustrates the structure of a Table of Contents.

Table of Contents

```
              IN THE

Supreme Court of the United States
             OCTOBER TERM, 1972


               No. 71-6356


          JOHN DOE, et al.,
                         Petitioners,

                  v.

        JOHN L. McMILLAN, et al.,
                         Respondents.


     ON WRIT OF CERTIORARI TO THE
  UNITED STATES COURT OF APPEALS FOR
   THE DISTRICT OF COLUMBIA CIRCUIT


        BRIEF FOR PETITIONERS


        URBAN LAW INSTITUTE

             JEAN CAMPER CAHN
             MICHAEL J. VALDER
             G. DAN BOWLING
             RONALD G. YELENIK
               Suite 509
               1145 19th Street, N.W.
               Washington, D.C. 20036
             Counsel for Petitioners
```

FIGURE 21–1. A Sample Cover from a Brief Submitted to the United States Supreme Court.

3. THE TABLE OF AUTHORITIES OR INDEX

This part of the appellate brief (called a Table of Authorities, or sometimes an Index) consists of a listing of:

a. each primary and secondary authority (p. 203) cited and relied upon in the brief;

b. the full citation to each authority;

c. the page or pages within the brief on which each authority is mentioned or discussed.

The Table of Authorities (or Index) is normally placed at the beginning of the brief, immediately following the Table of Contents. Group the various authorities into categories, listing separately all the opinions, all the federal constitutional provisions, all the state constitutional provisions, all the statutes, all the regulations, etc. Secondary authority such as treatises and law review articles are grouped together under a miscellaneous heading. Within each category, there should be a clear organization. Opinions, for example, should be cited in alphabetical order. The same is true of items listed in the miscellaneous category. Constitutional and statutory provisions, on the other hand, are listed in the order in which they appear in the Constitution or code, usually in numerical order. The following excerpt, from the respondent's brief in *United States v. Roberts,* illustrates this pattern:

Cases

United States v. Becker, 461 F.2d 230 (2nd Cir., 1972) 4

United States v. Pisacano, 459 F.2d 259, 264 (2nd Cir., 1972) 4, 5

United States v. Focarile, 340 F.Supp. 1033 (D.Md., 1972) 7

Statutes

18 U.S.C. § 245(a)(1) 8, 9

18 U.S.C. § 1952 3

18 U.S.C. § 2510 7

18 U.S.C. § 2516 . . . . .2, 3, 7, 8

18 U.S.C. § 2516(1) 2, 5, 6

18 U.S.C. § 2518(1)(a) 2

28 U.S.C. § 503 6

28 U.S.C. § 510 8

etc.

Section E. Jurisdiction Statement

In this section of the brief, there is a short statement explaining the subject-matter jurisdiction of the appellate court (p. 145). For example:

> This Court has jurisdiction under 28 U.S.C. § 1291 (1967).

The jurisdiction statement may point out some of the essential facts that relate to the jurisdiction of the appellate court such as how the case came up on appeal. For example:

> On January 2, 1978, a judgment was entered by the U.S. Court of Appeals for the Second Circuit. The U.S. Supreme Court granted certiorari on February 6, 1978. 400 U.S. 302.

Later in the brief there will be a Statement of the Case in which more detailed jurisdictional material is often included.

Section F. The Question(s) Presented

The question or questions presented provides the first major opportunity for advocacy in the appellate brief. The label used for this part of the brief varies. It may be called, "Questions Presented," "Points Relied upon for Reversal," "Points in Error," "Assignments of Error," "Issues Presented," etc. Regardless of the label, its substance is essentially the same: it is a statement of the issue or issues of law that the party wishes the appellate court to consider and decide.

The *location* of the statement of the issues within the brief, and even the *content* of the statement, may be regulated by court rule. The United States Supreme Court Rules, for example, provide that the question presented is to precede the statement of the case and the argument, and that it should be expressed ". . . in the terms of and circumstances of the case but without unnecessary detail . . ." Rule 15(1)(a). You should consult the court rules in your own jurisdiction for similar instructions.

The skill of identifying and stating issues of law has been treated elsewhere in this text (p. 225). Although the statement of the issues in an appellate brief will be based upon the errors of law that the appellant claims were made by the lower court (p. 280), the techniques of identifying and stating those issues are essentially the same as in other legal writing. As in an external memorandum such as a trial or hearing memorandum (p. 222), the statement of the issues in the appellate brief is very much a tool of persuasion. The writer's statement of the issues will generally be the first item that the judge will turn to in reading the brief. The manner in which the issues are phrased can have a significant impact upon his or her perspective in reading and evaluating the remaining portions of the brief.

A legal issue has two components: one or more rules of law, and facts that raise a question of the applicability of those rule(s) of law. We have already examined how advocates can phrase the same issue differently in a memorandum of law (p. 227). The same advocacy dynamics play a role in the phrasing of the rule of law and the fact components of issues in appellate briefs:

1. ADVOCACY IN THE RULE OF LAW COMPONENT OF THE ISSUE

There are two major advocacy techniques of stating the rule of law component of an issue.

The first is the selective use of quotations from the rule(s) of law being applied. You will often find that certain portions of a rule of law tend to favor the client while other portions are less favorable or are actually damaging. In drafting an issue, include a brief quotation of or other reference to the favorable language in the rule(s) of law involved in the issue. While it is not possible to "duck" the plain wording of a rule, your emphasis of the favorable language may encourage the reader to approach your argument on that issue in a "positive" frame of mind, making him or her more receptive to your interpretation of the damaging language in the rule.

A second method of achieving this end is to summarize or paraphrase the requirements and/or effects of the rule(s) in your statement of the issue. This technique is illustrated in the following opposing statements of an issue presented to the United States Supreme Court in a case on elections:

Appellant's Statement of Issue

Whether the totality of the general election ballot certification requirements imposed on minority political parties by the Texas Election Code, including provisions forcing such parties to obtain the notarized signatures of approximately 22,000 registered voters who have not previously participated during the same election year in a major party primary election or nominating convention, but limiting the time for obtaining such signatures to a period of approximately 55 days following the major party primary elections, and further requiring that a candidate formally file for office approximately nine months before the general election and approximately three months before the primary elections, abridges the rights of free association, liberty, due process and equal protection guaranteed by the First and Fourteenth Amendments?

Appellee's Statement of the Same Issue

Is it constitutionally permissible for the Texas Election Code to require that before the nominees of any new political party, or a political party whose nominee for governor at the last general election received less than 2% of the total vote cast for governor, or a previously existing party which did not have a nominee for governor in the last general election, can be placed upon the general election ballot, there must be a showing that the number of people participating in the party's precinct conventions or signing petitions to have the party's nominees on the general election ballot, was at least 1% of the vote for governor at the last general election?

The rule of law in this issue is a statute—the Texas Election Code. Note the different approach in each version of the issue. The appellant, who is seeking to have the statute ruled unconstitutional, emphasizes those aspects of the statute that it believes are unreasonable: the high number of signatures required, the short period of time available to obtain those signatures, etc. The appellee, on the other hand, ignores the time limitations completely and describes the rule of law in a manner that makes it appear to be much more reasonable. Note in particular the advocacy that is evident in the parties' description of the number of signatures required. The appellee describes the requirement as being "at least 1% of the vote for governor at the last general election," a figure that on its face would seem minimal and quite reasonable. The appellant, on the other hand, translates this percentage into the approximate number of signatures ("22,000") that would be necessary under this standard. The result is a figure that is more impressive and that tends to maximize the apparent unreasonableness of the requirement.

2. ADVOCACY IN THE FACTUAL COMPONENT OF THE ISSUE

Compare the use of facts in the following two statements of the same issue in opposing appellate briefs:

Petitioner's Statement of the Issue

Does the warrantless search of the contents of a briefcase made at the time of arrest pursuant to an arrest warrant for an alleged misdemeanor, in the absence of exigent circumstances, violate the Fourth and Fourteenth Amendments of the United States Constitution?

Respondent's Statement of the Same Issue

Whether an officer serving an arrest warrant for, among other things, carrying a concealed weapon, may constitutionally remove from the arrestee/driver's side of the car, a case from the floor of the car between the arrestee's feet and, feeling a bulky object like a weapon, may open the case and remove the weapon when he has previously been told the arrestee carried the weapon in just such a case?

Both parties describe the same situation or transaction in these issue statements, but there are significant differences. Each party begins by presenting a favorable fact. The petitioner begins its statement of the issue by stressing that no warrant was obtained for the *search,* a fact that is relevant to its contention that the search was unconstitutional. The respondent, on the other hand, begins by noting that the *arrest* that preceded the search *was* made with a warrant. In addition, the parties differ greatly in the extent to which they have described the facts. Petitioner, in an effort to minimize highly damaging facts, describes the arrest warrant broadly as being one "for an alleged misdemeanor," while the respondent emphasizes the damaging nature of the same fact by describing the circumstances in much more detail.

One final point should be mentioned concerning the statement of the issues. As discussed in Chapter 18, you must state and analyze some issues *on the assumption* that the court rules against you on issues treated early in your presentation (p. 228). The appellate brief should *not* be limited to those issues you are confident of winning. If the court eventually decides against you on an issue, other issues (which we have called *contingency* issues) may then arise that you must present in the light most favorable to the client. Suppose that the trial court found the defendant (the client) guilty of robbery and sentenced him or her to twenty years in prison. There are at least two issues that could exist: the legality of the conviction and the legality of the sentence. In the discussion of your first issue, you will focus on the impropriety of the conviction. If the appellate court eventually rules against you on the conviction issue (which, of course, you will not know at the time you are writing the appellate brief), you must be ready for the sentence issue, e.g., you may argue that the criminal statute does not authorize a sentence of over fifteen years for anyone convicted of robbery. Hence, the portion of the appellate brief in which you discuss the sentence issue might begin with a comment such as:

In the event that this court determines that the conviction was valid, the question then becomes whether the sentence. . . .

Section G.   Constitutional Provisions, Statutes, Regulations Involved

After stating the issues, you give the exact text (word for word) of any constitutional provisions, statutes, regulations, etc., that will be analyzed in the brief. If there are many of these rules of law or if any of them are very long, you can include them in the appendix of the brief. You would simply note in this early portion of the brief that the rules of law are printed in the appendix.

Section H. The Statement of the Case

The statement of the case, sometimes called the statement of the facts, will generally consist of the following four components:

1. A summary of the dispute;

2. A statement of the prior proceedings;

3. A brief summary of the judgment of the lower court and the court's reasoning; and

4. A narrative of the essential facts of the case.

As indicated earlier, some of this information may also be included in the jurisdiction Statement (p. 286).

It is a good practice to organize these components in the order they are listed above. The first three steps provide the court with an overview of the nature and status of the dispute and hence a context in which to read the factual narrative. The following statement from a brief filed in *Garrett Freightlines, Inc. v. United States* conforms to this pattern. (Tr. refers to pages in the transcript of the trial record.)

Statement of Facts

These are actions based upon the Federal Tort Claims Act, 28 U.S.C. § 1346(b), initiated by the appellants, Garrett Freightlines, Inc. and Charles R. Thomas in the United States District Court for the District of Idaho. The appellant alleged that appellee's employee, Randall W. Reynolds, while acting within the scope of his employment, negligently caused injury to appellants. The United States denied that the employee was acting within the scope of his employment.

On March 27, 1973, appellant Garrett made a motion for limited summary judgment as to whether Reynolds was acting within the scope of his employment when the collision occurred. The actions of Garrett and Thomas were consolidated by order of the court, and appellee later moved for summary judgment (Tr. 204).

The District Court held that under the authority of dicta in Berrettoni v. United States, 436 F.2d 1372 (9th Cir. 1970), that Reynolds was not within the scope of his employment when the accident occurred and granted appellee's motion for summary judgment. It is from that order and judgment that the injured now appeals.

Staff Sergeant Reynolds was a career soldier in the United States Military and, until November 9, 1970, stationed at Fort Rucker, Alabama. On or about July 30, 1970, official orders directed that Reynolds be reassigned to the Republic of Vietnam. In accordance with, and as a part of official orders, Reynolds was granted 45 days' delay en route leave which was authorized by his superiors (Tr. 240). Reynolds was also granted seven days' travel time not charged as leave. At the conclusion of leave and travel time, Reynolds was to report at Oakland, California, for transportation to Vietnam. Travel pay was authorized on an automobile mileage basis from Fort Rucker to Oakland for travel by private automobile by the serviceman (Tr. 301). Yet, Reynolds' household furniture was shipped at government expense to Portland, Oregon, at his designation. There is no doubt that Reynolds' Military Superiors were aware of his intentions to drive via Portland, Oregon—where he would leave his wife and spend the largest portion of his leave (Tr. 480). There is also no question but that Reynolds alone had the option of choosing the route which would take him to Oakland.

Reynolds and his wife left Fort Rucker on November 9, 1970, in accordance with his reassignment orders. The car, driven by Reynolds, collided on November 13, 1970, on the fifth day of travel, with a vehicle owned by the appellant Garrett and driven by appellant Thomas near Burley, Idaho (Tr. 320, 411).

The facts in the brief must be based upon the record below. You should attempt to describe them in a clear, concise, and easy-to-read fashion. Avoid tedious and unnecessary inventories of the transcripts and exhibits, and attempt to translate the evidence and findings into a vivid narrative that will hold the reader's attention. Above all, be accurate in your statement of the facts. False or misleading statements of fact, or the omission of an important but adverse fact, may well cause the court to question the accuracy and reliability of your entire brief.

Within the framework of these guidelines, there is a great deal of room for effective advocacy in stating the facts in the light most favorable to the client. Compare the following excerpts from the opposing briefs submitted to the United States Supreme Court in *Hardy v. Vuitch:*

Petitioner's Statement

Respondent, a physician licensed to practice medicine in the State of Maryland, was tried before a jury in the Circuit Court for Montgomery County, Maryland, on a charge of performing an abortion in a place other than a licensed and accredited hospital on November 23, 1968. Article 43, Section 137, et seq., Annotated Code of Maryland, 1971 Replacement Volume (App. 19a). The witness in that case, Rebekah Jayne Dodson, 19 years old, testified that she became pregnant and decided to have an abortion (Tr. 27). She was referred to Respondent's office, where she was examined by Respondent on November 21, 1968. Pursuant to his instructions, she returned to his office on November 23 with $300, at which time he performed an abortion.

. . . .

A pathologist, called to testify by Dr. Vuitch, who had examined placental tissue which had been removed from Miss Dodson, conceded that it was connected with a twelve week pregnancy (Tr. 32, 41).

Respondent's Statement

Dr. Milan V. Vuitch is duly licensed to practice medicine and surgery in the States of Maryland and New York, and the District of Columbia. He practices in the District where he is Medical Director of Laurel Clinic, Inc., and President of Laurel Hospital, Inc. Dr. Vuitch is a member of the District of Columbia Medical Society and the American Medical Association. He resides in Silver Spring, Maryland, with his wife and three sons. His medical training and extensive surgical experience are detailed in the Record (Tr. 14).

In July, 1969, Dr. Vuitch was tried on the charge of having violated Md.Code Ann., Art. 43, § 139, by performing a therapeutic abortion in a location which was not a general community hospital licensed by the State and accredited by the private, out-of-state-agency known as the Joint Commission on Accreditation of Hospitals (Tr. 30). There was no charge, nor any basis for charging, that Dr. Vuitch had other than excellent surgical qualifications, or that his medical facility was not well-equipped. There was no allegation nor evidence of malpractice, nor any other suggestion of impropriety. There was no evidence that the alleged patient could have secured a therapeutic abortion within her means and without substantial delay at a hospital. Neither the alleged patient nor her companion was charged with an offense. No Maryland law requires that any other medical procedure, regardless of complexity, be performed in a given type of clinical or hospital facility.

The trial led to a conviction, which was sustained throughout the Maryland appellate process, after which Dr. Vuitch sought and obtained a federal writ of habeas corpus upon the ground that the convicting statute was unconstitutional.

Petitioner, seeking to uphold the conviction, begins by stating that the respondent, a doctor, had been convicted of performing an abortion outside a hospital in a jury trial. Petitioner then proceeds to describe the incident in a relatively cold and matter-of-fact manner. Note in particular how petitioner stresses the age of the woman and the amount of the fee, facts that tend to suggest that the doctor was taking advantage of an innocent young woman for his own financial gain. The respondent (doctor), on the other hand, begins by elaborately describing his professional credentials, a fact that tends to detract from the alleged criminal nature of the act. His statement is drafted so as to focus on his competency to perform an abortion under such circumstances, and even suggests that the woman might otherwise have been unable to obtain the abortion at an accredited hospital. Note also the manner in which the two parties characterize the abortion. While the state refers to it simply as an "abortion," the doctor describes it as a "therapeutic abortion." Each side uses every opportunity to portray facts in a light most sympathetic to its position.

Section I. The Argument

The core of the appellate brief is the section that is often called the Argument. Here the parties analyze what they believe to be the controlling authorities on each issue in the brief. The Argument, usually placed after the Statement of the Case, constitutes the bulk of the brief.

The Argument is organized around *point headings* which are assertions by a party of the conclusions it is asking the court to adopt on the issues. The party's hope is that the appellate court will adopt or incorporate these point headings in the *holdings* of the court when it eventually writes its opinion.

Each point heading is presented and discussed, one at a time, in the body of the Argument. (As we saw earlier, the point headings are also printed within the Table of Contents at the beginning of the brief.) For relatively simple issues in the appellate brief, there is usually only one point heading. When the issue is more complex, you will often find a separate point heading devoted to each major premise in the analysis of that issue.

The most common method of writing a point heading is to rephrase an issue as an affirmative statement—capitalizing the first letter of all the important words. Here, for example, is an *issue* in an appellate brief:

Is the consensual appointment of a liquidating agent, who is not vested with title to the debtor's property and whose appointment does not affect the rights of creditors, the commission of an act of bankruptcy under Section 3a(5) of the Act, 11 U.S.C. § 21a(5)?

An appropriate *point heading* for the *Argument* on this issue could be formulated by rephrasing this issue as follows:

> The Consensual Appointment of a Liquidating Agent, Who Is Not Vested with Title to the Debtor's Property and Whose Appointment Does Not Affect the Rights of Creditors, Is Not the Commission of An Act of Bankruptcy.

Beneath each point heading in the Argument, there is a discussion of the authority that demonstrates why the assertion made in the heading should be adopted by the court. The most effective authority, as we saw in chapter 16, is mandatory primary authority, e.g., controlling statutes and case law (p. 204). In addition, the brief will use persuasive primary and secondary authority as deemed appropriate to the advocacy objectives of the client. The techniques of applying these kinds of authority are covered elsewhere in this book. The following themes reinforce this coverage in the context of the appellate brief:

1. using legislative history;
2. using similes and metaphors;
3. directly attacking your opponent's position;
4. evaluating the probable result; and
5. invoking tradition.

1. ARGUMENT USING LEGISLATIVE HISTORY

When an issue involves the application and interpretation of a statute, a major concern of the court will be to determine the intent of the authors of this law. Among the factors a court may consider in determining this intent is the legislative history of the statute, i.e., the various documents that record the legislature's deliberations on the provision in question. Some of the techniques of using legislative history in legal writing were discussed in Chapter 17 (p. 215). Despite the significant limitations on the utility of legislative history, it can be an effective tool of advocacy in constructing a legal argument. The following excerpt illustrates how the petitioner in *Edelman v. Jordan* used legislative history in an appellate brief that successfully persuaded the United States Supreme Court to deny retroactive welfare benefits to the respondents in that case:

> An examination of the committee report establishes an intent on the part of Congress to provide only for present need. There is no indication that Congress intended to fund payments for past needs when payments were not received by welfare recipients as a result of error and/or omission on the part of State welfare officials, or as a result of the construction given a federal statute by a State welfare official.
>
> For example, the House Ways and Means Committee on H.R. 7260, 74th Cong., 1st Sess., in Report Number 615, on the Social Security Act states as follows at page 3:
>
> > The need for legislation on the subject of Social Security is apparent at this time. On every hand the lack of such security is evidenced by human suffering, weakened morale, and increased public expenditures.

> This situation necessitates two complementary courses of action. We must relieve the *existing* distress and should devise measures to reduce destitution and dependency in the future. (Emphasis added.)

2. ARGUMENT BY USING SIMILES AND METAPHORS

Similes and metaphors are figures of speech used to compare one object with another. In a metaphor the writer directly identifies the two objects, equating the one with the other:

> Plaintiff, in attempting to argue that this transaction falls within the protection of the statute, is attempting to force a square peg into a round hole; it cannot be accomplished without doing great violence to both the peg and the hole.

A simile does not directly equate the two objects. It simply draws the comparison by the use of the terms *like* or *as:*

> Plaintiff's contention, like the sword of Damocles, hangs by the slenderest of threads.

Similes and metaphors will never win an argument; they are, in fact, no argument at all. They are useful in adding color and impact to an assertion, making your point much more vivid and memorable to the reader. These devices, however, should be used sparingly and cautiously. An argument that is inundated with trite and poorly chosen figures of speech is likely to irritate the reader.

3. ARGUMENT BY DIRECTLY ATTACKING YOUR OPPONENT'S POSITION

The direct attack is merely a form of counteranalysis (p. 231). The more persuasive your opponent's argument appears to be, the greater the need to present effective counteranalysis demonstrating that its position is an incorrect, or at least a less desirable, interpretation of the law. Note the direct attack in the following excerpt from a respondent's appellate brief:

> Petitioner's position would mean that while federal courts may invalidate and enjoin state *legislation* without running afoul or the Eleventh Amendment, federal courts may not require state officials to make restitution incident to the enjoining of illegal state *regulations* because of the Eleventh Amendment. To suggest that the former is not a suit against the state but the latter is, is capricious and illogical.

Another form of attack is to state your opponent's argument, but quickly and forcibly show that there are strong *policy* reasons why this argument should not be accepted by the court. This approach is outlined in (4) and (5) below.

4. ARGUMENT BY EVALUATING THE PROBABLE RESULT

Since opinions have precedential value in the future, the opinions act as a form of guidance to the public on what to do to avoid violating the law. Important opinions have a far-reaching impact not only on the parties before the court, but on society as a whole. Courts, of course, are aware of this impact. In reaching a decision, they may consider the broader social implications of that decision. After you have presented your arguments on the relevant mandatory and persuasive authority, you might argue that if your opponent's position is adopted, the result would:

a. be unfair;

b. be impractical;

c. be unduly burdensome;

d. be unenforceable;

e. be against public policy;

f. leave the party with no remedy;

g. permit the wrongdoer to profit from his or her wrong.

In *Lefkowitz. v. Turley,* the reply brief of the appellees used arguments of this kind:

> Taking into account the expansion of government activities in all fields, it takes little imagination to conclude that the disqualification to contract with the government may be a catastrophic limitation upon architects, engineers and others involved in government contracting. Also, such disqualification of a professional must certainly cast a shadow upon his reputation outside of the sphere of governmental contracting.
>
> . . . .
>
> Speaking in purely economic terms, disqualification from public contracting may be much more severe than individual loss of employment, and, unquestionably, the effect of disqualification upon professionals such as architects and engineers is much more serious than loss of employment on a sanitation truck.

5. ARGUMENT BY INVOKING TRADITION

Courts, like most institutions, have a great deal of respect for tradition, particularly as embodied in well-established principles of law. Generally, the longer a rule of law has been recognized, the more authority it has and the more reluctant the courts will be to reject it. The response to this position is to argue that times and practices have changed, and that the rule is therefore no longer appropriate.

There is a second and more important reason, however, for judicial reluctance to discard well-established rules: fairness. If people have been regulating their conduct to conform to the rule, it might be unfair to alter that rule in midstream.

The following excerpt illustrates how counsel for former President Nixon used an argument based on tradition in describing the doctrine of separation of powers to the United States Supreme Court:

> The concept of separation of governmental powers is deeply rooted in the history of political theory, finding its early expression in the works of Aristotle who recog-

nized the fundamental distinction between the legislative, executive and judicial functions. Although subsequently elaborated upon by many historians and scholars, the principle of separation of the branches of government was most familiar to colonial America in the writings of Locke and Montesquieu.

. . . .

The doctrine of separation of powers, as a vital and necessary element of our democratic form of government, has long been judicially recognized. United States v. Klein, 13 Wall (80 U.S.) 128 (1872). As early as 1879, this Court stressed the integrity and independence of each branch of the government.

Section J. The Conclusion

At the end of your argument on each issue, you state your conclusion. Generally this will consist of a single paragraph that briefly summarizes the major steps in your analysis and the result that flows from that analysis.

In addition to these summary conclusions as to individual issues, the brief should have an overall conclusion at the end. In most instances, this final conclusion will be no more than a terse, ritualized statement asking the court to take favorable action on the appeal. It often will consist of no more than a single sentence:

> For all the foregoing reasons, respondent (or petitioner) respectfully requests this court to affirm (or reverse) the judgment of the court below.

Note that this statement makes no attempt to summarize the party's argument on the various issues. Such a summary appears only in the individual conclusion to each major point or issue.

Section K. Appendix to the Brief

At the end of the brief, an appendix is often included. It mainly contains those portions of the record below that are pertinent to the appeal. Typically such an appendix will include copies of:

a. relevant docket entries;

b. relevant portions of the pleadings and other papers filed by the parties;

c. transcripts of relevant portions of the proceedings below;

d. exhibits introduced as evidence;

e. the lower court's judgment;

f. the lower court's opinion, if any.

The determination of which items in the record should be included in the appendix depends upon two factors: (a) the court rules, and (b) the needs of the party.

Most court rules specify that certain items such as the lower court's judgment *must* be included in the appendix of the brief. You should carefully read and comply with the rules in your own jurisdiction. The second factor to consider is the needs of the individual party. Whatever portions of the record you intend to rely on should be included in the appendix. If, for example, the appellant claims that the trial court erred in admitting certain testimony, it must include those portions of the transcript that contain its objection to the evidence as well as the transcript of the testimony itself.

Even though some of the items in the appendix may have their own internal page numbering, all the pages of the appendix should be numbered consecutively in order to permit easy reference to the various items in it.

Appendix A

Opinions to Be Used for Some of the Assignments

The PEOPLE, etc., Respondent, v. Howard SOHN, Appellant.

Supreme Court, Appellate Division, Second Department.
Dec. 10, 1973.
43 A.D.2d 716, 350 N.Y.S.2d 198 (1973).

Before LATHAM, Acting P. J., and SHAPIRO, GULOTTA, CHRIST and BENJAMIN, JJ.

MEMORANDUM BY THE COURT.

Appeal by defendant from a judgment of the Supreme Court, Queens County, rendered February 14, 1973, convicting him of assault in the second degree, after a nonjury trial, and sentencing him to probation for five years.

Judgment reversed, on the law and the facts and as a matter of discretion in the interests of justice, and indictment dismissed.

In our view the evidence failed to establish guilt beyond a reasonable doubt. The testimony as to how the incident began was extremely equivocal and it cannot be concluded beyond a reasonable doubt that appellant was the aggressor. A finding that appellant and his codefendants were the aggressors is inconsistent with the fact that they called the police and remained on the scene until their arrival. This, coupled with the fact that the complainant pled guilty to possession of a pistol during the incident, indicates that the People failed to meet their burden of proving guilt beyond a reasonable doubt.

Lillie BROWN, Appellant,
v.
SOUTHALL REALTY COMPANY,
Appellee.
No. 4199.

District of Columbia Court of Appeals.
Argued Dec. 11, 1967.
Decided Feb. 7, 1968.
Rehearing Granted March 27, 1968.
237 A.2d 834 (1968).

QUINN, Judge.

This appeal arises out of an action for possession brought by an appellee-landlord, against appellant-tenant, Mrs. Brown, for nonpayment of rent. The parties stipulated, at the time of trial, that the rent was in the arrears in the amount of $230.00. Mrs. Brown contended, however, that no rent was due under the lease because it was an illegal contract. The court held to the contrary and awarded appellee possession for nonpayment of rent.

Although counsel for appellant stated at oral argument before this court that Mrs. Brown had moved from the premises and did not wish to be returned to possession, she asserts that this court should hear this appeal because the judgment of the court below would render certain facts res judicata in any subsequent suit for rent.[1] In Bess v. David, supra, a suit by a landlord against a tenant for recovery of rent owed, defendant contended that he did not owe rent because he was not a tenant during the time alleged. The defendant was,

however, denied that defense, this court stating on appeal that "* * * we think *any* question of appellant's tenancy is foreclosed by the judgment in the previous *possessory* action." (Emphasis supplied.) 140 A.2d 317.

Thus, because the validity of the lease and the determination that rent is owing will be irrevocably established in this case if the judgment of the trial court is allowed to stand,[2] we feel that this appeal is timely made.

Although appellant notes a number of errors, we consider the allegation that the trial court erred in failing to declare the lease agreement void as an illegal contract both meritorious and completely dispositive, and for this reason we reverse.

The evidence developed, at the trial, revealed that prior to the signing of the lease agreement, appellee was on notice that certain Housing Code violations existed on the premises in question. An inspector for the District of Columbia Housing Division of the Department of Licenses and Inspections testified that the violations, an obstructed commode, a broken railing and insufficient ceiling height in the basement, existed at least some months prior to the lease agreement and had not been abated at the time of trial. He also stated that the basement violations prohibited the use of the entire basement as a dwelling place. Counsel for appellant at the trial below elicited an admission from the appellee that "he

---

1. Edwards v. Habib, D.C.App., 227 A.2d 388 (1967); Bess v. David, D.C.Mun.App., 140 A.2d 316 (1958); David v. Nemerofsky, D.C.Mun.App., 41 A.2d 838 (1945).

2. Note in Bess v. David, supra, this court cited with approval the following language from McCotter v. Flinn, 30 Misc. 119, 61 N.Y.S. 786, 787 (1899): "A judgment taken by default in summary proceedings by a landlord for non-payment of rent is conclusive between the parties as to the existence and *validity* of the lease, the occupation by the tenant, and that *rent is due*, and also as to any other facts alleged in the petition or affidavit which are required to be alleged as a basis of the proceedings." (Emphasis supplied.)

told the defendant after the lease had been signed that the back room of the basement was habitable despite the Housing Code Violations." In addition, a Mr. Sinkler Penn, the owner of the premises in question, was called as an adverse witness by the defense. He testified that "he had submitted a sworn statement to the Housing Division on December 8, 1964 to the effect that the basement was unoccupied at that time and would continue to be kept vacant until the violations were corrected."

This evidence having been established and uncontroverted, appellant contends that the lease should have been declared unenforceable because it was entered into in contravention to the District of Columbia Housing Regulations, and knowingly so.

Section 2304 of the District of Columbia Housing Regulations reads as follows:

> No persons shall rent or offer to rent any habitation, or the furnishings thereof, unless such habitation and its furnishings are in a clean, safe and sanitary condition, in repair, and free from rodents or vermin.

Section 2501 of these same Regulations, states:

> Every premises accommodating one or more habitations shall be maintained and kept in repair so as to provide decent living accommodations for the occupants. This part of the Code contemplates more than mere basic repairs and maintenance to keep out the elements; its purpose is to include repairs and maintenance designed to make a premises or neighborhood healthy and safe.

It appears that the violations known by appellee to be existing on the leasehold at the time of the signing of the lease agreement were of a nature to make the "habitation" unsafe and unsanitary. Neither had the premises been maintained or repaired to the degree contemplated by the regulations, i.e., "designed to make a premises * * * healthy and safe." The lease contract was, therefore, entered into in violation of the Housing Regulations requiring that they be safe and sanitary and that they be properly maintained.

In the case of Hartman v. Lubar, 77 U.S.App.D.C. 95, 96, 133 F.2d 44, 45 (1942), cert. denied, 319 U.S. 767, 63 S.Ct. 1329, 87 L.Ed. 1716 (1943), the court stated that, "[t]he general rule is that an illegal contract, made in violation of the statutory prohibition designed for police or regulatory purposes, is void and confers no right upon the wrongdoer."[3] The court in Lloyd v. Johnson, 45 App.D.C. 322, 327 (1916), indicated:

> To this general rule, however, the courts have found exceptions. For the exception, resort must be had to the intent of the legislature, as well as the subject matter of the legislation. The test for the application of the exception is pointed out in Pangborn v. Westlake, 36 Iowa 546, 549, and approved in Miller v. Ammon, 145 U.S. 421, 426, 36 L.Ed. 759, 762, 12 Sup.Ct.Rep. 884, as follows: "We are, therefore, brought to the true test, which is, that while, as a general rule, a penalty implies a prohibition, yet the courts will always look to the subject matter of it, the wrong or evil which it seeks to remedy or prevent, and the pur-

---

3. See also Kirschner v. Klavik, D.C.Mun.App., 186 A.2d 227 (1962), and Rubin v. Douglas, D.C.Mun.App., 59 A.2d 690 (1948).

pose sought to be accomplished in its enactment; and if, from all these, it is manifest that it was not intended to imply a prohibition or to render the prohibited act void, the court will so hold and construe the statute accordingly."

Applying this general rule to the Housing Regulations, it may be stated initially that they do provide for penalties for violations.[4] A reading of Sections 2304 and 2501 infers that the Commissioners of the District of Columbia, in promulgating these Housing Regulations, were endeavoring to regulate the rental of housing in the District and to insure for the prospective tenants that these rental units would be "habitable" and maintained as such.[5] The public policy considerations are adequately stated in Section 2101 of the District of Columbia Housing Regulations, entitled "Purpose of Regulations." To uphold the validity of this lease agreement, in light of the defects known to be existing on the leasehold prior to the agreement (i.e., obstructed commode, broken railing, and insufficient ceiling height in the basement), would be to flout the evident purposes for which Sections 2304 and 2501 were enacted. The more reasonable view is, therefore, that where such conditions exist on a leasehold prior to an agreement to lease, the letting of such premises constitutes a violation of Sections 2304 and 2501 of the Housing Regulations, and that these Sections do indeed "imply a prohibition" so as "to

render the prohibited act void." Neither does there exist any reason to treat a lease agreement differently from any other contract in this regard.[6]

Thus, for this reason and those stated above, we reverse.

Reversed.

Montie D. STEPHENS, Appellant,

v.

DEPARTMENT OF STATE POLICE and Holly V. Holcomb, Superintendent, State Police, Respondents.

Court of Appeals of Oregon.

Argued and Submitted Aug. 23, 1974.

Decided Sept. 30, 1974.

526 P.2d 1043 (Or. App. 1974).

Before SCHWAB, C. J., and LANG-TRY and FOLEY, JJ.

LANGTRY, Judge.

This appeal is from a judgment of the circuit court in a writ of review proceeding under ORS 34.010 et seq. The proceeding from which the writ was taken was a disciplinary matter heard by a trial board of the Oregon State Police pursuant to the proceedings provided for in an ORS ch. 181. The plaintiff was a trooper in the Oregon State Police who applied, as a United States Army reserve officer, to take and was accepted for a nine-week military training course in the United States Army Infantry

---

4. See Washington, D. C., Housing Regulations, § 2104 (1955).

5. Note the use of the word "shall" in both §§ 2304 and 2501 of the Housing Regulations. The word "shall" ordinarily connotes language of command. Anderson v. Yunkgau, 329 U.S. 482, 485, 67 S.Ct. 428, 91 L.Ed. 436 (1947); Ballou v. Kemp, 68 U.S. App.D.C. 7, 92 F.2d 556 (1937).

6. See Jess Fisher & Co. v. Hicks, D.C.Mun.App., 86 A.2d 177 (1952), where a lease agreement was held ineffective because it violated the District of Columbia Rent Control Act. Cf. Amos v. Cummings, D.C.Mun.App., 67 A.2d 687 (1949).

School at Fort Benning, Georgia. He had been refused permission for the leave of absence by his commanding police officer and had been given written orders to report for regular duty on the morning on which he had left. He did not report for duty on that morning. The training course was extended to a total of 12 weeks, after which he reported for police duty. This led to the disciplinary proceeding which resulted in his removal from the police force. The trial board of police officers found that he was guilty of being absent without authorization and of insubordination by reason of his violation of a direct order to report for duty. These specifications were stated to be in violation of Article VIII, Section 1; Article II, Section 9(w) and Article IV, Section 6 of the Department of State Police Manual (1968). The circuit court after hearing affirmed the action of the superintendent in removing plaintiff pursuant to the findings of the trial board.

Our review is pursuant to ORS 34.040, which provides in pertinent part that a writ shall be "allowed" where the tribunal, in this case the trial board of officers, "(3) [m]ade a finding or order not supported by reliable, probative and substantial evidence; or (4) [i]mproperly construed the applicable law." ORS 34.100 provides that on appeal we may "affirm, modify, reverse or annul the decision."

The first finding of the trial board was that plaintiff was "wilfully absent from duty * * * without the consent of his superior officers, in violation of Article VIII, Section 1, Department of State Police Manual." In arriving at this finding the trial board relied upon a 1967 opinion of the Attorney General of Oregon which held that ORS 408.240,

giving public employes a right to military leave of absence without pay for periods of active service does not apply to periods of duty over 15 days at a time which are exclusively for training. 33 Op.Att'y Gen. 319 (Or. 1967). The opinion is quite involved but it concludes that ORS 408.240 does not apply to military training leaves of absence like that here in question. The statute (ORS 408.240) states:

(1) Whenever any public officer or employe leaves a position after June 24, 1950, whether voluntarily or involuntarily, in order to perform military duty, such office or position shall not become vacant, nor shall the officer or employe be subject to removal as a consequence thereof. * * *

ORS 408.210 defines military duty as

* * * *training* and service *performed by* an inductee, enlistee or *reservist* or any entrant into a temporary component of the Armed Forces of the United States, * * * but does not include active duty training as a reservist in the Armed Forces of the United States or as a member of the National Guard of the United States where the call is for a period of 15 days or less. (Emphasis supplied.)

Plaintiff testified that he had contemplated resigning from the state police in order to take the training course. But he consulted legal counsel before doing so, and we can only conclude that counsel advised him that the plain wording of these statutes meant that he was entitled to the leave without sacrificing his position.

(1). The wording of these statutes would seem to support plaintiff's position. Military leave is granted by the statute automatically. There is no discretion on the part of any department or official to grant or deny the leave. The statute on its face is unconditional.

Defendants argue that the granting of military leave under ORS 408.240 is mandatory only for periods of military training combined with service. They interpret the statute as saying that military leave for purposes of training only is a matter of departmental policy—in this case left to the discretion of the police department. They base this conclusion on the Attorney General's opinion interpreting the statutes in question. We must make an independent determination of the meaning of the statutes.

The Attorney General's opinion notes that, when the legislature was considering ORS 408.210 and 408.240 in 1951, it appeared to have had before it the "Model State Law Relating to Military Leave" contained in "Suggested State Legislation—Program for 1951—Developed by the Council of State Governments." The definition of military duty contained in ORS 408.210 is taken almost verbatim from the "Suggested State Legislation" except for one important difference. The original definition contained the qualification, "'* * * Provided, That "military duty" shall not include active duty training as a reservist in the armed forces of the United States or as a member of the National Guard of the United States *where the call is for training only.*'" (Emphasis supplied.) The Attorney General said this provision was persuasive to demonstrate that the definition of military duty in its original form, and as enacted, was never meant to include periods of training only. Perhaps this was so, but the

legislature, while using the rest of the definition, chose to eliminate the emphasized words, substituting other words about 15-days-or-less leaves of absence from the final draft of the statute. If the elimination of the "training only" limitation from the definition of military duty as enacted is significant at all, it would seem to demonstrate that the legislature meant to broaden the definition to include periods for training only.

ORS 408.210 seems to use the terms "training *and* service" and "training *or* service" interchangeably, implying that there is no intent to distinguish between the two terms.

* * * [T]he court is not authorized to rewrite a statute or to ignore the plain meaning of unambiguous words * * *.

"* * * The court's province, after all, is to ascertain what the legislature intended from *the language used*, with such aid as may be found in the rules of interpretation and legitimate extrinsic sources; to construe statutes, not to enact them; to declare what the legislature has done, not what it should have done. * * *" * * * Lane County v. Heintz Const. Co. et al., 228 Or. 152, 157, 364 P.2d 627, 630 (1961).

We conclude that under the definition of "military duty" as contained in ORS 408.210 there is no distinction between periods of service and periods of training only.

The state argues that it would be an "absurd result which would follow from construing ORS 408.240 to permit all state employes from taking unlimited leave for voluntary military training * * *." We can see that it might well be an unsatisfactory result. We can hardly agree that it would be absurd, however. In fact, the record contains an exhibit which is an official statement from the Governor of Oregon urging that such leaves of absence be granted without loss of vacation time. If the results from this statutory language are unsatisfactory, and not what the legislature intended, it may readily remedy the situation.

(2). Trooper Stephens disobeyed a direct order of his superior to report to work. Defendants argue that because of this action Stephens' dismissal for insubordination is justified. Stephens had had a similar request denied on a previous occasion, and presumably knew of the interpretation of the law that was made in the Attorney General's opinion. He testified that he had contemplated resignation from the state police in order to take training in the Army.

ORS 181.290 gives the Superintendent of State Police power to remove any police officer for "insubordination." A search reveals no Oregon cases dealing with the meaning of this term as used in the statute, nor does it turn up any Oregon cases dealing with permissible grounds for the removal of police officers. Cases from other jurisdictions will give some idea of what other courts allow to come under the heading of "insubordination."

It is axiomatic that continued public employment cannot be conditioned on the abrogation of a constitutional right. *See* Slochower v. Board of Education, 350 U.S. 551, 76 S.Ct. 637, 100 L.Ed. 692 (1956), where a teacher had been fired for his exercise of Fifth Amendment rights. However, public employment may be conditional on the giving up of some privileges which other citizens possess. Slocum v. Fire and Police Com. of Peoria, 8 Ill.App. 3d 465, 290 N.E.2d 28 (1972).

In California "insubordination" can be rightfully predicated only upon refusal to obey some order which a superior officer is entitled to give and is entitled to have obeyed. Parrish v. Civil Service Commission, 66 Cal.2d 260, 57 Cal.Rptr. 623, 425 P.2d 223 (1967); Sheehan v. Board of Police Commrs., 197 Cal. 70, 239 P. 844 (1925); Garvin v. Chambers, 195 Cal. 212, 232 P. 696 (1924); Forstner v. City etc. of San Francisco, 243 Cal.App.2d 625, 52 Cal.Rptr. 621 (1966).

Courts emphasize that an order which infringes on constitutional rights is void in this context and insubordination cannot be predicated thereon. *Cf.* Parrish v. Civil Service Commission, supra, and Roller v. Stoecklen, 75 Ohio Law Abst. 453, 143 N.E.2d 181 (CP Montgomery County 1957).

However, in the latter case, where a constitutional right was infringed by the order, the court said:

> Where a simple doubt exists as to the reasonableness or legality of an order of a superior and time is not made of the essence of the order * * * some other method might be selected * * * for its determination. * * * 75 Ohio Law Abst. at 457, 143 N.E.2d at 184.

We have already noted that there was ample time for Stephens to have anticipated the order and to have chosen another method of determining the matter.

ORS 180.060(2) provides that the Attorney General shall give opinions such as was given here. ORS 180.220 provides that the Attorney General shall be counsel for heads of departments and that they cannot have other counsel. In State ex rel. v.

Mott, 163 Or. 631, 640, 97 P.2d 950 (1940), speaking of reliance upon opinions of the Attorney General, the court said:

> * * * While the secretary of state was not bound to follow such opinion, he had the right to do so and is protected while acting in good faith even though it is assumed the same was erroneous * * *. If the law were otherwise few responsible administrative officers would care to assume the hazards of rendering close decisions in public affairs. Officers acting in good faith have a right to rely on the opinion of the attorney general, as he is the officer designated by law to render such service * * *.

While the general rule appears to be that an officer is not insubordinate for refusing to obey an order that is not legally valid, under the peculiar facts of this case we find an exception to exist. When the officer deliberately chose the method he did to test the law, it was at the risk of losing his position.

Affirmed.

FOLEY, Judge (dissenting).

I agree with the conclusion of the majority that the 1967 opinion of the Attorney General was incorrect and the majority statement that

> * * * [m]ilitary leave is granted by the statute automatically. There is no discretion on the part of any department or official to grant or deny the leave. The statute on its face is unconditional.

The superintendent's order that the trooper report for police duty, in the face of the statute, was thus illegal. Upon that basis I do not agree with the conclusion of the majority that an officer must obey an illegal order or be discharged as insubordinate unless he chooses a method other than refusal to obey to test the legality of the order.

While I am in sympathy with the state's concern that the statutes involved pose problems for state employers, I agree with the majority's statement that:

> * * * If the results * * * are unsatisfactory, and not what the legislature intended, it may readily remedy the situation.

As the majority points out, our review includes whether the trial board of officers " '* * * [i]mproperly construed the applicable law' " The superintendent of the state police relied upon an Attorney General's opinion, the appellant upon private legal counsel. The Attorney General's opinion was incorrect and obviously the opinion of the trooper's attorney interpreting the statute in question was correct. I see no reason why the trooper was not as entitled, at his risk, to rely upon his counsel as was the superintendent to rely upon the opinion of the Attorney General. There is no claim that the trooper failed to give his superiors reasonable notice of his military orders.

The wording of the statute is clear:

> (1) Whenever any * * * employe leaves a position * * * whether *voluntarily* or *involuntarily*, in order to perform military duty, such office or position shall not become vacant, *nor shall the * * * employe be subject to removal as a consequence thereof. * * ** (Emphasis supplied.) ORS 408.240(1).

The effect of the action of the majority is to rewrite the statute to ignore the word "voluntarily" in it and to eliminate the words "nor shall the

* * * employe be subject to removal as a consequence thereof." I do not think this court should assume such broad legislative powers.

I would reverse the judgment of the circuit court. I dissent.

Michael NICHOLSON et al.
v.
The CONNECTICUT HALF-WAY HOUSE, INC.

Supreme Court of Connecticut.
March 16, 1966.
153 Conn. 507, 218 A.2d 383 (1966).

KING, C. J., ALCORN, SHANNON, HOUSE and THIM, JJ.

THIM, Acting Justice.

The plaintiffs are property owners and residents of Irving Street in Hartford. The defendant is the owner of a residential dwelling at 10–12 Irving Street. Shortly after taking title to this property, the defendant announced plans to maintain it as a residence for persons paroled from the Connecticut State Prison, under a program having as a primary objective the assistance of such persons in making a favorable and responsible adjustment to society. In this action the plaintiffs sought to enjoin the proposed use of the defendant's property on the ground of nuisance, alleging that the peaceful use and enjoyment of the surrounding properties were threatened. The court concluded that the anticipated use of the property constituted a nuisance in fact and granted a permanent injunction, from which the defendant has appealed.

The finding discloses the following facts: Irving Street, as it pertains to this case, runs between Albany Avenue and Homestead Avenue in a middle-class neighborhood of Hartford. With the exception of the two lots abutting Albany Avenue, it is devoted exclusively to residential uses. There are twenty-nine residences on the block in question, most of which are three-story dwellings housing a separate family on each floor. They are on lots with frontages averaging fifty to sixty feet. The numerous children who live on the block play in front of their houses, on the sidewalk, or in the street. Albany Avenue, which provides the closest bus line to the defendant's property, is almost completely commercial on the street level. Homestead Avenue is primarily residential but is also the site of the Veeder Root factory, which is situated opposite the end of Irving Street.

The defendant's property is a three-family house located on the east side of Irving Street and three lots from Homestead Avenue. It was purchased with the intent of providing a temporary residence for selected parolees from the state prison. The residence is referred to as "Half-Way House." The defendant plans to house up to fifteen men at one time, excluding, under its present policy, sex offenders, drug addicts, and alcoholics. As a prerequisite to parole, these men will have either secured or been promised outside employment. The primary purpose of the defendant's undertaking is to provide these men with a home and an extensive counseling program under the guidance of a resident director trained in the field of rehabilitation. The proposed use does not violate any zoning restrictions, and the sole question is whether it constitutes an equitably abatable nuisance.

A principal claim of the defendant is that the subordinate facts, as found by the trial court, provide an insufficient basis for the granting of an injunction. Stated alternatively, the defendant's claim is that the facts do not bring the present situation within the definition of nuisance as recognized by this court.

The issue of the reasonableness of the use of one's property, in relation to the rights of abutting and neighboring property owners, has been before us on other occasions. If the elements of a nuisance are clearly demonstrated, and if irreparable harm cannot otherwise be prevented, the court may enjoin the use objected to. See Brainard v. Town of West Harford, 140 Conn. 631, 636, 103 A.2d 135; 66 C.J.S. Nuisances § 114. One basic element of nuisance, as that term is used to describe an abatable use of private property, is that the use of the land be unreasonable. "We concede that the law will not interfere with a use that is reasonable." Hurlbut v. McKone, 55 Conn. 31, 42, 10 A. 164, 165. "It is the duty of every person to make a reasonable use of his own property so as to occasion no unnecessary damage or annoyance to his neighbor." Nailor v. C. W. Blakeslee & Sons, Inc., 117 Conn. 241, 245, 167 A. 548, 549. A fair test of whether a proposed use constitutes a nuisance is "the reasonableness of the use of the property in the particular locality under the circumstances of the case." Wetstone v. Cantor, 144 Conn. 77, 80, 127 A.2d 70, 72. To meet this test in the instant case, the evidence must show that the defendant's proposed use of the property under the circumstances is unreasonable.

Here the proposed use of the defendant's property, in and of itself is lawful. The only factual grounds offered to support the relief granted are the fears of the plaintiffs that the residents of defendant's halfway house will commit criminal acts in the neighborhood and the finding that the proposed use has had a depreciative effect on land values in this area. The first of these grounds goes to the core of the plaintiffs' complaint. The real objection of the plaintiffs is to the presence in the neighborhood of persons with a demonstrated capacity for criminal activity. They fear future manifestations of such activity in their neighborhood. This present fear of what may happen in the future, although genuinely felt, rests completely on supposition. The anticipation by the plaintiffs of the possible consequences of the defendant's proposed use of the property can be characterized as a speculative and intangible fear. They have neither alleged nor offered evidence to prove any specific acts or pattern of behavior which would cause them harm so as to warrant the drastic injunctive relief granted by the court.

It is clear that the power of equity to grant injunctive relief may be exercised only under demanding circumstances. Leo Foundation v. Cabelus, 151 Conn. 655, 657, 201 A.2d 654. "No court or equity should ever grant an injunction merely because of the fears or apprehensions of the party applying for it. Those fears or apprehensions may exist without any substantial reason. Indeed they may be absolutely groundless. Restraining the action of an individual or a corporation by injunction is an extraordinary power, always to be exercised with caution, never without the most satisfactory reasons." Goodwin v. New York, N. H. & H. R. Co., 43 Conn. 494, 500; Ginsberg v. Mascia, 149 Conn. 502, 505, 182 A.2d 4. The fears and apprehensions of the plaintiffs in the present case, based as they are on speculation, cannot justify the granting of injunctive relief. See 66 C.J.S. Nuisances § 113, and cases cited.

The plaintiffs' claim of depreciated property values is likewise ineffective as a basis for supporting the issuance of an injunction. The mere depreciation of land values, caused in this case by the subjective apprehensions of neighboring property owners and their potential buyers, cannot sustain an injunction sought on the ground of nuisance. See Cawley v. Housing Authority, 146 Conn. 543, 546, 152 A.2d 923; 39 Am.Jur., Nuisance, §§ 28, 157.

The plaintiffs have cited Brainard v. Town of West Hartford, 140 Conn. 631, 103 A.2d 135, for the proposition that an unreasonable use of property which is merely anticipatory may be enjoined. In that case, however, the proposed use, a town dump in a residential area, was a known quantity whose attributes as a nuisance could be readily adjudged prior to the undertaking.[1] A similar factual showing has not been produced in the present case. The plaintiffs have also cited Jack v. Torrant, 136 Conn. 414, 71 A.2d 705, in support of their overall position. That case involved the operation of an embalming and undertaking establishment in a residential district and is clearly distinguishable on its facts from the present situation.

Our conclusion is not intended to serve as a comment on the future operations of the defendant. We only hold that, under the present circumstances, there has been an insufficient factual showing that the defendant will make any unreasonable use of its property or that the prospective residents of its halfway house will engage in unlawful activities in the surrounding neighborhood. For the reasons already discussed, the granting of the injunction by the trial court was not justified at this time. Our holding on this issue makes a review of the remaining assignments of error unnecessary.

There is error, the judgment is set aside and the case is remanded with direction to render judgment for the defendant.

In this opinion the other judges concurred.

State of CONNECTICUT
v.
Patrick MENILLO.
No. 74–1569.
Nov. 11, 1975.
423 U.S.9, 96 S.Ct. 170, 46 L.Ed.
2d 152 (1975).

PER CURIAM.

In 1971 a jury convicted Patrick Menillo of attempting to procure an abortion in violation of Connecticut's criminal abortion statute. Menillo is not a physician and has never had any medical training. The Connecticut Supreme Court nevertheless overturned Menillo's conviction, holding that under the decisions in *Roe v. Wade*, 410 U.S. 113, 93 S.Ct. 705, 35 L.Ed.2d 147 (1973), and *Doe v. Bolton*, 410 U.S. 179, 93 S.Ct. 739, 35 L.Ed.2d 201 (1973), the Connecticut statute was a "nullity." As we think the Connecticut court misinterpreted *Roe* and *Doe*, we grant

---

1. The trial court in the *Brainard* case found that "[t]he establishment of a dump on the land purchased by the defendant would greatly depreciate the value of the plaintiffs' land, creating a noxious smoke, litter, offensive and unhealthy odors, rats, vermin, insects and fire danger." A–316 Rec. & Briefs, back of p. 7.

the State's petition for certiorari and vacate the judgment.

The statute under which Menillo was convicted makes criminal an attempted abortion by "any person."[1] The Connecticut Supreme Court felt compelled to hold this statute null and void, and thus incapable of constitutional application even to someone not medically qualified to perform an abortion, because it read *Roe* to have done the same thing to the similar Texas statutes. But *Roe* did not go so far.

In *Roe* we held that Texas Penal Code Art. 1196, which permitted termination of pregnancy at any stage only to save the life of the expectant mother, unconstitutionally restricted a woman's right to an abortion. We went on to state that as a result of the unconstitutionality of Art. 1196 the Texas abortion statutes had to fall "as a unit," 410 U.S., at 166, 93 S.Ct., at 733, and it is that statement which the Connecticut Supreme Court and courts in some other States have read to require the invalidation of their own statutes even as applied to abortions performed by nonphysicians.[2] In context, however, our statement had no such effect. Jane Roe had sought to have an abortion " 'performed by a competent, licensed physician, under safe, clinical conditions,' " *id.*, at 120, 93 S.Ct., at 710, and our opinion recognized only her right to an abortion under those circumstances. That the

Texas statutes fell as a unit meant only that they could not be enforced, with or without Art. 1196, in contravention of a woman's right to a clinical abortion by medically competent personnel. We did not hold the Texas statutes unenforceable against a nonphysician abortionist, for the case did not present the issue.

Moreover, the rationale of our decision supports continued enforceability of criminal abortion statutes against nonphysicians. *Roe* teaches that a State cannot restrict a decision by a woman, with the advice of her physician, to terminate her pregnancy during the first trimester because neither its interest in maternal health nor its interest in the potential life of the fetus is sufficiently great at that stage. But the insufficiency of the State's interest in maternal health is predicated upon the first trimester abortion being as safe for the woman as normal childbirth at term, and that predicate holds true only if the abortion is performed by medically competent personnel under conditions insuring maximum safety for the woman. See 410 U.S., at 149–150, 163, 93 S.Ct. at 724–725, 731; cf. *Cheaney v. Indiana*, 410 U.S. 991, 93 S.Ct. 1516, 36 L.Ed.2d 189 (1973), denying cert. to 259 Ind. 138, 285 N.E. 2d 265 (1972). Even during the first trimester of pregnancy, therefore, prosecutions for abortions conducted by nonphysicians infringe upon no realm of personal privacy

---

1. Conn.Gen.Stat.Ann. § 53–29 (Supp.1975):

"Any person who gives or administers to any woman, or advises or causes her to take or use anything, or uses any means, with intent to procure upon her a miscarriage or abortion, unless the same is necessary to preserve her life or that of her unborn child, shall be fined not more than one thousand dollars or imprisoned in the State Prison not more than five years or both."

2. See, *e.g.*, *State v. Hultgren*, 295 Minn. 299, 204 N.W.2d 197 (1973); *Commonwealth v. Jackson*, 454 Pa. 429, 312 A.2d 13 (1973). The highest courts of other States have held that their criminal abortion laws can continue to be applied to laymen following *Roe* and *Doe*. E.g., *People v. Bricker*, 389 Mich. 524, 208 N.W.2d 172 (1973); *State v. Norflett*, 67 N.J. 268, 337 A.2d 609 (1975).

secured by the Constitution against state interference. And after the first trimester the ever increasing state interest in maternal health provides additional justification for such prosecutions.

As far as this Court and the Federal Constitution are concerned, Connecticut's statute remains fully effective against performance of abortions by nonphysicians. We express no view, of course, as to whether the same is now true under Connecticut law. Accordingly, the petition for certiorari is granted, the judgment of the Supreme Court of Connecticut is vacated, and we remand the case to that court for its further consideration in light of this opinion.

Vacated and remanded.

Mr. Justice WHITE concurs in the result.

———

Albert G. MUMMA, Jr., Appellant,

v.

Jean M. MUMMA, Appellee.

No. 5574.

District of Columbia Court of Appeals.
Argued April 13, 1971.
Decided Aug. 6, 1971.
280 A.2d 73 (D.C. 1971).

Before GALLAGHER, REILLY and YEAGLEY, Associate Judges.

PER CURIAM:

This is an appeal from certain supplementary provisions contained in a judgment granting a wife an absolute divorce. The husband in this appeal does not challenge the divorce decree itself but assigns as error, portions of the judgment relating to (a) division of holdings in real property, (b) the amount of alimony and child support, (c) payment of fees to the wife's attorney, and (d) a restriction on the husband's visitational rights to his children.

The parties to this litigation were married in 1952 and the issue of the marriage consists of three children, all minors. During their married life the family was supported by the husband's earnings as an architect, but it was not until 1963 that he began to practice his profession independently in an office he opened in Georgetown. At about this period the husband purchased a house for the family residence on nearby 35th Street, and subsequently, a small building on Wisconsin Avenue with space for an architect's office and a three room apartment. There is a first mortgage on both properties. Title to both places was in the name of husband and wife as tenants by the entirety, although interest and amortization payments to the mortgagees were provided by the husband. Prior to the divorce proceedings, the husband had also become the owner of two unimproved parcels of land in Langley, Virginia. Title to these lots was in the husband's name alone.

In January of 1968, the couple separated. This parting was the result of a violent altercation in the late evening between wife and husband, culminating in police intervention. The husband was taken to a precinct station—at the wife's request—where he was detained overnight, and on the next day, determined not to return to the marital abode. On that same day, unknown to him, the wife retained an attorney.

In the following month the husband met a lady employed as a writer by a government agency. Shortly thereafter they decided to live together and at the time of the hearing in the court below, were occupying the apartment in the building where the husband had his office. This relationship, which the husband did not deny, was the basis for the wife's obtaining a divorce on the ground of adultery, although, as the trial judge pointed out, she was also entitled to a decree—as two years had elapsed since cohabitation—on the basis of desertion or voluntary separation.

Besides awarding custody of the children, alimony, child support allowance, and specified legal expenses to the wife, the trial judge also made a division of real property. The court awarded the office building to the husband and the 35th Street house and its contents to the wife, the tenancy by the entirety in each property having been dissolved by entry of the divorce decree pursuant to the provisions of D.C.Code 1967, § 16–910. With respect to the land in Langley, Virginia, the court ordered the wife to be given an equal share, despite the fact that title to such property was held only by the husband and that the wife had advanced no money for its purchase.

The husband's first objection to the court's decree with respect to the real estate is to the disposition of the Georgetown properties, his contention being that the equity in the marital abode was substantially more valuable than his corresponding investment in the Wisconsin Avenue building.[1] He argues that this feature of the award was inequitable under the statute providing for dissolution of a joint tenancy or tenancy by the entirety upon a final decree of absolute divorce, and authorizing court apportionment "in a manner that seems to him equitable, just, and reasonable". D.C.Code 1967, § 16–910.

It is well established, however, that this section of the code vests the trial judge with considerable discretion. Slaughter v. Slaughter, 83 U.S.App.D.C. 301, 171 F.2d 129 (1948), and does not require fiscal equality, Oxley v. Oxley, 81 U.S.App.D.C. 346, 159 F.2d 10 (1946); Richardson v. Richardson, 72 App.D.C. 67, 112 F.2d 19 (1940). Accordingly, there are no grounds for overruling this portion of the decree.

The objection to the disposition of the Virginia property is well taken, however. It appears on the face of the statute that only jointly held property may be apportioned pursuant thereto, and that has been the interpretation adopted by the courts. Hunt v. Hunt, D.C.App., 208 A.2d 731 (1965); Mazique v. Mazique, D.C. App., 206 A.2d 577 (1965), aff'd on other grounds, 123 U.S.App. D.C. 48, 356 F.2d 801, cert. denied, 384 U.S. 981, 86 S.Ct. 1882, 16 L.Ed.2d 691 (1966); Posnick v. Posnick, D.C.Mun.App., 160 A.2d 804 (1960); Tendrich v. Tendrich, 90 U.S.App.D.C. 61, 193 F.2d 368 (1951); Wheeler v. Wheeler, 88 U.S.App.D.C. 193, 188 F.2d 31 (1951); Reilly v. Reilly, 86 U.S. App.D.C. 345, 182 F.2d 108, cert. denied 340 U.S. 865, 71 S.Ct. 90, 95 L.Ed. 632 (1950).

Any judicial authority to award property not jointly held has been found rather in the general equity power. In *Wheeler, supra*, a suit for absolute divorce, where the court below had awarded the wife a portion of the husband's solely owned property, the court, after rejecting the contention that such property could be awarded under a previous version

---

1. The husband's financial statement, filed July 23, 1968 with the court, indicates an equity of $46,000 in the marital abode and of $23,000 in the Wisconsin Avenue property.

of D.C.Code 1967, § 16–910, set out the standard applicable to this case:

> If the wife were found to have some interest, some claim of right, whether legal or equitable, in the property involved, the answer would be at hand: it is settled that in a divorce proceeding the court may adjudicate the property rights of the spouses, and award the wife property which belongs to her. Reilly v. Reilly, 86 U.S. App.D.C. 345, 182 F.2d 108. It is not clear whether the instant case was decided on such a basis. We cannot tell from the findings made by the District Court whether it predicated the award upon a determination that the wife had a legal or equitable interest in the property, or whether it merely decided that because of the contributions she had made toward the maintenance of the household she should be given a share of the property. If the court acted upon the latter premise, the award does not fall within the ambit of the Reilly decision, and the question remains whether the court exceeded its authority. *Wheeler, supra,* 188 F.2d at 32.

The courts have been hesitant to find such an "interest" or "claim of right". Appellee cites only one case, *Hunt, supra,* which does so, and we have been unable to find others. In *Hunt,* property held jointly by the parties had been conveyed to the husband's mother without compensation in an admitted attempt to avoid creditors and to enable the husband to proceed in forma pauperis in a pending criminal case. The mother died prior to the divorce, leaving this property to the husband. The court, holding that the wife had remained an equitable owner of the property when it was conveyed without compensation to the mother, awarded a half-interest to the wife. No such circumstances appear in the present case.

After a careful review of the record with particular attention to the wife's contribution to the family finances, we find no adequate basis for the trial court's award to her of a one-half interest in the Virginia property. Although she performed sporadic clerical services for the husband for an undetermined period when he was beginning his architectural practice in 1963, we hold this an insufficient contribution to justify the award of a one-half interest in property purchased by the husband in 1965, and paid for by him over the two succeeding years, particularly in view of the disposition of the marital abode.

Appellant also contends that the trial court erred in awarding $200 a month alimony to the wife, $500 per month support for the children, $2,500 in counsel fees, and $500 in costs to be paid by the husband. This means that the husband, in addition to attorney's fees and costs, must pay $8,400 a year for alimony and child support. The husband's business records disclosed that his net income after taxes in 1968 was $9,422 and in 1969 was $12,726. If these records accurately refelect the appellant's income, there is some substance to this objection, particularly with respect to the amount allowed for legal expense and the absence of any provisions for adjustment commensurate with fluctuations in net earnings. The transcript discloses, however, that the trial court did not accept these figures as definitive, for it characterized the husband's testimony as "poor-mouthing" and not "creditable". But the court made no finding as to the actual or even the approximate amount of the husband's income.

Appellee defends this portion of the decree on the ground that the husband's tax returns did not take into account his entire cash income, noting that (a) deductions were claimed for depreciation of office equipment and payments to employees, and (b) he received certain gifts from his parents and the corespondent. We do not know whether or not such matters shaped the thinking of the court below. If consideration were given to such factors, the decree is questionable for obviously depreciation, overhead expense, and gifts, do not constitute income. We recognize that trial judges have a considerable measure of discretion in determining the appropriate amount of alimony and child support, but it is essential that in exercising such discretion the trial court first determine the net income (or a reasonable approximation of such) from which a portion is to be set aside for alimony and support payments, as these items are recurring expenditures. Such a determination is also relevant to the question of the appropriate sum to be allowed the opposing party for counsel fees[2] and other expenses incident to the litigation. This observation is prompted by the trial court's award of $8,400 for alimony and child support in the face of a showing by petitioner from business records of income amounting only to $12,726 in 1969.

Accordingly in the absence of any finding with respect to the husband's net income, we remand the case to the trial court for rehearing and further findings. At such rehearing, the court in the absence of affirmative evidence showing otherwise might accept the husband's 1971 income tax returns as a guide to his actual net income. In light of evidence developed at such hearing the court, if it sees fit, may determine that alimony and child support payments should be based on a percentage of income rather than a fixed amount. Pending a new determination as a result of such rehearing, the most recent decree with respect to such payments shall remain in effect unless and until modified by further order of this court.

Appellant also asserts that the trial court exceeded its authority in setting down for further hearing the question of the college education of the oldest child of the parties. It is clear that the trial court may properly require the husband to contribute to his daughter's further education until she reaches majority, Spence v. Spence, D.C.App., 266 A.2d 29 (1970), providing she has the requisite capacity and he can afford to do so. Hoffman v. Hoffman, 210 A.2d 549 (1965), Pincus v. Pincus, D.C.App., 197 A.2d 854 (1964). Setting down these issues for further hearing was, accordingly, proper. In view of our disposition of this case, however, the hearing on these issues should be combined with the hearing on the issues remanded to the trial court.

We have considered appellant's other objections to the decree, including the restriction placed upon visitation rights, but are not persuaded that the trial court's disposition of these matters was beyond the scope of its discretion.

Affirmed in part. Reversed and remanded in part.

---

2. Unless the income of petitioner is considerably higher than appears in his business records, the counsel fees awarded by the trial court would appear excessive.

Irene OWEN, Plaintiff

v.

**ILLINOIS BAKING
CORPORATION,
an Illinois corporation,
Defendant.
Civ.A. No. 4619.**

United States District Court
W.D.Michigan, S.D.
Feb. 7, 1966.
260 F.Supp. 820 (W.D.Mich.1966).

FOX, District Judge.

After a trial by jury, a judgment of $30,000 was returned in favor of plaintiff's husband in companion case 4618, for injuries received in an automobile collision between cars driven by plaintiff's husband and an employee of defendant. In the instant case, a judgment of $5,000 was returned in favor of plaintiff for loss of consortium as a result of the accident.

Defendant has moved the court to set aside the judgment in case 4619, and seeks a new trial in case 4618, D.C., 235 F.Supp. 257.

The basis on which the court is requested to set aside the judgment of $5,000 is that under the decided cases in Indiana, which was the situs of the accident, there is no right of a wife to recover damages for loss of consortium, although such right is recognized as to a husband. Burk v. Anderson, 232 Ind. 77, 109 N.E.2d 407 (1953). The opinion in that case expressed marked dissatisfaction with the rule, but felt that under the decided precedents, no other decision was possible.

In the opinion of this court, following the reasoning of the United States Court of Appeals for the District of Columbia Circuit, modern concepts of the marital relationship do not allow such anachronistic practices to be perpetuated in the law. In the case of Hitaffer v. Argonne Co., 87 U.S.App.D.C. 57, 183 F.2d 811, 23 A.L.R.2d 1366, cert.den. 340 U.S. 852, 71 S.Ct. 80, 95 L.Ed. 624, the court held that a husband and wife have, in the marriage relation, equal rights which will receive equal protection of the law. In the subsequent case of Smither & Co. v. Coles, 100 U.S.App. D.C. 68, 242 F.2d 220, cert.den. 354 U.S. 914, 77 S.Ct. 1299, 1 L.Ed.2d 1129, the District of Columbia Circuit overruled the decision in the Hitaffer case inasmuch as it related to the scope of exclusive liability provisions in the District of Columbia Workmen's Compensation Act, D.C. Code 1961, § 36–501 et seq. However, it recognized the holding in that case that a wife has a protected right to maintain an action for loss of consortium.

As pointed out by the Hitaffer court, the right existed at common law, and when female emancipation resulted in the passage of enabling legislation removing previous disabilities on a woman's right to act in her own behalf before the law, the last barrier to the maintenance of such a suit should have been removed. (Id. 183 F.2d at 816.)

In Indiana, two theories have been advanced to support the existing rule. In Brown v. Kistleman, 177 Ind. 692, 98 N.E. 631, 40 L.R.A.,N.S., 236 (1912), the court held that this interest of the wife was not a property right or derived from a contract of bargain and sale, and it lies in an area which the law will not enter except out of necessity. However the right is characterized, it arises from the marital relation, and to say that it inheres in the husband but not the wife is to indulge in what the Hitaffer court termed "legal gymnastics." And to grant a husband the right to sue on this right while denying the wife access to the courts in the assertion of this same right is too clearly a violation of Fourteenth Amendment equal protection guarantees to require citation of authority.

In Boden v. Del-Mar Garage, 205 Ind. 59, 185 N.E. 860, the court concluded that all actions for loss of consortium were in fact actions for loss of services, and stated that it was unaware of any case which had been maintained solely for loss of consortium. This rationale is effectively refuted by the more recent Indiana case of Burk v. Anderson, supra, which recognized explicitly that services are only one element of the right which the law designates as consortium, and stated that the husband has a right of action for loss of all the elements of consortium, and not merely services, as intimated by the court in Boden, supra.

Thus again, to say that the husband has a right of action for all the elements of his consortium, but the wife does not, runs afoul of Fourteenth Amendment guarantees.

Under the Erie doctrine, federal courts are bound to follow the substantive law of the states in diversity cases. However, when, as here, a federal question is presented, the court does not look to the law of the state, but to federal law as interpreted by the United States Supreme Court, Porter Royalty Pool Co. v. C.I.R., 165 F.2d 933, (CCA 6, 1948), cert.den. 334 U.S. 833, 68 S.Ct. 1347, 92 L.Ed. 1760 (1948).

Thus, this court determines that the denial of the right to sue for loss of consortium, when applied to a wife but not a husband, is clearly a violation of the wife's right to equal protection of the laws under the Fourteenth Amendment to the Federal Constitution. To draw such a distinction between a husband and wife is a classification which is unreason-

able and impermissible, and likewise a violation of the Fourteenth Amendment guarantees.

The motion to set aside the judgment in favor of Irene Owen in Civil Action 4619 is hereby denied. An order may be drawn accordingly.

THOMPSON et al.
v.
ROYALL et al.

Supreme Court of Appeals of Virginia.
Sept. 20, 1934.
163 Va. 492, 175 S.E. 748 (1934).

HUDGINS, Justice.

The only question presented by this record is whether the will of Mrs. M. Lou Bowen Kroll had been revoked shortly before her death.

The uncontroverted facts are as follows: On the 4th day of September, 1932, Mrs. Kroll signed a will, typewritten on five sheets of legal cap paper; the signature appeared on the last page duly attested by three subscribing witnesses. H. P. Brittain, the executor named in the will, was given possession of the instrument for safe-keeping. A codicil typed on the top third of one sheet of paper dated September 15, 1932, was signed by the testatrix in the presence of two subscribing witnesses. Possession of this instrument was given to Judge S. M. B. Coulling, the attorney who prepared both documents.

On September 19, 1932, at the request of Mrs. Kroll, Judge Coulling and Mr. Brittain took the will and the codicil to her home where she told her attorney, in the presence of Mr. Brittain and another, to destroy both. But, instead of destroying the papers, at the suggestion of Judge Coulling, she decided to retain them as memoranda, to be used as such in the event she decided to execute a new will. Upon the back of the manuscript cover, which was fastened to the five sheets by metal clasps, in the handwriting of Judge Coulling, signed by Mrs. Kroll, there is the following notation: "This will null and void and to be only held by H. P. Brittain instead of being destroyed as a memorandum for another will if I desire to make same. This 19 Sept. 1932. M. Lou Bowen Kroll."

The same notation was made upon the back of the sheet on which the codicil was written, except that the name S. M. B. Coulling was substituted for H.P. Brittain; this was likewise signed by Mrs. Kroll.

Mrs. Kroll died October 2, 1932, leaving numerous nephews and nieces, some of whom were not mentioned in her will, and an estate valued at approximately $200,000. On motion of some of the beneficiaries, the will and codicil were offered for probate. All the interested parties including the heirs at law were convened, and on the issue devisavit vel non the jury found that the instruments dated September 4 and 15, 1932, were the last will and testament of Mrs. M. Lou Bowen Kroll. From an order sustaining the verdict and probating the will this writ of error was allowed.

For more than 100 years, the means by which a duly executed will may be revoked have been prescribed by statute. These requirements are found in section 5233 of the 1919 Code, the pertinent parts of which read thus: "No will or codicil, or any part thereof, shall be revoked, unless * * * by a subsequent will or codicil, or by some writing declaring an intention to revoke the same, and executed in the manner in which a will is required to be executed, or by the testator, or some person in his presence

and by his direction cutting, tearing, burning, obliterating, canceling, or destroying the same, or the signature thereto, with the intent to revoke."

The notations, dated September 19, 1932, are not wholly in the handwriting of the testatrix, nor are her signatures thereto attached attested by subscribing witnesses; hence under the statute they are ineffectual as "some writing declaring an intention to revoke." The faces of the two instruments bear no physical evidence of any cutting, tearing, burning, obliterating, canceling, or destroying. The only contention made by appellants is that the notation written in the presence, and with the approval, of Mrs. Kroll, on the back of the manuscript cover in the one instance, and on the back of the sheet containing the codicil in the other, constitute "canceling" within the meaning of the statute.

Both parties concede that to effect revocation of a duly executed will, in any of the methods prescribed by statute, two things are necessary: (1) The doing of one of the acts specified, (2) accompanied by the intent to revoke—the animo revocandi. Proof of either, without proof of the other, is insufficient. Malone v. Hobbs, 1 Rob. (40 Va.) 346, 39 Am.Dec. 263; 2 Minor Ins. 925.

The proof established the intention to revoke. The entire controversy is confined to the acts used in carrying out that purpose. The testatrix adopted the suggestion of her attorney to revoke her will by written memoranda, admittedly ineffectual as revocations by subsequent writings, but appellants contend the memoranda, in the handwriting of another, and testatrix' signatures, are sufficient to effect revocation by cancellation. To support this contention, appellants cite a number of authorities which hold that the modern definition of cancellation includes "any act which would destroy, revoke, recall, do away with, overrule, render null and void, the instrument."

Most of the authorities cited that approve the above or a similar meaning of the word were dealing with the cancellation of simple contracts, or other instruments that require little or no formality in execution. However, there is one line of cases which apply this extended meaning of "canceling" to the revocation of wills. The leading case so holding is Warner v. Warner's Estate, 37 Vt. 356. In this case proof of the intent and the act were a notation on the same page with, and below the signature of, the testator, reading: "This will is hereby cancelled and annulled. In full this 15th day of March in the year 1859," and written lengthwise on the back of the fourth page of the foolscap paper, upon which no part of the written will appeared, were these words, "Cancelled and is null and void. (Signed) I. Warner." It was held this was sufficient to revoke the will under a statute similar to the one here under consideration.

In Evans' Appeal, 58 Pa. 238, the Pennsylvania court approved the reasoning of the Vermont court in Warner v. Warner's Estate, supra, but the force of the opinion is weakened when the facts are considered. It seems that there were lines drawn through two of the three signatures of the testator appearing in the Evans will, and the paper on which material parts of the will were written was torn in four places. It therefore appeared on the face of the instrument, when offered for probate, that there was a sufficient defacement to bring it within the meaning of both obliteration and cancellation.

The construction of the statute in Warner v. Warner's Estate, supra has been criticized by eminent text-writers on wills, and the courts in the majority of the states in construing similar statutes have refused to follow the reasoning in that case. Jarman on Wills (6th Ed.) 147, note 1; Schouler on Wills (5th Ed.) § 391; Redfield on the Law of Wills (4th Ed.) 323–325; 28 R. C. L. 180; 40 Cyc. 1173; Dowling v. Gilliland, 286 Ill. 530, 122 N.E. 70, 3 A.L.R. 829; Freeman's notes to Graham v. Burch, 28 Am.St.Rep. 339, 351; Will of Ladd, 60 Wis. 187, 18 N.W. 734, 50 Am.Rep. 355; Howard v. Hunter, 115 Ga. 357, 41 S.E. 638, 639, 90 Am.St.Rep. 121; Sanderson v. Norcross, 242 Mass. 43, 136 N.E. 170; Gay v. Gay, 60 Iowa, 415, 14 N.W. 238, 46 Am. Rep. 78; Brown v. Thorndike, 15 Pick. (Mass.) 388; Noesen v. Erkenswick, 298 Ill. 231, 131 N.E. 622.

The above, and other authorities that might be cited, hold that revocation of a will by cancellation within the meaning of the statute contemplates marks or lines across the written parts of the instrument, or a physical defacement, or some mutilation of the writing itself, with the intent to revoke. If written words are used for the purpose, they must be so placed as to physically affect the written portion of the will, not merely on blank parts of the paper on which the will is written. If the writing intended to be the act of canceling does not mutilate, or erase, or deface, or otherwise physically come in contact with, any part of written words of the will, it cannot be given any greater weight than a similar writing on a separate sheet of paper, which identifies the will referred to, just as definitely as does the writing on the back. If a will may be revoked by writing on the back, separable from the will, it may be done by a writing not on the will. This the statute forbids.

The learned trial judge, A. C. Buchanan, in his written opinion, pertinently said:

"The statute prescribes certain ways of executing a will, and it must be so executed in order to be valid, regardless of how clear and specific the intent. It also provides certain ways of revoking and it must be done so in order to [be] a valid revocation, regardless of intent. As said in Will of Ladd, 60 Wis. 187, 18 N.W. 734, 50 Am.Rep. at pages 362, 363:

"'The difficulty with the rule contended for is that it gives to the words written in pencil, although not attested, witnessed, nor executed in the manner prescribed by statute, the same force as though they had been so attested, witnessed and executed, for the purpose of proving that the act of putting the words there was with the "intention" of revoking the will. It is the language, the expression by written words alone, which is thus sought to be made effectual; whereas the statute in effect declares that such written words shall have no force or effect as such unless executed, attested and subscribed as required.'

"The same reasoning led the Illinois court to the same conclusion in Dowling v. Gilliland, * * * (supra), where it is said:

"'The great weight of authority is to the effect that the mere writing upon a will which does not in any wise physically obliterate or cancel the same is insufficient to work a destruction of a will by cancellation, even though the writing may express an intention to revoke and cancel. This appears to be the better rule. To hold otherwise would be to give to words written in pencil, and not attested to by witnesses nor executed in the manner provided by the statute, the same effect as if they had been so attested.'

"The same rule seems to prevail in New York, Massachusetts and North Carolina. The Georgia cases are to the same effect, although it does not appear that the Georgia statute is the same as ours.

"A different rule seems to be followed in Tennessee, as shown by Billington v. Jones, 108 Tenn. 234, 66 S.W. 1127, 56 L.R.A. 654, 91 Am.St.Rep. 751, but the court there points out that Tennessee has no statute on the subject, and says the same thing is true in Connecticut, where Witter v. Mott, 2 Conn. 67, was decided."

The attempted revocation is ineffectual, because testatrix intended to revoke her will by subsequent writings not executed as required by statute, and because it does not in any wise physically obliterate, mutilate, deface, or cancel any written parts of the will.

For the reasons stated, the judgment of the trial court is affirmed.

Affirmed.

———

MacPHERSON
v.
BUICK MOTOR CO.

(Court of Appeals of New York. March 14, 1916.)
217 N.Y. 382, 111 N.E. 1050 (1916).

CARDOZO, J. The defendant is a manufacturer of automobiles. It sold an automobile to a retail dealer. The retail dealer resold to the plaintiff.

While the plaintiff was in the car it suddenly collapsed. He was thrown out and injured. One of the wheels was made of defective wood, and its spokes crumbled into fragments. The wheel was not made by the defendant; it was bought from another manufacturer. There is evidence, however, that its defects could have been discovered by reasonable inspection, and that inspection was omitted. There is no claim that the defendant knew of the defect and willfully concealed it. The case, in other words, is not brought within the rule of Kuelling v. Lean Mfg. Co., 183 N.Y. 78, 75 N.E. 1098, 2 L.R.A.(N.S.) 303, 111 Am.St.Rep. 691, 5 Ann.Cas. 124. The charge is one, not of fraud, but of negligence. The question to be determined is whether the defendant owed a duty of care and vigilance to any one but the immediate purchaser.

The foundations of this branch of the law, at least in this state, were laid in Thomas v. Winchester, 6 N.Y. 397, 57 Am.Dec. 455. A poison was falsely labeled. The sale was made to a druggist, who in turn sold to a customer. The customer recovered damages from the seller who affixed the label. "The defendant's negligence," it was said, "put human life in imminent danger." A poison, falsely labeled, is likely to injure any one who gets it. Because the danger is to be foreseen, there is a duty to avoid the injury. Cases were cited by way of illustration in which manufacturers were not subject to any duty irrespective of contract. The distinction was said to be that their conduct, though negligent, was not likely to result in injury to any one except the purchaser. We are not required to say whether the chance of injury was always as remote as the distinction assumes. Some of the illustrations might be rejected to-day. The principle of the distinction is, for present purposes, the important thing. Thomas v. Winchester became quickly a landmark of the law. In the application of its principle there may, at times, have been uncertainty or even error. There has never in this state been doubt or disavowal of the principle itself. The chief cases are well known, yet to recall some of them will be helpful. Loop v. Litchfield, 42 N.Y. 351, 1 Am.Rep. 513, is the earliest. It was the case of a defect in a small balance wheel used on a circular saw. The manufacturer pointed out the defect to the buyer, who wished a cheap article and was ready to assume the risk. The risk can hardly have been an imminent one, for the wheel lasted five years before it broke. In the meanwhile the buyer had made a lease of the machinery. It was held that the manufacturer was not answerable to the lessee. Loop v. Litchfield was followed in Losee v. Clute, 51 N.Y. 494, 10 Am.Rep. 638, the case of the explosion of a steam boiler. That decision has been criticized (Thompson on Negligence, 233; Shearman & Redfield on Negligence [6th Ed.] § 117); but it must be confined to its special facts. It was put upon the ground that the risk of injury was too remote. The buyer in that case had not only accepted the boiler, but had tested it. The manufacturer knew that his own test was not the final one. The finality of the test has a bearing on the measure of diligence owing to persons other than the purchaser. Beven, Negligence (3d Ed.) pp. 50, 51, 54; Wharton, Negligence (2d Ed.) § 134.

These early cases suggest a narrow construction of the rule. Later cases, however, evince a more liberal spirit. First in importance is Devlin v.

Smith, 89 N.Y. 470, 42 Am.Rep. 311. The defendant, a contractor, built a scaffold for a painter. The painter's servants were injured. The contractor was held liable. He knew that the scaffold, if improperly constructed, was a most dangerous trap. He knew that it was to be used by the workmen. He was building it for that very purpose. Building it for their use, he owed them a duty, irrespective of his contract with their master, to build it with care.

From Devlin v. Smith we pass over intermediate cases and turn to the latest case in this court in which Thomas v. Winchester was followed. That case is Statler v. Ray Mfg. Co., 195 N.Y. 478, 480, 88 N.E. 1063. The defendant manufactured a large coffee urn. It was installed in a restaurant. When heated, the urn exploded and injured the plaintiff. We held that the manufacturer was liable. We said that the urn "was of such a character inherently that, when applied to the purposes for which it was designed, it was liable to become a source of great danger to many people if not carefully and properly constructed."

It may be that Devlin v. Smith and Statler v. Ray Mfg. Co. have extended the rule of Thomas v. Winchester. If so, this court is committed to the extension. The defendant argues that things imminently dangerous to life are poisons, explosives, deadly weapons—things whose normal function it is to injure or destroy. But whatever the rule in Thomas v. Winchester may once have been, it has no longer that restricted meaning. A scaffold (Devlin v. Smith, supra) is not inherently a destructive instrument. It becomes destructive only if imperfectly constructed. A large coffee urn (Statler v. Ray Mfg. Co., supra) may have within itself, if

negligently made, the potency of danger, yet no one thinks of it as an implement whose normal function is destruction. What is true of the coffee urn is equally true of bottles of aerated water. Torgesen v. Schultz, 192 N.Y. 156, 84 N.E. 956, 18 L.R.A.(N.S.) 726, 127 Am.St. Rep. 894. We have mentioned only cases in this court. But the rule was received a like extension in our courts of intermediate appeal. In Burke v. Ireland, 26 App.Div. 487, 50 N.Y.Supp. 369, in an opinion by Cullen, J., it was applied to a builder who constructed a defective building; in Kahner v. Otis Elevator Co., 96 App.Div. 169, 89 N.Y.Supp. 185, to the manufacturer of an elevator; in Davies v. Pelham Hod Elevating Co., 65 Hun, 573, 20 N.Y.Supp. 523, 20 N.Y.Supp. 523, affirmed in this court without opinion, 146 N.Y. 363, 41 N.E. 88, to a contractor who furnished a defective rope with knowledge of the purpose for which the rope was to be used. We are not required at this time either to approve or to disapprove the application of the rule that was made in these cases. It is enough that they help to characterize the trend of judicial thought.

Devlin v. Smith was decided in 1882. A year later a very similar case came before the Court of Appeal in England (Heaven v. Pender, 11 Q.B.D., 503). We find in the opinion of Brett, M.R., afterwards Lord Esher, the same conception of a duty, irrespective of contract, imposed upon the manufacturer by the law itself:

Whenever one person supplies goods or machinery, or the like, for the purpose of their being used by another person under such circumstances that every one of ordinary sense would, if he thought, recognize at once that unless he used ordinary care and skill with regard to the condition of the thing supplied, or the mode of supplying it, there will be danger of injury to the person or property of him for whose use the thing is supplied, and who is to use it, a duty arises to use ordinary care and skill as to the condition or manner of supplying such thing.

He then points out that for a neglect of such ordinary care or skill whereby injury happens, the appropriate remedy is an action for negligence. The right to enforce this liability is not to be confined to the immediate buyer. The right, he says, extends to the persons or class of persons for whose use the thing is supplied. It is enough that the goods "would in all probability be used at once * * * before a reasonable opportunity for discovering any defect which might exist," and that the thing supplied is of such a nature "that a neglect of ordinary care or skill as to its condition or the manner of supplying it would probably cause danger to the person or property of the person for whose use it was supplied, and who was about to use it." On the other hand, he would exclude a case "in which the goods are supplied under circumstances in which it would be a chance by whom they would be used or whether they would be used or not, or whether they would be used before there would probably be means of observing any defect," or where the goods are of such a nature that "a want of care or skill as to their condition or the manner of supplying them would not probably produce danger of injury to person or property." What was said by Lord Esher in that case did not command the full assent of his associates. His opinion has been criticized "as requiring

every man to take affirmative precautions to protect his neighbors as well as to refrain from injuring them." Bohlen, Affirmative Obligations in the Law of Torts, 44 Am.Law Reg. (N.S.) 341. It may not be an accurate exposition of the law of England. Perhaps it may need some qualification even in our own state. Like most attempts at comprehensive definition, it may involve errors of inclusion and of exclusion. But its tests and standards, at least in their underlying principles, with whatever qualification may be called for as they are applied to varying conditions, are the tests and standards of our law.

We hold, then, that the principle of Thomas v. Winchester is not limited to poisons, explosives, and things of like nature, to things which in their normal operation are implements of destruction. If the nature of a thing is such that it is reasonably certain to place life and limb in peril when negligently made, it is then a thing of danger: Its nature gives warning of the consequences to be expected. If to the element of danger there is added knowledge that the thing will be used by persons other than the purchaser, and used without new tests, then, irrespective of contract, the manufacturer of this thing of danger is under a duty to make it carefully. That is as far as we are required to go for the decision of this case. There must be knowledge of a danger, not merely possible, but probable. It is possible to use almost anything in a way that will make it dangerous if defective. That is not enough to charge the manufacturer with a duty independent of his contract. Whether a given thing is dangerous may be sometimes a question for the court and sometimes a question for the jury. There must also be knowledge that in the usual course of events the danger will be shared by others than the buyer. Such knowledge may often be inferred from the nature of the transaction. But it is possible that even knowledge of the danger and of the use will not always be enough. The proximity or remoteness of the relation is a factor to be considered. We are dealing now with the liability of the manufacturer of the finished product, who puts it on the market to be used without inspection by his customers. If he is negligent, where danger is to be foreseen, a liability will follow.

We are not required, at this time, to say that it is legitimate to go back of the manufacturer of the finished product and hold the manufacturers of the component parts. To make their negligence a cause of imminent danger, an independent cause must often intervene; the manufacturer of the finished product must also fail in his duty of inspection. It may be that in those circumstances the negligence of the earlier members of the series is too remote to constitute, as to the ultimate user, an actionable wrong. Beven on Negligence (3d Ed.) 50, 51, 54; Wharton on Negligence (2d Ed.) § 134; Leeds v. N. Y. Tel. Co., 178 N.Y. 118, 70 N.E. 219; Sweet v. Perkins, 196 N.Y. 482, 90 N.E. 50; Hayes v. Hyde Park, 153 Mass. 514, 516, 27 N.E. 522, 12 L.R.A. 249. We leave that question open. We shall have to deal with it when it arises. The difficulty which it suggests is not present in this case. There is here no break in the chain of cause and effect. In such circumstances, the presence of a known danger, attendant upon a known use, makes vigilance a duty. We have put aside the notion that the duty to safeguard life and limb, when the consequences of negligence may be foreseen, grows out of

contract and nothing else. We have put the source of the obligation where it ought to be. We have put its source in the law.

From this survey of the decisions, there thus emerges a definition of the duty of a manufacturer which enables us to measure this defendant's liability. Beyond all question, the nature of an automobile gives warning of probable danger if its construction is defective. This automobile was designed to go 50 miles an hour. Unless its wheels were sound and strong, injury was almost certain. It was as much a thing of danger as a defective engine for a railroad. The defendant knew the danger. It knew also that the car would be used by persons other than the buyer. This was apparent from its size; there were seats for three persons. It was apparent also from the fact that the buyer was a dealer in cars, who bought to resell. The maker of this car supplied it for the use of purchasers from the dealer just as plainly as the contractor in Devlin v. Smith supplied the scaffold for use by the servants of the owner. The dealer was indeed the one person of whom it might be said with some approach to certainty that by him the car would not be used. Yet the defendant would have us say that he was the one person whom it was under a legal duty to protect. The law does not lead us to so inconsequent a conclusion. Precedents drawn from the days of travel by stagecoach do not fit the conditions of travel today. The principle that the danger must be imminent does not change, but the things subject to the principle do change. They are whatever the needs of life in a developing civilization require them to be.

In reaching this conclusion, we do not ignore the decisions to the contrary in other jurisdictions. It was held in Cadillac Co. v. Johnson, 221 Fed. 801, 137 C.C.A. 279, L.R.A.1915E, 287, that an automobile is not within the rule of Thomas v. Winchester. There was, however, a vigorous dissent. Opposed to that decision is one of the Court of Appeals of Kentucky. Olds Motor Works v. Shaffer, 145 Ky. 616, 140 S.W. 1047, 37 L.R.A.(N.S.) 560, Ann. Cas.1913B, 689. The earlier cases are summarized by Judge Sanborn in Huset v. J. I. Case Threshing Machine Co., 120 Fed. 865, 57 C.C.A. 237, 61 L.R.A. 303. Some of them, at first sight inconsistent with our conclusion, may be reconciled upon the ground that the negligence was too remote, and that another cause had intervened. But even when they cannot be reconciled; the difference is rather in the application of the principle than in the principle itself. Judge Sanborn says, for example, that the contractor who builds a bridge, or the manufacturer who builds a car, cannot ordinarily foresee injury to other persons than the owner as the probable result. 120 Fed. 865, at page 867, 57 C.C.A. 237, at page 239, 61 L.R.A. 303. We take a different view. We think that injury to others is to be foreseen not merely as a possible, but as an almost inevitable, result. See the trenchant criticism in Bohlen, supra, at page 351. Indeed, Judge Sanborn concedes that his view is not to be reconciled with our decision in Devlin v. Smith, supra. The doctrine of that decision has now become the settled law of this state, and we have no desire to depart from it.

In England the limits of the rule are still unsettled. Winterbottom v. Wright, 10 M. & W. 109, is often cited. The defendant undertook to provide a mail coach to carry the mail bags. The coach broke down from latent defects in its construction. The defendant, however, was not the manufacturer. The court held that he was not liable for injuries to a passenger. The case was decided on a demurrer to the declaration. Lord Esher points out in Heaven v. Pender, supra, at page 513, that the form of the declaration was subject to criticism. It did not fairly suggest the existence of a duty aside from the special contract which was the plaintiff's main reliance. See the criticism of Winterbottom v. Wright, in Bohlen, supra, at pages 281, 283. At all events, in Heaven v. Pender, supra, the defendant, a dock owner, who put up a staging outside a ship, was held liable to the servants of the shipowner. In Elliot v. Hall, 15 Q.B.D. 315, the defendant sent out a defective truck laden with goods which he had sold. The buyer's servants unloaded it, and were injured because of the defects. It was held that the defendant was under a duty "not to be guilty of negligence with regard to the state and condition of the truck." There seems to have been a return to the doctrine of Winterbottom v. Wright in Earl v. Lubbock, [1905] 1 K.B. 253. In that case, however, as in the earlier one, the defendant was not the manufacturer. He had merely made a contract to keep the van in repair. A later case (White v. Steadman, [1913] 3 K.B. 340, 348) emphasizes that element. A livery stable keeper who sent out a vicious horse was held liable, not merely to his customer, but also to another occupant of the carriage, and Thomas v. Winchester was cited and followed, White v. Steadman, supra, at pages 348, 349. It was again cited and followed in Dominion Natural Gas Co. v. Collins, [1909] A.C. 640, 646.

From these cases a consistent principle is with difficulty extracted. The English courts, however, agree with ours in holding that one who invites another to make use of an appliance is bound to the exercise of reasonable care. Caledonian Ry. Co. v. Mulholland, [1898] A.C. 216, 227; Inderman v. Dames, L.R. [1 C.P.] 274. That at bottom is the underlying principle of Devlin v. Smith. The contractor who builds the scaffold invites the owner's workmen to use it. The manufacturer who sells the automobile to the retail dealer invites the dealer's customers to use it. The invitation is addressed in the one case to determinate persons and in the other to an indeterminate class, but in each case it is equally plain, and in each its consequences must be the same.

There is nothing anomalous in a rule which imposes upon A., who has contracted with B., a duty to C. and D. and others according as he knows or does not know that the subject-matter of the contract is intended for their use. We may find an analogy in the law which measures the liability of landlords. If A. leases to B. a tumble-down house, he is not liable, in the absence of fraud, to B.'s guests who enter it and are injured. This is because B. is then under the duty to repair it, the lessor has the right to suppose that he will fulfill that duty, and, if he omits to do so, his guests must look to him. Bohlen, supra, at page 276. But if A. leases a building to be used by the lessee at once as a place of public entertainment, the rule is different. There injury to persons other than the lessee is to be foreseen, and foresight of the consequences involves the creation of a duty. Junkermann v. Tilyou R. Co., 213 N.Y. 404, 108 N.E. 190,

L.R.A.1915F, 700, and cases there cited.

In this view of the defendant's liability there is nothing inconsistent with the theory of liability on which the case was tried. It is true that the court told the jury that "an automobile is not an inherently dangerous vehicle." The meaning, however, is made plain by the context. The meaning is that danger is not to be expected when the vehicle is well constructed. The court left it to the jury to say whether the defendant ought to have foreseen that the car, if negligently constructed, would become "imminently dangerous." Subtle distinctions are drawn by the defendant between things inherently dangerous and things imminently dangerous, but the case does not turn upon these verbal niceties. If danger was to be expected as reasonably certain, there was a duty of vigilance, and this whether you call the danger inherent or imminent. In varying forms that thought was put before the jury. We do not say that the court would not have been justified in ruling as a matter of law that the car was a dangerous thing. If there was any error, it was none of which the defendant can complain.

We think the defendant was not absolved from a duty of inspection because it bought the wheels from a reputable manufacturer. It was not merely a dealer in automobiles. It was a manufacturer of automobiles. It was responsible for the finished product. It was not at liberty to put the finished product on the market without subjecting the component parts to ordinary and simple tests. Richmond & Danville R. R. Co. v. Elliott, 149 U.S. 266, 272, 13 Sup.Ct. 837, 37 L.Ed. 728. Under the charge of the trial judge nothing more was required of it. The obligation to inspect must vary with the nature of the thing to be inspected. The more probable the danger the greater the need of caution.

There is little analogy between this case and Carlson v. Phoenix Bridge Co., 132 N.Y. 273, 30 N.E. 750, where the defendant bought a tool for a servant's use. The making of tools was not the business in which the master was engaged. Reliance on the skill of the manufacturer was proper and almost inevitable. But that is not the defendant's situation. Both by its relation to the work and by the nature of its business, it is charged with a stricter duty.

Other rulings complained of have been considered, but no error has been found in them.

The judgment should be affirmed, with costs.

WILLARD BARTLETT, C. J. (dissenting). The plaintiff was injured in consequence of the collapse of a wheel of an automobile manufactured by the defendant corporation which sold it to a firm of automobile dealers in Schenectady, who in turn sold the car to the plaintiff. The wheel was purchased by the Buick Motor Company, ready made, from the Imperial Wheel Company of Flint, Mich., a reputable manufacturer of automobile wheels which had furnished the defendant with 80,000 wheels, none of which had proved to be made of defective wood prior to the accident in the present case. The defendant relied upon the wheel manufacturer to make all necessary tests as to the strength of the material therein, and made no such test itself. The present suit is an action for negligence, brought by the subvendee of the motor car against the manufacturer as the original vendor. The evidence warranted a finding by the jury that the wheel which collapsed was defective when it left the hands of the defendant. The automobile was being prudently operated at the time of the accident, and was moving at a speed of only eight miles an hour. There was no allegation or proof of any actual knowledge of the defect on the part of the defendant, or any suggestion that any element of fraud or deceit or misrepresentation entered into the sale.

The theory upon which the case was submitted to the jury by the learned judge who presided at the trial was that, although an automobile is not an inherently dangerous vehicle, it may become such if equipped with a weak wheel; and that if the motor car in question, when it was put upon the market was in itself inherently dangerous by reason of its being equipped with a weak wheel, the defendant was chargeable with a knowledge of the defect so far as it might be discovered by a reasonable inspection and the application of reasonable tests. This liability, it was further held, was not limited to the original vendee, but extended to a subvendee like the plaintiff, who was not a party to the original contract of sale.

I think that these rulings, which have been approved by the Appellate Division, extend the liability of the vendor of a manufactured article further than any case which has yet received the sanction of this court. It has heretofore been held in this state that the liability of the vendor of a manufactured article for negligence arising out of the existence of defects therein does not extend to strangers injured in consequence of such defects, but is confined to the immediate vendee. The exceptions to this general rule which have thus far been recognized in New York are cases in which the article sold was of such a character that danger to life or limb was involved in the ordinary use thereof; in other words, where the article sold was inherently dangerous. As has already been pointed out, the learned trial judge instructed the jury that an automobile is not an inherently dangerous vehicle.

The late Chief Justice Cooley of Michigan, one of the most learned and accurate of American law writers, states the general rule thus:

> The general rule is that a contractor, manufacturer, vendor or furnisher of an article is not liable to third parties who have no contractual relations with him, for negligence in the construction, manufacture, or sale of such article. 2 Cooley on Torts (3d Ed.), 1486.

The leading English authority in support of this rule, to which all the later cases on the same subject refer, is Winterbottom v. Wright, 10 Meeson & Welsby, 109, which was an action by the driver of a stagecoach against a contractor who had agreed with the postmaster general to provide and keep the vehicle in repair for the purpose of conveying the royal mail over a prescribed route. The coach broke down and upset, injuring the driver, who sought to recover against the contractor on account of its defective construction. The Court of Exchequer denied him any right of recovery on the ground that there was no privity of contract between the parties, the agreement having been made with the postmaster general alone.

> If the plaintiff can sue, said Lord Abinger, the Chief Baron, every passenger or even any person passing along the road who was injured by the upsetting of the coach might bring a similar action. Unless we confine the operation of such contracts as this to the parties who enter into them the most absurd and outrageous consequences, to which I can see no limit, would ensue.

The doctrine of that decision was recognized as the law of this state by the leading New York case of Thomas v. Winchester, 6 N.Y. 397, 408, 57 Am.Dec. 455, which, however, involved an exception to the general rule. There the defendant, who was a dealer in medicines, sold to a druggist a quantity of belladonna, which is a deadly poison, negligently labeled as extract of dandelion. The druggist in good faith used the poison in filling a prescription calling for the harmless dandelion extract, and the plaintiff for whom the prescription was put up was poisoned by the belladonna. This court held that the original vendor was liable for the injuries suffered by the patient. Chief Judge Ruggles, who delivered the opinion of the court, distinguished between an act of negligence imminently dangerous to the lives of others and one that is not so, saying:

> If A. build a wagon and sell it to B., who sells it to C., and C. hires it to D., who in consequence of the gross negligence of A. in building the wagon is overturned and injured, D. cannot recover damages against A., the builder. A.'s obligation to build the wagon faithfully arises solely out of his contract with B. The public have nothing to do with it. * * * So, for the same reason, if a horse be defectively shod by a smith, and a person hiring the horse from the owner is thrown and injured in consequence of the smith's negligence in shoeing, the smith is not liable for the injury.

In Torgesen v. Schultz, 192 N.Y. 156, 159, 84 N.E. 956, 18 L.R.A.(N.S.) 726, 127 Am.St.Rep. 894, the defendant was the vendor of bottles of aerated water which were charged under high pressure and likely to explode unless used with precaution when exposed to sudden changes of temperature. The plaintiff, who was a servant of the purchaser, was injured by the explosion of one of these bottles. There was evidence tending to show that it had not been properly tested in order to insure users against such accidents. We held that the defendant corporation was liable notwithstanding the absence of any contract relation between it and the plaintiff—

> under the doctrine of Thomas v. Winchester, supra, and similar cases based upon the duty of the vendor of an article dangerous in its nature, or likely to become so in the course of the ordinary usuage to be contemplated by the vendor, either to exercise due care to warn users of the danger or to take reasonable care to prevent the article sold from proving dangerous when subjected only to customary usage.

The character of the exception to the general rule limiting liability for negligence to the original parties to the contract of sale, was still more clearly stated by Judge Hiscock, writing for the court in Statler v. Ray Manufacturing Co., 195 N.Y. 478, 482, 88 N.E. 1063, where he said that:

> In the case of an article of an inherently dangerous nature, a manufacturer may become liable for a negligent construction which, when added to the inherent character of the appliance, makes it imminently dangerous, and causes or contributes to a resulting injury not necessarily incident to the use of such an article if properly constructed, but naturally following from a defective construction.

In that case the injuries were inflicted by the explosion of a battery of steam-driven coffee urns, constituting an appliance liable to become dangerous in the course of ordinary usage.

The case of Devlin v. Smith, 89 N.Y. 470, 42 Am.Rep. 311, is cited as an authority in conflict with the view that the liability of the manufacturer and vendor extends to third parties only when the article manufactured and sold is inherently dangerous. In that case the builder of a scaffold 90 feet high, which was erected for the purpose of enabling painters to stand upon it, was held to be liable to the administratrix of a painter who fell therefrom and was killed, being at the time in the employ of the person for whom the scaffold was built. It is said that the scaffold, if properly constructed, was not inherently dangerous, and hence that this decision affirms the existence of liability in the case of an article not dangerous in itself, but made so only in consequence of negligent construction. Whatever logical force there may be in this view it seems to me clear from the language of Judge Rapallo, who wrote the opinion of the court that the scaffold was deemed to be an inherently dangerous structure, and that the case was decided as it was because the court entertained that view. Otherwise he would hardly have said, as he did, that the circumstances seemed to bring the case fairly within the principle of Thomas v. Winchester.

I do not see how we can uphold the judgment in the present case without overruling what has been so often said by this court and other courts of like authority in reference to the absence of any liability for negligence on the part of the original vendor of an ordinary carriage to any one except his immediate vendee. The absence of such liability was the very point actually decided in the English case of Winterbottom v. Wright, supra, and the illustration quoted from the opinion of Chief Judge Ruggles in Thomas v. Winchester, supra, assumes that the law on the subject was so plain that the statement would be accepted almost as a matter of course. In the case at bar the defective wheel on an automobile, moving only eight miles an hour, was not any more dangerous to the occupants of the car than a similarly defective wheel would be to the occupants of a carriage drawn by a horse at the same speed, and yet, unless the courts have been all wrong on this question up to the present time, there would be no liability to strangers to the original sale in the case of the horsedrawn carriage.

The rule upon which, in my judgment, the determination of this case depends, and the recognized exceptions thereto, were discussed by Circuit Judge Sanborn, of the United States Circuit Court of Appeals in the Eighth Circuit, in Huset v. J. I. Case Threshing Machine Co., 120 Fed. 865, 57 C.C.A. 237, 61 L.R.A. 303, in an opinion which reviews all the leading American and English decisions on the subject up to the time when it was rendered (1903). I have already discussed the leading New York cases, but as to the rest I feel that I can add nothing to the learning of that opinion or the cogency of its reasoning. I have examined the cases to which Judge Sanborn refers, but if I were to discuss them at length, I should be forced merely to paraphrase his lan-

guage, as a study of the authorities he cites has led me to the same conclusion; and the repetition of what has already been so well said would contribute nothing to the advantage of the bench, the bar, or the individual litigants whose case is before us.

A few cases decided since his opinion was written, however, may be noticed. In Earl v. Lubbock, [1905] L.R. 1 K.B. Div. 253, the Court of Appeal in 1904 considered and approved the propositions of law laid down by the Court of Exchequer in Winterbottom v. Wright, supra, declaring that the decision in that case, since the year 1842, had stood the test of repeated discussion. The Master of the Rolls approved the principles laid down by Lord Abinger as based upon sound reasoning; and all the members of the court agreed that his decision was a controlling authority which must be followed. That the federal courts still adhere to the general rule, as I have stated it, appears by the decision of the Circuit Court of Appeal in the Second Circuit, in March, 1915, in the case of Cadillac Motor Car Co. v. Johnson, 221 Fed. 801, 137 C.C.A. 279, L.R.A.1915E, 287. That case, like this, was an action by a subvendee against a manufacturer of automobiles for negligence in failing to discover that one of its wheels was defective, the court holding that such an action could not be maintained. It is true there was a dissenting opinion in that case, but it was based chiefly upon the proposition that rules applicable to stagecoaches are archaic when applied to automobiles, and that if the law did not afford a remedy to strangers to the contract, the law should be changed. If this be true, the change should be effected by the Legislature and not by the courts. A perusal of the opinion in that case and in the

Huset Case will disclose how uniformly the courts throughout this country have adhered to the rule and how consistently they have refused to broaden the scope of the exceptions. I think we should adhere to it in the case at bar, and therefore I vote for a reversal of this judgment.

HISCOCK, CHASE, and CUDDEBACK, JJ., concur with CARDOZO, J., and HOGAN, J., concurs in result. WILLARD BARTLETT, C. J., reads dissenting opinion. POUND, J., not voting.

Judgment affirmed.

**Jack R. GOLDBERG,
Commissioner of
Social Services of the City of
New York, Appellant,
v.
John KELLY et al.
No. 62**

Argued Oct. 13, 1969.
Decided March 23, 1970.
397 U.S. 254, 90 S.Ct. 1011, 25
L.Ed.2d 287 (1970).

Mr. Justice BRENNAN delivered the opinion of the Court.

The question for decision is whether a State that terminates public assistance payments to a particular recipient without affording him the opportunity for an evidentiary hearing prior to termination denies the recipient procedural due process in violation of the Due Process Clause of the Fourteenth Amendment.

This action was brought in the District Court for the Southern District of New York by residents of New York City receiving financial aid under the federally assisted program of Aid to Families with Dependent Children (AFDC) or under New York State's general Home Relief program.[1] Their complaint alleged that the New York State and New York City officials administering these programs terminated, or were about to terminate, such aid without prior notice and hearing, thereby denying them due process of law.[2] At the time the suits were filed there was no requirement of prior notice or

---

1. AFDC was established by the Social Security Act of 1935, 49 Stat. 627, as amended, 42 U.S.C. §§ 601–610 (1964 ed. and Supp. IV). It is a categorical assistance program supported by federal grants-in-aid but administered by the States according to regulations of the Secretary of Health, Education, and Welfare. See N. Y. Social Welfare Law §§ 343–362 (1966). We considered other aspects of AFDC in King v. Smith, 392 U.S. 309, 88 S.Ct. 2128, 20 L.Ed.2d 1118 (1968), and in Shapiro v. Thompson, 394 U.S. 618, 89 S.Ct. 1322, 22 L.Ed.2d 600 (1969).

Home Relief is a general assistance program financed and administered solely by New York state and local governments. N. Y. Social Welfare Law §§ 157–165 (1966), since July 1, 1967, Social Services Law §§ 157–166. It assists any person unable to support himself or to secure support from other sources. *Id.*, § 158.

2. Two suits were brought and consolidiated in the District Court. The named plaintiffs were 20 in number, including intervenors. Fourteen had been or were about to be cut off from AFDC, and six from Home Relief. During the course of this litigation most, though not all, of the plaintiffs either received "fair hearing" (see *infra*, at 332–333) or were restored to the rolls without a hearing. However, even in many of the cases where payments have been resumed, the underlying questions of eligibility that resulted in the bringing of this suit have not been resolved. For example, Mrs. Altagracia Guzman alleged that she was in danger of losing AFDC payments for failure to cooperate with the City Department of Social Services in suing her estranged husband. She contended that the departmental policy requiring such cooperation was inapplicable to the facts of her case. The record shows that payments to Mrs. Guzman have not been terminated, but there is no indication that the basic dispute over her duty to cooperate has been resolved, or that

hearing of any kind before termination of financial aid. However, the State and city adopted procedures for notice and hearing after the suits were brought, and the plaintiffs, appellees here, then challenged the constitutional adequacy of those procedures.

The State Commissioner of Social Services amended the State Department of Social Services' Official Regulations to require that local social services officials proposing to discontinue or suspend a recipient's financial aid do so according to a procedure that conforms to either subdivision (a) or subdivision (b) of § 351.26 of the regulations as amended.[3] The City of New York elected to promulgate a local procedure according to subdivision (b). That subdivision, so far as here pertinent, provides that the local procedure must include the giving of no-

tice to the recipient of the reasons for a proposed discontinuance or suspension at least seven days prior to its effective date, with notice also that upon request the recipient may have the proposal reviewed by a local welfare official holding a position superior to that of the supervisor who approved the proposed discontinuance or suspension, and, further, that the recipient may submit, for purposes of the review, a written statement to demonstrate why his grant should not be discontinued or suspended. The decision by the reviewing official whether to discontinue or suspend aid must be made expeditiously, with written notice of the decision to the recipient. The section further expressly provides that "[a]ssistance shall not be discontinued or suspended prior to the date such notice of decision is sent to the recipient and his representative,

---

the alleged danger of termination has been removed. Home Relief payments to Juan DeJesus were terminated because he refused to accept counseling and rehabilitation for drug addiction. Mr. DeJesus maintains that he does not use drugs. His payments were restored the day after his complaint was filed. But there is nothing in the record to indicate that the underlying factual dispute in his case has been settled.

3. The adoption in February 1968 and the amendment in April of Regulation § 351.26 coincided with or followed several revisions by the Department of Health, Education, and Welfare of its regulations implementing 42 U.S.C. § 602(a)(4), which is the provision of the Social Security Act that requires a State to afford a "fair hearing" to any recipient of aid under a federally assisted program before termination of his aid becomes final. This requirement is satisfied by a post-termination "fair hearing" under regulations presently in effect. See HEW Handbook of Public Assistance Administration (hereafter HEW Handbook), pt. IV, §§ 6200–6400. A new HEW regulation, 34 Fed.Reg. 1144 (1969), now scheduled to take effect in July 1970, 34 Fed.Reg. 13595 (1969), would require continuation of AFDC payments until the final decision after a "fair hearing" and would give recipients a right to appointed counsel at "fair hearings." 45 CFR § 205.10, 34 Fed.Reg. 1144 (1969); 45 CFR § 220.25, 34 Fed.Reg. 1356 (1969). For the safeguards specified at such "fair hearings" see HEW Handbook, pt. IV, §§ 6200–6400. Another recent regulation now in effect requires a local agency administering AFDC to give "advance notice of questions it has about an individual's eligibility so that a recipient has an opportunity to discuss his situation before receiving formal written notice of reduction in payment or termination of assistance." Id., pt. IV, § 2300(d)(5). This case presents no issue of the validity of construction of the federal regulations. It is only subdivision (b) of § 351.26 of the New York State regulations and implementing procedure 68–18 of New York City that pose the constitutional question before us. Cf. Shapiro v. Thompson, 394 U.S. 618, 641, 89 S.Ct. 1322, 1335, 22 L.Ed.2d 600 (1969). Even assuming that the constitutional question might be avoided in the context of AFDC by construction of the Social Security Act or of the present federal regulations thereunder, or by waiting for the new regulations to become effective, the question must be faced and decided in context of New York's Home Relief program, to which the procedures also apply.

if any, or prior to the proposed effective date of discontinuance or suspension, whichever occurs later."

Pursuant to subdivision (b), the New York City Department of Social Services promulgated Procedure No. 68-18. A caseworker who has doubts about the recipient's continued eligibility must first discuss them with the recipient. If the caseworker concludes that the recipient is no longer eligible, he recommends termination of aid to a unit supervisor. If the latter concurs, he sends the recipient a letter stating the reasons for proposing to terminate aid and notifying him that within seven days he may request that a higher official review the record, and may support the request with a written statement prepared personally or with the aid of any attorney or other person. If the reviewing official affirms the determination of ineligibility, aid is stopped immediately and the recipient is informed by letter of the reasons for the action. Appellees' challenge to this procedure emphasizes the absence of any provisions for the personal appearance of the recipient before the reviewing official, for oral presentation of evidence, and for confrontation and cross-examination of adverse witnesses.[4] However, the letter does inform the recipient that he may request a post-termination "fair hearing."[5] This is a proceeding before an independent state hearing officer at which the recipient may appear personally, offer oral evidence, confront and cross-examine the witnesses against him, and have a record made of the hearing. If the recipient prevails at the "fair hearing" he is paid all funds erroneously withheld.[6] HEW Handbook, pt. IV, §§ 6200–6500; 18 NYCRR §§ 84.2–84.23. A recipient

---

4. These omissions contrast with the provisions of subdivision (a) of § 351.26, the validity of which is not at issue in this Court. That subdivision also requires written notification to the recipient at least seven days prior to the proposed effective date of the reasons for the proposed discontinuance or suspension. However, the notification must further advise the recipient that if he makes a request therefor he will be afforded an opportunity to appear at a time and place indicated before the official identified in the notice, who will review his case with him and allow him to present such written and oral evidence as the recipient may have to demonstrate why aid should not be discontinued or suspended. The District Court assumed that subdivision (a) would be construed to afford rights of confrontation and cross-examination and a decision based solely on the record. Kelly v. Wyman, 294 F.Supp. 893, 906–907 (1968).

5. N. Y. Social Welfare Law § 353(2) (1966) provides for a post-termination "fair hearing" pursuant to 42 U.S.C. § 602(a)(4). See n. 3, *supra*. Although the District Court noted that HEW had raised some objections to the New York "fair hearing" procedures, 294 F.Supp., at 898 n. 9, these objections are not at issue in this Court. Shortly before this suit was filed, New York State adopted a similar provision for a "fair hearing" in terminations of Home Relief. 18 NYCRR §§ 84.2–84.23. In both AFDC and Home Relief the "fair hearing" must be held within 10 working days of the request, § 84.6, with decision within 12 working days thereafter, § 84.15. It was conceded in oral argument that these time limits are not in fact observed.

6. Current HEW regulations require the States to make full retroactive payments (with federal matching funds) whenever a "fair hearing" results in a reversal of a termination of assistance. HEW Handbook, pt. IV, §§ 6200(k), 6300(g), 6500(a); see 18 NYCRR § 358.8. Under New York State regulations retroactive payments can also be made, with certain limitations, to correct an erroneous termination discovered before a "fair hearing" has been held. 18 NYCRR § 351.27. HEW regulations also authorize, but do not require, the State to continue AFDC payments without loss of federal matching funds pending completion of a "fair hearing." HEW Handbook, pt. IV, § 6500(b). The new HEW regulations presently scheduled to become effective July 1, 1970, will supersede all of these provisions. See n. 3, *supra*.

whose aid is not restored by a "fair hearing" decision may have judicial review. N.Y.Civil Practice Law and Rules, Art. 78 (1963). The recipient is so notified, 18 NYCRR § 84.16.

I

The constitutional issue to be decided, therefore, is the narrow one whether the Due Process Clause requires that the recipient be afforded an evidentiary hearing *before* the termination of benefits.[7] The District Court held that only a pretermination evidentiary hearing would satisfy the constitutional command, and rejected the argument of the state and city officials that the combination of the post-termination "fair hearing" with the informal pretermination review disposed of all due process claims. The court said: "While post-termination review is relevant, there is one overpowering fact which controls here. By hypothesis, a welfare recipient is destitute, without funds or assets. * * * Suffice it to say that to cut off a welfare recipient in the face of * * * 'brutal need' without a prior hearing of some sort is unconscionable, unless overwhelming considerations justify it." Kelly v. Wyman, 294 F.Supp. 893, 899, 900 (1968). The court rejected the argument that the need to protect the public's tax revenues supplied the requisite "overwhelming

consideration." "Against the justified desire to protect public funds must be weighed the individual's overpowering need in this unique situation not to be wrongfully deprived of assistance. * * * While the problem of additional expense must be kept in mind, it does not justify denying a hearing meeting the ordinary standards of due process. Under all the circumstances, we hold that due process requires an adequate hearing before termination of welfare benefits, and the fact that there is a later constitutionally fair proceeding does not alter the result." *Id.*, at 901. Although state officials were party defendants in the action, only the Commissioner of Social Services of the City of New York appealed. We noted probable jurisdiction, 394 U.S. 971, 89 S.Ct. 1469, 22 L.Ed.2d 751 (1969), to decide important issues that have been the subject of disagreement in principle between the three-judge court in the present case and that convened in Wheeler v. Montgomery, 397 U.S. 280, 90 S.Ct. 1026, 25 L.Ed.2d 307. We affirm.

Appellant does not contend that procedural due process is not applicable to the termination of welfare benefits. Such benefits are a matter of statutory entitlement for persons qualified to receive them.[8] Their termination involves state action that adjudicates important rights. The

---

7. Appellant does not question the recipient's due process right to evidentiary review *after* termination. For a general discussion of the provision of an evidentiary hearing prior to termination, see Comment, The Constitutional Minimum for the Termination of Welfare Benefits: The Need for and Requirements of a Prior Hearing, 68 Mich.L.Rev. 112 (1969).

8. It may be realistic today to regard welfare entitlements as more like "property" than a "gratuity." Much of the existing wealth in this country takes the form of rights that do not fall within traditional common-law concepts of property. It has been aptly noted that

"[s]ociety today is built around entitlement. The automobile dealer has his franchise, the doctor and lawyer their professional licenses, the worker his union membership, contract, and pension rights, the executive his contract and stock options; all are devices to aid security and independence. Many of the most important of these entitlements now flow from government: subsidies to farmers and businessmen, routes for airlines and channels for television stations;

constitutional challenge cannot be answered by an argument that public assistance benefits are "a 'privilege' and not a 'right'" Shaprio v. Thompson, 394 U.S. 618, 627 n. 6, 89 S.Ct. 1322, 1327 (1969). Relevant constitutional restraints apply as much to the withdrawal of public assistance benefits as to disqualification for unemployment compensation, Sherbert v. Verner, 374 U.S. 398, 83 S.Ct. 1790, 10 L.Ed.2d 965 (1963); or to denial of a tax exemption, Speiser v. Randall, 357 U.S. 513, 78 S.Ct. 1332, 2 L.Ed.2d 1460 (1958); or to discharge from public employment, Slochower v. Board of Higher Education, 350 U.S. 551, 76 S.Ct. 637, 100 L.Ed. 692 (1956).[9] The extent to which procedural due process must be afforded the recipient is influenced by the extent to which he may be "condemned to suffer grievous loss," Joint Anti-Fascist Refugee Committee v. McGrath, 341 U.S. 123, 168, 71 S.Ct. 624, 647, 95 L.Ed. 817 (1951) (Frankfurter, J., concurring), and depends upon whether the recipient's interest in avoiding that loss outweighs the governmental interest in summary adjudication. Accordingly, as we said in Cafeteria & Restaurant Workers Union, etc. v. McElroy, 367 U.S. 886, 895, 81 S.Ct. 1743, 1748–1749, 6 L.Ed.2d 1230 (1961), "consideration of what procedures due process may require under any given set of circumstances must begin with a determination of the precise nature of the government function involved as well as of the private interest that has been affected by governmental action." See also Hannah v. Larche, 363 U.S. 420, 440, 442, 80 S.Ct. 1502, 1513, 1514, 4 L.Ed. 2d 1307 (1960).

It is true, of course, that some governmental benefits may be administratively terminated without affording the recipient a pre-termination evidentiary hearing.[10] But we agree with the District Court that when welfare is discontinued, only a pre-termination evidentiary hearing pro-

---

long term contracts for defense, space, and education; social security pensions for individuals. Such sources of security, whether private or public, are no longer regarded as luxuries or gratuities; to the recipients they are essentials, fully deserved, and in no sense a form of charity. It is only the poor whose entitlements, although recognized by public policy, have not been effectively enforced."

Reich, Individual Rights and Social Welfare: The Emerging Legal Issues, 74 Yale L.J. 1245, 1255 (1965). See also Reich, The New Property, 73 Yale L.J. 733 (1964).

9. See also Goldsmith v. United States Board of Tax Appeals, 270 U.S. 117, 46 S.Ct. 215, 70 L.Ed. 494 (1926) (right of certified public accountant to practice before the Board of Tax Appeals); Hornsby v. Allen, 326 F.2d 605 (C.A. 5th Cir. 1964) (right to obtain a retail liquor store license); Dixon v. Alabama State Board of Education, 294 F.2d 150 (C.A. 5th Cir.), cert. denied, 368 U.S. 930, 82 S.Ct. 368, 7 L.Ed.2d 193 (1961) (right to attend a public college).

10. One Court of Appeals has stated: "In a wide variety of situations, it has long been recognized that where harm to the public is threatened, and the private interest infringed is reasonably deemed to be of less importance, an official body can take summary action pending a later hearing." R. A. Holman & Co. v. SEC, 112 U.S.App. D.C. 43, 47, 299 F.2d 127, 131, cert. denied, 370 U.S. 911, 82 S.Ct. 1257, 8 L.Ed.2d 404 (1962) (suspension of exemption from stock registration requirement). See also, for example, Ewing v. Mytinger & Casselberry, Inc., 339 U.S. 594, 70 S.Ct. 870, 94 L.Ed. 1088 (1950) (seizure of mislabeled vitamin product); North American Cold Storage Co. v. Chicago, 211 U.S. 306, 29 S.Ct. 101, 53 L.Ed. 195 (1908) (seizure of food not fit for human use); Yakus v. United States, 321 U.S. 414, 64 S.Ct. 660, 88 L.Ed. 834 (1944) (adoption of wartime price regulations); Gonzalez v. Freeman, 118 U.S.App.D.C. 180, 334 F.2d 570 (1964) (disqualification of a contractor to do business with the Government). In Cafeteria & Restaurant Workers Union, etc. v. McElroy, *supra*, 367 U.S. at 896, 81 S.Ct. at 1749, summary dismissal of a public employee was upheld because "[i]n [its] proprietary military capacity, the Federal Gov-

vides the recipient with procedural due process. Cf. Sniadach v. Family Finance Corp., 395 U.S. 337, 89 S.Ct. 1820, 23 L.Ed.2d 349 (1969). For qualified recipients, welfare provides the means to obtain essential food, clothing, housing, and medical care.[11] Cf. Nash v. Florida Industrial Commission, 389 U.S. 235, 239, 88 S.Ct. 362, 366, 19 L.Ed.2d 438 (1967). Thus the crucial factor in this context—a factor not present in the case of the blacklisted government contractor, the discharged government employee, the taxpayer denied a tax exemption, or virtually anyone else whose governmental entitlements are ended—is that termination of aid pending resolution of a controversy over eligibility may deprive an *eligible* recipient of the very means by which to live while he waits. Since he lacks independent resources, his situation becomes immediately desperate. His need to concentrate upon finding the means for daily subsistence, in turn, adversely affects his ability to seek redress from the welfare bureaucracy.[12]

Moreover, important governmental interests are promoted by affording recipients a pre-termination evidentiary hearing. From its founding the Nation's basic commitment has been to foster the dignity and well-being of all persons within its borders. We have come to recognize that forces not within the control of the poor contribute to their poverty.[13] This perception, against the background of our traditions, has significantly influenced the development of the contemporary public assistance system. Welfare, by meeting the basic demands of subsistence, can help bring within the reach of the poor the same opportunities that are available to others to participate meaningfully in the life of the community. At the same time, welfare guards against the societal malaise that may flow from a widespread sense of unjustified frustration and insecurity. Public assistance, then, is not mere charity, but a means to "promote the general Welfare, and secure the Blessings of Liberty to ourselves and our Posterity." The same governmental interests that counsel the provision of welfare, counsel as well its uninterrupted provision to those eligible to receive it; pre-termination evidentiary hearings are indispensable to that end.

Appellant does not challenge the force of these considerations but argues that they are outweighed by countervailing governmental interests in conserving fiscal and administrative resources. These interests, the argument goes, justify the delay of any evidentiary hearing until after discontinuance of the grants. Summary adjudication protects the public fisc by stopping payments promptly upon discovery of reasons to believe that a recipient is no longer

---

ernment, * * * has traditionally exercised unfettered control," and because the case involved the Government's "dispatch of its own internal affairs." Cf. Perkins v. Lukens Steel Co., 310 U.S. 113, 60 S.Ct. 869, 84 L.Ed. 1108 (1940).

11. Administrative determination that a person is ineligible for welfare may also render him ineligible for participation in state-financed medical programs. See N. Y. Social Welfare Law § 366 (1966).

12. His impaired adversary position is particularly telling in light of the welfare bureaucracy's difficulties in reaching correct decisions on eligibility. See Comment, Due Process and the Right to a Prior Hearing in Welfare Cases, 37 Ford.L.Rev. 604, 610–611 (1969).

13. See, *e.g.*, Reich, *supra*, n. 8, 74 Yale L.J., at 1255.

eligible. Since most terminations are accepted without challenge, summary adjudication also conserves both the fisc and administrative time and energy by reducing the number of evidentiary hearings actually held.

We agree with the District Court, however, that these governmental interests are not overriding in the welfare context. The requirement of a prior hearing doubtless involves some greater expense, and the benefits paid to ineligible recipients pending decision at the hearing probably cannot be recouped, since these recipients are likely to be judgment-proof. But the State is not without weapons to minimize these increased costs. Much of the drain on fiscal and administrative resources can be reduced by developing procedures for prompt pre-termination hearings and by skillful use of personnel and facilities. Indeed, the very provision for a post-termination evidentiary hearing in New York's Home Relief program is itself cogent evidence that the State recognizes the primacy of the public interest in correct eligibility determinations and therefore in the provision of procedural safeguards. Thus, the interest of the eligible recipient in uninterrupted receipt of public assistance, coupled with the State's interest that his payments not be erroneously terminated, clearly outweighs the State's competing concern to prevent any increase in its fiscal and administrative burdens. As the District Court correctly concluded, "[t]he stakes are simply too high for the welfare recipient, and the possibility for honest error or irritable misjudgment too great, to allow termination of aid without giving the recipient a chance, if he so desires, to be fully informed of the case against him so that he may contest its basis and produce evidence in rebuttal." 294 F.Supp., at 904–905.

II

We also agree with the District Court, however, that the pre-termination hearing need not take the form of a judicial or quasi-judicial trial. We bear in mind that the statutory "fair hearing" will provide the recipient with a full administrative review.[14] Accordingly, the pre-termination hearing has one function only: to produce an initial determination of the validity of the welfare department's grounds for discontinuance of payments in order to protect a recipient against an erroneous termination of his benefits. Cf. Sniadach v. Family Finance Corp., 395 U.S. 337, 343, 89 S.Ct. 1820, 1823, 23 L.Ed.2d 349 (1969) (Harlan, J., concurring). Thus, a complete record and a comprehensive opinion, which would serve primarily to facilitate judicial review and to guide future decisions, need not be provided at the pre-termination stage. We recognize, too, that both welfare authorities and recipients have an interest in relatively speedy resolution of questions of eligibility, that they are used to dealing with one another informally, and that some welfare departments have very burdensome caseloads. These considerations justify the limitation of the pre-termination hearing to minimum procedural safeguards, adapted to the particular characteristics of welfare recipients, and to the limited nature of the controversies to be re-

---

14. Due process does not, of course, require two hearings. If, for example, a State simply wishes to continue benefits until after a "fair" hearing there will be no need for a preliminary hearing.

solved. We wish to add that we, no less than the dissenters, recognize the importance of not imposing upon the States or the Federal Government in this developing field of law any procedural requirements beyond those demanded by rudimentary due process.

"The fundamental requisite of due process of law is the opportunity to be heard." Grannis v. Ordean, 234 U.S. 385, 394, 34 S.Ct. 779, 783, 58 L.Ed. 1363 (1914). The hearing must be "at a meaningful time and in a meaningful manner." Armstrong v. Manzo, 380 U.S. 545, 552, 85 S.Ct. 1187, 1191, 14 L.Ed.2d 62 (1965). In the present context these principles require that a recipient have timely and adequate notice detailing the reasons for a proposed termination, and an effective opportunity to defend by confronting any adverse witnesses and by presenting his own arguments and evidence orally. These rights are important in cases such as those before us, where recipients have challenged proposed terminations as resting on incorrect or misleading factual premises or on misapplication of rules or policies to the facts of particular cases.[15]

We are not prepared to say that the seven-day notice currently provided by New York City is constitutionally insufficient *per se*, although there may be cases where fairness would require that a longer time be given. Nor do we see any constitutional deficiency in the content or form of the notice. New York employs both a letter and a personal conference with a caseworker to inform a recipient of the precise questions raised about his continued eligibility. Evidently the recipient is told the legal and factual bases for the Department's doubts. This combination is probably the most effective method of communicating with recipients.

The city's procedures presently do not permit recipients to appear personally with or without counsel before the official who finally determines continued eligibility. Thus a recipient is not permitted to present evidence to that official orally, or to confront or cross-examine adverse witnesses. These omissions are fatal to the constitutional adequacy of the procedures.

The opportunity to be heard must be tailored to the capacities and circumstances of those who are to be heard.[16] It is not enough that a welfare recipient may present his position to the decision maker in writing or second-hand through his caseworker. Written submissions are an unrealistic option for most recipients, who lack the educational attainment necessary to write effectively and who cannot obtain professional assistance. Moreover, written submissions do not afford the flexibility of oral presentations; they do not permit the recipient to mold his argument to the issues the decision maker appears to regard as

---

15. This case presents no question requiring our determination whether due process requires only an opportunity for written submission, or an opportunity both for written submission and oral argument, where there are no factual issues in dispute or where the application of the rule of law is not intertwined with factual issues. See FCC v. WJR, 337 U.S. 265, 275–277, 69 S.Ct. 1097, 1103–1104, 93 L.Ed. 1353 (1949).

16. "[T]he prosecution of an appeal demands a degree of security, awareness, tenacity, and ability which few dependent people have." Wedemeyer & Moore, The American Welfare System, 54 Calif.L.Rev. 326, 342 (1966).

important. Particularly where credibility and veracity are at issue, as they must be in many termination proceedings, written submissions are a wholly unsatisfactory basis for decision. The second-hand presentation to the decision maker by the caseworker has its own deficiencies; since the caseworker usually gathers the facts upon which the charge of ineligibility rests, the presentation of the recipient's side of the controversy cannot safely be left to him. Therefore a recipient must be allowed to state his position orally. Informal procedures will suffice; in this context due process does not require a particular order of proof or mode of offering evidence. Cf. HEW Handbook, pt. IV, § 6400(a).

In almost every setting where important decisions turn on questions of fact, due process requires an opportunity to confront and cross-examine adverse witnesses. E.g., ICC v. Louisville & N. R. Co., 227 U.S. 88, 93–94, 33 S.Ct. 185, 187–188, 57 L.Ed. 431 (1913); Willner v. Committee on Character & Fitness, 373 U.S. 96, 103–104, 83 S.Ct. 1175, 1180–1181, 10 L.Ed.2d 224 (1963). What we said in Greene v. McElroy, 360 U.S. 474, 496–497, 79 S.Ct. 1400, 1413, 3 L.Ed.2d 1377 (1959), is particularly pertinent here:

> Certain principles have remained relatively immutable in our jurisprudence. One of these is that where governmental action seriously injures an individual, and the reasonableness of the action depends on fact findings, the evidence used to prove the Government's case must be disclosed to the individual so that he has an opportunity to show that it is untrue. While this is important in the case of documentary evidence, it is even

more important where the evidence consists of the testimony of individuals whose memory might be faulty or who, in fact, might be perjurers or persons motivated by malice, vindictiveness, intolerance, prejudice, or jealousy. We have formalized these protections in the requirements of confrontation and cross-examination. They have ancient roots. They find expression in the Sixth Amendment * * *. This Court has been zealous to protect these rights from erosion. It has spoken out not only in criminal cases, * * * but also in all types of cases where administrative * * * actions were under scrutiny.

Welfare recipients must therefore be given an opportunity to confront and cross-examine the witnesses relied on by the department.

"The right to be heard would be, in many cases, of little avail if it did not comprehend the right to be heard by counsel." Powell v. Alabama, 287 U.S. 45, 68–69, 53 S.Ct. 55, 64, 77 L.Ed. 158 (1932). We do not say that counsel must be provided at the pre-termination hearing, but only that the recipient must be allowed to retain an attorney if he so desires. Counsel can help delineate the issues, present the factual contentions in an orderly manner, conduct cross-examination, and generally safeguard the interests of the recipient. We do not anticipate that this assistance will unduly prolong or otherwise encumber the hearing. Evidently HEW has reached the same conclusion. See 45 CFR § 205.10, 34 Fed. Reg. 1144 (1969); 45 CFR § 220.25, 34 Fed.Reg. 13595 (1969).

Finally, the decision maker's conclusion as to a recipient's eligibility must rest solely on the legal rules and evidence adduced at the hearing. Ohio Bell Tel. Co. v. PUC, 301 U.S. 292, 57 S.Ct. 724, 81 L.Ed. 1093 (1937); United States v. Abilene & S. R. Co. 265 U.S. 274, 288–289, 44 S.Ct. 565, 569–570, 68 L.Ed. 1016 (1924). To demonstrate compliance with this elementary requirement, the decision maker should state the reasons for his determination and indicate the evidence he relied on, cf. Wichita R. & Light Co. v. PUC, 260 U.S. 48, 57–59, 43 S.Ct. 51, 54–55, 67 L.Ed. 124 (1922), though his statement need not amount to a full opinion or even formal findings of fact and conclusions of law. And, of course, an impartial decision maker is essential. Cf. In re Murchison, 349 U.S. 133, 75 S.Ct. 623, 99 L.Ed. 942 (1955); Wong Yang Sung v. McGrath, 339 U.S. 33, 45–46, 70 S.Ct. 445, 451–452, 94 L.Ed. 616 (1950). We agree with the District Court that prior involvement in some aspects of a case will not necessarily bar a welfare official from acting as a decision maker. He should not, however, have participated in making the determination under review.

Affirmed.

Mr. Justice BLACK, dissenting.

In the last half century the United States, along with many, perhaps most, other nations of the world, has moved far toward becoming a welfare state, that is, a nation that for one reason or another taxes its most affluent people to help support, feed, clothe, and shelter its less fortunate citizens. The result is that today more than nine million men, women, and children in the United States receive some kind of state or federally financed public assistance in the form of allowances or gratuities, generally paid them periodically, usually by the week, month, or quarter.[1] Since these gratuities are paid on the basis of need, the list of recipients is not static, and some people go off the lists and others are added from time to time. These ever-changing lists put a constant administrative burden on government and it certainly could not have reasonably anticipated that this burden would include the additional procedural expense imposed by the Court today.

The dilemma of the ever-increasing poor in the midst of constantly growing affluence presses upon us and must inevitably be met within the framework of our democratic constitutional government, if our system is to survive as such. It was largely to escape just such pressing economic problems and attendant government repression that people from Europe, Asia, and other areas settled this country and formed our Nation. Many of those settlers had personally suffered from persecutions of various kinds and wanted to get away from governments that had unrestrained powers to make life miserable for their citizens. It was for this reason, or so I believe, that on reaching these new lands the early settlers undertook to curb their governments by confining their powers within written boundaries, which eventually became written constitu-

---

1. This figure includes all recipients of Old-age Assistance, Aid to Families with Dependent Children, Aid to the Blind, Aid to the Permanently and Totally Disabled, and general assistance. In this case appellants are AFDC and general assistance recipients. In New York State alone there are 951,000 AFDC recipients and 108,000 on a general assistance. In the Nation as a whole the comparable figures are 6,080,000 and 391,000. U. S. Bureau of the Census, Statistical Abstract of the United States: 1969 (90th ed.), Table 435, p. 297.

tions.[2] They wrote their basic charters as nearly as men's collective wisdom could do so as to proclaim to their people and their officials an emphatic command that: "Thus far and no farther shall you go; and where we neither delegate powers to you, nor prohibit your exercise of them, we the people are left free."[3]

Representatives of the people of the Thirteen Original Colonies spent long, hot months in the summer of 1787 in Philadelphia, Pennsylvania, creating a government of limited powers. They divided it into three departments—Legislative, Judicial, and Executive. The Judicial Department was to have no part whatever in making any laws. In fact proposals looking to vesting some power in the Judiciary to take part in the legislative process and veto laws were offered, considered, and rejected by the Constitutional Convention.[4] In my judgment there is not one word, phrase, or sentence from the beginning to the end of the Constitution from which it can be inferred that judges were granted any such legislative power. True, Marbury v. Madison, 1 Cranch 137, 2 L.Ed. 60 (1803), held, and properly, I think, that courts must be the final interpreters of the Constitution, and I recognize that the holding can provide an opportunity to slide imperceptibly into constitutional amendment and law making. But when federal judges use this judicial power for legislative purposes, I think they wander out of their field of vested powers and transgress into the area constitutionally assigned to the Congress and the people. That is precisely what I believe the Court is doing in this case. Hence my dissent.

The more than a million names on the relief rolls in New York,[5] and the more than nine million names on the rolls of all the 50 States were not put there at random. The names are there because state welfare officials believed that those people were eligible for assistance. Probably in the officials' haste to make out the lists many names were put there erroneously in order to alleviate immediate suffering, and undoubtedly some people are drawing relief who are not entitled under the law to do so. Doubtless some draw relief checks from time to time who know they are not eligible, either because they are not actually in need or for some other reason. Many of those who thus draw undeserved gratuities are without sufficient property to enable the government to collect back from them

2. The goal of a written constitution with fixed limits on governmental power had long been desired. Prior to our colonial constitutions, the closest man had come to realizing this goal was the political movement of the Levellers in England in the 1640's. J. Frank, The Levellers (1955). In 1647 the Levellers proposed the adoption of An Agreement of the People which set forth written limitations on the English Government. This proposal contained many of the ideas which later were incorporated in the constitutions of this Nation. *Id.* at 135–147.

3. This command is expressed in the Tenth Amendment:
"The powers not delegated to the United States by the Constitution, nor prohibited by it to the States, are reserved to the States respectively, or to the people."

4. It was proposed that members of the judicial branch would sit on a Council of Revision which would consider legislation and have the power to veto it. This proposal was rejected. J. Elliot, 1 Elliot's Debates 160, 164, 214 (Journal of the Federal Convention); 395, 398 (Yates' Minutes); vol. 5 pp. 151, 161–166, 344–349 (Madison's Notes) (Lippincott ed. 1876). It was also suggested that The Chief Justice would serve as a member of the President's executive council, but this proposal was similarly rejected. *Id.*, vol. 5, pp. 442, 445, 446, 462.

5. See n. 1, *supra.*

any money they wrongfully receive. But the Court today holds that it would violate the Due Process Clause of the Fourteenth Amendment to stop paying those people weekly or monthly allowances unless the government first affords them a full "evidentiary hearing" even though welfare officials are persuaded that the recipients are not rightfully entitled to receive a penny under the law. In other words, although some recipients might be on the lists for payment wholly because of deliberate fraud on their part, the Court holds that the government is helpless and must continue, until after an evidentiary hearing, to pay money that it does not owe, never has owed, and never could owe. I do not believe there is any provision in our Constitution that should thus paralyze the government's efforts to protect itself against making payments to people who are not entitled to them.

Particularly do I not think that the Fourteenth Amendment should be given such an unnecessary broad construction. That Amendment came into being primarily to protect Negroes from discrimination, and while some of its language can and does protect others, all know that the chief purpose behind it was to protect ex-slaves. Cf. Adamson v. California, 332 U.S. 46, 71–72, and n. 5, 67 S.Ct. 1672, 1686, 91 L.Ed. 1903 (1947) (dissenting opinion). The Court, however, relies upon the Fourteenth Amendment and in effect says that failure of the government to pay a promised charitable instalment to an individual deprives that individual of *his own property*, in violation of the Due Process Clause of the Fourteenth Amendment. It somewhat strains credulity to say that the government's promise of charity to an individual is prop-

erty belonging to that individual when the government denies that the individual is honestly entitled to receive such a payment.

I would have little, if any, objection to the majority's decision in this case if it were written as the report of the House Committee on Education and Labor, but as an opinion ostensibly resting on the language of the Constitution I find it woefully deficient. Once the verbiage is pared away it is obvious that this Court today adopts the views of the District Court "that to cut off a welfare recipient in the face of * * * 'brutal need' without a prior hearing of some sort is unconscionable," and therefore, says the Court, unconstitutional. The majority reaches this result by a process of weighing "the recipient's interest in avoiding" the termination of welfare benefits against "the governmental interest in summary adjudication." *Ante*, at 334. Today's balancing act requires a "pre-termination evidentiary hearing," yet there is nothing that indicates what tomorrow's balance will be. Although the majority attempts to bolster its decision with limited quotations from prior cases, it is obvious that today's result doesn't depend on the language of the Constitution itself or the principles of other decisions, but solely on the collective judgment of the majority as to what would be a fair and humane procedure in this case.

The decision is thus only another variant of the view often expressed by some members of this Court that the Due Process Clause forbids any conduct that a majority of the Court believes "unfair," "indecent," or "shocking to their consciences." See, *e.g.*, Rochin v. California, 342 U.S. 165, 172, 72 S.Ct. 205, 209, 96 L.Ed. 183 (1952). Neither these words nor any like them appear anywhere in the Due Process Clause. If they did, they would leave the majority of Justices free to hold any conduct unconstitutional that they should conclude on their own to be unfair or shocking to them.[6] Had the drafters of the Due Process Clause meant to leave judges such ambulatory power to declare laws unconstitutional, the chief value of a written constitution, as the Founders saw it, would have been lost. In fact, if that view of due process is correct, the Due Process Clause could easily swallow up all other parts of the Constitution. And truly the Constitution would always be "what the judges say it is" at a given moment, not what the Founders wrote into the document.[7] A written constitution, designed to guarantee protection against governmental abuses, including those judges, must have written standards that mean something definite and have an explicit content. I regret very much to be compelled to say that the Court today makes a drastic and dangerous departure from a Constitution written to control and limit the government and the judges and moves toward a constitution designed to be no more and no less than what the judges of a particular social and economic philosophy declare on the one hand to be fair or on the other hand to be shocking and unconscionable.

The procedure required today as a matter of constitutional law finds no precedent in our legal system. Reduced to its simplest terms, the problem in this case is similar to that frequently encountered when two parties have an ongoing legal relationship that requires one party to make periodic payments to the other. Often the situation arises where the party "owing" the money stops paying it and justifies his conduct by arguing that the recipient is not legally entitled to payment. The recipient can, of course, disagree and go to court to compel payment. But I know of no situation in our legal system in which the person alleged to owe money to another is required by law to continue making payments to a judgment-proof claimant without the benefit of any security or bond to insure that these payments can be recovered if he wins his legal argument. Yet today's decision in no way obligates the welfare recipient to pay back any benefits wrongfully received during the pretermination evidentiary hearings or post any bond, and in all "fairness" it could not do so. These recipients are by definition too poor to post a bond or to repay the benefits that, as the majority assumes, must be spent as received to insure survival.

The Court apparently feels that this decision will benefit the poor and needy. In my judgment the eventual result will be just the opposite. While today's decision requires only

---

6. I am aware that some feel that the process employed in reaching today's decision is not dependent on the individual views of the Justices involved, but is a mere objective search for the "collective conscience of mankind," but in my view that description is only a euphemism for an individual's judgment. Judges are as human as anyone and as likely as others to see the world through their own eyes and find the "collective conscience" remarkably similar to their own. Cf. Griswold v. Connecticut, 381 U.S. 479, 518–519, 85 S.Ct. 1678, 1700–1701, 14 L.Ed.2d 510 (1965) (Black, J., dissenting); Sniadach v. Family Finance Corp., 395 U.S. 337, 350–351, 89 S.Ct. 1820, 1827, 23 L.Ed.2d 349 (1969) (Black, J., dissenting).

7. To realize how uncertain a standard of "fundamental fairness" would be, one has only to reflect for a moment on the possible disagreement if the "fairness" of the procedure in this case were propounded to the head of the National Welfare Rights Organization, the president of the national Chamber of Commerce, and the chairman of the John Birch Society.

an administrative, evidentiary hearing, the inevitable logic of the approach taken will lead to constitutionally imposed, time-consuming delays of a full adversary process of administrative and judicial review. In the next case the welfare recipients are bound to argue that cutting off benefits before judicial review of the agency's decision is also a denial of due process. Since, by hypothesis, termination of aid at that point may still "deprive an *eligible* recipient of the very means by which to live while he waits," *ante,* at 335, I would be surprised if the weighing process did not compel the conclusion that termination without full judicial review would be unconscionable. After all, at each step, as the majority seems to feel, the issue is only one of weighing the government's pocketbook against the actual survival of the recipient, and surely that balance must always tip in favor of the individual. Similarly today's decision requires only the opportunity to have the benefit of counsel at the administrative hearing, but it is difficult to believe that the same reasoning process would not require the appointment of counsel, for otherwise the right to counsel is a meaningless one since these people are too poor to hire their own advocates. Cf. Gideon v. Wainwright, 372 U.S. 335, 344, 83 S.Ct. 792, 796, 9 L.Ed.2d 799 (1963). Thus the end result of today's decision may well be that the government, once it decides to give welfare benefits, cannot reverse that decision until the recipient has had the benefits of full administrative and judicial

review, including, of course, the opportunity to present his case to this Court. Since this process will usually entail a delay of several years, the inevitable result of such a constitutionally imposed burden will be that the government will not put a claimant on the rolls initially until it has made an exhaustive investigation to determine his eligibility. While this Court will perhaps have insured that no needy person will be taken off the rolls without a full "due process" proceeding, it will also have insured that many will never get on the rolls, or at least that they will remain destitute during the lengthy proceedings followed to determine initial eligibility.

For the foregoing reasons I dissent from the Court's holding. The operation of a welfare state is a new experiment for our Nation. For this reason, among others, I feel that new experiments in carrying out a welfare program should not be frozen into our constitutional structure. They should be left, as are other legislative determinations, to the Congress and the legislatures that the people elect to make our laws.

BRUBAKER v. DICKSON.

310 F.2d 30 (9th Cir. 1962)

BROWNING, Circuit Judge.

Appellant was convicted in the Superior Court of Los Angeles County of murder in the first degree. He was sentenced to death. After exhausting state remedies,[1] appellant filed a petition for habeas corpus in the District Court. That court denied the

---

1. The conviction was affirmed by the Supreme Court of California on direct appeal. People v. Brubaker, 53 Cal.2d 37, 346 P.2d 8 (1959). Appellant filed petitions for habeas corpus in the Marin County Superior Court and in the Supreme Court of California. They were denied without hearing. A petition for certiorari to the Supreme Court of the United States was denied, the order noting that Mr. Justice Douglas was of the opinion that certiorari should be granted. Brubaker v. Dickson, 365 U.S. 824, 81 S.Ct. 703, 5 L.Ed.2d 702 (1961).

petition after oral argument. Appellant then filed an identical petition in this Court. We declined to entertain it, transferring the application back to the District Court for "hearing and determination."[2] The District Court again dismissed the petition on oral argument, rejecting affidavits offered by both sides and declining to receive further evidence.

I.

Appellant alleged that he had been denied effective aid of counsel at his trial in the state court. He alleged that through lack of investigation and preparation his court-appointed trial counsel failed to discover and present substantial defenses which appellant had to the charge against him. These defenses were said to be (1) that at the time of the homicides appellant could not have had the specific intent required for first-degree murder; and (2) that certain confessions, which were the sole evidence of appellant's guilt, were obtained in violation of his constitutional rights. He further alleged that trial counsel inexcusably failed to discover and present evidence in mitigation of

sentence, although substantial evidence was available. . . .

A. The factual allegations in support of a defense based upon appellant's mental state when the crime was committed may be summarized as follows.

Electroencephalographic (EEG) examinations made subsequent to appellant's conviction revealed organic brain damage.[3] His prior medical history contained episodes of head injury and infantile illness from which the brain damage could have resulted; there were no such incidents subsequent to the homicides. Medical opinion indicated that the damage was such as to render appellant "definitely seizure prone" and was "of a type often associated with abnormal and otherwise unexplainable conduct." There was psychiatric opinion based upon post-conviction evaluations that appellant, while not "insane," had a compulsive personality marked by strong emotional instability.[4] There was substantial evidence of hypersensitivity to alcohol;[5] and the record established that immediately prior to the homicides appellant had drunk heavily.[6] There

---

2. 28 U.S.C.A. § 2241(b).

3. The examinations were conducted by doctors at San Quentin Prison. A report of examination by that institution's Neuropsychiatric Committee stated, "His EEG shows abnormal tracings with localizing in the right temporal parietal area, where he has a scar from an old head injury in 1942, when he claims he was unconscious for 36 hours."

4. The report of the San Quentin Prison Neuropsychiatric Committee stated, "We are agreed that his personality structure may best be described as a Passive-Aggressive Personality with Emotional Instability, Neurotic and Dissociative Features with Overcompensatory Aggressive behavior." A psychological evaluation of appellant prepared by a San Quentin Prison clinical psychologist noted indications of "emotional lability and compulsive tendencies," and stated that under the stimulus of alcohol "he has a definite tendency to act-out in an hysterical, impulsive manner,"

5. Affidavits of two of appellant's work supervisors over a five-year period, and of his landlady, his mother, and his wife, related incidents involving violence and loss of memory following consumption by appellant of relatively minor quantities of alcoholic beverages.

6. The confessions recited the consumption by appellant of a can of beer, two drinks of vodka, and close to an additional one-half pint of vodka, immediately before the homicides. The autopsy physician testified at trial that the alcohol blood content of the female victim, whom appellant matched "drink for drink," was above the level indicating intoxication. Also, appellant's affidavit stated that he had consumed additional substantial quantities of alcohol during the preceding twenty-four hours.

was competent medical opinion to support the view that, in the light of these and other factors, appellant was incapable of entertaining the specific intent required for first-degree murder at the time and in the circumstances of the homicides.[7]

B. The following factual allegations were made in support of the inadmissibility of the confessions.

Appellant was arrested on a Tuesday evening. He was taken to the police station and booked. He told the arresting officers he wished to contact an attorney; they said he could get his attorney "later." He repeated this request twice more in the course of the evening. The requests were denied. The following morning he again asked to see his attorney; the officers said, "You'll see him."[8]

Appellant was questioned briefly the evening of his arrest. The following day he was subjected to lie detector tests and questioned intermittently from about 9:00 a.m. until about 2:30 in the afternoon when he first confessed. This confession, much longer than those subsequently taken, was recorded, but was later destroyed and was not introduced at trial. After further questioning, a typewritten statement was prepared which appellant signed and which was introduced at trial. The questioning resumed the following day. A tape-recorded confession taken that afternoon was also introduced at trial.

At the time of his arrest appellant was employed as a service station attendant. He had a tenth grade education, having failed the eleventh grade. He was thirty-nine years old. As noted, his pesonality was characterized by "emotional instability" and "neurotic and dissociative features." He did not know of his right to remain silent when questioned by the police. The officers did not advise him of his right; he was told that his interest lay in telling them his story fully and accurately before trial.[9]

---

7. The affidavit of Dr. John J. Preisinger stated that even before the electroencephalogram was available "there was little doubt in my mind that Mr. Brubaker had organic brain disease which would affect his behavior while drinking," and concluded, "I do not see how he could form any intent to do wrong (with even vague responsibility) if he were drinking." The affidavit of one of appellant's present attorneys stated that he submitted the same documentary material that Dr. Preisinger had seen to Dr. Edward T. Colbert, of Santa Monica, California, and that Dr. Colbert "substantially corroborates the opinion of Dr. Preisinger," and was further of the opinion that at the time of the homicides "retreat was impossible for a person of petitioner's compulsive and unstable psychic makeup."

The affidavit of Dr. Bernard L. Diamond, member of the American Psychiatric Association and author in forensic psychiatry, expressed the view that existing data indicated the desirability of further examination of appellant to determine his mental state at the time of the homicides. Dr. A. A. Marinacci, head of the Departments of Electroencephalography, Los Angeles County General Hospital, University of Southern California, and Good Samaritan Hospital, Los Angeles, agreed to examine appellant's electroencephalograms. Appellant's present attorney sought but was denied the opportunity to arrange for such examinations.

8. A memorandum prepared by a Deputy Public Defender following an interview with appellant shortly after his arraignment contained the notation, "Says denied atty at 1st." Affidavits of the two arresting officers "lodged" with the District Court but not accepted for filing, acknowledged a conversation with appellant regarding an attorney, although denying that he requested permission to telephone counsel.

9. Nothing in the confessions or elsewhere in the record indicates that appellant knew or was advised of his constitutional rights. The following excerpts from the tape-recorded confession reflect the substance of the advice given appellant by the officers: "It's much better for you if you are going to find you told something wrong to tell us now than it is to wait until we get in court,

From the final refusal of his request to contact a lawyer, appellant inferred that he would not be permitted to see a lawyer until he confessed. Before he confessed, one of the officers told him they had "other ways" to make him talk, which appellant took as a threat of violence. Appellant states that he confessed in fear, and in ignorance of his rights; that he had no clear recollection of the critical events surrounding the commission of the crime and that the details which appear in the recorded confessions were suggested to him by the officers as the way things must have happened.

C. The factual allegations in support of the contention that trial counsel failed to investigate and present appellant's defenses were as follows.

Appellant's trial counsel, a Deputy Public Defender, was appointed shortly after arraignment. Appellant told trial counsel that he knew nothing of the law, and placed himself entirely in trial counsel's hands.[10] Trial counsel initially recommended to appellant that he plead guilty. In the three-and-a-half months between arraignment and trial, trial counsel saw appellant on three occasions for a total of about an hour. Two of the conferences were devoted largely to matters other than appellant's defense.[11]

Trial counsel was aware of appellant's history of head injury and extended unconsciousness and of the heavy drinking that occurred on the night of the homicide[12] Nonetheless, he made no effort to elicit appellant's personal history, made no inquiries of appellant's family, friends or employers (although furnished the names by appellant), and failed to arrange a private examination of appellant by an independent psychiatrist (although funds were available for that purpose), because he mistakenly supposed that the communica-

---

and meanwhile have us find out, and possibly get proof that something you told us was not right. * * * If you can think of anything important to this case, tell us about it now. Because we don't want to go to court and prove you a liar. * * * If there's anything that you can straighten out now, you straighten it out in your story, and we won't have to go to court later and prove that this happened and you didn't tell us about it."

10. In an affidavit lodged with the District Court but not received for filing, trial counsel stated that appellant "placed his trust completely in me—more than once he said to me, 'I don't know anything about the law. I'll do whatever you say.'" The affidavit continued, "I never had any occasion to talk with Mr. Brubaker about what his rights might be and how he could exercise them if he was not satisfied with my representation of him. The occasion never arose for me to talk with Mr. Brubaker along these lines because he was so thoroughly cooperative."

11. It is alleged that the first conference concerned the necessity of seeking a continuance because of counsel's commitments on other cases, and that the second was devoted largely to explaining to appellant and his mother that counsel was abandoning a defense of insanity because of the report of the court-appointed psychiatrist (see note 12), and that they should be prepared for the death penalty. The affidavit of appellant's mother confirmed the latter conversation in part.

12. Appellant was examined by a court-appointed psychiatrist prior to the appointment of trial counsel. The letter report of this psychiatrist to the court found no evidence of mental illness, but recited appellant's history of head injury and extended unconsciousness, and a statement by appellant that his recollection of the crucial events was in "some parts * * * clouded up." (Letter from Dr. McNiel to Judge Nye, Oct. 2, 1958.) Trial counsel's affidavit and the trial transcript indicated that he was aware of the contents of the confessions later introduced at trial which recited in detail the drinking that occurred immediately prior to the homicides.

tions would not be privileged.[13] Trial counsel was told of the circumstances surrounding the taking of the confessions, including the refusal of appellant's prior requests for access to counsel, but he did not pursue the matter.[14] Trial counsel did not exercise his right to obtain a copy of the initial recorded interrogation of appellant by the police, since destroyed, although it contained material of value to the defense.[15]

The only evidence offered at trial to prove appellant's commission of the homicides was appellant's two confessions, but trial counsel made no effort to exclude them, announcing "no objections" to the admission of the first, and stipulating to the admission of the second. When the State rested, appellant's trial counsel approached the bench with appellant, stating that he did not intend to put appellant on the stand and "would like an expression of consent or lack of consent for the record at this time." Appellant consented. Trial counsel then rested for the defense, calling no witnesses as to the appellant's mental condition or any other matter. Trial counsel did not consult with appellant during the trial or between court sessions.

Trial counsel argued in summation that appellant lacked the necessary intent for first-degree murder, relying entirely upon the immediate details of the crime as indicated in the confessions, and by the physical circumstances. None of the facts and contentions summarized above relating to the admissibility of the confessions and the bearing of appellant's mental condition and intoxication upon the issue of specific intent was presented to the court or jury either through cross-examination, by affirmative evidence, or in argument.

The separate hearing on penalty required by California law was scheduled to be held four days following appellant's conviction. The California statute provides that "Evidence may be presented at the further proceedings on the issue of penalty, of the circumstances surrounding the crime, of the defendant's background and history, and of any facts in aggravation or mitigation of the penalty."[16] Appellant's trial counsel had assumed from the outset that a first-degree conviction was probable, yet he made no preparation for the penalty hearing. He did not see appellant during the four days between verdict and hearing. As the hearing was about to convene he spoke with appellant for five minutes, telling him that he "ought not to be disappointed" if he received a death sentence.

---

13. The affidavit of one of appellant's present counsel recited conversation with trial counsel to this effect. Present counsel cite In re Ochse, 38 Cal.2d 230, 238 P.2d 561 (1951), as establishing that under California law such communications are within the attorney-client privilege and as such are protected from disclosure.

14. Trial counsel's affidavit states, "I probably told [appellant] * * * that I thought it would be a futile act to object to the introduction of the confessions into evidence."

15. Present counsel argue that this initial recording, concededly much more extensive than in the later confessions introduced in trial, would have supported appellant's assertions that he was encouraged in the mistaken belief that he had no right to remain silent and his interest lay in full pretrial disclosure, that he was threatened, and that the details in the later confessions originated with the officers and were suggested to appellant, and would also have reflected appellant's confusion and remorse.

16. Cal.Pen.Code § 190.1.

The State offered evidence in aggravation of the penalty.[17] Appellant's trial counsel offered none in mitigation. When the State rested, appellant's counsel approached the bench with appellant, stating, "I would like the record to show that I have advised the defendant that, in my opinion, we have no evidence which would be of assistance to him in mitigation, and for that reason, I have recommended that he not testify." Appellant was asked to state for the record that counsel had so advised him and that he did not wish to testify; he responded, "That's correct." Trial counsel then rested. Substantial affirmative evidence in mitigation could have been secured by reasonable diligence,[18] but none was introduced because as trial counsel stated, he was not aware that any was available.

Trial counsel's summation challenging particulars of the State's argument in aggravation of sentence could only have prejudiced appellant. The prosecution argued that appellant was "a madman, a sex fiend"; trial counsel responded that "there is not one iota of evidence concerning this man's mental condition. * * * He is presumed to be sane." The prosecutor argued that appellant had shown no remorse; trial counsel responded that, although appellant had "concededly lied" when first questioned, he had then determined to tell the truth, though perhaps this decision was "self serving" and reached "only * * * because he thought it would help him," and the jury should consider the fact that he had cooperated.

II.

The test to be applied in determining the legal adequacy of the allegations of appellant's petition is readily stated: "The requirement of the Fourteenth Amendment is for a fair trial";[19] the due process clause "prohibits the conviction and incarceration of one whose trial is offensive to the common and fundamental ideas of fairness and right."[20] Compliance with this standard required that appellant, charged with a capital offense, be represented at trial by counsel.[21]

---

17. Trial counsel said he did not know what evidence the State intended to offer, though the principal witness was a cousin of appellant's wife. The hearing was delayed to permit trial counsel to examine the State's exhibits reflecting appellant's prior record, which trial counsel said he had not seen.

18. As evidence relevant to mitigation, appellant's present counsel pointed to material relating to appellant's organic brain damage, compulsive and unstable personality, and hypersensitivity to alcohol; his background and personal history: the deformities, illnesses and insecurities of his childhood, the absence from his record of any prior convictions of felony or of assaultive crimes, and the reputation which he bore among his work supervisors, fellow employees, friends and neighbors. Illustrative of supporting affidavits in the latter category was that of a plant superintendent under whom appellant worked continuously for four years: "Charlie Brubaker has been a very good friend of mine and has been out to my house many times. * * * He was a gentleman at all times and always thoughtful. * * * To kill someone was just not like him. * * * He is a very fine boy. * * * He was very good as a worker—one of the fastest men I had. * * * I know * * * that when he drinks, he just goes out of his head—just one beer and he doesn't even know his own name. * * * Charlie never hurt anybody he ever worked with. He was a friendly person who never intended any harm to anyone. He used to go around and take up a collection for anyone in our shop who was in trouble and his own two bucks would go into the hat first."

19. Massey v. Moore, 348 U.S. 105, 108, 75 S.Ct. 145, 147, 99 L.Ed. 135 (1954).

20. Betts v. Brady, 316 U.S. 455, 473, 62 S.Ct. 1252, 1262, 86 L.Ed. 1595 (1942).

21. Powell v. Alabama, 287 U.S. 45, 53 S.Ct. 55, 77 L.Ed 158 (1932).

But the constitutional requirement of representation at trial is one of substance, not of form. It could not be satisfied by a pro forma or token appearance. Appellant was entitled to "effective aid in the preparation and trial of the case."[22]

This does not mean that trial counsel's every mistake in judgment, error in trial strategy, or misconception of law would deprive an accused of a constitutional right. Due process does not require "errorless counsel, and not counsel judged ineffective by hindsight, but counsel reasonably likely to render *and rendering* reasonably effective assistance."[23] Determining whether the demands of due process were met in such a case as this requires a decision as to whether "upon the whole course of the proceedings," and in all the attending circumstances, there was denial of fundamental fairness;[24] it is inevitably a question of judgment and degree.

From the allegations of the petition, the defenses available but not presented by trial counsel appear to have been substantial.

Under California law "on the trial of the issues raised by a plea of not guilty to a charge of a crime which requires proof of a specific mental state, competent evidence that because of mental abnormality not amounting to legal insanity defendant did not possess the essential specific mental state is admissible." Such evidence "is received not as a 'complete defense' negating capacity to commit any crime but as a 'partial defense' negating specific mental state essential to a particular crime."[25] Evidence as to appellant's mental state was also relevant to the question of penalty, and might well have been persuasive.[26]

The allegations of the petition made out a prima facie case for the excludability of appellant's confessions under the rule announced in Crooker v. California.[27]

Facts are alleged from which it would appear that these potential defenses would have suggested themselves to a reasonably diligent trial counsel. The defense actually tendered was so insubstantial in relation to those not offered as to cast doubt upon the hypothesis that trial counsel made a deliberate informed choice.[28] The failure of trial counsel to contact obvious witnesses lends

---

22. Powell v. Alabama, 287 U.S. 45, 71, 53 S.Ct. 55, 65, 77 L.Ed. 158 (1932).

23. MacKenna v. Ellis, 280 F.2d 592, 599 (5th Cir. 1960), modified 289 F.2d 928 (5th Cir. 1961).

24. Malinski v. New York, 324 U.S. 401, 416, 65 S.Ct. 781, 789, 89 L.Ed. 1029 (1945) (concurring opinion); Betts v. Brady, 316 U.S. 455, 62 S.Ct. 1252, 86 L.Ed. 1595 (1942). "What due process requires in one situation may not be required in another, and this, of course, because the least change of circumstances may provide or eliminate fundamental fairness." Crooker v. California, 357 U.S. 433, 441 n. 6, 78 S.Ct. 1287, 1292, 2 L.Ed.2d 1448 (1958).

25. People v. Gorshen, 51 Cal.2d 716, 336 P.2d 492, 498–499 (1959), and authorities cited; People v. Wells, 33 Cal.2d 330, 202 P.2d 53, 61–70 (1949).

26. This is also true of the evidence relating to appellant's background and personal history. See note 18.

27. 357 U.S. 433, 78 S.Ct. 1287 (1958).

28. It is difficult to credit the suggestion, for example, that trial counsel deliberately chose to stipulate to the admission of confessions which were the sole evidence of appellant's guilt and which were at least arguably excludable under the rule announced in *Crooker,* on the theory that it would be better strategy to invoke the sympathy of the jury by a display of candor, especially since under California procedure the objection to the confessions could have been submitted initially to the court out of the presence of the jury.

further credence to the allegation that counsel did not undertake the investigation and research essential to adequate trial presentation. In any event it would not seem proper to dispose of so substantial a showing "by a resort to speculation and surmise"[29] as to possible explanations for trial counsel's inaction.

Upon an examination of the whole record, we conclude that appellant alleged a combination of circumstances, not refuted by the record, which, if true, precluded the presentation of his available defenses to the court and the jury through no fault of his own, and thus rendered his trial fundamentally unfair. Appellant does not complain that after investigation and research trial counsel made decisions of tactics and strategy injurious to appellant's cause; the allegation is rather that trial counsel failed to prepare, and that appellant's defense was withheld not through deliberate though faulty judgment, but in default of knowledge that reasonable inquiry would have produced and hence in default of any judgment at all.[30] The omissions alleged by appellant "were not mere mistakes of counsel or errors in the course of the trial. If true, they constituted a total failure to present the cause of the accused in any fundamental respect. Such a proceeding would not constitute for the accused the fair trial contemplated by the due process clause * * *"[31] It follows that appellant must have an opportunity to support the allegations of his petition, by proof, in a hearing before the District Court.

It should be noted that none of the reasons which have sometimes prompted denial of a factual hearing on allegations of inadequate representation by counsel are present in this case. The ease with which plausible but unfounded allegations may be made against trial counsel, the temptation of the convicted to blame their attorneys rather than themselves, and the weakness of the threat of perjury against those confined in prison or facing execution did not contribute to the allegations of this petition which was prepared and carefully documented by responsible counsel. The reputation of the Office of the Public Defender of Los Angeles County and of trial counsel in this case negated any possibility that available defenses were deliberately withheld to win delay and give accused two chances to prevail. The stresses imposed upon state-federal relations by differing determinations of the same factual issues could not arise here for no state court had considered the factual issues which the federal District Court will now determine for the first time on remand. . . .

Remanded for further proceedings.

In re HAWLEY.

63 Cal. Rptr. 831, 433 P.2d 919 (1967)

PETERS, Justice.

In June of 1966 petitioner pleaded guilty to murder in the first degree and was sentenced to life imprisonment. He did not appeal. On May 1, 1967, he filed a petition for a writ of

---

29. Palmer v. Ashe, 342 U.S. 134, 137, 72 S.Ct. 191, 193, 96 L.Ed. 154 (1951).

30. "Pro forma entry of an appearance without study or preparation for useful participation in the trial is not a satisfaction of the constitutional rights of an accused." Turner v. Maryland, 303 F.2d 507, 511 (4th Cir. 1962). The importance of reasonable investigation and preparation in determining whether challenged representation meets constitutional standards was emphasized by the court in Powell v. Alabama, 287 U.S. 45, 57–58, 53 S.Ct. 55, 77 L.Ed. 158 (1932).

31. Jones v. Huff, 80 U.S.App.D.C. 254, 152 F.2d 14, 15 (1945).

habeas corpus seeking reversal of the judgment on the ground of ineffective aid of counsel at the time of his plea.

Petitioner's allegations and exhibits submitted by him, including the transcript of the grand jury proceedings, may be summarized as follows:

He is a 29-year-old American Indian. He had been drinking almost continuously from March 7, 1966, until the date of the homicide on March 19, 1966. On that day he met a woman in Sacramento's West End. They spent the morning drinking wine and in the evening decided to have intercourse. Petitioner remembered seeing a mattress in an abandoned hotel. They entered the hotel and went into a small dark room where decedent, Alejandro Lopez, also under the influence of liquor, was sleeping on the mattress. Petitioner woke Lopez and asked him to leave. He got up, said something in Spanish and tried to kick petitioner, who knocked Lopez down with his fist. Hawley then had intercourse with his lady friend. Afterwards, Lopez made a remark that petitioner did not understand. Petitioner grabbed a stick and hit Lopez with it until he stopped talking. He then dragged the still-alive Lopez into another room 50 feet away. He gathered papers and small sticks together around Lopez and lit them. Petitioner does not remember any of the details, nor does he remember dragging Lopez or lighting the fire. Petitioner then went out of the building, his lady friend left him, and he met and started to drink with a male friend. Petitioner noticed there was no fire in the building he had vacated and took his friend inside. The friend saw the body, and called the police. The two men waited until the officers arrived. Petitioner then related these facts to the officers and signed a statement. An autopsy revealed that the fire caused Lopez's death. The only damage to the building was a charring of the floor by the body.

Petitioner was indicted for murder and arson. He was represented by the public defender, who requested Dr. S. Green to prepare a psychiatric study of petitioner. In his report, Dr. Green reviewed petitioner's background. It showed that petitioner's mother, father and girl friend had all been killed in separate automobile accidents while they were intoxicated. Petitioner had only completed the 10th grade in school. Since 1954 he spent about 10 months of every year in prison, each incident resulting in his incarceration occurring while he was intoxicated. Dr. Green found physical deterioration and dilapidation with consequential impairment of retention, memory and vocabulary. Petitioner expressed no guilt about his actions and little concern over his fate. Dr. Green found him to be presently sane and responsible, but concluded as to his condition at the time of the crimes:

At the time of the alleged crime of arson, the effect of prolonged alcoholism would be so severe it would contaminate any intent he may have had. Furthermore, the amount of wilfulness and maliciousness would be severely restricted and he would be inable [sic] to comprehend such an action or govern himself.

Regarding the charge of murder, this man was severely intoxicated and does have a type of mental disease that rendered him incapable to do his duty to govern his actions in accord with the duty imposed by law. He did not act with malice aforethought, and in my opinion he cannot be guilty of murder. The necessary ingredients to kill, which are the result of deliberation and must depend upon a pre-existing reflection, were not present due to his state of mind.

"It is my opinion that this man's action can only be understood in the light of severe personality problems and mental disease which existed at the time of the alleged crimes. The intoxication involved him to a degree that he did not know right from wrong. He had aggressive feelings to such a degree that he was psychotic, mentally ill, a dangerous man; but he could not do anything about it."

Counsel also had available a report by Dr. W. Rapaport, prepared upon request of the district attorney. Dr. Rapaport reviewed petitioner's present condition and concluded: "While he states that he was drunk at the time, examination indicates he was not unconscious. Examination shows no evidence of mental illness either at the time of the homicide or at the time of the examination. Examination reveals that he was not acting under an irresistable [sic] impulse or that he was under the influence or direction of any unusual power."

Under these circumstances, the public defender entered into an agreement with the prosecution to the effect that if petitioner would plead guilty to first degree murder, the prosecution would recommend life imprisonment instead of the death penalty and would move to dismiss the arson charge. Petitioner alleges that counsel advised him to plead guilty, to take the compromise, and thereby to avoid the danger of risking the death penalty. Petitioner does not allege that his counsel was unaware or failed to discuss with him the possible defenses of insanity (see People v. Wolff, 61 Cal.2d 795, 799–803, 40 Cal. Rptr. 271, 394 P.2d 959)

or of diminished capacity (see People v. Conley, 64 Cal.2d 310, 322, 49 Cal.Rptr. 815, 411 P.2d 911).

Petitioner contends that the public defender's recommendation under these circumstances that he plead guilty to first degree murder was a denial of effective representation. This depends on whether the record shows that counsel's advice to plead guilty improperly deprived petitioner of the defenses mentioned.

Reliance is placed on People v. Ibarra, 60 Cal.2d 460, 34 Cal.Rptr. 863, 386 P.2d 487. There the defendant was convicted of possession of heroin in violation of Health and Safety Code section 11500. The conviction was reversed on the ground that the defendant was denied effective assistance of counsel because the record showed that counsel did not know of the rule that defendant could challenge the legality of the search and seizure despite his denial that the heroin was taken from him and his failure to claim a proprietary interest in the premises which were entered. Counsel's actions foreclosed the determination of crucial factual issues determinative of defendant's defense. It was stated that "It is counsel's duty to investigate carefully all defenses of fact and of law that may be available to the defendant, and if his failure to do so results in withdrawing a crucial defense from the case, the defendant has not had the assistance to which he is entitled." (Id. at p. 464, 34 Cal.Rptr. at p. 486, 386 P.2d at p. 490.)

We agree that the right of a defendant to assistance of counsel applies not only during trial, as in *Ibarra*, but also when the defendant is advised to plead guilty, and that the competency of counsel is subject to review in both instances. Counsel by advising his client to plead guilty cannot be permitted to evade his responsibility to adequately research the facts and the law.

Bargaining for pleas is, of course, an important factor in the administration of the criminal law.[1] But at the time of determining whether to accept such a bargain the accused is entitled to the advice and assistance of counsel, based upon an investigation of the facts and law of his case. The plea of guilty "constitutes an admission of every element entering into the offense charged, and constitutes a conclusive admission of defendant's guilt." (People v. Outcault, 90 Cal.App.2d 25, 29, 202 P.2d 602, 604.) Counsel is particularly qualified to make such a recommendation because it is he, not his client, who possesses the skills to analyze the nature of the charges, to evaluate the evidence, and to make informed recommendations.[2]

Deprivation of the right to counsel at the pleading stage because of incompetency can well constitute a deprivation of due process. Although plea bargains may expedite proceedings in the criminal courts, such expedition cannot be a substitute for due process. Thus, if incompetency of counsel were here shown, it would be a ground for relief.

But no such showing is made. There is no showing that counsel was not aware of the facts or the law, or that he was unfamiliar with a crucial defense. In fact the record shows quite the contrary. Obviously, counsel knew the facts of the case. In view of the confession and the facts admitted therein, the only possible defense related to the mental condition of the client. That the attorney was well aware of this possible defense is indicated by the fact that he secured the psychiatric report of Dr. Green.

Under the gruesome facts existing here, and in view of the conflicting evidence on the mental condition of petitioner, we cannot say that counsel was incompetent because he advised petitioner to plead guilty. While, if counsel had had a substantially conclusive defense it would have been a deprivation of counsel to urge the guilty plea, that is not this case. Here the evidence as to the defense was highly conflicting. Under such circumstances the paramount consideration of the lawyer is to determine whether it is reasonably possible that he could convince a jury of his version of the facts. Where there is a significant possibility that the jury might impose the death penalty, counsel's wisest alternative may well be a plea bargain.

That is this case. Here, there is no showing that counsel did not research the facts or the law, or that he was ignorant of a crucial defense, or that he did not talk these matters

---

1. For the fiscal year 1965 to 1966, 69.0% of the criminal cases in the superior courts were disposed of before trial. (Judicial Council of California, 1967 Annual Report of the Administrative Office of the California Courts, table XIX, p. 201.)

2. "Few, if any, intelligent and well educated laymen are schooled in the science of law, and if charged with a crime are capable of determining for themselves whether the indictment is good or bad. They are unfamiliar with the rules of evidence, lacking both the skill and knowledge to adequately prepare their defense, even though they may have a perfect one. They require the guiding hand of counsel at every step of the proceeding. Though they be not guilty, they face the danger of conviction because they do not know how to establish their innocence. If this be true of a man of intelligence how much more true is it of those without adequate schooling and experience." (People v. McGarvy, 61 Cal.App.2d 557, 562, 142 P.2d 92, 95.)

over with petitioner.[3] While counsel possessed substantial evidence supporting the possible defenses of insanity or diminished responsibility,[4] including some substantiation from the district attorney as to defendant's intoxication,[5] he also knew that such evidence had been directly contradicted by Dr. Rapaport. He also knew that the facts were quite gruesome, and that defendant's admitted conduct indicated a degree of premeditation and malice. He knew that in a trial the death penalty was a real possibility. Under such circumstances he cannot be charged with incompetency in seeking and advising a plea bargain. . . .

The order to show cause is discharged and the petition is denied.

TRAYNOR, C. J., and McCOMB, TOBRINER, MOSK, BURKE, and SULLIVAN, JJ., concur.

IOWA DEPT. OF SOCIAL SERVICES
v.
IOWA MERIT EMPLOYMENT DEPT.

261 N.W.2d 161 (Iowa, 1977)

HARRIS, Justice.

This dispute between two state administrative agencies arose from the attempt of Cynthia Gunther (the intervenor) to raise her employment classification at the men's reformatory. The Iowa department of social services, men's reformatory (the department) has the ultimate responsibility for the operation of the men's reformatory at Anamosa. The Iowa merit employment department, Iowa merit employment commission (the commission) is charged with enforcing the Merit System Act (ch. 19A, The Code). The controlling question is whether a bona fide occupational qualification exception (BFOQ) exists which prevents a woman employee from undertaking the duties of a reformatory corrections officer II (CO II). The trial court determined no BFOQ existed for the position. The trial court ordered the intervenor to be placed in the CO II classification. At the same time the trial court ordered, in view of the intervenor's status as a woman, that she be exempted from certain duties routinely required of men in the same classification. We agree there are certain duties routinely required of a CO II which, as a practical matter, are impossible for a woman to perform. We believe such impossibility renders the CO II classification a proper subject for a BFOQ. We reverse the trial court.

The most significant facts in this dispute are (1) that all inmates of the Iowa men's reformatory are males, and (2) the intervenor is female. . . .

---

3. In order to secure habeas corpus relief, petitioner must allege and prove all the facts upon which he relies to overturn the judgment. (See e.g., In re Shipp, 62 Cal.2d 547, 553, 43 Cal.Rpts. 3, 399 P.2d 571; In re Dixon, 41 Cal.2d 756, 760, 264 P.2d 513.) A general allegation of "ineffective counsel" is not a sufficient basis for relief.

4. People v. Conley, supra, 64 Cal.2d 310, 49 Cal.Rptr. 815, 411 P.2d 911, decided three months before petitioner changed his plea to guilty, first applied the diminished capacity defense to a situation where the defendant was intoxicated; however, the defense, generally, has been well recognized since People v. Wells, 33 Cal.2d 330, 202 P.2d 53. Compare also People v. Gorshen, 51 Cal.2d 716, 336 P.2d 492.

5. The prosecutor in his statement of the facts said to the court: "Essentially, this defendant had been drinking with companions in the West End. They had been drinking wine. Mr. Hawley stated to me that this conduct had been going on over the last two or three days. We had corroborated the fact that he had been drinking, just prior to this incident."

Thirty-five percent of inmates at the reformatory have been convicted of crimes of violence, including sex offenses. Clearly the inmate population at the reformatory has a far greater tendency to violence than does the general population. The inmates are deprived of normal sexual experiences. Many of them react spontaneously with little thought of consequences.

The correction officers who make up the operating personnel of the reformatory are of four classifications. The first classification is that of correction officer I (CO I). This is generally the beginning classification for a new officer at the reformatory. A CO I rotates through various tasks on a somewhat limited basis. A number of officers, by reason of age, physical condition, or perhaps for various other reasons are never elevated beyond the CO I classification.

CO II's are subject to general duty throughout the institution. They can perform all the functions of a CO I and significant additional tasks such as riot control, patrol of cell blocks, and superintending inmates' bath and shower rooms. CO II's conduct frequent "pat searches" and "strip searches" of the inmates. While patrolling cell blocks CO II's are in full view of the cells themselves. They can, and frequently do, view the inmates' toilet. In general CO II's are in much closer and direct personal contact with the inmates than are CO I's. The record is clear a female CO II would be in very real danger of sexual attack.

Some CO II's advance to higher classifications as CO III and CO IV officers. Some CO II's do not so advance. With each advancement authority and pay increase.

Petitioner is a four-year college graduate. Except for her sex and lack of institutional experience there is no question that, with additional training, she would possess the qualifications of a CO II officer. When employed as a CO I officer she was assigned duty in the visitors rooms, central control, and tower watch. Eventually she sought advancement to CO II which will cause her to be rotated through all assignments. Because some assignments as a CO II officer would be impractical for any woman the department refused to promote her. The department also refused to create a distinct classification for her by calling her a CO II and omitting the duties she could not perform. Petitioner thereafter appealed to the merit commission which ruled in her favor. The commission directed that she be given the CO II classification but in effect created a new and distinct classification by exempting her from "pat" or "strip" searches and from assignments to the cell blocks.

On appeal the trial court affirmed the merit commission "* * * with the common sense exemption noted both by the agency below and the *Reynolds* court [*Reynolds v. Wise*, 375 F.Supp. 145, (N.D. Tex.)] that these officers should not be placed in job duties that may reasonably be expected to breach inmates' justified expectations of personal privacy." The reformatory appealed to this court. . . .

All parties concede the intervenor cannot perform all tasks routinely assigned to male CO II's. In her brief and argument intervenor states:

"Admittedly there are certain job duties and job functions which the intervenor cannot perform either because of inmate privacy rights, or the necessity to avoid compromising positions. However, that is not to say that the intervenor cannot be pro-

moted through the classification system. * *." (Emphasis added.) The commission eliminated from the intervenor's duties "* * * assignment to dormitories [cell houses?] or shakedown * * * to insure privacy."

For reasons which will appear we agree and hold the intervenor's womanhood prevents her from performing all CO II functions at the men's reformatory.

The parties point to provisions of different but somewhat related Code chapters. The department points to chapter 601A, The Code (Iowa Civil Rights Act of 1965). Section 601A.6(1)(a) provides in part:

"It shall be an unfair or discriminatory practice for any * * * [p]erson to refuse to hire, accept, register, classify, or refer for employment, to discharge an employee, or to otherwise discriminate in employment against any applicant for employment or any employee because of * * * sex * * * *unless based upon the nature of the occupation [the BFOQ exception].* * * *." (Emphasis added.)

The commission points to chapter 19A, The Code, (the Merit System Act). Section 19A.18 provides:

"No person shall be appointed or promoted to, or demoted or discharged from, any position in the merit system, or in any way favored or discriminated against with respect to employment in the merit system because of his * * * sex * * *." Chapter 19A contains no BFOQ clause.

Section 19A.22 provides:

"The provisions of this chapter, including but not limited to its provisions on employees and positions to which the merit system apply, shall prevail over any inconsistent provisions of the Code and all subsequent Acts unless such subsequent Acts provide a specific exception from the merit system."

The commission argues the absence of a BFOQ from chapter 19A combined with the provisions of 19A.22 show the legislature intended to deny any BFOQ exemption for Iowa merit employees such as the intervenor....

Turning to the two Code chapters referred to we do not believe the legislature's failure to include a BFOQ provision in § 19A.18 indicates a total prohibition of BFOQ provisions for that chapter. We note that § 356.5(6), The Code, requires jailers "[t]o have a matron on the jail premises at all times during the incarceration of any one or more female prisoners * * *."

We do not think the department of transportation is prohibited from hiring male attendants for male restrooms or females for female restrooms in highway rest stops. But the commission's interpretation of § 19A.18, precluding BFOQ exceptions, would make such hiring practices impossible. Similarly, we do not believe male officers could be required, for lack of a BFOQ clause, for a CO II position at the women's reformatory at Rockwell City.

In any event the absence of a BFOQ provision in § 19A.18 could not justify an unconstitutional invasion of the inmates' rights to human dignity and privacy....

The parties, the commission, and the trial court conceded the obvious when they recognized the existence of a personal right of privacy with respect to one's own body and bodily functions. Such a right is guaranteed by several provisions of the federal Constitution. See *Hodgson v. Robert Hall Clothes, Inc.*, 326 F.Supp. 1264, 1269 (D.C. Del.1971); *Henderson v. United States*, 390 F.2d 805, 807–808 (9 Cir. 1967). See also *York v. Story*, 324 F.2d 450, 455 (9 Cir. 1963) where it is said: "We cannot conceive of a more basic subject of privacy than the naked body. The desire to shield one's unclothed figure from view of strangers, and particularly strangers of the opposite sex, is impelled by elementary self-respect and personal dignity."

In general prisoners possess sensibilities to exposure of the body and its functions approximating those of people in a free society....

Of course, "* * * [l]awful incarceration brings about the necessary withdrawal or limitation of many privileges and rights, a retraction justified by the considerations underlying our penal system. * * *." *Price v. Johnston*, 334 U.S. 266, 285, 68 S.Ct. 1049, 1060, 92 L.Ed. 1356, 1369 (1948)....

However to the extent consistent with those considerations, prisoners retain a residuum of constitutional rights. *Wolff v. McDonnell*, 418 U.S. 539, 556–572, 94 S.Ct. 2963, 2974–2982, 41 L.Ed.2d 935, 950–960 (1974)....

It is not suggested by any party the exposed cells of the reformatory should be modified. No one suggests supervision of prisoners as they toilet or shower can be eliminated. No one claims strip searches of the inmates can be abandoned. It seems continuous supervision by male guards will be necessary security requirements at the reformatory. It is apparent, and is undisputed, there would be a constitutional violation of inmates' rights if the guards were women. Cases from other jurisdictions indicate continuous surveillance by one of the opposite sex violates a right of personal privacy. *In re Long*, Cal.App., 127 Cal.Rptr. 732 (1976); *Long v. California State Personnel Board*, 41 Cal.App.3d 1000, 116 Cal.Rptr. 562 (1974); *City of Philadelphia v. Pennsylvania Hum. Rel. Com'n,*, 7 Pa.Cmwlth. 500, 300 A.2d 97 (1973).

We hold the absence of a BFOQ provision in § 19A.18 cannot justify an invasion of inmates' constitutional rights....

We come then to the central and fighting issue in this suit. Are the duties which the intervenor cannot perform crucial to her job classification? If not the commission and trial court were right in ordering the intervenor to be classified as CO II and at the same time exempting her from performance of those duties. We fully recognize and subscribe to the goals of the Iowa Civil Rights Act of 1965 and the Merit System Act. At the same time we think it is more than apparent that, under the facts in this case as found by the commissioner, the duties the intervenor cannot perform are the very core and substance of the CO II classification.

The commissioner's findings of fact were supported by the record. They can be summarized as follows:

a. Cell houses and other areas frequented by CO II's are places where bodily functions are performed and showers taken in full view of correctional officers at all times.

b. By reason of the physical arrangement at the reformatory, the spacing of buildings, towers, etc., there are places which cannot be observed from towers or by other means so that correctional officers on general duty are frequently alone with inmates. Even where more than one officer is on duty in an area the officers are normally not in view of one another.

c. Daily required "pat searches" of inmates are an essential duty of a CO II.

d. Strip searches are frequent and, although usually two officers are present, one could not be a woman.

e. No place in the reformatory could be considered safe from danger. A female would be more subject to an assault, especially a sexual assault.

f. Surprise is essential for a correction officer. To announce a correctional officer's presence in order to avoid embarassment of inmates would eliminate this important factor for effective performance.

g. It would be economically unsound, would present serious scheduling problems, would destroy essential flexibility in the assignment of CO II's, and cause discontent among male CO II's to limit the functions of a female CO II.

j. The question of invasion of the privacy of inmates by a female CO II is so serious it could cause protest if females worked in certain areas. This would lead to serious confrontation if the protests were ignored. Male inmates have fixed ideas as to female roles. Confrontations and testing are certain to be frequent.

k. The inmate population at the reformatory has a greater tendency to violence than does the general population. Inmates react spontaneously with little thought of consequences and without mature judgment. Anything which upsets the balance ignites these factors, affects the rehabilitation program, and requires countermeasures (which always take time) in order to get things back to normal).

1. There have already been inmate protests concerning their privacy because the intervenor worked in the tower. This example of the reactions of the male inmates is typical.

From the findings we conclude it is impossible to separate the CO II classification from the duties the intervenor cannot perform. A CO II is an officer whose essential function, though flexible, demands the closest personal contact with reformatory inmates. Physical contact and inti-mate surveillance are essential and common. It is apparent that the basic distinction between CO I's and CO II's lies in the ability of CO II's, by such personal contact, to bring the authority of the institution to bear directly on the person of each inmate. This conclusion is supported by the fact that some CO II's, because of advancing age, or fear, voluntarily take demotions to a CO I classification, and "sit it out on the tower before they retire."

We do not believe the institution should be required to substantially adjust its physical plant or procedure in order to support the imposition of a classification. The following from *Long v. California State Personal Board, supra*, 41 Cal.App.3d at 1015, 116 Cal.Rptr. at 572 (3 Dist. 1974) is pertinent:

"Argument was presented and even evidence to the effect that physical adjustments could be made to prevent these incidents. [Potential sexual attack on a woman chaplain by male prisoners.] Security guards could be hired, alarm systems could be expanded, buildings could be moved, and procedures changed. However we do not view the duty of an employer to refrain from discrimination based upon sex as requiring him to alter substantially his facility and procedure to suit the sex of the person involved. Certainly reasonable adjustments should be made, otherwise equal protection rights of either sex could be thwarted by contrived nonsensical conditions."

Under the closely similar federal civil rights acts, 42 U.S.C. 2000e–2(e), a discriminatory practice cannot be justifed by administrative convenience, *Schaefer v. Tannian*,

394 F. Supp. 1128, 1134 (E.D.Mich. 1974), or in the private sector by a "business purpose." *Robinson v. Lorillard Corporation*, 444 F.2d 791, 796–797 (4 Cir. 1971). On the other hand it is permissible to discriminate on the basis of sex on the ground of "business necessity", that is, where the practice is "necessary to the safe and efficient operation of the business." *Robinson supra*, 444 F.2d at 797–798. The civil rights act permits reasonable classifications of employees based on sex, and an employer is required to neither pattern a job for a woman or a man, nor accept an inefficient mode of operation. 14 C.J.S.Supp. Civil Rights § 68, p. 120 (1974). See *Dothard v. Rawlinson*, 97 S.Ct. 2720, 2728, 53 L.Ed.2d 786, 799 (1977) n. 14.

We hold the decisions of the commission and the trial court . . . were spawned by an erroneous understanding of the law. . . .

REVERSED.

FORTS
v.
WARD.

621 F.2d 1210 (2d Cir. 1980).

NEWMAN, Circuit Judge:

The modern sensitivity to the significance of gender in American life and law has made it inevitable that cases will arise where gender-based legal contentions conflict. This case arises in a context where that conflict can be expected to recur with some frequency: privacy rights versus employment rights. Members of one sex assert a privacy right not to have their unclothed bodies viewed by members of the opposite sex. At the same time, members of one sex assert an employment right not to be discriminated against in job opportunities because of their gender. In this case, the privacy right is asserted by female prisoners, and the employment right is asserted by male prison guards, but the potential conflict of rights transcends the particular alignment of genders. Indeed, in this very case the challenged discrimination against the male guards is alleged to result in the impairment of employment rights of female guards. Resolution of such cases requires a careful inquiry as to whether the competing interests can be satisfactorily accommodated before deciding whether one interest must be vindicated to the detriment of the other. Fortunately this case is one where that inquiry yields a result that respects both privacy and employment rights.

The case is here on appeal and cross-appeal from an order of the United States District Court for the Southern District of New York (Richard Owen, Judge), which seeks to protect the privacy interests of women inmates at the Bedford Hills Correctional Facility ("Bedford Hills") a women's prison operated by the State of New York. *Forts v. Ward*, 471 F.Supp. 1095 (S.D.N.Y. 1978). The order, *id.* at 1102–03, imposed various requirements, including a prohibition on the assignment of male guards to certain duties in the infirmary and housing units of the prison. The suit was brought by ten women inmates against State correction and personnel officials ("State defendants") and the state-wide union[1] representing correction

---

1. The union is Security Unit Employees Council 82, American Federation of State, County and Municipal Employees, AFL-CIO (Council 82).

officers and two union officials ("union defendants"). The State defendants have not appealed. The union defendants have appealed only to challenge the portion of Judge Owen's order that enjoins male guards from assignment to duties requiring observation of female inmates through the windows of their cell doors during nighttime hours. The plaintiffs have cross-appealed to challenge the denial of their motion for class certification.[2]

The background and procedural history of this litigation require some explanation. In February, 1977, pursuant to a change in state policy,[3] male correction officers were assigned for the first time to duties within the living and sleeping corridors of Bedford Hills. Several months later, the inmate plaintiffs commenced the action, pursuant to 42 U.S.C. § 1983, on behalf of themselves and an alleged class of approximately 400 other women inmates at Bedford Hills.[4] Their complaint alleged that the assignment of male guards to areas of the prison where inmates were involuntarily exposed to view while partially or completely unclothed denied the inmates their constitutional right to privacy. In June, 1977, the District Court granted the plaintiffs' motion for a preliminary injunction against assignment of male correction officers to parts of the housing and hospital units of Bedford Hills. *Forts v. Ward*, 434 F.Supp. 946 (S.D.N.Y.1977). Upon appeal by all defendants, this Court reversed and remanded for an evidentiary hearing on the injunction motion, having concluded that disputed issues of fact existed. *Forts v. Ward*, 566 F.2d 849 (2d Cir. 1977).

Upon remand, Judge Owen combined the hearing on the preliminary injunction with the trial on the merits and held a twelve-day non-jury trial in December, 1977 and January, 1978. Forty-three witnesses testified, and Judge Owen, accompanied by counsel, made a personal inspection of Bedford Hills. At Bedford Hills each inmate occupies an individual solid-walled cell measuring seven

---

2. Plaintiffs initially cross-appealed more broadly, challenging the District Court's order for failing to provide greater protection for their privacy rights. This aspect of their appeal has been withdrawn, the plaintiffs preferring to determine whether implementation of the order in practice warrants any further relief. Judge Owen explicitly retained jurisdiction to modify the order.

3. "This new assignment policy was an attempt by the Department of Correctional Services to eliminate sex certification in the assignment and transfer of correction officers and to implement the collective bargaining agreement between the State and the correction officers' union." *Forts v. Ward*, 566 F.2d 849, 850–51 (2d Cir. 1977) (footnotes omitted). Aware that the new assignment policy might result in some invasions of inmate privacy, the State of New York issued a set of guidelines in May, 1977, to govern job assignments of prison guards. These guidelines prohibit assignments that require a guard "to conduct strip frisks of inmates of the opposite sex," and they prohibit permanent assignment of a guard to areas where inmates of the opposite sex are "open to view" while showering. In addition, the guidelines provide that "At least one officer of the same sex as the inmate population at a facility must be assigned to each housing block." *Forts v. Ward, supra*, 471 F.Supp. at 1097 n.3.

4. The complaint also sought certification of a sub-class consisting of the approximately 100 Muslim women at Bedford Hills. The complaint alleged that as a result of the complained of assignment practices, the members of the sub-class were forced to expose their bodies to males "in violation of their religious beliefs" and their First Amendment rights to the free exercise of their religion. On their cross-appeal, the inmate plaintiffs have not contested the denial of their request for certification of the sub-class. On the merits, the free exercise of religion claim was deemed not to warrant any additional relief beyond that extended to the inmate population. 471 F.Supp. at 1102 & n.25.

feet by ten feet and containing a bed and a toilet. Each cell has a solid door, controlled by guards at the end of each corridor. Each cell door has a clear glass window measuring six inches by nine inches. The interior of the cell, including the bed and the toilet, is visible to anyone in the corridor looking through the cell door window. Prison rules permit an inmate during the day to request that her cell door be closed and allow her to cover the cell door window for fifteen-minute intervals. At night the door is kept closed, but the window may not be covered.

On November 20, 1978, Judge Owen issued his decision, *Forts v. Ward, supra*, 471 F.Supp. 1095. He found that female inmates, while completely or partially unclothed, had been subjected to "a certain amount of viewing" by male correction officers and that such incidents were "certain to occur again with some frequency" given the physical setup and rules of Bedford Hills, *id.* at 1097–98. The Court noted that though an "individual's normal right of privacy must necessarily be abridged upon incarceration" in the interest of prison security, *id.* at 1098, inmates do retain some residual privacy rights, *id.* at 1099. With respect to the guards' interest in equal job opportunity, the Court

found "no dispute that the job of a correction officer at Bedford Hills can be equally well performed by any qualified and trained man or woman" but concluded that "equal job opportunity must in some measure give way to the right of privacy." *Ibid.* Specifically, the Court ruled that the women inmates were entitled to be protected from being viewed by male guards when they were partially or completely unclothed—while receiving medical treatment at the prison hospital or while showering, using toilet facilities, or sleeping in the housing units. The opinion contemplated protecting the inmates' privacy by a combination of changes in guards' work assignments and minor structural alterations.

Judge Owen found no reason to bar male guards from assignment to the housing corridors during the daytime hours since prison rules permitted an inmate to protect her privacy during those hours by covering the cell door window for up to fifteen-minute intervals while dressing or attending to personal needs. However, he found that because prison rules prohibited covering the door windows during nighttime hours, the assignment of male guards to the corridors during those time periods violated the inmates' right of privacy.[5] *Id.* at 1100–1101. Judge

---

5. Judge Owen's opinion also found that the assignment of male guards to the corridors during the morning count violated the inmates' right to privacy:

> . . . somewhere between 6:30 and 6:45 in the morning, the inmates are awakened and all the cell doors are simultaneously rolled open by a master switch. . . . At that point, the inmates obviously do not have even the door to protect them from anything. Some inmates may wish to use the toilet upon arising; some, while waiting, may wish to change from night clothes into day clothes; one may find her night clothes and bedding visibly soiled from an unexpected menstrual flow and wish to clean up; yet the present rules for the security of the prison require that each inmate present herself to be counted at that hour regardless of the state of her clothing or the calls of nature.

471 F.Supp. at 1101 (footnote omitted). Prior to the entry of his final order, the prison procedures respecting the morning count were changed. Thus, Judge Owen's order merely called for a continuation of the "present procedure . . . insofar as inmates are told five minutes before the count that the count will occur, and that under normal circumstances, during this five minute period no male officers shall enter the housing unit corridors." *Id.* at 1102–03. On appeal, the union defendants have raised no objection to this portion of Judge Owen's order.

Owen also found that the invasions of privacy occurring while inmates were showering or changing into and out of their clothes could be easily corrected by installation in the shower facilities of appropriate screens. *Id.* at 1101.

Rather than immediately issuing an order implementing his opinion, Judge Owen directed the State defendants to submit a proposed order that, "while maximizing equal job opportunity, will afford each inmate the minimal privacy to which the court concludes she is entitled." *Id.* at 1102. The proposed order submitted by the State defendants suggested two solutions to prevent viewing through the cell door window during nighttime hours: issuing to each inmate upon request, a set of one-piece pajamas, commonly known as "Dr. Denton's," and changing the prison rules to permit inmates to cover their cell door windows at night for the same fifteen-minute intervals permitted during the daytime. The order entered by Judge Owen on April 12, 1979, rejected both of these suggestions in favor of an absolute prohibition against the assignment of male correction officers to duties during the nighttime "which require them under normal circumstances to observe female inmates through the windows of each inmate's cell." *Forts v. Ward, supra*, 471 F.Supp. at 1102. The rationale for this change was explained to the parties by Judge Owen at a conference held in late February, 1979:

> . . . I do not think it appropriate to say to a woman, "In order to protect your privacy, you have got to be ensconced in a two-legged bag over the night or give up the right to privacy. It seems to me that she

has the right to select appropriate sleep wear . . . because I don't see any prison necessity for a particular designation of sleep wear and I don't see that a person has to sleep in a Dr. Denton, if the temperature hits 90 or 95 . . . in order that a man may have the privilege of walking up and down the corridor and looking in upon her. . . .

Having decided to prohibit guards from nighttime corridor assignments primarily because he found the State's sleepwear proposal unacceptable, Judge Owen found it unnecessary to accept the State's additional suggestion that cell door windows could be covered for intervals during the night.

The nature of the issues presented on appeal has been significantly shaped by the fact that the State defendants have elected not to challenge Judge Owen's order. The acquiescence of the State defendants means that there is no longer any dispute between the inmate plaintiffs and New York as to whether the nighttime viewing of completely or partially unclothed women inmates by male prison guards violates the constitutional privacy rights of the inmates. We may assume for purposes of this appeal that such viewing is a denial of constitutional rights. But that issue remains whether the District Court's remedy impairs protected rights of the prison guards. On their behalf the union defendants contend that the portion of the remedy removing them from nightime shifts in the housing units is unjustifiable gender-based employment discrimination in violation of Title VII of the Civil Rights Act of 1964, 42 U.S.C. § 2000e *et seq.* (1970 ed. and Supp. V).[6] . . .

---

6. The pertinent provisions of Title VII make it unlawful for an employer to discriminate with respect to "terms, conditions, or privileges of employment" or "to limit, segregate, or classify his

The merits of the guards' Title VII defense appears to place their equal employment rights in opposition to the inmates' privacy rights.[7] While this Title VII grievance is asserted on behalf of men, we note that gender-based discrimination in prison employment opportunities generally disadvantages women. See, *e. g.*, *Dothard v. Rawlinson*, 433 U.S. 321, 97 S.Ct. 2720, 53 L.Ed.2d 786 (1977); *Gunther v. Iowa State Men's Reformatory*, 462 F.Supp. 952 (N.D. Iowa 1979); see "Balancing Inmates' Right to Privacy with Equal Employment for Prison Guards," 4 Women's Rights Law Reporter 243 (1978). Moreover, even in this case, we are informed that removal of men from night shift duties would impair the employment opportunities of female employees at Bedford Hills by bumping them from preferred daytime shifts to which they would normally be entitled by virtue of seniority.

In most respects Judge Owen skillfully avoided an ultimate conflict between employment and privacy rights by carefully tailored adjustments to either facilities or work assignments. In protecting the inmates' privacy at the prison hospital, the judge prohibited the stationing of male guards at locations where inmates could be viewed completely or partially unclothed. That precise limitation on job assignments has apparently caused no removal of male guards from normally assigned shifts. However, the remedy adopted to protect the privacy of the inmates in their cells during nighttime hours has placed privacy and employment rights in direct conflict and resulted in a denial of equal employment opportunities for the male guards and, as a consequence of their reassignment, for the female guards as well. We believe the process of making careful adjustments, which Judge Owen pursued for most of the disputes before him, can be continued to resolve the contested matter of nighttime observations.

The male guards have been prohibited from the nighttime shifts to avoid the opportunity for them to view women inmates on those infrequent occasions when the inmates are completely or partially unclothed. There are obviously two ways to avoid that opportunity in every circumstance in which it exists: remove the men or obstruct their view. The availability of this choice of remedies to protect the privacy of the inmates was fully recognized by the District Court with respect to a portion of this case. For example, the inmates complained that their privacy was impaired when male guards had the opportunity to view them taking showers during daytime hours. Instead of removing male guards from daytime shifts, Judge Owen ordered installation of a translucent screen, which permitted only enough visibility to ascertain that the shower area was occupied. See *Forts v. Ward, supra*, 471 F.Supp. at 1101.

[*sic*] employees . . . in any way which would deprive or tend to deprive any individual of employment opportunities," because of such individual's sex. 42 U.S.C. § 2000e-2(a).

7. We note that the dispute raised on this appeal does not involve a conflict between privacy interests and prison security interests. *See Dothard v. Rawlinson*, 433 U.S. 321, 97 S.Ct. 2720, 53 L.Ed.2d 786 (1977). The prison authorities at Bedford Hills have not asserted that any security interest requires unrestricted opportunity for male guards to view inmates at all times. In fact the record gives some indication that some of the women inmates believe their security interests will be enhanced if male guards are permitted to remain on duty during nighttime shifts.

We need not decide in this case to what extent an employer may be required to expend money or alter procedures to avoid a situation that, if uncorrected, would justify gender-based discrimination. In this case, the employer has already acknowledged its willingness to make necessary changes to eliminate the opportunity for viewing in the two circumstances that impair the privacy of the inmates during the nighttime hours.

The first circumstance concerns the sporadic situations when the inmates are subject to viewing through the cell door window while they are changing clothes or using the toilet. The prison authorities offered to prevent these opportunities for viewing by amending the prison rules to permit the inmates to cover the window for fifteen-minute intervals during the nighttime hours, just as they are currently permitted to during the daytime. There is nothing in the record to indicate why that proposed rule change would not protect privacy at nighttime as satisfactorily as it does during the daytime.[8]

The second circumstance concerns the opportunity for viewing the inmates while asleep, during which time their nighttime garments may fail to conceal private parts of their bodies. The prison authorities offered to solve this problem by issuing one-piece pajamas to any inmate who felt that her present sleepwear provided ineffective covering. Judge Owen found that proposal unsatisfactory, apparently because the item of clothing suggested by the prison authorities, a "Dr. Denton," was unattractive ("a two-legged bag") and uncomfortably warm on hot nights. We seriously doubt that the inmates' interests in style or even in avoiding the occasional discomfort of warmth from a sleeping garment are of sufficient gravity to justify denial of equal employment opportunities. However, we need not resolve the appropriateness of any particular sleepwear, because we do not believe the District Court adequately explored with the State defendants the range of available clothing that might be obtained. The State defendants represented their willingness to provide a suitable nighttime garment,[9] and we cannot believe that there do not exist on the market sufficient items from which a satisfac-

---

8. At a conference in which the State defendants' proposed order was considered, Judge Owen questioned whether the proposal for fifteen-minute covering of cell door windows during nighttime hours might create some security problem in connection with the time period just prior to the morning count. Since the State defendants proposed the fifteen-minute covering during nighttime hours, we assume they were satisfied that no security interests would be impaired. We note that the State defendants' proposal does not preclude female guards from entering cells during intervals when the cell door windows are covered. However, we do not mean to foreclose the prison authorities from presenting legitimate security concerns, either upon remand or thereafter, if experience indicates unanticipated problems. Nor do we mean to foreclose the inmates from pursuing any claim that the fifteen-minute window covering is not achieving adequate protection of their privacy. On the present record, the fifteen-minute covering appears to be an acceptable way of accommodating both the inmates' privacy interests and the employees' equal employment rights. Even if some further refinements in the State defendants' proposal is warranted, we would expect every effort to be made, by all sides, to assist the District Court in formulating a final decree that provides adequate protection to all concerned.

9. When the proposed order was discussed, it was acknowledged by counsel that the suggesting of issuing a "Dr. Denton's" was an unfortunate one and that this item was not the only sleepwear the State defendants were willing to furnish. Specifically mentioned was a set of two-piece pajamas.

tory choice can be made. Moreover, we do not think it is imposing on counsel to suggest that they can negotiate this aspect of the case without further litigation in a United States District Court. The privacy interest entitled to protection concerns the involuntary viewing of private parts of the body by members of the opposite sex. Since appropriate sleepwear can sufficiently protect that interest, its use should be preferred to any loss of employment opportunities. We do not agree with the inmates that their privacy interest extends to a protection against being viewed while sleeping by male guards so long as suitable sleepwear is provided. Nor do we agree that any legally enforceable rights of inmates sufficient to impair employment rights can arise from an inmate's preference for sleepwear of her choice or for none at all.

We therefore vacate so much of the order appealed from as prohibits the assignment of male guards to the nighttime shifts in dormitories of Bedford Hills and remand for further proceedings to revise the order with appropriate means to eliminate the opportunities for viewing that have been found to impair the privacy rights of the inmates.[10] In doing so, we do not minimize in any way the significance of the privacy interests of the inmates that the District Court has sought to protect. We do not elevate the employment rights of the guards above any protectible privacy rights of the inmates. We simply conclude that in the circumstances of this case the remedy proposed by the State will accord adequate protection to the privacy interests of the inmates by means that will avoid any denial of the guards' rights to equal employment opportunities. Since that is so, it is important for the employment opportunties of both sexes that the portion of the District Court's remedy requiring unjustified gender-based discrimination be set aside.

As to plaintiffs' cross-appeal from the denial of class certification, we find no basis to disturb the District Court's exercise of discretion. The order appealed from benefits all members of the alleged class, and the State defendants have not appealed and have explicitly indicated a willingness to comply. In these circumstances, class certification would be "largely a formality," *Galvan v. Levine*, 490 F.2d 1255, 1261 (2d Cir. 1973), *cert. denied*, 417 U.S. 936, 94 S.Ct. 2652, 41 L.Ed.2d 240 (1974), and was properly denied, wholly apart from the issue of whether disputes within the class concerning the scope of relief impaired the capacity of the named plaintiffs adequately to represent the class.

Vacated and remanded for further proceedings consistent with this opinion.

---

10. This decision is not intended to preclude the District Court from continuing the present order in effect, on an interim basis, pending entry and implementation of a revised final decree.

Appendix B

Suggested Responses to Some of the Assignments

Suggested Response to Assignment #5
(supra, p. 58)

Tom sues Jim. Tom's *cause of action* is breach of contract. Jim *moves* that the court dismiss the case since Tom has *failed to state a cause of action.* (Alternative terminology: Jim files a *demurrer,* or Jim *moves* to dismiss for *failure to state a claim upon which relief can be granted.*) The court denies this *motion.* In Jim's *answer,* he states a *counterclaim* in which he says that Tom breached the contract. After *discovery,* Tom files a *motion for a summary judgment.* This *motion* is denied.

Suggested Response to Assignment #7
(supra, p. 71)

6(a) PEOPLE v. SOHN

The *Sohn* opinion is quite unusual: the court cites *no* authority in support of its conclusion. This does not mean, however, that no authority is relied upon. Assault in the second degree is probably a statutory crime in New York. The court simply decided not to give us its citation.

The main standard being applied in the opinion is "proof beyond a reasonable doubt." This standard (which is a rule of law) has common law origins and is now part of our constitutional law. Again, there are no citations to any common law opinions or constitutional provisions provided by the court. If you wanted to find out more about this area of the law, independent research on your part would be needed.

Why are there no citations to authority in *Sohn*? First of all, the court probably wanted to keep its opinion brief and not clutter it with citations. More important, the court undoubtedly felt that there was no controversy over the *meaning* of the rules of law covered in the opinion (assault in the second degree, and proof beyond a reasonable doubt); the only area of dispute was the *application* of these rules to the facts. When this is so, a court may feel less of a need to give citations. Finally, these rules of law may be so widely known in New York that the court felt that citations were unnecessary.

Nevertheless, it must be said that the absence of any citations in an opinion is unusual.

7(b) STEPHENS v. DEPT. OF STATE POLICE

[S] ORS 34.010 et seq.

[S] ORS ch. 181

[R] Dept. of State Police Manual, Art. VIII, section 1; Article II, section 9(w); Article IV, section 6

[S] ORS 34.040 (3) and (4)

[S] ORS 34.100

[S] ORS 408.240

[OAG] 33 Op.Att'y Gen. 319

[S] ORS 408.210

[O] "Model State Law Relating to Military Leave" in "Suggested State Legislation—Program for 1951—Developed by the Council of State Governments"

[OTJ] Lane County v. Heintz Const. Co.

[O] Statement from the Governor

[S] ORS 181.290

[OOJ] Slochower v. Board of Education

[OOJ] Slocum v. Fire and Police Com. of Peoria

[OOJ] Parrish v. Civil Service Commission

[OOJ] Sheehan v. Board of Police Commrs.

[OOJ] Garvin v. Chambers

[OOJ] Forstner v. City etc. of San Francisco

[OOJ] Roller v. Stoecklen

[S] ORS 180.060(2)

[S] ORS 180.220

[OTJ] State ex rel. v. Mott

Comments

1. Note that the first citation you find is within the caption of the opinion: 526 P.2d 1043 (Or.App.1974). This is a cite to the *Stephens* case you are reading.

The court that wrote *Stephens* (Court of Appeals of Oregon) also lists events that occurred earlier in the case, e.g., decisions of the circuit court and the trial board. Are these decisions authorities? No. They are part of the prior proceedings of the *Stephens* opinion. The court is simply telling us what happened below.

2. The court does not give us the abbreviation of ORS. However, several places in the opinion the court refers to the legislature as having written the ORS sections that are cited. The court also refers to them as "statutes." Hence, we have so designated them above.

3. The Model State Law is designated [O] above. It is not a law itself. It is part of the legislative history (p. 215) of the statute being interpreted. The legislature considered this document when it passed the statute.

4. The statement from the Governor is also relied upon by the court. The court uses the statement to bolster its interpretation of the statute or, more accurately, to counter the interpretation of the statute urged by the state. The Governor's statement is not a law. The Governor was "urging" someone (perhaps the legislators) to take a certain position.

7(c) NICHOLSON v. CONN. HALF-WAY HOUSE, INC.

[OTJ] Brainard v. Town of West Hartford

[E] 66 C.J.S. Nuisances § 114

[OTJ] Hurlbut v. McKone

[OTJ] Nailor v. C. W. Blakeslee & Sons, Inc.

[OTJ] Wetstone v. Cantor

[OTJ] Leo Foundation v. Cabelus

[OTJ] Goodwin v. New York, N. H. & H. R. Co.

[OTJ] Ginsberg v. Mascia

[E] 66 C.J.S. Nuisances § 113

[OTJ] Cawley v. Housing Authority

[E] 39 Am.Jur., Nuisance, §§ 28, 157

[OTJ] the trial court decision in *Brainard* quoted in A–316 Rec. & Briefs, back of p. 7

[OTJ] Jack v. Torrant

Comments

1. Note that the court tells us that it is treating principles of equity. Many of the opinions cited by the court deal with the law of equity.

2. C.J.S. stands for *Corpus Juris Secundum,* a legal encyclopedia published by West. Am.Jur. stands for *American Jurisprudence,* a legal encyclopedia published by Lawyers Co-operative. Both these texts constitute secondary authority (p. 203).

3. Footnote 1 refers to "A 316 Rec. & Briefs, back of p. 7." This is probably a reference to the record below and the appellate briefs filed in the case we are reading: *Nicholson.* In the record or appellate briefs filed by one or both of the attorneys in *Nicholson,* there was a quote from a finding from the trial court stage of the *Brainard* opinion that we have already labeled [OTJ], a Connecticut state case. Since *Brainard* is [OTJ], the trial court decision in *Brainard* is also [OTJ].

Suggested Response to Assignment #8 (supra, p. 86)

8(a) PEOPLE v. SOHN

Parties:

People/State/prosecutor below/respondent here

v.

Sohn/accused/defendant below/appellant here

Comment The *Sohn* opinion is an unusually short opinion. This does not necessarily make the opinion easier to understand. Much of the information essential to a comprehensive brief of *Sohn* is not spelled out by the court. It must be *inferred* from the information we *are* given. For example, with respect to the parties, the opinion never characterizes the People (of New York) as "the prosecutor." This must be inferred from the fact that the opinion concerns a criminal prosecution and that "the People," i.e., the state government, is customarily the prosecutor in such cases.

8(b) BROWN v. SOUTHALL REALTY CO.

Parties:

Brown/tenant/defendant below/appellant here

v.

Southall Realty Co./landlord/plaintiff below/appellee here

Comment While the present litigation status of each party here is listed in the caption of the opinion, the original status of the parties is not. We had to determine this status by reading the opinion. Although the opinion never specifically states that the Realty Co. was the original plaintiff and Brown the original defendant, this can be inferred from the first line of the opinion: "This appeal arises out of an action for possession *brought by* appellee-landlord, *against* appellant-tenant...." [Emphasis added.] From this statement it can be inferred that the Realty Co., the party *bringing* the action, was the plaintiff below. Brown, the party *against* whom the action was brought, was the defendant below.

8(c) STEPHENS v. DEPT. OF STATE POLICE

Parties:

Stephens/state trooper/employee/plaintiff below/appellant here
v.
Dept. of State Police and another/state agency/employer/
defendant below/respondent here

8(d) NICHOLSON v. CONN. HALF-WAY HOUSE, INC.

Parties:

Nicholson and others/residential property owners/plaintiffs
below/appellees here
v.
Conn. Half-Way House, Inc./neighborhood treatment program/
defendant below/appellant here

8(e) CONN. v. MENILLO

Parties:

Conn./State/prosecutor below/appellant here
v.
Menillo/accused/defendant below/appellee here

Comment In this opinion we must *infer* the litigation status, both present and original, of each party. Since the first sentence speaks of Menillo's being "convicted" under a "criminal abortion statute," we can assume that he was originally a defendant and that the State of Connecticut was the prosecutor. The status of the parties at the time this opinion was written may be inferred from the fact that, following the overturning of Menillo's conviction by the Connecticut Supreme Court, it was the State that petitioned the United States Supreme Court (the court writing this opinion) for certiorari (p. 52). Hence the State is the appellant and Menillo is the appellee or respondent.

Suggested Response to Assignment #10 (supra, p. 95)

10(a) PEOPLE v. SOHN

OBJECTIVES:

- The People (the prosecutor) want to convict and punish Sohn for assault in the second degree.

CAUSE OF ACTION:
DEFENSE:

- Sohn wants to avoid conviction and punishment.
- Prosecution for assault in the second degree.
- Denial: assault in the second degree has not been established.

10(b) BROWN v. SOUTHALL REALTY CO.

OBJECTIVES:

- Southall wants to evict Brown and regain possession of the rented premises.
- Brown initially wanted to avoid being evicted and now wants to avoid having to pay rent.

CAUSE OF ACTION:

- Brown breached the duty under the lease to pay rent.

DEFENSE:

- The lease is illegal and no rent need be paid under it because of a violation of §§ 2304 and 2501 of the D.C. Housing Regulations.

Comments

1. Note that Brown's objective changed between the time of the initial proceeding before the trial court and the present appeal. At the time the litigation began, her objective was to avoid being evicted. Otherwise why would the landlord have to bring a *possessory* action against her, i.e., an action to have the court force her to return possession of the premises? However, by the time the dispute reached the court of appeals (which wrote the *Brown* opinion), Brown had moved from the premises and was no longer concerned about being evicted. Her objective at this point was solely to avoid paying rent.

2. We are not told whether the landlord's cause of action is based upon a common law theory (breach of lease) or upon a statute that gives a landlord the right to evict a tenant for not paying the rent.

10(c) STEPHENS v. DEPT. OF STATE POLICE

OBJECTIVES:

- The Department of State Police wants to fire Stephens as a state police trooper.
- Stephens wants to avoid being fired.

CAUSE OF ACTION:

- Absence without authorization and insubordination in violation of Article VIII, § 1; Article II, § 9(w); and Article IV, § 6 of the Department of State Police Manual; and removal for insubordination pursuant to ORS 181.290.

DEFENSE:

- Stephens contends that what he did was authorized under ORS 408.240 and ORS 408.210; therefore, no violations of the Manual occurred.

Comment Since it appears from the opinion that the formal decision to terminate Stephens did not occur until after the administrative hearing had been held by the Trial Board of the Oregon State Police, the Department's objective at the initial stage of the litigation (i.e., at the administrative hearing) was to fire Stephens from his job. If, on the other hand, Stephens had been terminated *before* the hearing, the Department's objective at the hearing would be to avoid having to reinstate Stephens.

10(d) NICHOLSON v. CONN. HALF-WAY HOUSE, INC.

OBJECTIVES:	• Nicholson and the others want to prevent the defendant from using its property as a halfway house.
	• Defendant wants to use its property as a halfway house.
CAUSE OF ACTION:	• Nuisance that can be enjoined.
DEFENSE:	• Denial that the proposed use constitutes a nuisance.

10(e) CONN. v. MENILLO

OBJECTIVES:	• The state wants to convict and punish Menillo for attempting to procure an abortion.
	• Menillo wants to avoid conviction and punishment.
CAUSE OF ACTION:	• Violation of Conn.Gen.Stat.Ann. § 53–29 (Supp.1975).
DEFENSE:	• A conviction under Conn.Gen.Stat.Ann. § 53–29 is unconstitutional and therefore invalid.

Comment We are not told what constitutional provisions Menillo claimed the conviction violated. All we know is that the constitutional claim involved "personal privacy."

Suggested Response to Assignment #12 (supra, p. 101)

12(a) PEOPLE v. SOHN

PRIOR PROCEEDINGS:	(1) TRIAL: Sohn was tried for assault in the second degree in the Supreme Court, Queens County. RESULT: Convicted and sentenced.

PRESENT
PROCEEDING: (2) APPEAL: Sohn now appeals to the Supreme Court, Appellate Division, Second Department.

12(b) BROWN v. SOUTHALL REALTY CO.

PRIOR
PROCEEDINGS: (1) TRIAL: Southall Realty Co. sued Brown for possession of its rented premises for nonpayment of rent. RESULT: Judgment for Southall, awarding it possession of the premises.

PRESENT
PROCEEDING: (2) APPEAL: Brown now appeals the judgment of the lower court to the District of Columbia Court of Appeals.

12(c) STEPHENS v. DEPT. OF STATE POLICE

PRIOR
PROCEEDINGS: (1) ADMINISTRATIVE HEARING: The Department of State Police brought Stephens before a trial board on disciplinary charges. RESULT: The board found that Stephens was absent without authorization and was insubordinate. Pursuant to these findings, Stephens was removed from his job by the Superintendent of State Police.

     (2) APPEAL I: Stephens brought a writ of review proceeding in the circuit court. RESULT: Superintendent's decision affirmed.

PRESENT
PROCEEDING: (3) APPEAL II: Stephens now appeals to the Court of Appeals of Oregon.

Comments

1. The administrative proceedings could be presented as one proceeding, as we have listed it here, or as two proceedings, one before the trial board and a second before the Superintendent. It is a common practice in administrative proceedings to have a two-step decision-making process. A hearing is held by an examiner or a board that makes findings of fact and a *recommended* decision. These findings and the recommendation are then reviewed by the head of the agency who has the power to reject, modify, or adopt the recommended decision (p. 19).

2. Stephens's first appeal was to a court described only as "the circuit court." It is not possible to tell from the opinion whether this is a court of middle appeals or a trial level court that has appellate jurisdiction over the agency.

12(d) NICHOLSON v. CONN. HALF-WAY HOUSE, INC.

PRIOR PROCEEDINGS:	(1) TRIAL: Nicholson and others filed suit against defendant for an injunction on the ground of nuisance. RESULT: Judgment for Nicholson and others, permanent injunction issued.
PRESENT PROCEEDING:	(2) APPEAL: Conn. Half-way House now appeals to the Supreme Court of Connecticut.

Comment There is no indication that there was an appeal to a middle appeals court or, indeed, that such a court exists in Connecticut.

12(e) CONN. v. MENILLO

PRIOR PROCEEDINGS:	(1) TRIAL: Menillo was prosecuted for attempting to procure an abortion. RESULT: Conviction.
	(2) APPEAL I: Menillo appealed to the Connecticut Supreme Court. RESULT: Lower court reversed, conviction overturned.
PRESENT PROCEEDING:	(3) APPEAL II: The State now appeals to the United States Supreme Court for a writ of certiorari.

Comment This case, like that in Assignment 12(d), involves Connecticut law. Note again that the appeal seemed to go from the trial court directly to the Connecticut Supreme Court.

Suggested Response to Assignment #15 (supra, p. 109)

a. premises
   dwelling place
   habitation
   living accommodation

   housing
   rental unit
   leasehold

Suggested Response to Assignment #16
(supra, p. 112)

a. Would the court have concluded that the lease was void if the housing code violations consisted of a broken railing and insufficient height in the basement even though the commode functioned properly?

or:

How important or crucial was it to the court's holding (voiding the lease) that a malfunctioning commode was among the code violations?

b. Would the court have concluded that the lease was void if the housing code violations were not in existence at the time the lease agreement was signed, but occurred subsequently?

or:

How important or crucial was it to the court's holding (voiding the lease) that the housing code violations were in existence at the time the lease agreement was signed?

Suggested Response to Assignment #18(1)
(supra, p. 127)

(1) **(a)** Internal opinions *followed* by the Brown court:
> Bess v. David
> McCotter v. Flinn
> Hartman v. Lubar
> Kirschner v. Klavik
> Rubin v. Douglas
> Lloyd v. Johnson
> Pangborn v. Westlake
> Miller v. Ammon
> Anderson v. Yungkau
> Ballou v. Kemp
> Jess Fisher & Co. v. Hicks
> Amos v. Cummings

(b) Internal opinions *extended* by the Brown court:
> Bess v. David
> Jess Fisher & Co. v. Hicks

(c) Internal opinions *distinguished* by the Brown court:
> None

(d) Internal opinions *overruled* by the Brown court:
> None

(e) Internal opinions rejected by the Brown court for any other reason:
> None

(f) Internal opinions whose use by the court is unclear:

Edwards v. Habib

David v. Nemerofsky

Comments

1. It is not always easy to tell when a court is *following* an internal opinion. A court may simply quote from or refer to an internal opinion and not tell us that it approves or adopts the quote or other reference to the internal opinion. Yet the context of the quote or other reference to the internal opinion will usually be a sufficient indication of whether the court is accepting or following it.

2. *Edwards v. Habib* and *David v. Nemerofsky* are placed in the unclear category above. They are cited in the first footnote after an assertion by the tenant. We don't know whether these are simply cases that the tenant cited in support of her position, or whether the court is relying on them in any way. *Bess v. David* is also listed in this footnote, but elsewhere the Brown court gives us clear indications of how it is using this internal opinion.

3. *Bess v. David* and *Jess Fisher & Co. v. Hicks* are listed as being extended by the Brown court. They are certainly being followed since the court cites them with approval. Because of fact differences with the Brown facts, however, they are also being extended. In *Bess v. David,* the defendant said that he was not a tenant during the time alleged, whereas Mrs. Brown never denied that she was a tenant. Similarly, the Jess Fisher case involved a violation of the Rent Control Act, whereas *Brown* involved a violation of the Housing Regulations.

4. It is clear that the Brown court is following *McCotter v. Flinn* (footnote 2), but it is not clear whether the Brown court is extending it because we are given so few of the facts in McCotter. The same is true of the following internal opinions that are followed: *Hartman, Kirschner, Rubin, Lloyd, Pangborn, Miller, Anderson, Ballou,* and *Amos.*

5. We have listed *Amos v. Cummings* (footnote 6) as having been followed by the Brown court. The court uses the following notation before this internal opinion: "Cf." Literally, this means "compare," but it is a signal that the internal opinion is sufficiently similar or analogous to lend support to the proposition that it is cited for.

Suggested Response to Assignment #19
(supra, p. 146)

19(a) PEOPLE v. SOHN

Issue: Was guilt of assault in the second degree established beyond a reasonable doubt?

Holding: No.

Comments

1. There is only one legal issue in this opinion. Yet two rules of law are involved in the issue: a particular crime (assault in the second degree), and the standard of proof needed to convict (beyond a reasonable doubt).

2. What is the alleged error below? We are not explicitly told. We can infer, however, that the defendant-appellant (Sohn) is claiming that the trial court erred in coming to the conclusion that guilt was established beyond a reasonable doubt. Sohn is the party who appealed. Hence we can also infer that he and the People (the prosecution) disagree about how the two rules of law apply to his case.

19(b) BROWN v. SOUTHALL REALTY CO.

Issue I: Does res judicata require this court to hear the appeal?

Holding I: Yes.

Issue II: Is the lease void because of a violation of §§ 2304 and 2501?

Holding II: Yes.

Comments

1. The first issue is an example of one of the major exceptions to the requirement that legal issues must be based on an alleged error below (p. 144). The first issue is *not* dependent on an alleged error below. It is an issue of appealability based on what happened *after* the prior proceeding (the trial) was over. Mrs. Brown moved from the premises and does not wish to return. Southall originally sued for possession, which it now has. Mrs. Brown no longer wants possession. Hence, why allow an appeal? Mrs. Brown *is* appealing. We can infer that Southall is trying to prevent the appeal on the ground that the case is now moot. Hence the first issue concerns the appealability of the case, which is not dependent on any alleged errors made below at the trial.

2. Res judicata is a common law doctrine (p. 10). If this term is new to you, you should briefly examine the topic in a legal encyclopedia or in a civil procedure treatise.

3. The second issue *is* dependent on an alleged error below. Mrs. Brown is claiming that "the trial court erred in failing to declare the lease agreement void" because of a violation of various sections of the Housing Code. This issue involves the interrelationship among at least three rules of law: the applicability of two sections of the Housing Code and the legality of the lease, which is a contract or agreement.

19(c) STEPHENS v. DEPT. OF STATE POLICE

Issue I: Did the appellant have a right to a leave of absence under ORS 408.240 and ORS 408.210?

Holding I: Yes.

Issue II: Can the appellant be fired for insubordination under ORS 181.290?

Holding II: Yes.

Comments

1. There is some suggestion in the opinion that there may have been another issue: the appealability of the case. At the beginning of the first two paragraphs of the opinion, we are given citations to the statutes that the court interprets as allowing it to hear this appeal. By implication, is the court telling us that one of the parties objected to this appellate court's taking the case? It is unclear. The court may simply be stating what its subject-matter jurisdiction is (p. 145), even though neither party may have raised any objections as to its existence in this case. Yet, one can still suspect that there is at least a minor issue here in view of the prominence that the court gives to this topic.

2. You will note that the above two issues do not refer to the provisions of the Police Manual, which is probably a set of state regulations (p. 65). Shouldn't these regulations be included in the issues as rules of law in contention along with the ORS statutes? Technically, yes. The parties are in disagreement about the legality of the regulations that were interpreted by the Board (and apparently by the circuit court) as denying the leave and as authorizing termination. The issues, therefore, could have been rephrased to ask whether the interpretation of the provisions of the Police Manual (denying the leave and authorizing the termination for insubordination) was inconsistent with the ORS statutes. Since, however, the main focus of the opinion is on the ORS statutes, we have limited the statement of the issues in the suggested response to the meaning and applicability of these statutes.

3. What are the errors below? By implication, we are told that Stephens felt that the police agency, the trial board, and the affirming circuit court misinterpreted ORS 408.240, 408.210, and 181.290.

4. The dissenting opinion of Judge Foley confirms our view that the two issues in the majority opinion are the right to a leave and the legality of the termination. Foley also addresses both issues.

19(d) NICHOLSON v. CONN. HALF-WAY HOUSE, INC.

ISSUE: Is there an equitable abatable nuisance due to an unreasonable use of land?

Holding: No.

Comments

1. Arguably, there are two issues in this opinion. First, does a nuisance exist? Second, if there is a nuisance, can it be enjoined? The court itself, however, treats both issues together. It refers to the "sole" issue in the case. The phrase "equitably abatable nuisance" combines the two issues. It appears that the resolution of both issues is dependent on the reasonableness of the use of the land. Hence both issues are treated together as one issue above. It would not be incorrect, however, to separate it into two issues.

2. The court tells us that one of the elements of nuisance is unreasonableness. The latter is part of the definition of nuisance. Indeed, it is this component of nuisance that is in contention in this opinion. Hence, it is included in the issue as the main component of the rule of law in contention.

19(e) CONN. v. MENILLO

Issue: Does a conviction of a layperson for violating the abortion statute (§ 53–29) violate the constitutional right to personal privacy?

Holding: No.

Comments

1. This legal issue involves the interrelationship between two rules of law: a statute and a constitutional right.

2. The court does not give a clear reference to the constitutional provision involved. There is no citation to the Constitution. Several times the court refers to a "right to an abortion." Toward the end of the opinion, there is a more direct reference to the Constitution: "personal privacy secured by the Constitution." The court is referring to the Constitution by concept rather than by citation. To obtain more background on this area of the law, you might want to check a legal encyclopedia, a constitutional law treatise, or you might want to read some of the internal opinions cited by the court, e.g., *Roe v. Wade.*

3. What is the alleged error below? The State (i.e., the prosecutor) is saying that the Connecticut Supreme Court failed to apply the U.S. Constitution, as interpreted in *Roe,* correctly.

Suggested Response to Assignment #21 (supra, p. 162)

21(a) PEOPLE v. SOHN, p. 299.

Rules of law (or elements thereof) being applied:

- Assault in the second degree
- Beyond a reasonable doubt

Kind of contention:

- Assault in the second degree: Do the facts fit?
- Beyond a reasonable doubt: Do the facts fit?

Comments

1. The court appears to deal with each rule of law as a whole rather than with its particular elements. Note, however, that a major concern of the court is the concept of aggression or being the aggressor. It is not clear whether aggression is an element of the crime of assault in the second degree. It probably is, but we are not given quotations or descriptions of the crime that would enable us to determine for sure whether aggression is an element.

2. Note also that we are given *no* definitions of any of the rules of law in this short opinion. This is probably due to the fact that none of the definitions appear to have been in dispute. In each instance, the contention was over whether the facts fit within the rules.

21(b) BROWN v. SOUTHALL REALTY CO., p. 300

Rules of law (or elements thereof) being applied:

- res judicata
- § 2304 and § 2501

Kind of contention:

- res judicata: Do the facts fit?
- § 2304 and § 2501: What is the definition?

Comments

1. The elements of res judicata are not given. This rule of law is not defined and there is no indication that the parties disagreed over the definition. The question is whether the facts fit within the concept of res judicata.

2. The court *does* refer to specific elements of §§ 2304 and 2501 (habitation, healthy, safe, etc.), but there does not appear to be any disagreement over these references. The landlord is not denying that the premises constituted an unhealthy and unsafe habitation. The dispute centers on the penalty that should flow therefrom.

3. The landlord knew that the violations existed when he rented the premises. This is conceded. Hence, again, there is no contention concerning *whether* §§ 2304 and 2501 were violated, i.e., there is no dispute over whether the facts fit within these rules of law. The contention over them was definitional. There are penalties for violating the Housing Code. The question is whether these penalties "imply a prohibition" that renders the lease void. This is a definitional question. Specific terms in §§ 2304 and 2501 are not being defined. The court examines the purpose of the Housing Code as a whole, and, in effect, reads this prohibition into it. The definitional question could be phrased as follows: Can we interpret the Housing Code to include the prohibition? or, Did the authors of the Code (the Commissioners) include this prohibition by implication?

21(c) STEPHENS v. DEPT. OF STATE POLICE, p. 302.

Rules of law (or elements thereof) being applied:

- ORS 408.240 and ORS 408.210: "military duty"
- ORS 181.290: "insubordination"

Kind of contention:

- ORS 408.240 and ORS 408.210: What is the definition?
- ORS 181.290: What is the definition?

21(d) NICHOLSON v. CONN. HALF-WAY HOUSE, INC., p 307.

Rules of law (or elements thereof) being applied:

• Equitably abatable nuisance: irreparable harm, reasonableness

Kind of contention:

• Equitably abatable nuisance: irreparable harm, reasonableness: Do the facts fit?

21(e) CONNECTICUT v. MENILLO, p. 309.

Rule of law (or elements thereof) being applied:

• § 53–29 (statute)
• Personal privacy (constitutional doctrine)

Kind of contention:

• § 53–19 and personal privacy: Is there consistency?

Comment The central dispute is whether the *interpretation* of a Connecticut statute (§ 53–29) by the state courts is consistent with the constitutional right of personal privacy.

Suggested Response to Assignment #22 (supra, p. 165)

22(a) PEOPLE v. SOHN

Reasoning: The evidence is conflicting as to how the incident began and what happened after the incident. Hence, there is reasonable doubt of guilt. The court's reasoning is largely based on some *implied* observations about human nature. For example, someone who commits a crime usually flees. The defendant did not flee. In fact, he called the police and waited until they came. Also how trustworthy can the complainant (i.e., the alleged victim) be when the latter pled guilty to possession of a pistol during the incident? All this adds up to reasonable doubt that the defendant committed the assault.

Comment The reasoning is based on the interpretation of assault and of the reasonable-doubt standard needed to establish guilt for this crime. Assault is a crime of aggression. Reasonable doubt means the existence of significant uncertainty as to any of the necessary elements of the crime. Aggression appears to be one of these elements. (See p. 380, Comment 1.) The evidence shows significant uncertainty as to who was the aggressor. Hence, there should have been no conviction.

To show doubt, the court is relying on its concept of human nature. A good guy/bad guy reasoning is implicit in the conclusion of the court as it draws the logical connections between this conclusion and the facts of the case. If you are a "bad guy," it is human nature to stay away from the police. Can

Sohn be a "bad guy" if he actually called the police and waited until they arrived? Also, it is usually only "good guys" that complain about being the victim of crime. Can the complainant be a "good guy" if he pled guilty to possessing a pistol during this same incident in which Sohn was supposed to have been the aggressor?

22(b) BROWN v. SOUTHALL REALTY CO.

Reasoning for Issue I: The court allowed this appeal because of the consequences of the doctrine of res judicata. If the appeal were not allowed, the trial court decision on the issue of rent would be final. The issue of *possession* may now be moot since the tenant no longer wants possession. But the *rent* issue is still alive. If it is not resolved now, then res judicata will prevent the tenant from later claiming that she does not owe rent in the event that the landlord later sues for rent.

Reasoning for Issue II: It was the intent of the Commissioners (who wrote the Housing Code) to have a lease declared void when the landlord enters it knowing that there are unsafe and unsanitary conditions that make the rented premises uninhabitable. To infer any other intent would contradict the purpose of §§ 2304 and 2501, which is to insure that housing is livable.

Comments

Reasoning for Issue I: The reasoning is based on the meaning of res judicata. The court does not describe this common law doctrine in any detail; it assumes that you know what it means. If this doctrine is new to you, you need to spend a few moments obtaining some background on the doctrine in a legal encyclopedia or civil procedure treatise (p. 28).

Res judicata prevents a relitigation of all matters resolved by a final judgment. A judgment is not final until the trial is over and all the regular appeals have been completed (or the time for such appeals has expired). In the trial judgment here, the lower court said that Mrs. Brown owed rent. This judgment would become final unless she was allowed to appeal. If she is not allowed to do so, then she could not later claim that she does not owe rent in a subsequent action brought by the landlord to collect it. Res judicata would prevent the relitigation of the matter of rent. The court relies on *Bess v. David* to explain the meaning and consequences of the doctrine of res judicata.

Reasoning for Issue II: The reasoning is based on the intent of the authors of the regulations. The court inferred this intent. It is important to note that the Housing Code is silent as to what happens if a lease is knowingly entered in violation of the Code. We are told that there are penalties for violating the Code (see footnote 4), but nowhere in the Code does it say that one of the penalties is the voidness of the lease itself. The court, however, infers that this must have been the intent of the authors of the Code in view of the purpose of §§ 2304 and 2501 to provide habitable (livable) housing for tenants. The court uses *Lloyd v. Johnson* as guidance in inferring this intent. The penalties in the Code "imply a prohibition," which, in view of the purpose of the Code, leads to the conclusion that the authors also intended that the lease be declared void. See p. 381, Comment 3, on why issue II is really a definitional issue.

22(c) STEPHENS v. DEPT. OF STATE POLICE

Reasoning for Issue I: The meaning of the language used by the legislature in ORS 408.240 and 408.210 is clear. It shows an intent to allow a leave of absence for training only. The statute is unconditional. It is *not* dependent on the discretion of the employer. The right to take leave under the statute is not dependent on training being combined with service.

Reasoning for Issue II: Insubordination includes challenging the legality of a questionable order by deliberately disobeying it when there is time to use other methods to challenge the order.

Comments

Reasoning for Issue I: The court's reasoning on the first issue is an excellent presentation on the separation of powers between the judicial and legislative branches of government. A court is not a legislative body. Courts must carry out the intent of the legislature as manifest in the language of the statutes of the legislature. The court suggests that ORS 408.240 and 408.210, as interpreted, might pose some administrative problems for the police department. But this is a problem of the *wisdom* of the statute. It is not the function of a court to second-guess the wisdom of the legislature. The court's function is to interpret and apply the policy that the legislature has laid out in the statute (assuming the statute does not violate some superior authority such as the Constitution). If the police department has problems with the statute, it should ask the legislature, not the courts, to change the statute. In effect, the court is saying that it does not want to rewrite the statute under the guise of interpreting it. (However, this is precisely what the dissenting judge charges the majority with doing—but for the second issue, not the first.)

Reasoning for Issue II: A similar reasoning is used for Issue II. The court begins by trying to determine what the legislature meant by "insubordination" in ORS 181.290. As in Issue I, the starting point is the search for legislative intent. Here, however, there is no plain meaning of the statute. The meaning of "insubordination" in ORS 181.290 is not clear, and there are no Oregon cases interpreting it. The court, therefore, looks to the case law of other states—California and Ohio—to see how these states have handled similar problems. The court likes the approach of Ohio (in *Roller v. Stoecklen*) and adopts it. The Ohio case requires some other method of testing a legally questionable order when there is time to do so. By implication, the court is telling us that when the Oregon legislature wrote the insubordination statute, it probably intended to include the same kind of requirement.

The dissent, however, says that the court's holding on the second issue misinterprets ORS 408.240, which says that there shall be no removal for taking a leave. Judge Foley charges that the majority opinion is rewriting the statute by ignoring this provision on removal.

The role of the Attorney General's opinion in the court's reasoning needs to be examined. The court emphasizes the fact that the police department relied in good faith on the opinion of the Attorney General. The court says that this reliance should be protected and encouraged. The suggestion of the court, through its use of the quote from the *Mott* opinion, is that the opposite would occur if the court failed to find insubordination in this case. Does this reasoning make sense? Is it true that government officials will be less likely to rely on the Attorney General if the court reinstates Mr. Stephens in this case? What "hazards" (quoting *Mott*) do such officials face? Personal suits against them?

There is no discussion by the court of the peculiar nature of the employment in this case—police work. Discipline is traditionally very important in such settings. Do you think that this point influenced the court in its reasoning on the insubordination holding?

22(d) NICHOLSON v. CONN. HALF-WAY HOUSE, INC.

Reasoning: To constitute a nuisance, there must be an unreasonable use of land. There is no showing of unreasonableness here. To enjoin or abate a nuisance, there must be a concrete showing of irreparable harm. Specificity is required in view of the drastic nature of an injunction. Fears and speculation are not concrete enough.

Comment Nuisance is a common law doctrine. Injunction and abatement are equitable doctrines. The reasoning of the opinion is fairly simple. It is based solely on the meaning of nuisance and on the conditions that must exist before an injunction will be granted. Injunction (or abatement) is a "drastic" remedy. This is all the more reason why the court insists on specificity in the evidence. It takes an extreme case to warrant an injunction. By definition, a case based on speculation and fear is not extreme enough. The facts here do not fit the definition of nuisance or the conditions for an injunction.

22(e) CONN. v. MENILLO

Reasoning: The state does not have a sufficiently great interest in maternal health during the first trimester so long as the abortion is performed by medically competent personnel under safe conditions. This requirement is not met when the abortion is performed by an untrained nonphysician. When this occurs, the state's interest is strong enough to prohibit the abortion. The statute, therefore, *is* consistent with the constitutional right to an abortion when the statute is applied to an untrained nonphysician.

Comment This reasoning is based on the court's prior opinions of *Roe v. Wade* and *Doe v. Bolton*, particularly the former. The court summarizes its reasoning in *Roe* and tells us how the reasoning should affect someone like Mr. Menillo. The Court is saying, in effect, that the Connecticut Supreme Court failed to identify the reasoning in *Roe* properly. The Connecticut Court read the reasoning in *Roe* too broadly. The reasoning in *Roe*, which led to striking down a Texas abortion statute applied to a doctor, does not extend to an abortion statute that is applied to an untrained nonphysician.

The court gives us the test for determining whether a woman's right to privacy has been invaded. The test balances her interest with the interest of the state in protecting her health. This test is the court's way of interpreting the meaning of the right to personal privacy in the Constitution.

Suggested Response to Assignment #24
(supra, p. 166)

24(a) PEOPLE v. SOHN

Key Facts: Defendant was convicted of assault in the second degree. The evidence was extremely equivocal and inconsistent.

Issue: Has guilt of assault in the second degree been established beyond a reasonable doubt when the evidence at the trial was extremely equivocal and inconsistent?

Holding: No.

Comments

1. The fact that the defendant was convicted was *obviously* key. The holding reversed the conviction. To reverse a conviction, there obviously must be a conviction to reverse.

2. The court itself uses the *fact categorizations* of "extremely equivocal" and "inconsistent" to describe the individual facts. We are given three major individual facts: defendant called the police, he waited until the police came, the complainant pled guilty to possession of a pistol during the incident. It is very difficult to say with certainty that any of these individual facts are key. The removal of any one of them would arguably have produced the same result. None of these individual facts are listed in the issue since they are probably not key. It would not have been incorrect, however, to have included some or all of them in the issue as *context* facts (p. 139).

3. The *reasoning* of the court supports the conclusion that the broader fact categorizations (extremely equivocal/inconsistent) are key. Reasonable doubt means significant uncertainty. If the evidence is extremely equivocal and inconsistent, then significant uncertainty exists. If the evidence had not been extremely equivocal and inconsistent, but rather had clearly pointed to Sohn's being the aggressor, then we can safely say that the court would have reached a different holding and would have found that there was no reasonable doubt as to guilt.

4. *Sohn* should be shepardized to determine what other opinions, if any, have said about the facts in *Sohn*.

24(b) BROWN v. SOUTHALL REALTY CO.

Key Facts for Issue I: Landlord wins a judgment against tenant. Tenant wants to appeal this judgment.

Issue I: Can a tenant appeal a judgment awarding possession to the landlord due to nonpayment of rent when the judgment would be res judicata on matters such as whether rent is due even though the tenant no longer wants possession of the premises?

Holding I: Yes.

Key Facts for Issue II: Code violations existed at the beginning of the lease that rendered the premises unsafe and unsanitary. The landlord knew of these violations at the time the lease was entered.

Issue II: Is a lease void when the landlord knows before entering the lease that there are unsafe and unsanitary conditions in the rented premises in violation of §§ 2304 and 2501 of the D.C. Housing Code?

Holding II: Yes.

Comments

Issue I

1. The first issue is a procedural issue. Hence, the key facts will involve procedural or litigation facts.

2. The *reasoning* of the court supports the selection of the above facts as key for the first issue. As the court interprets the meaning of res judicata, the only way to prevent the lower court judgment from becoming final on all matters such as rent is to allow this appeal from the judgment.

3. It is *not* a key fact that Mrs. Brown has moved out and no longer wants possession. The landlord probably argued that this was key on the ground that this fact makes the entire case moot. Not so according to the *reasoning* used by the court on this issue. Res judicata would finalize matters such as rent. There is more at stake here than the question of who is entitled to possession. According to the court, there is no need for Mrs. Brown to want possession in order for her to claim that she owes no past rent. But she cannot have this claim resolved unless she is allowed to appeal. If she does not have it resolved in *this* proceeding, res judicata will bar her from raising the claim in a subsequent proceeding if the landlord later tries to sue her for back rent.

Note the "even though" fact in the statement of Issue I. An "even though" fact is a fact that one of the parties incorrectly argued was key. As indicated earlier, it is proper to include such facts in your statement of the issue (p. 139).

Issue II

4. Unsafe and unsanitary is a *fact categorization* used by the court to describe the individual facts of obstructed commode, broken railing, and insufficient ceiling height. The *reasoning* of the court also supports the conclusion that unsafe and unsanitary is a key fact. The court tells us that the intent of the authors of the Housing Code is to void those leases on premises that have Code violations rendering the premises uninhabitable (unlivable). Every Code violation would not necessarily make the premises uninhabitable. Only the most serious would qualify, i.e., those that make the premises unsafe and unsanitary. The reasoning, therefore, supports the broader fact categorization as key.

5. Several times in the opinion the court *repeats* two facts that are arguably critical: The conditions existed before the lease was entered and the landlord knew this. The court gives considerable emphasis to these facts. It would be useful to shepardize the *Brown* opinion to see if other opinions that cite *Brown* also stress these facts.

One *internal opinion* supports the conclusion that it was key that the violations existed when the lease was entered. The court cites *Hartman v. Lubar,* which said that a contract is void if it is "made" in violation of the statute. The emphasis of the *Hartman* opinion is on a contract that violated the law when it was entered or "made." A lease agreement is a contract.

From another perspective, however, it can be argued that it was *not* key that the violations existed at the time the lease was entered and that the landlord knew of these violations. The reasoning of the court is broad enough to enable us to argue that a lease on premises that are unsafe and unsanitary is void regardless of whether these conditions existed at the beginning of the lease or arose sometime thereafter. If the "public policy" of the Code is to provide habitable premises, then it should make no difference *when* the serious conditions arose, *whether* the landlord knew about them, or *when* the landlord found out about them. One can argue that the court is being overly restrictive in interpreting the intent of the authors of the Code.

6. One might also argue that it was *not* key that the opinion involved a landlord-tenant relationship and a lease. Is *any* agreement or contract void if knowingly entered into in violation of legal requirements? Does the court's reliance on the internal opinion of *Hartman v. Lubar* support this view of the second holding of *Brown? Hartman* was apparently not a landlord-tenant case. The same is probably true of the *Pangborn* and *Miller* opinions relied upon by the court.

24(c) STEPHENS v. DEPT. OF STATE POLICE

Key Facts for Issue I: A public employee took a leave of absence to attend a military training course.

Issue I: Does a state trooper who is a public employee have a right under ORS 408.240 and 408.210 to a "military duty" leave of absence to attend a military training course even though the training is not combined with service and the employee is denied permission to attend?

Holding I: Yes.

Key Facts for Issue II: A public employee was discharged when he deliberately disobeyed an order not to take a leave of absence. The legality of the order was questionable. He had time to use other methods of testing the legality of the order.

Issue II: Can a public employee (state trooper) be discharged for "insubordination" under ORS 181.290 when he deliberately disobeyed a questionable order not to take a leave of absence and there was time to use some other method to test the legality of the order even though the order turned out to be illegal?

Holding II: Yes.

Comments

Issue I

1. The employer argued that two facts were key: the training was not combined with service, and the employee was not given permission to go. The court, however, emphatically tells us that neither is required. In effect, neither are key facts. Under the *reasoning* of the court, the legislature intended the leave to be unconditional. Both these facts are stated in the first issue as "even though" or context facts—facts that one of the parties vigorously but incorrectly argued were key, p. 139.

2. It is not key that Stephens was a state trooper. The broader *fact categorization* of public officer or employee is key. Issue I, however, lists Stephens as a state trooper as a background or context fact.

Issue II

3. Very emphatic language is also used by the court when discussing those facts that will constitute insubordination. Indeed, the court is so direct that it is *obvious* what facts were key to the second holding. See, for example, the court's quote from *Roller,* which begins with a "Where" clause (third last paragraph of the majority opinion). Also, see the "When" clause in the last sentence of the majority opinion. The court clearly conditions its holding on the existence of certain facts: the existence of time to try another method to challenge the order, and the deliberate nature of the disobedience.

4. Are the following facts also key: (a) the police department relied in good faith on the advice of the Attorney General, and (b) the police department requires considerable discipline from its officers? See discussion in the Suggested Response to Assignment #22(c), p. 385.

5. *Stephens* should be shepardized to see what other opinions, if any, have said about the facts of *Stephens.*

24(d) NICHOLSON v. CONN. HALF-WAY HOUSE, INC.

Key Facts: The proposed use of the land by the defendant as a halfway house does not violate any law. The plaintiffs fear that harm will result from this use, but there is no specific evidence to substantiate this harm.

Issue: Is there an equitably abatable nuisance due to the unreasonable use of land as a halfway house when the use of the land is otherwise legal and there is fear of irreparable harm, but no specific evidence of it?

Holding: No.

Comments

1. Property values in the area have actually depreciated. The court, however, emphatically tells us that this is *not* a key fact; the depreciation resulted from fears and speculation only. "The mere depreciation of land values, caused in this case by subjective apprehensions * * * cannot sustain an injunction * * *." It is *obvious,* therefore, that the depreciation here is not a key fact.

2. Twice the court *repeats* the fact that the use of the land is legal. "The proposed use does not violate any zoning restrictions * * *." "Here the proposed use of the defendant's property in and of itself is lawful." This repetition is some support for the keyness of this fact.

3. The *reasoning* of the court is based on the meaning of nuisance and injunction. There must be a showing of unreasonableness. Unreasonableness requires a concrete indication of interference with the use of someone else's land. There is no such evidence here. This lack of evidence is key. An injunction requires a showing of irreparable harm. It is key that all we have here is sheer speculation of harm—no specific evidence of it.

4. The court's reliance on the *internal opinions* of *Brainard v. Town of West Hartford* and *Jack v. Torrent* supports the above selection of key facts. The harm in *Brainard* and *Torrent* was based on specific harm—not sheer speculation. These cases support the *fact categorization* of fear as key. Furthermore, there is a good deal of *repetition* of the fact that our case involves fear only.

5. In the issue, we have stated the proposed use of the land as a halfway house. This is a background or context fact (p. 139), not a key fact. It is clear that the court would have reached the same holding if some other similar legal use were involved such as a drugstore.

6. *Nicholson* should be shepardized to see what other opinions, if any, have said about the facts of *Nicholson*.

24(e) CONN. v. MENILLO

Key Facts: A nonphysician was convicted of performing an abortion.

Issue: When a state convicts a nonphysician for performing an abortion, is there a violation of a woman's constitutional right to privacy in having the abortion?

Holding: No.

Comments

1. The court's discussion of the *internal opinion* of *Roe v. Wade* clearly establishes nonphysician as key (see, however, comment 2 below). The court says that *Roe* does not apply to a nonphysician, i.e., *Roe* still allows a conviction of a nonphysician. The court's *reasoning* also supports nonphysician as key. The state can prevent an abortion during the first trimester only if the abortion is performed safely by medically competent personnel. The court suggests that a nonphysician cannot provide this safety. Throughout the opinion, the court *repeats* the fact that the defendant was not a physician.

2. For the purposes of argument, separate two concepts: (a) a nonphysician, and (b) an untrained nonphysician. The former is a broader category. Nonphysicians could arguably be trained to perform safe abortions. Which is key in the opinion: (a) or (b)? Several times the court suggests that the critical fact is the absence of medically competent personnel. A trained nonphysician would not necessarily fall into this category. In the first paragraph of the opinion, the court tells us that the defendant was a nonphysician "and" never had any medical training. Arguably, the opinion is ambiguous as to whether both facts were key to the holding.

3. *Menillo* should be shepardized to see what other opinions, if any, have said about the facts of *Menillo*.

Suggested Response to Assignment #26
(supra, p. 170)

26(a) PEOPLE v. SOHN

Disposition: Judgment is reversed; indictment is dismissed.

26(b) BROWN v. SOUTHALL REALTY CO.

Disposition: Judgment for landlord is reversed.

26(c) STEPHENS v. DEPT. OF STATE POLICE

Disposition: Circuit Court judgment is affirmed.

26(d) NICHOLSON v. CONN. HALF-WAY HOUSE, INC.

Disposition: Judgment for plaintiffs is set aside. The case is remanded to the lower court to enter judgment for the defendant.

26(e) CONN. v. MENILLO

Disposition: The petition for certiorari is granted. The judgment of the Supreme Court of Conn. is vacated, and the case is remanded to that court.

Appendix C

Citations: How and When to Use Them

The purpose of this appendix is to provide a set of basic rules on proper citation form for the most common types of authority used in legal writing. For situations not covered by these rules, see *A Uniform System of Citation,* Fourteenth Edition (1986).

I. General Considerations

1. Every time you quote from or otherwise rely upon any type of authority in your writing, you *must* provide a complete citation to that authority in your writing.

2. Citations to authority in legal memoranda and appellate briefs should be placed in the text of your argument rather than footnoted; in other kinds of nonadversary writing, such as books and articles, it is permissible to place the citations in footnotes.

3. The purpose of a citation is to advise the reader of (a) the identity, and (b) the location of each item of authority that you rely upon in your writing. When you are in doubt as to the proper citation form and are unable to locate a rule that governs the authority, give enough information to advise the reader of these two essential details. In doing so, err on the side of giving too much rather than too little information.

II. Enacted Law

A. CONSTITUTIONS AND CHARTERS

Constitutions and charters are cited to (a) the abbreviated name of the constitution or charter, (b) the article, and (c) the section to which you are referring. Usually, no date is needed in the cite.

Example
"No Bill of Attainder or ex post facto Law shall be passed." U.S.Const. art. I, § 9, cl. 3.

B. FEDERAL STATUTES

1. Most federal statutes are collected in chronological order of passage in the *United States Statutes at Large* (Stat.) and subsequently are arranged by subject matter in the *United States Code* (U.S.C.). The general practice is to cite only to the United States Code.

Statutes in the United States Code are cited to (a) the title number, (b) the abbreviated name of the code, (c) the number of the section and, if relevant, the subsection to which you are referring, and (d) the date of the code *edition* you are using. Where appropriate, you may also indicate the name of the statute or act at the beginning of the citation.

Example
42 U.S.C. § 3412(a) (1940).
or
Narcotic Rehabilitation Act of 1966, 42 U.S.C. § 3412(a) (1970).

2. Some federal statutes are not published in the United States Code. Such statutes must be cited to the United States Statutes at Large as follows: (a) the volume in which the statute appears, (b) the abbreviated name of the compilation (Stat.), (c) the page number on which the statute begins, and (d) the year of the volume in which the statute appears. Where appropriate, you may also indicate the name of the statute at the beginning of the citation.

Example
80 Stat. 1444 (1966).
or
Narcotic Addict Rehabilitation Act, 80 Stat. 1444 (1966).

3. Recently enacted federal statutes that have not yet been published in U.S. Statutes at Large or the U.S. Code should be cited to (a) the public law number, (b) if relevant, the number of the particular title and section within the act, and (c) the exact date (day, month, and year) of enactment. Where appropriate, you may also indicate the name of the statute at the beginning of the citation.

Example
Narcotic Addict Rehabilitation Act of 1966, Pub.L. 89–793, Title III, § 302 (Nov. 8, 1966).

C. STATE STATUTES

1. Like federal statutes, the statutes of the various states are compiled in two kinds of collections, *state codes* (arranged by subject matter), and *session laws* (arranged in chronological order of enactment).

2. Citations to state statutes should generally include (a) the title or chapter number of the statute, (b) the abbreviated name of the code or session laws, (c) the number of the section within the statute to which you are referring, and (d) the date. Use the year that appears on the spine of the code, or the latest year that appears on the title page, or the latest copyright year—in this order of preference. The order in which these four components (a–d) must be presented in the citation will vary a great deal from state to state. You must familiarize yourself with the system used in your state.

D. ADMINISTRATIVE REGULATIONS

1. Federal administrative regulations are published in the *Federal Register* (Fed.Reg.) and are later codified by subject matter in the *Code of Federal Regulations* (C.F.R.).

2. Federal regulations that appear in the *Code of Federal Regulations* are cited to (a) the title number in which the regulation appears, (b) the abbreviated name of the code, (c) the number of the particular section to which you are referring, and (d) the date of the code edition which you are using.

Example
29 C.F.R. § 102.60(a) (1975).

3. Federal Regulations that have not yet been codified into the *Code of Federal Regulations* are cited to the *Federal Register* using (a) the volume in which the regulation appears, (b) the abbreviation "Fed.Reg.," (c) the page on which the regulation appears, and (d) the date of the *Federal Register* that you are using.

Example
27 Fed.Reg. 2092 (1962).

4. The regulations of state administrative agencies are not always codified, and the manner of citation may vary not only from state to state but from agency to agency. In those states that do codify administrative regulations, the system of citation will generally be very similar to that described above for federal administrative regulations.

III. Case Law

We have already examined the basic citation structure for court opinions (p. 25). The following general citation rules should be kept in mind:

1. Give a complete cite. This includes the official cite and the standard unofficial cites, if any. (See Examples A, D, and E below.) The official cite comes first.

2. The date of the decision goes in parenthesis at the end of the cite. (See Examples A to G below.)

3. Do not include the abbreviation of the court in the parenthesis at the end of the cite unless the court is *not* the highest court in the jurisdiction or it is otherwise unclear what court wrote the opinion. (Compare Examples D and E below.)

4. Cites to opinions in F.Supp. and to F. or F.2d must include the abbreviation of the court in the parenthesis at the end of the cite. These opinions will have no parallel cites. (See Examples B and C below.)

5. The following rules apply to the names of the parties:

    a. Use only the last name of persons.

    b. Do not include the party's litigation status (e.g., appellant).

    c. Do not use the title of a party (e.g., Secretary).

    d. If there are multiple parties on each side of the litigation, include only the first party mentioned on each side (omit phrases such as "et al.").

    e. If the opinion consolidates two or more different cases, use the parties from the first case listed in the caption.

    f. Do not place the names of the parties in capital letters (all caps) unless this is the actual way the party spells its name.

    g. Use abbreviations. Corporation = Corp. Incorporated = Inc. Company = Co. Board = Bd. Commission = Comm'n Committee = Comm. Department = Dep't Government = Gov't National = Nat'l Railroad = R.R. Association = Ass'n

6. Do not abbreviate United States.

7. Do not use the docket number in the cite.

Example A
Format of a Citation to
an Opinion of the Highest Federal Court
(the United States Supreme Court):

Taglianetti v. United States, 394 U.S. 316, 89 S.Ct. 1099, 22 L.Ed.2d 302 (1969) [according to some, a more correct format would be *Taglianetti v. United States,* 394 U.S. 316 (1969). This format uses only the official cite; parallel cites are not included.]

Example B
Format of a Citation to
an Opinion of a Federal Middle Appeals Court
(the United States Court of Appeals, Second Circuit):

Sterling Nat'l Bank and Trust Co. of N.Y. v. Fidelity Mortgage Investors, 510 F.2d 870 (2nd Cir. 1975)

Example C
Format of a Citation to
an Opinion of a Federal Trial Court
(the United States District Court, Western District in Wisconsin):

Stone v. Schmidt, 398 F.Supp. 768 (W.D.Wisc.1975)

Example D
Format of a Citation to
an Opinion of the Highest State Court
(New Jersey Supreme Court)

Petlin Associates, Inc. v. Township of Dover, 64 N.J. 327 316 A.2d 1 (1974)

Example E
Format of a Citation to
an Opinion of a Lower State Court
(Conn. Superior Court, Appellate Session):

Huckabee v. Stevens, 32 Conn.Supp. 511, 338 A.2d 512 (Conn. Super. Ct., 1975)

Example F
Format of a Citation to
an Administrative Decision
(National Labor Relations Board):

Standard Dry Wall Products, Inc., 91 N.L.R.B. 544 (1950)

Example G
Format of a Citation to
an Opinion of the Attorney General:

---

40 Op.Atty.Gen. 423 (1945)

When quoting from or referring to specific language in an opinion, you must list both the number of the page on which the *opinion* begins and the number of the page on which the *quoted language* begins in the official and unofficial cites. In the following example, the quote is found on page 20 of Maryland Reports (abbreviated Md.) and on page 379 of Atlantic Reporter, Second Series (abbreviated A.2d).

Example

"Even though laches may not apply, one must use reasonable promptness when seeking judicial protection." *Bridgeton Education Ass'n v. Board of Education,* 147 Md. 17, 20, 334 A.2d 376, 379 (1975).

IV. Secondary Authority

1. Treatises and other books are cited to (a) the number of the volume being referred to, if part of a multi-volume set, (b) the full surname and first initial of the author, (c) the title of the book, (d) the number of the section and/or page to which you are referring, (e) the edition of the book, if other than the first, and (f) the date of publication.

Example

---

6 M. Belli, *Modern Trials,* § 289 (1963)
and
G. Osborne, *Handbook on the Law of Mortgages,* § 211, p. 370 (2d ed. 1970).

2. Law review *articles* are cited by reference to (a) the full surname of the author, (b) the title of the article, (c) the number of the volume in which the article appears, (d) the abbreviated name of the law review, (e) the number of the page on which the article appears, and (f) the date of publication. The title of the article should be italicized or underscored.

Example
Catz & Robinson, *Due Process and Creditor's Remedies,* 28 Rutgers L.Rev. 541 (1975).

3. Law review *notes* and *comments* are cited in the same manner as law review articles (see #2 above), except that the name of the author is omitted.

Example
Note, *Second-Class Postal Rates and the First Amendment,* 28 Rutgers L.Rev. 693 (1975).

4. Legal encyclopedias are cited by reference to (a) the number of the volume, (b) the abbreviated name of the encyclopedia, (c) the subject heading to which you are referring, (d) the number of the section to which you are referring, and (e) the date of the publication of the volume you are citing.

Example
83 C.J.S. *Subscriptions* § 3 (1953) and 77 Am.Jur.2d *Vendor and Purchaser* § 73 (1975).

5. Restatements of the Law published by the American Law Institute are cited by reference to (a) the title of the Restatement, (b) the edition being referred to (if other than the first edition), (c) the number of the section being referred to, and (d) the date of publication.

Example
Restatement (Second) of Agency § 37 (1957).

Appendix D

Quotation Marks, Brackets, and Ellipsis Dots

When you quote something, use quotation marks and cite the source of your quote. For example, "The equitable lien in its most simple form is simply a lien for the amount of money to which the plaintiff is entitled." Dobbs, D., *Handbook on the Law of Remedies,* 250 (1973).

An exception exists to the rule on using quotation marks when your quote is fifty words or more. Do not use quotation marks for such quotes. Instead, indent the quote as in the following example from a memorandum of law.

> There are many ways in which administrative agencies handle the problem of too many formal hearings:
>
>> Faced with the need to make an enormous number of decisions quickly, many of the agencies which process individual claims have developed sophisticated informal procedures in an effort to minimize the use of formal hearings. One of the most familiar examples is the Internal Revenue Service. Despite the formidable complexity of tax laws, the IRS has developed forms which are relatively simple to complete. . . .
>
> Gellhorn & Boyer, *Administrative Law and Process,* 117 (2d ed. 1981). The same is true of the claims structure in our case.

Since this quote is over fifty words, no quotation marks are used and the entire quote is indented. If the quote is forty-nine words or less, use quotation marks and do not indent unless you feel that added emphasis should be given to the quote.

Note that a complete citation to the source of the quote is provided. This is extremely important to avoid a charge of plagiarism. If you are using another person's words, you must acknowledge the source. Suppose that you are only paraphrasing: rewording someone else's ideas. The same rule applies: a complete citation is needed. Unfortunately, a great many people take liberties with the writing of others. It is very tempting to rephrase someone else's thoughts to make them *appear* to be your own. This is dangerous and may be illegal.

Often you will be mixing some of your own thoughts with those of others. To be safe, you should still provide the citation. It is too easy to fall back on the excuse that you do not have to cite any sources because you are unable to separate your own thoughts from all the sources that you have been checking. The reality, however, is that if you are determined at the outset to attempt such a separation, you will be able to accomplish it. Furthermore, when there is reasonable doubt about whether a thought is original or borrowed, you should resolve the doubt by providing the citation.

Students sometimes want to impress the reader by making him or her think that all the ideas in the memorandum are original. There is also the possibility that a student may feel somewhat embarrassed by a memorandum that relies too much on secondary sources since most of the analysis should consist of primary authority. Hence the student tries to paraphrase a hornbook or other secondary authority without providing any citations. This approach is improper for a number of reasons. First, it will often be obvious to the experienced reader that the student is relying on secondary authority even though the citations are absent. Second, it is no shame to use secondary authority so long as you lay a proper foundation for it (p. 212) and you acknowledge the source by a complete citation. To be sure, it is much more difficult to analyze opinions, statutes, and other primary authority than it is to "lift" material out of hornbooks, legal encyclopedias, and other secondary authority. The risks you run in doing so, however, are very serious.

After you have properly quoted from any enacted law, use quotation marks when you subsequently refer to any language in your quote. Compare the following two excerpts from legal memos in which statutory material is quoted and discussed:

> Section 20 provides: "All documentation must be completed before the committee begins its deliberation." Mass.Code Ann. Ch. 14, § 3 (1950). The defendant's submission of the entire portfolio should constitute the requisite documentation. Furthermore, it is our view that the committee did not begin its deliberation until June 4, 1976.

More accurately, the memo should have been written as follows:

> Section 20 provides: "All documentation must be completed before the committee begins its deliberation." Mass.Code Ann. Ch. 14, § 3 (1950). The defendant's submission of the entire portfolio should constitute the requisite "documentation." Furthermore, it is our view that the committee did not begin its "deliberation" until June 4, 1976.

Note that in the second excerpt, the words "documentation" and "deliberation" are in quotation marks because these are the exact words of the statute; whenever you use language from something you have just quoted, quotation marks are needed.

Very often, particularly within opinions, you will find quotations within quotations. In such situations, place the main quote in double quotation marks and the quote within the quote in single quotation marks.

Examples: Tom said, "When I arrived at the store, the manager told me to 'get out,' which I immediately began to do when he said 'this is the last time I will ever let you in here.' "

In Jones v. Jones, 245 Mass. 32, 36, 108 N.E.2d 14, 17 (1950), the court said, "we have always followed the *Durant* rule that 'mortgage payment schedules are integral parts of the mortgage agreement.' Durant v. Morgan Trust, 109 F.2d 157, 160 (2nd Cir. 1932)."

Note the three quotation marks (' ") used at the end of the first example indicating the close of the quote within the quote *and* the close of the main quote.

The next major concern about quotations is how to indicate when you have *altered* something in the quote. The following rules apply:

Altering Quotations
1. Use brackets when changing a letter from a capital letter to a small letter.

What You Are Quoting	Correct Form
At no time will delays be permitted. X v. Y, 20 F.Supp. 109, 111, (N.D.Cal. 1950).	The court said that "[a]t no time will delays be permitted." X v. Y, 20 F.Supp. 109, 111 (N.D.Cal.1950).

2. Use brackets when changing a letter from a small letter to a capital letter.

While appellate courts are bound by the fact findings of a trial court, the higher court can determine that such fact findings are not supported by the evidence. A v. B, 22 F.2d 91, 95 (8th Cir. 1925).	"[T]he higher court can determine that such fact findings are not supported by the evidence." A v. B, 22 F.2d 91, 95 (8th Cir. 1925).

3. Use brackets when you are adding anything to the quote for purposes of clarity.

What You Are Quoting	Correct Form
Factual questions cannot be resolved without proper instructions. E. v. F, 52 N.J. 871, 875, 109 N.E. 3, 7 (1940).	"Factual questions cannot be resolved [by the jury] without proper instructions." E v. F, 52 N.J. 871, 875, 109 N.E. 3, 7 (1940).

4. If you want to underline or italicize anything in the quote, say "emphasis added" in parenthesis or brackets after the quote.

Concerning the issues raised by plaintiff, we will discuss only those that relate to the assumption of risk defense. C v. D, 49 F.2d 307, 310 (1st Cir. 1950).	"Concerning the issues raised by plaintiff we will discuss *only* those that relate to the assumption of risk defense." C v. D, 49 F.2d 307, 310 (1st Cir. 1950) (Emphasis added).

There are two circumstances when you need to alert the reader that you are *not* altering anything in the quote:

> **1. If the original source of the quote has italicized certain words within it, you should say "emphasis in original" in parenthesis or brackets at the end of the quote to avoid the suggestion that you did the italicizing.**

What You Are Quoting	Correct Form
At no time will any county officer be allowed to determine *on his own* that eligibility has not been established. G v. H, 89 F.Supp. 1124, 1130 (S.D.N.Y.1970).	"At no time will any county officer be allowed to determine *on his own* that eligibility has not been established." G v. H, 89 F.Supp. 1124, 1130 (S.D.N.Y.1970) (Emphasis in original).

> **2. If the material you are quoting contains a significant mistake, you should include the notation "sic" in brackets immediately after the error to avoid the suggestion that the mistake was made by you in copying the quote.**

What You Are Quoting	Correct Form
The judgment of the district court are reversed. J v. K, 300 U.S. 41, 45 (1960).	"The judgment of the district court are [sic] reversed." J v. K, 300 U.S. 41, 45 (1960).

Finally, we need to consider the use of ellipsis dots (. . .) to indicate the removal of anything from a quote. Some writers like to use asterisks (* * *) instead of ellipsis dots to identify omissions, although the latter is preferred. The following rules apply:

1. All omissions from a quote must be signaled by ellipsis dots except an omission at the beginning of a quote. Do not use ellipsis dots to begin a quotation.

2. Three dots are used to indicate an omission within a sentence except that:

- if the omission is from the end of a sentence, a total of four dots are needed (. . . .), three to indicate the omission and one to indicate the end of the sentence;

- if the omission includes a comma or semicolon, use three dots; do not include the comma or semicolon unless this punctuation is needed to understand the sentence with the omission.

3. If an entire paragraph is omitted, four dots (. . . .) are used at the point at which the paragraph would have begun if it had not been omitted.

What follows is an illustration of these rules. In excerpt I, the original material to be quoted (from Smith v. Smith, 32 F.2d 819, 821 (10th Cir. 1930)) is presented. In excerpt II, the material is presented with the proper use of ellipsis dots to indicate the omissions.

I

This is a direct appeal from a jury verdict and judgment by the district court for the State. The defendant argued that the lower court erred in failing to exclude certain medical testimony, and that his error was prejudicial, in violation of the law and unfair.

At no time during the trial did the defendant object to the admission of this testimony. The objection is raised for the first time on appeal. Due to this failure to object below, we shall not consider this issue on appeal.

Additionally, the defendant argues that he was denied the effective assistance of counsel, the right to dismiss his counsel, and the right to be present during sentencing. We find no merit to any of these contentions and deny the appeal.

II

"This is a[n]...appeal from a...judgment by the district court for the State. The defendant argued that the lower court erred in failing to exclude certain medical testimony, and that this error was prejudicial...and unfair.

    . . . .

"Additionally, the defendant argues that he was denied...the right to be present during sentencing. We find no merit to any of these contentions...." Smith v. Smith, 32 F.2d 819, 821 (10th Cir. 1930).

Appendix E

Research Overview on Case Law

I. Techniques for Finding Case Law on Point

1. If you already have a statute, shepardize the statute to find cases interpreting the statute.

2. If you already have a constitutional provision, shepardize the provision to find cases interpreting it.

3. If you already have a federal regulation in C.F.R., shepardize the regulation to find cases interpreting it.

4. Check the *American Digest System* (or any other digest that gives small paragraph summaries of the cases of the courts in which you are interested). Use the Descriptive Word Index of these digests to find the topic of your research. You will be lead to key topics and numbers where the cases are summarized or digested.

5. Use the indexes to *American Law Reports:* ALR, ALR2d, ALR3d, ALR4th, ALR Fed. Find annotations on the topic of your research. These annotations are extensive research papers giving numerous citations to cases.

6. Use the indexes of the following books to find the topic of your research. In the footnotes of these books, you will often find extensive references to cases:

- legal encyclopedias (C.J.S. and AmJur.2d)
- treatises on the law

7. Find law review literature on the topic of your research. This literature will often have extensive footnote references to cases. There are three main indexes to locate periodical or law review literature:

- Index to Legal Periodicals
- Current Law Index
- Legal Resource Index

8. Use the legal research computers, e.g., WESTLAW, LEXIS.

9. Find a loose-leaf service on the topic of your research.

II. Techniques for Finding *Additional* Case Law Once You Already Have One Case on Point

1. Shepardize the case you have.

2. Get the key topic and numbers at the beginning of the case as printed in a reporter of West. Take these key topics and numbers to the digests of West. There you should find additional cases on the same area of the law.

3. Find out if your case has been noted in the law reviews. You do this by checking the tables of cases in the following indexes:

- Index to Legal Periodicals
- Current Law Index
- Legal Resource Index

4. Check the *American Law Reports* (ALR, ALR2d, ALR3d, ALR4th, ALR Fed.). Use the indexes for each of these units. Find annotations on the same topics that were covered in the case you already have.

5. Check the table of cases in major treatises that deal with the same area of the law covered in the case you have. See if the treatise comments on your case. If so, the commentary may include references to other cases on the same area of the law.

Appendix F

Bibliography

GENERAL BIBLIOGRAPHIES

"Law and Language: A Selected Annotated Bibliography on Legal Writing" by T. Collins & D. Hattenhauer, 33 *Journal of Legal Education* 141 (1983).

"Research on Legal Writing: A Bibliography" by P. Kolin & R. Marquardt, 78 *Law Library Journal* 493 (1986).

TREATISES

Advocacy: The Art of Pleading a Case, 2d ed. by R. Givens (Shepard's, 1984).

Appeals by M. Houts (Matthew Bender, 1981–).

Appellate Judicial Opinions by R. Leflar (West, 1974).

Art of Advocacy (Matthew Bender, 1978–).

Brief Writing and Argumentation, 3rd ed. by M. Pittoni (Foundation Press, 1967).

Brief Writing and Oral Argument, 4th ed. by E. Re (Oceana, 1973).

Clear and Effective Legal Writing by V. Charrow & M. Erhardt (Little, Brown, 1986).

The Bramble Bush by K. Llewellyn (Oceana, 1960).

The Common Law by O. W. Holmes (Little, Brown, 1881).

The Common Law Tradition: Deciding Appeals by K. Llewellyn (1960).

The Concept of Law by H.L.A. Hart (Oxford Univ. Press, 1976).

Effective Legal Communications by I. Mehler (Philgor, 1975).

Effective Legal Writing, 3d ed. by G. Block (Foundation, 1986).

409

The Fundamentals of Legal Writing, 2d ed. by R. Dickerson (Little, Brown, 1986).

Handbook of Appellate Advocacy, 2d ed. by UCLA Moot Court Honors Program (West, 1986).

Introduction to Advocacy, 3d ed. by the Harvard Board of Student Advisors (Foundation, 1981).

The Language of the Law by D. Melinkoff (Little, Brown, 1963).

Law and the Modern Mind by J. Frank (1930).

The Legal Imagination: Studies in the Nature of Legal Thought and Expression by J. White (Little, Brown, 1973).

Legal Writing by N. Brand & N. White (1976).

Legal Writing in a Nutshell by M. Rombauer (West, 1982).

Legal Writing: Sense and Nonsense by D. Melinkoff (West, 1982).

Legal Writing Style, 2d ed. by H. Weihofen (West, 1980).

Legislative Analysis and Drafting, 2d ed. by W. Statsky (West, 1984).

The Nature of the Judicial Process by B. Cardozo (Yale Univ. Press, 1921).

A Practical Guide to Legal Writing and Legal Method by J. Dernbach & R. Singleton (Rothman, 1981).

A Streamlined Briefing Technique by C. Emery (Bancroft-Whitney, 1960).

Supreme Court Practice, 6th ed. by R. Stern (BNA, 1986).

Tactics of Legal Reasoning by P. Schlag & D. Skover (Carolina Academic Press, 1986).

When Lawyers Write by R. Weisberg (Little, Brown, 1987).

Writing from a Legal Perspective by G. Gopen (West, 1981).

Writing in Law Practice by F. Cooper (Bobbs-Merrill, 1963).

Writing Persuasive Briefs by G. Peck (Little, Brown, 1984).

Written and Oral Advocacy by M. Fontham (Wiley, 1985).

CURRENT LAW INDEX (CLI) & LEGAL RESOURCE INDEX (LRI)

In the CLI and LRI, look for references to periodical literature under the following subject headings:

Bill Drafting
Briefs
Common Law
Decision Making
Forms (Law)

Legal Authorities
Legal Composition
Legal Documents
Legal Drafting

INDEX TO LEGAL PERIODICALS (ILP)

In the ILP, look for references to legal periodical literature under the following subject headings:

Bibliography

Briefs

Common Law

Judge-Made Law

Language

Legal Education

Legal Drafting

Legal Terminology

Legislative Drafting

Index

413